Superstition as Ideology in Iranian Politics
From Majlesi to Ahmadinejad

A superstitious reading of the world based on religion may be harmless at a private level. Yet, employed as a political tool, it can have more sinister implications. As this fascinating book by Ali Rahnema, a distinguished Iranian intellectual, relates, superstition and mystical beliefs have endured and influenced ideology and political strategy in Iran from the founding of the Safavi (Safavid) dynasty in the sixteenth century to the present day. The endurance of these beliefs has its roots in a particular brand of popular Shi'ism, which was compiled and systematized by the eminent cleric Mohammad Baqer Majlesi in the seventeenth century. Majlesi, who is considered by some to be the father of Iranian Shi'ism, encouraged believers to accept fantastical notions as part of their faith and to venerate their leaders as superhuman. As Rahnema demonstrates through a close reading of the Persian sources and with examples from contemporary Iranian politics, it is this supposed connectedness to the hidden world that has allowed leaders such as Muhammad Reza Shah Pahlavi and Mahmud Ahmadinejad to present themselves and their entourage as representatives of the Divine, and their rivals as the embodiment of evil.

Ali Rahnema is Professor of Economics and Director of the Master of Arts program in Middle East and Islamic Studies at The American University of Paris. His many publications include *An Islamic Utopian: A Political Biography of Ali Shariati* (1998, 2000); *Pioneers of Islamic Revival* (1994, 2006); *Islamic Economic Systems* (with Farhad Nomani, 1994); and *The Secular Miracle: Religion, Politics, and Economic Policy in Iran* (with Farhad Nomani, 1990).

Cambridge Middle East Studies 35

Cambridge Middle East Studies has been established to publish books on the nineteenth- to twenty-first-century Middle East and North Africa. The aim of the series is to provide new and original interpretations of aspects of Middle Eastern societies and their histories. To achieve disciplinary diversity, books are solicited from authors writing in a wide range of fields including history, sociology, anthropology, political science, and political economy. The emphasis is on producing books offering an original approach along theoretical and empirical lines. The series is intended for students and academics, but the accessible and wide-ranging studies will appeal to the interested general reader.

A list of books in this series can be found after the index.

Superstition as Ideology in Iranian Politics

From Majlesi to Ahmadinejad

ALI RAHNEMA
The American University of Paris

CAMBRIDGE
UNIVERSITY PRESS

CAMBRIDGE
UNIVERSITY PRESS

University Printing House, Cambridge CB2 8BS, United Kingdom

One Liberty Plaza, 20th Floor, New York, NY 10006, USA

477 Williamstown Road, Port Melbourne, VIC 3207, Australia

314-321, 3rd Floor, Plot 3, Splendor Forum, Jasola District Centre, New Delhi - 110025, India

79 Anson Road, #06-04/06, Singapore 079906

Cambridge University Press is part of the University of Cambridge.

It furthers the University's mission by disseminating knowledge in the pursuit of education, learning and research at the highest international levels of excellence.

www.cambridge.org
Information on this title: www.cambridge.org/9780521182218

First published 2011

A catalogue record for this publication is available from the British Library

Library of Congress Cataloging in Publication data
Rahnema, 'Ali.
Superstition as ideology in Iranian politics: from Majlesi to Ahmadinejad / Ali Rahnema.
   p.   cm. – (Cambridge Middle East studies)
Includes bibliographical references and index.
ISBN 978-1-107-00518-1 (hardback) – ISBN 978-0-521-18221-8 (paperback)
1. Iran – Politics and government – Psychological aspects.   2. Ideology – Iran –
History.   3. Islam and politics – Iran – History.   4. Shi'ah – Iran –
History.   5. Political psychology – Case studies.   6. Superstition – Religious
aspects – Islam.   I. Title.   II. Series.
DS274.R325   2011
320.95501´9–dc22   2010040797

ISBN 978-1-107-00518-1 Hardback
ISBN 978-0-521-18221-8 Paperback

Contents

Preface and Acknowledgements

This book is the result of certain academic and intellectual questions and problems that gradually became puzzles and enigmas in my understanding of the debates conducted by certain twentieth-century Shiʿi reformers in Iran. My study of Shariʿat Sangelaji and ʿAli Shariʿati convinced me that, despite their differences, both men felt compelled at a certain point in their intellectual development to grapple with one towering religious figure of the past. In tune with their different temperaments, educational back-grounds, styles, degrees of scholarly thoroughness and religio-political agenda each engaged Mohammad-Baqir Majlesi as the symbol, architect and archetype of what needed to be reformed in Shiʿi Islam. From the works of these reformers, it seemed as though serious and meaningful reform of Shiʿism had to start with a critique of Majlesi. By 1997, it became evident to me that understanding modern Shiʿi reformism meant under-standing Majlesi, who seemed to be its nemesis in the eyes of these early reformers. So the original idea of this book started with an interest in Mohammad-Baqir Majlesi's life, works, religious culture and politics, only to understand the arguments against and attacks on his colossal influence on popular Shiʿism. Needless to say that having started with the works of his critics, my reading of Majlesi was coloured by their criticisms.

The end of my study of Majlesi and Sangelaji overlapped with the flurry of news and rumours from Iran about supernatural observations, experi-ences, and statements among different segments of the society. Of prime significance was that from the latter half of 2005; the floodgate of reports in the media on such supernatural experiences was opened by a series of religious superstitious accounts pronounced by politicians in power. The taboo on un-nuanced, direct and public reference to religious superstitious experiences or so-called supernatural facts by men in positions of political and religious leadership was broken, which then seemed to liberate the repressed superstitious feelings of a segment of the population. It was also

important to me that the widespread and thorough reporting on religious
and political superstition and the important social debate that it caused
was almost entirely a domestic one, and the clerical and non-clerical critics
of religious superstition came from different national political spectrums.
As the heated debate continued, two ideas associated with it informed my
original project.

First, was it possible and/or useful to trace certain key elements of the
twenty-first-century resurgence in the debate on superstition in Iran to the
ideas that Majlesi had so diligently and painstakingly compiled and propagated long ago? If so, were the reformists not justified in their obsession to
confront Majlesi as the source of much deviation in the faith, lay bare his
religious and political agenda and move on with reforming Shiʿism? Did
not the deconstruction and dialectical transcendence of Majlesism lie at
the core of Shiʿi reformism? Was not a proper and thorough settlement of
scores with Majlesism the Achilles' heel of reforming Shiʿism? Majlesi
seems to have coloured and moulded Shiʿism to such an extent that few
from the ranks of the official clergy felt at ease criticizing him for fear of
being accused of criticizing Shiʿism proper. Was society prepared for a first
round of intellectual debate on Majlesism? Was Iranian society in 2010 so
divided that part may feel insulted by the opening of such a debate while
the other cast it aside as marginal and dated given the rapid sociopolitical
transformations in the country?

Second, following certain reported remarks and practices of the president and his entourage since 2005, the sensitive concept of religious superstition had entered the public realm and come under sharp criticism by
a wide spectrum of the Shiʿi clergy. For the first time in the history of the
Islamic Republic, the topic of religious superstition, its various forms and
manifestations, its perpetrators and the school of thought that propagated
it, the political and religious goals of its advocates, its social and political
consequences and the degree to which such superstitious claims had proper
religious credentials or were rooted in solid Shiʿi proofs was opened up
for debate and scrutiny. What seemed to have been lost in the debate was
that the president's behaviour and utterances and those of his proponents
were neither exceptional nor isolated cases in historical terms. Previous
Iranian leaders and rulers had made similar claims to being connected with
the hidden world and had engaged in similar superstitious practices. My
search for such cases was not to be a thorough historical study of superstition among Iranian rulers throughout history, but a selected study that
would examine and exemplify the degree of persistence of religious superstition among them. One object of this selective and anecdotal survey was

to assess the worldly political benefits drawn from such pious claims to supernatural connectedness. The other was to reflect on the impact and consequences of such claims on the rational capacity of the people who were expected to believe such quasi-religious superstitions. Did religious superstition act as a vehicle to numb the minds of the common folk in order to prevent them from independent reflection, keeping them resigned, docile and manageable?

Based on these two ideas associated with the superstition debate in Iran, the project spread from a study of Majlesi to include a short survey of the nature, prevalence and role of religious superstition during the reign of two monarchs and a president. One thread that weaves through the book is a reflection on the right to engage in rational and independent thought from a Shi'i perspective and whether Shi'ism respects and promotes such a right. Can Shi'ism's deep commitment to justice as an inalienable right allow it to consider independent and rational thought as the prerogative and privilege of a few, or does Shi'ism inevitably consider independent thought as the religious, natural and human right of all Shi'i? Majlesism and its present-day clerical and non-clerical followers in Iran argue that rational and independent thought by the common people is not only incompatible with Shi'ism but that it is its antithesis. Yet they arrogate the right to interpret and apply independent thought, which they label as dangerous to the common man, to themselves so as to impose their own manual of personal, social, political and religious behaviour on society in order to engineer the lives of the common folk. If people are to be denied the right to reason and to stand by their own deductions, their thinking would need to be replaced by something else. In the name of Shi'ism, a Majlesian or neo-Majlesian state would subsequently need to promote the antithesis of reasoning – superstition and irrational thought – to ensure the common folk's eternal subservience and loyalty. Majlesism as an anti-rational and pro-superstition school of thought fostered and promoted as state ideology, therefore, constitutes the nexus of this study.

In writing this book, I am indebted to many people. Yahya helped me out patiently with tracking down and finding relevant books. Once his student, always his student: in my mind, he was my imaginary thesis director to whom I felt responsible to provide a progress report each step of the way. Purandokht, the ever-graceful professional, facilitated my access to the rich library stacks. Anvar, the wise sage with an incredible breadth and depth of knowledge, read the part on Majlesi, applied his encyclopaedic knowledge base, unfaltering memory and scholarly method and provided me with sharp, insightful and specific comments and criticisms. Shahram

Ghanbari read parts of the manuscript and as usual provided me with his nuanced and useful comments. He prodded me to employ a standardized Farsi transliteration, convinced me that Arab-language scholars correctly use their own transliteration and Farsi-language writers should use their own. He helped me diligently with the laborious process of producing an appropriate Farsi transliteration for the relevant terms used in this book. I decided that a thorough Farsi transliteration, such as distinguishing between the short and long *alef* (A), would make the text too awkward to the eyes of most readers, and so decided on a partial one. The Farsi transliteration of Qur'an is Qor'an and that of Islam is Eslam. Even though I have adopted a partial Farsi transliteration in this text, I have continued to use the Arabic transliteration of well-established terms such as Qur'an, Islam, Shi'i and Imam. Where I have used Farsi transliteration of words such as *jahad* and *'olama*, which I thought may confuse or bother readers familiar with their Arabic transliteration, I have bracketed and placed the familiar Arabic transliteration, *jihad* and *ulema*, next to the Farsi transliteration when used for the first time in the text. My anonymous readers picked up the weaknesses in the text that I had ignored, leading to final changes and amendments in the introduction. Lisa Damon carefully read the new introduction and helped to improve it where it became too wordy. I discussed the original form of this project, different from the present book, with Charles Tripp in 2007. As usual, I am indebted to him for his encouragement, understanding and support.

Then there are those who hear bits and pieces of a writing project during different parts of its construction. I am thankful to Soraya, Mariam, Zahra, Reza and Lisa for becoming involuntarily subjected to hearing about this story, sometimes inquisitively, sometimes disapprovingly and sometimes in silence. Finally this book is dedicated to a people whose *Jesus* does not walk on water but *rises with the dawn*, teaching a tolerant Islam and a democratic Iran, and when gagged and chained in the lion's den, it is he who roars for his people against irreligious, oppressive and unjust rulers.

Introduction

The 1979 Iranian revolution culminating in the Islamic Republic of Iran was an untimely rooster that perplexed analysts, academics and journalists. In the late twentieth century, long after religion had been called the opium of the masses, Islam became the primary mobilizing force of a potent revolutionary ideology, which was to mark indelibly the subsequent three decades of world history. In search of labelling, understanding and naming the events in Iran, a flurry of Western neologisms were coined. Epithets such as fundamentalism, with a Christian genealogy, were excavated and soon became household terms designating this "new brand" of Islam. Islam was made out to be a uniform and undifferentiated monolith. This blanket concept, most suitable for rhetorical tagging, concealed the most rudimentary differences among Muslims. It placed the Sunnis and Shi'is and their different subsets along with the mystics and Sufis, with their own multiple offshoots, and the modernists and traditionalists, only to mention a few, in the same jar and slapped a single label on it.

At the risk of schematizing, the encounter between nascent neo-conservative Western governments, taken off guard, and the Islamic resurgence can be outlined in a four-step process. First, Islam was homogenized; then the essence of this "undistinguishable mass" was identified as "aggressive and violent"; subsequently, it was attributed a "threatening" political goal and posture; and finally, "suitable" policies of containment, pre-emptive and punitive strikes were developed and employed to counter the perceived "danger" of this newly erupted Islam. This new encounter spawned its own vocabulary bringing into circulation terms such as "Islamo-fascism", "jihadism", "Islamism" and "takfirism". The naivety of such politically motivated and sensationalist appellations can only be understood in the context of the variety of Islamic creeds and schools of thought. Back in the twelfth century, the Islamic scholar, Mohammad ebn Adbolkarim ebn Ahmad Shahrestani, had referred to more than 70 different

Islamic schools of thought and sects in his classical work, *al-Melal va al-Nehal*.

Islam is a religion composed of a core of principles relating to belief; its orthodoxy and doctrine. The core principles are accompanied by rites and rituals of worship and a set of laws dealing with family, commercial and criminal affairs. This outer circle constitutes Islam's orthopraxy or the correct action and practice. To the modern-day average Westerner, who is constantly told that Islam is a political faith, a word of explanation is in order. Those Muslims who believe that the object and mission of the faith is to attain greater proximity to God through individual devotion, betterment and piety think of their religion as a personal act of belief. They look at this world as a transitory space and to the hereafter as the permanent abode. Real rewards are to be sought in the hereafter, through the proper following of the Shari'at (Shari'a) in this world. Concerns of this world, other than private religiously defined obligations, do not fall into the realm of religious responsibilities. On the Day of Judgement, each person is believed to stand alone before God and no one's good or bad actions are considered to be counted towards that of anyone else's. Individuals are responsible for their own religious or irreligious acts, which eventually determine their final abode of paradise or hell. Other than paying *zakat*, which is a personal devotional obligation, Muslims have no social, collective or political obligations. Spiritual Islam confines religion to the private realm and has no preconceptions or value judgements about the "correct" political, social and economic system.

POLITICAL ISLAM

In the aftermath of colonial expansion in India, North Africa and the Middle East, starting in the eighteenth century and consolidated in the nineteenth and twentieth centuries, colonized Muslims, whose world had been destabilized by a violent intrusion, sought to find appropriate responses to their predicament. To intellectuals and people of reflection in this part of the world, both clerical and lay, regaining political independence became a major preoccupation. Searching in their own repositories of knowledge and tradition, some came to identify a grand theory based on Islam. In Islam, they found a social, political and economic theory, as well as a plan for action. Political Islam, as we know it today, came to the foreground as a liberation theory and a political agenda for a particular purpose. Contrary to spiritual Islam, which was concerned with regulating the individual's private relation with God for primarily the hereafter, political Islam emphasized the here and the now. Its ideologues and theoreticians maintained that Islam had a sociopolitical theory, enabling Muslims to deduce appropriate courses of action in the face of different predicaments. In political Islam, temporal issues of social justice, equity and independence became as important as rewards and punishments in the hereafter. The responsibility of the good Muslim became first and foremost national, social and collective.

To generations of anti-colonial Muslims, Islam became a religion of resistance, protest and insurgence against the occupying forces. In the highly charged political atmosphere of rolling back colonial incursions, spiritual Islam became associated with apolitical Islam and was looked down upon as a collaborationist position, invariably playing into the hands of the colonialists. Yet great multitudes of Muslims continued to live out their private apolitical spiritual Islam. For the most part, they frustrated the hopes and aspirations of those who wished to transform abruptly the religiosity of the people into a colossal anti-colonial wave. Some 205 years after the British East India Company defeated Mirza Mohammad Seraj al-Dowleh, the Nawab of Bengal at Plassey, Algeria obtained its independence in 1962. For two centuries, the political Islam of intellectuals and political leaders kindled underneath the dry forest of spiritual Islam, never really catching like wildfire, yet constantly challenging the rule of the colonialists.

The political Islam resulting from colonial penetration was primarily grounded in a soul-searching quest to find out why the colonialists had won, what was the key to their success and how Islam, relying on its own resources, could make a comeback. This was an Islamic discourse in opposition to the colonial political economy, their rule and their local middlemen. It was therefore a discourse about ideals, which would put to shame the ugly realities of subjugation, exploitation, injustice and violation of national sovereignty.

Yet before Western colonization, other kinds of political Islam ruled over the Muslim world. Except during the Crusades and the Mongol invasion of the mid thirteenth century, Islam in power was not threatened by a non-Islamic religious, philosophical, political and economic system, against which it needed to rally the pious people. It had neither an insurrectionary nor an oppositional political posture, as it constituted the political status quo. It needed to convince the people that the actual existing state of political, social and economic affairs was a reflection of the ideal Islam. So it derived its legitimacy to rule and presumed prerogative to blind obedience from the Muslim people by claiming to be the genuine administrator of Islam and the defender of its values as was practiced by the Prophet.

Naturally, instead of looking into Islam to find a critical and dynamic discourse of change, protestation and reformation, pre-colonial political Islam sought to consolidate its rule by prohibiting and discouraging dissent. In their worldly endeavour, the pre-colonial Islamic rulers evoked Islam as a tool to justify and maximize their rule. The discourse and expectation of political Islam *in power* is very different from political Islam *in opposition*. In times of peace, the former seeks a docile, neutralized, stupefied and apolitical public, which would facilitate its hegemony and tenure. Political Islam in opposition, however, seeks an awakened, engaged, alert and politicized community, enabling it to rally a successful rebellion against the false, non-Islamic or anti-Islamic forces. In the process of both defending worldly political power and challenging a political status quo, in the name of Islam, the key issue of what constitutes Islam comes to depend on who speaks for the faith and whether they employ the faith as an offensive or defensive political tool. Political Islam, either in opposition or as a ruling power, holds that the object of the faith is to usher in, construct and maintain a preconceived type of society imprinted by Islamic values. The modality of how to attain this objective and the levers employed to attain and retain power in the name of Islam can vary. A standard blueprint addressing these issues does not exist.

This book focuses on religious superstition used as a tool by Iranian Shiʻi political leaders to maintain their political hold on the people during the span of some 500 years. It seeks to investigate how superstition has been consistently cloaked in religious concepts, precepts and teachings to shape and numb popular behaviour and judgement in order to justify political hegemony and maintain power. The hypothesis that religion for temporal reasons has employed and spawned superstition and relied upon it to buttress its political, social and economic status applies equally to all three Abrahamic faiths. While superstitious ideas may have been equally common among Christians and Muslims up to the sixteenth century, it can be argued that due to the Reformation Movement in Europe, the intensity and prevalence of superstition as a religious discourse in the Christian world ebbed more dramatically and palpably than it did subsequently in the Muslim world. This book seeks to study how superstition as a religious discourse for political purposes, albeit with changes and mutations, has lingered on in Iran.

BELIEF, RELIGION, SUPERSTITION AND POLITICAL SUPERSTITION

In this book, beliefs and practices found and performed on the basis of an irrational cause and effect relation is considered superstitious. It is said that among the Irish, if you hear a cuckoo on your right you will have good luck for a year. Once such a belief becomes popular and common, it becomes folkloric. It may have been a legend particular to Ireland, or it may have been an old farmers' or old wives' tale. Breaking a mirror, walking under a ladder, coming across a black cat or an owl and spilling salt are just a few of the commonly shared superstitions among the people of the world. In all these cases, ominous outcomes are associated with unreasonably established causes. These beliefs can be considered as myths and fairy tales, resulting from the fictive minds of their propagators, mistaking false cause fallacies for acceptable explanations of truths. In the folklores and fairy tales, irrational causal relations happen automatically and in an unmanaged or unengineered fashion. The cuckoo sings, the cat or owl appear and the salt is accidentally spilt. There is no intended intervention to control, manipulate and change the course of the natural order. According to these folkloric myths, the natural order is altered as a result of an accident, and those who believe it attribute predictability to an event that, due to its irrational foundation, cannot be predictable. This is accidental or autonomous superstition.

Belief in sorcery, witchcraft and all sorts of magic, both black and white, can also be considered as superstition. Yet this type of superstitious belief is different from accidental or autonomous superstition. In these cases, the believer is convinced that someone can alter and change the laws of nature through the manipulation of some sort of supernatural force. This type of belief is not accidental but induced or caused by humans. The human agency is believed to have a supernatural power or be capable of mobilizing and controlling such powers to disrupt or alter the course of nature or history. In this case, the outcome of events or situations is also believed to be alterable through an object. This type of superstition is based on human engineering, and even though it may be traced to the Celts, their religion and the druids, their priests, through time, this type of magical manipulation has become detached from religion and has attained an unreligious if not anti-religious status. Belief in the power of magicians, witches and soothsayers to effectuate supernatural acts is human-driven superstition.

This work is not concerned with the above two types of superstition, since it is assumed that belief in them does not necessarily imply a false cause relation in which the outcome is attributed to the Divine or an intercessor in contact with the Divine. These folkloric, magical and basically none-divinely associated or ascribed irrational relations are certainly a part of the body of superstitious thought but do not constitute the type of superstition on which this study is focusing. The superstitious beliefs that this study is interested in can be considered as a religious subset of superstition. It involves belief in those irrational causal relations that are argued to be possible because of religiously justifiable arguments attributed to the interventionist agency of God or someone claiming some sort of representation, appointment, delegation or trusteeship from Him. Green may be considered by some as a colour bearing good luck. If the justification for it is not rooted in some religious explanation tracing it to some direct or indirect Divine will, plan or interpretation, it will not be considered as religious superstition. But if a priest or a clergy makes a claim to the luck-bearing property of the colour green, then such a belief will be considered as religious superstition and hence becomes a concern of this study.

Muslims articulate their belief in the existence and singularity of the Almighty by giving testimony that there is no God but God, and Mohammad is His Prophet. Muslims believe that the Qur'an is the word of God revealed to Mohammad. From the pages of the Qur'an, certain attributes of God can be gleaned. Among other attributes, God is believed to be eternal, the creator of the universe, the life giver and taker and the single Lord to be worshipped. He is most gracious and merciful. God is omnipotent. He has power over all things, and when He decrees something, it is done. He is omnipresent, seeing and hearing all things. God is omniscient, and nothing on earth or in heaven is hidden from Him. To Him belongs the dominion of heaven and earth, and He has no partner in his dominion. Nothing resembles God, as He is perfect, and nothing should be feared but Him. All will return to Him, and He shall gather everyone on the Day of Judgement. God is man's ultimate protector or helper. The order of the universe and natural cycles are His work and constitute signs for people who understand. God is the ultimate planner. Even when people take false gods, it is according to God's plan.

To Muslims, as to all monotheists, the ultimate cause of all things is God. Belief in God as the creator of the universe also implies the belief in God's natural order in the material world. The Qur'an reminds human beings that God created heaven and earth and all that is between them, "not for idle sport" or as a "pastime" (21:16–17).[1] Time and again, the Qur'an reiterates that creation is an orderly, systematic and carefully organized endeavour following the laws that the Almighty has set for it and synchronized it by. God invites human beings to reflect upon the methodical and precise operation of nature in order to see the signs of His glory. The Qur'an says:

He created the heavens and the earth in true (proportions): He makes the Night overlap the Day, and the Day overlap the Night. He has subjected the sun and the moon (to His Law): each follow a course for a time appointed. Is He not the exalted in power. (39:5).

According to the Qur'an, the earth has been "set in order" by God (7:56). He "regulates all affairs" in the universe, "explaining the Signs in detail" (13:2). It is the power of God that holds birds poised in the midst of the sky (16:79). God invites human beings to reflect on the perfect natural order that He has created as a proof of his omnipotence (2:164). He invites human beings in whatever condition they may be to "contemplate (the wonders of) creation in the heaven and the earth, (with the thought): 'Our Lord! Not for naught hast thou created (all) this! Glory to Thee!'" (3:191). Despite the accounts of the Prophet's earliest biographers, Muslims believe that, on the basis of the Qur'an, Mohammad's only miracle was the recitation of the Qur'an, as he was incapable of reading and writing at the time of the revelations. This was the self-evident Sign from God for those "endowed with knowledge" (29:48–49).

God is the supernatural creator of the universal natural order. The human capacity to speculate over, understand and decipher the secrets of this natural order is also a God-given power. We have come to understand God's rules of nature in this world through our reasoning. Yet we do not know of the natural flow of events or rules of nature in the hidden world, including the hereafter. Clearly, what is considered "natural" on earth could not be the same in the hidden world. What concerns us here is the operation of the temporal world. Only God has the power to contravene in the natural order that He has established in the universe and that human beings have gradually come to understand through their reflection and reasoning. The curiosity of human beings has motivated them to push for greater understanding of the universe and its laws as already defined and set out by God. God enjoined them to observe and think about creation.

---

[1] The numbers in brackets refer to the Surah and Ayah in *The Holy Qur'an*, (tr.) A. Y. 'Ali (Hertfordshire, 2000).

If, through some supernatural act, God were to intervene in His own natural laws, which have come to be the ones also understood and accepted by human beings in this world, the outcome would seem contradictory to human reasoning. Believers are convinced that God can intervene in the course of events in this world. Yet believers can also be convinced that God does not meddle with his own perfect creation. As the causality, modality and proof of any given claimed intervention remains beyond human understanding, believers could doubt the claim of other believers who maintain that they have witnessed God's agency. When human beings claim to have observed or witnessed an act of intervention by God, how can they convince others of their experience? Such claims remain only presumptions, as they can neither obtain God's explicit confirmation that a supernatural act resulted from His will nor can they be verified by any other means. The fact that God can transform or revoke the natural order that He has promulgated does not mean that He would do so. Why create the order to disrupt it? God is omnipotent; yet He warns that the creation of heaven and earth and all that is between them was "not for idle sport", as "a pastime" or purposeless (21:16–17; 3:191). He emphasizes that "We created them not except for just ends: but most of them do not understand" (44:38–39). The belief that the natural rules of this world could be tampered with, circumvented, outwitted, deceived, short-circuited and bent through the performance of certain mechanical rites, rituals or processes by evoking God's omnipotence contradicts the purposefulness, justice and, most important of all, God's signs of perfection and proof of omnipotence.

A superstitious reading of the world based on religion evokes God's supernatural powers and seeks to harness and manipulates them to undermine, distort and second-guess the orderly perfection of His creation for personal material ends in this world. A superstitious mindset seeks "special favours" from God in this world knowing that such demands are "exceptional cases". Demands for such favours are submitted to God or some holy figure who can secure God's power of intercession. The usual means of gaining special favours or expecting superstitious results is through the performance of "special" rituals, supplications or incantations. If the favours are granted every time that they are demanded, the attainment of supernatural results becomes a general rule, defeating the purpose of using God to outwit the natural order that He has created. The superstitious mind, in search of supernatural results expects God to violate his own rules arbitrarily and inequitably just for the sake and interest of an individual. It may be hypothesized that when the Qur'an speaks of those who do not understand that the world was created only "for just ends" (44:38–39), it may be referring to the superstitious.

It could be argued that, to the religious superstitious, creation may indeed seem like an "idle sport" and a "pastime", a plaything capable of manipulation to obtain desired supernatural ends and results at will. The religiously superstitious subconsciously believe that those whom they call upon as intercessors to effectuate their "un-natural" wish have the power to call successfully upon and obtain God's powers to intervene in the natural order. In other cases, religious superstition claims that the practice of certain rites, rituals, prayers or use of certain objects may produce exceptional or supernatural results. In both these cases, the religiously superstitious subconsciously believe that creations of God, animate or inanimate, can control and dictate God's actions and powers. At this point, the monotheist can slip into polytheism.

Throughout history, numerous factors have been cited as the source of superstitious drives. Any combination of real or imagined fear, anxiety, desperation, helplessness and powerlessness, on the one hand, or excessiveness, on the other hand, can trigger superstition. The precariousness, arbitrariness and insecurity of life characterized by low life expectancy, high death rates, poor sanitation and health conditions; widespread plagues and natural disasters; ignorance and illiteracy; low levels of technology in agriculture; famine, malnutrition and poverty; and finally wars, violence, expropriations, lootings, despotic rulers and lawlessness in the Middle Ages and the Early Modern period can be considered as the context in which superstitious beliefs flourished. Superstitious beliefs are argued to reflect "the hazards of an intensely insecure environment".[2]

Superstition is argued to be caused primarily by the fact that human beings cannot "govern all their circumstances by set rules" and that their fortunes and well-being ascends and descends independent of their control.[3] According to Baruch Spinoza, an excommunicated Jew who was groomed to become a rabbi, superstition "comes to all men naturally" even though it is said to spring not from reason.[4] To Spinoza who lived in Amsterdam at the same time as Mohammad-Baqer Majlesi lived in Esfahan, superstition kicks in when "hope and fear are struggling for mastery".[5] To Spinoza, Alexander of Macedonia was the perfect example

---

[2] K. Thomas, *Religion and the Decline of Magic* (London, 1991), p. 5.
[3] B. A. Spinoza, *Theologico-Political Treatise and Political Treatise*, (tr.) R. H. M. Elwis (New York, 2004), p. 3.
[4] Ibid., p. 4.   [5] Ibid., p. 3.

of a superstitious person. He sought the council of seers and fortune-tellers when he feared the outcome of a campaign. However, having defeated Darius the mighty Persian King, Alexander ceased to consult his sooth-sayers. But once again, after having been frightened by reverses, abandoned by his allies and fallen sick, he returned to superstition.[6]

Faced with unpredictable, unmanageable and gloomy private, social and political conditions, people turn to exceptional and supernatural measures and methods. Religion and men of religion as self-professed experts on God are the most obvious sources of consultation and solace. The extraordinary solutions demanded by the flocks are not materially within the power and capacity of the men of religion. Yet certain men of religion within all three Abrahamic faiths pretended to possess or were believed capable of mustering supernatural powers. They laid their claim to possessing and providing supernatural solutions on the account that they were the servants of God and therefore more familiar with His ways than others. Even if they did not believe this to be true, their flock pressed them to prove themselves useful and provide ready-made solutions. According to Spinoza, popular or superstitious religion, which he calls "heathen superstition", is "summed up as respect for ecclesiastics".[7] The process of sanctifying and adulating the ecclesiastics leads faiths to become "mere compounds of credulity and prejudices", "carefully fostered for the purpose of extinguishing the last spark of reason".[8]

It could be argued that for believers who feel that faith in God, the source and origin of all phenomena, is too abstract and impalpable a concept, superstition may act as a substitute to facilitate bridging the mental gap between the idea of God and feeling or sensing God. Such a bridge-building process could eventually lead to disbelief. The belief in predetermination or free volition, and even a combination of both, need not necessarily create a space for superstition. The pious could believe that God may intervene in the material world in mysterious ways. But such a position does not necessitate the belief that He is in need of agents or things in the material world to delegate his powers, in order to carry out His design, and to represent Him. The notion of intercession and the role of a holy personality as intermediary between human beings and God open the door to granting powerful agency to particular individuals, only indirectly in relation with and connected to God. When this Janus-faced being, the intercessor, becomes the object of adulation and is effectively and implic-itly yet not officially and explicitly substituted for God, then superstition

---

[6] Ibid., p. 4.   [7] Ibid., p. 6.   [8] Ibid., p. 7.

transforms monotheism to polytheism. This substitution process attributes to mortals those functions and characteristics that are specific to God. Thus a space is created for human godheads or idols to be re-created and conjured on earth to conserve a humanized image of the sacred too complicated to fathom, philosophically and intellectually, in its intangible pure form. From the perspective of non-superstitious believers, it could be argued that the inability of naive believers to comprehend or come to grips with God, the impalpable Absolute Truth, spawns an ideal condition for power-seeking ecclesiastics and rulers to come forward, purporting to assuage the fears and needs that lie at the root of superstitious beliefs by laying claim to Divine powers.

Institutionalized religions systematize, articulate and popularize God's messages, designs and intentions. The men of religion act as interpreters and spokesmen of God's messages. In this role, they can blur the fine line between God's supernatural powers that are solely His dominion and the superstitious claims of men to somehow control and channel these powers. The belief that in some way and for some unknown reason God's systematic natural order can be interfered, meddled and tampered with in His name is passed off as God's omnipotence. Religions can claim superiority by cultivating the superstitious notion that they are the best mediums to effectuate and deliver supernatural feats. They thus pretend to be the vendors of merchandise that they do not possess; they therefore become false pretenders of false religions.

The Divine or hidden world and all that belongs to it is ruled and managed by laws that are different from the laws governing our temporal world and are unknown to human beings. What may be considered as supernatural and extra-rational explanations in the material world may very well apply to the natural course of events in the hidden world. In the hidden world, rationality, the human toolbox for resolving problems in the material world is rendered completely superfluous and ineffectual before the far superior and powerful original source, God. In the Divine world, the cause of events and conditions are divinely willed and beyond the grasp of human reason and rationality. It is inevitably the outcome of God's will. It has taken centuries for human beings to develop their understanding of the rules and laws of the material world, the orderly creation of God. The laws that govern the material world are partially known to human beings. That which is known could be argued to be only a part of what God has created and put into motion. Thus we are dealing with the two very different worlds of the material (earth) and the hidden (heaven and hell).

Separating the two worlds does not undermine belief in God or the hereafter. The relation between seeking proximity to God and performing good deeds in this world in light of expecting rewards and salvation in the next is not ruptured by arguing that the laws of heaven and earth are different. Belief in the causal relation between piety in this world and salvation in the hereafter does not necessarily presuppose the belief in the intervention of the hidden world through the intermediary of a mortal in the material world. Expecting punishments and rewards in the hereafter for behaviour and acts in the material world is a matter of belief and faith in an otherwise unverifiable principle. This principle, however, does not necessarily foster superstition. Rewards and punishments in the hereafter, expressed in a language understandable to human beings is an experience that the pious can believe in but will be able to experience and verify only after they have passed away.

As long as belief in the two worlds, their main actors and agents, motives, laws, problem-solving toolboxes, modes of operation and objectives does not imply daily criss-crossing, slipping and overlapping between them, superstition may not find room to grow. The claim to "happenings" resulting from alterations in the natural course of events, alien to and inexplicable by rational and scientific means, can be labelled as superstition. The label superstition rather than spiritual experience is used when an attempt is made to systematize and institutionalize a supernatural alteration. The case of a person experiencing a religious visitation or inspiration, for which there can be no scientific proof in the material world, is different from the person reciting a prayer given to him by a priest for the purpose of warding off highway robbers or a person who goes on pilgrimage to a shrine that has been identified by a religious institution as holy and where miracles occur. In the first case, there is no bargain. Nothing is offered for a gain. Something otherworldly, beyond the grasp of the laws of our material world, may have occurred. In the second case, a bargain is sought. Gain is maximized and loss is minimized through the claim that God will use His omnipotence to give satisfaction, having heard a prayer or having observed one of His close servants being revered. To assume that God is needy and will intervene in His own perfect creation to alter the course of events just because some priest, sincere or insincere, has provided a prayer formula or an incantation that would secure God's approval is a case of superstition.

On a personal and private level, individuals can believe in the idea that God could alter the natural course of events. Belief in different degrees of Providence resulting from His autonomous will and design is part and parcel of faith and does not imply a superstitious outlook, unless Providence is assumed to be non-autonomous and induced by mortals and things. Throughout history, personal religious or supernatural experiences have acted as important shifting factors in the life of individuals. These spiritual or mystical experiences have cleared the vision and illuminated the heart of ordinary men. To those who claim to have experienced them, they have provided certitude in the face of deep scepticism, saving them from the pits of desperation and providing them with hope and a purpose in life. The lives and legends of the Catalan Ramon Lull and the Persian Jalal ad-Din Mohammad Rumi in the thirteenth century and the Frenchman Louis Massignon and the Iranian ʿAli Shariʿati in the twentieth century can be seen as cases of men who, according to their own accounts, underwent such experiences. The alteration in the course of events does not result from an institutionalized attempt, request or demand. It is a one-on-one relation between human beings and God with no official intermediaries to render services or draw benefit from the success of the results obtained. Such experiences do not bear material or political benefits for the individuals claiming to have undergone them. It remains a private source of energy, sealed from social, economic and political manipulations and capitalizations. As such, private spiritual experiences are different from institutionalized, commodified and politicized spiritual experiences, even though both lay claim to a supernatural experience.

Whereas personal supernatural experiences, if unpublicized, can hardly be abused to foster hegemonic power relations, the intentional public communication of such experiences shifts their significance and implication from the private realm to a public one. It concomitantly lays the groundwork for the emergence of a top-down power structure where the selected few with self-proclaimed access to God's omnipotence stand at the apex of this pyramid and the masses, devoid of such abilities, spread out at the base. Religiously, politically and socially, this unequal "condition of connectedness" to God institutionalizes a relationship of dominance and dependence. The act of publicizing and politicizing a personal "supernatural experience" implies reaching a wider public to impact, impress or convince them of the sacredness of the person involved. Claiming a privileged superhuman status provides an effective springboard for an over-ambitious political or religious leader wishing to impress the simple common folk.

By proclaiming or hinting at access to powers that are God's monopoly, a claimant to "superhuman status" is effectively expecting the respect, obedience and even worship that are reserved for God. In societies where, at some point in their history, certain segments of the population accept the claim of their rulers, clergy and/or lay to connectedness with God and come to believe in their power to alter the natural order of events, political superstition feeding on religious superstition enters the sociopolitical scene as a new force competing for public respectability and allegiance.

Rich traditions of superstitious beliefs have flourished in all societies at some point in their history, and lent themselves to embracing political superstition or acceptance of a mortal as a divinely guided leader. Once society accepts a leader as divinely selected and supported, an unfettered sociopolitical control mechanism, the ultimate objective of such politically inspired superstitious claims, is put into place. The self-proclaimed vice-gerent of God arrogates absolutist rule and demands unquestioned obedience and allegiance from his believing and complying subjects. A seemingly harmless superstitious tradition and culture becomes the cradle of political despotism and absolutism. Political superstition is the outcome of the desire of power-seeking individuals, instrumentalizing and manipulating spiritualism, to present the laws and modes of operation of the hidden world as constantly intervening and operating in the material world in their favour and in line with their political designs.

For Muslims, those who pretend connectedness with the hidden world cannot claim to have a direct relation with God, as believers maintain that God speaks through Angel Gabriel only to His prophets. Divination or the ability to foretell the future assumes foreknowledge of the future through some Divine agency. Any foretelling of the future for political ends, be it through divination by dreams or the type of necromancy reported in the case of Shah Esmaʿil (Ismail) when he hears a voice forbidding him to pursue Shahi Beyg in the river, lest he would fall into a deadly whirlpool and be killed, is an act of political superstition. A politician laying claim to directly or indirectly possessing any of the powers that are in God's monopoly is an impostor hoping that the credulity of the common folk would allow him to realize his plans by abusing religiosity and faith. Reciting a set of prayers chosen by the clergy and said to produce supernatural material results due to their intrinsic capacity to move God to approve such results are also exercises in superstition. The fact that the pious come to believe in objects, words and mortals, possessing powers capable of moving the Divine to effectuate supernatural outcomes for their individual benefits, reflects an unconscious state of idolatry as human beings effectively project the powers of God onto others or other things.

LEGACY OR AHISTORICISM

The resilience and endurance of an almost time-resistant set of quasi-religious and superstitious characteristics attributed to Iranian political leaders is the main focus of this study. The notion that Persian rulers possess some sort of Divine attribute is probably as ancient as Persian history. Pre-Islamic Persian kings were always said to be vested with a God-given fortune (*farnah*).[9] The term *farr-e izadi* (*farnah-e izadi*) or the Divine Fortune, as used in the *Zand-Avesta*, the sacred book of Zoroastrians, refers to a Divine illumination that, once shone upon a person's heart, would set him apart from others, identifying him as the King, the chosen one.[10] As a consequence of this Divine illumination, the King obtains perfection in religious and material realms. The ancient Persian kings were legitimized and differentiated from their subjects by an assumed "special relationship" with Ahura Mazda and other gods. This special connection, in turn, conferred upon them the "Divine Right" to rule.

According to Ferdowsi's myth-based history of Persia, Jamshid, the first of kings, is said to have been invulnerable, in possession of magical powers, capable of seeing the unseen and foretelling the future with the help of his magical cup (*jam-e jam*) and special ring, sometimes referred to as Solomon's ring. Jamshid was the first to possess the "Divine Fortune" or the royal glory. After some 550 years, Jamshid is said to have lost his "Divine Fortune" and subsequently his throne after having lied, grown arrogant and claimed divinity for himself.[11]

After Persia became Muslim, the pre-Islamic notion of kings possessing a God-given fortune (*farnah or farr*) underwent a subtle transformation in form but not in content. The kings' God-given fortune takes the much more descriptive form and image of the shadow of God on earth (*zell-ollah*). This royal title retained the superhuman and sacred characteristic of the kings. Mohammad-Baqer Majlesi refers to Shah Soltan Hoseyn, the last Safavi (Safavid) king, as the "Shah of Shahs (*Shahanshah*) of an army of angels", the "embodiment of all Divine graces" and "the shadow of God on earth".[12] The notion of king as shadow of God on earth and the embodiment of all Divine graces sought to convince the people that kings

---

[9] J. Wiesehofer, *Ancient Persia* (London, 1996), p. 30.
[10] M. Moin, *Farhang Farsi*, vol. II (Tehran, 1364), p. 2493.
[11] M. Omidsalar, 'Jamshid in Persian Literature', in *Encyclopedia Iranica*, Vol. XIV, Fascicle 5: pp. 522–528.
[12] M. B. Majlesi, *Haq al-Yaqin* (Tehran, n.d), p. 2.

possessed Divine attributes and Divine missions. It implied that kings were connected with the hidden world and were divinely guided and protected. Their subjects, the people, were thus not only supposed to be obedient to them because of their worldly military might, but primarily because of their special connection with God and their appointment by Him. Why else would the Shi'i king be a shadow of God, if God did not will him to be so?

It was, therefore, not surprising that certain Safavi clerics maintained that the political rule and power of Shi'i leaders was willed and approved by God, the Prophet and the imams.[13] Chardin, who visited Persia three times during the reigns of Shah 'Abbas II and Shah Soleyman Safavi, wrote that the majority of Iranians believed that their kings were the representatives of the imams and the deputy of the Hidden Imam during his occultation. According to Chardin, once the Twelfth Imam reappears, the Shah would willingly pass on to him all his powers and responsibilities. On that day, the Shah would humbly hold the rein of the Imam's horse and walk in front of the holy horseman.[14] According to Chardin, a common belief among Iranians of the late Safavi period was that not only is the Shah the deputy of the Imam, but he is also endowed with some sort of supernatural power such as healing the sick.[15]

This study spans some 500 years of Iranian history seeking to understand and explain the role, practice and influence of superstition with an emphasis on political superstition. The main hypothesis of this study is that political superstition has crept into and at times become imbued with a particular and hegemonic reading of Shi'ism. The fact that Twelver Shi'ism became the dominant religion of Persians after the founding of the Safavi dynasty in 1501 enabled this particular brand of superstitious Shi'ism to develop widely and propagate its tenants as a state religion and ideology. The lion's share of systematizing, institutionalizing and subsequently popularizing this superstitious brand of Shi'ism goes to Mohammad-Baqer Majlesi, who lived under five Safavi shahs. This book seeks to demonstrate that, despite the passage of some three centuries from the death of Majlesi, this brand of superstitious Shi'ism, which will be called Majlesism, continues to clasp tenaciously at the mind and belief of some Iranians. The claim to the historical tenacity of superstition does not suggest that the

---

[13] M. Sefatgol, *Sakhtar, Nehad va Andisheh Dini dar Iran-e asr Safavi* (Tehran, 1381), pp. 514–515.

[14] J. Chardin, *Voyages de Monsieur le chevalier Chardin en Perse et autres liux d'Orient*, Tome 2 (Amsterdam, 1711), p. 207. Chardin uses the Persian expression of 'Gelaudar Imam'.

[15] Ibid., p. 209.

influence and popularity of this discourse has not considerably diminished in time, but the mere fact that a twenty-first-century politician believes that this type of a discourse can fall on receptive ears implies that such ideas continue to resonate with some segments of the Iranian people.

Case studies of Shah Esmaʿil Safavi of the sixteenth century and Mohammad-Reza Shah Pahlavi and President Mahmud Ahmadinejad of the twentieth and twenty-first century aim to show the historical obstinacy of religiously based superstitious discourses among both the Iranian public and its political leaders. Shah Esmaʿil Safavi's rise to power and the accounts of his political superstition predate the birth of Majlesi by some 110 years. Shah Esmaʿil was reared and seeped in the extremist and superstitious Shiʿi doctrines of his forefathers, Sheykh Joneyd and Heydar. Majlesi borrowed from and was influenced by the discourse of the Safavi dynasty's founders. However, on the basis of his own research, supported by the Safavi court, he further compiled, codified and systematized a politically superstitious discourse. In his role as a most prominent Shiʿi jurist, he gave religious credence to this particular reading of Shiʿism by seeking and obtaining support for it mainly in reports attributed to the imams that had long been discarded or banished by mainstream Shiʿi jurists. Given his official position in the court of Safavi Shahs, Majlesi was successful in propagating and officializing a superstition-based Shiʿism, Majlesism, which as an ideology sought to assure the absolute rule of the shahs while keeping the people docile and subdued by maintaining them immersed in superstitious beliefs.

Claims made by both Mohammad-Reza Pahlavi, the King of Kings and the Love or Light of the Aryans (*Aryamehr*), and Mahmud Ahmadinejad, the sixth President of the Islamic Republic of Iran, demonstrate how modern-day Iranian political leaders have continued this tradition of impressing upon the people their "witnessed" supernatural experiences. By making such public claims, they seek to attribute to themselves supernatural powers for the purpose of commanding authority and respect while disarming the rational faculties of the pious. Can it be maintained that Mohammad-Reza Pahlavi and Mahmud Ahmadinejad have drawn from Majlesi's writings? Is it necessary to establish such a link? The establishment of a direct causal relationship between Majlesi's discourse and the behaviour of modern Iranian Shiʿi is difficult if not impossible. Yet the cyclical resurgence of claims and accounts, which echo Majlesi's religious discourse, provides circumstantial evidence that the actual existing Shiʿi culture continues to be influenced by Majlesism. It may even be argued that certain Shiʿi strands believe Majlesism to be the authentic

reading of Shi'i Islam. Recent events in Iran have once more demonstrated
the power and deep roots of Majlesism.

Majlesi's works have continued to exercise an undisputable authority
among the guild of Shi'i preachers who are key propagators of popular
Shi'ism among the common folk. These indispensable religious emissaries
acting as intermediaries between the clerical establishment, *rowhaniyyat*,
and the people are the *vo'az* (preachers), the *maddah*s (eulogizers of the
imams) and the *rowzeh khanha* (mourners of the imams). The common
folk obtain a significant part of their religious education from this guild,
which in turn relies heavily on the plethora of Majlesi's writings as the
prime source of their sermons and speeches. Even those who use other
sources invariably draw upon works that have been modelled and crafted
on the basis of Majlesi's. Sheykh 'Abbas Qomi, whose popular book,
Mafateeh al-Jennan, is a major source of reference for this guild, considers
himself a loyal follower of Majlesi's style and path. The Majlesi Shi'i
culture, his particular discourse, methodology, language, interpretations,
value system, historiography, messianism, hagiography, demonizations
and accounts of events have, for centuries, found their way to the psyche
of believers and continue to shape and colour their minds.

Majlesi's zealous supporters concur with his ardent opponents on the
compelling, singular and seemingly interminable influence and imprint of
his discourse on Iranian Shi'ism. They differ substantially, however, on
their respective assessment of Majlesi's contribution to the understanding,
interpretation, presentation, orientation, image and long-term viability of
Shi'ism as a living faith that needs to guide believers in an evolving world
and provide answers for their emerging problems. The major bone of
contention in the debate between his proponents and opponents is whether
Majlesi's brand of Shi'ism and its sociopolitical and economic consequences constitute a true reflection of Shi'ism based on proper Shi'i sources or
whether it is a deviation from and a distortion of genuine Shi'ism. In this
work, the arguments of his numerous ardent supporters and admirers is
not reviewed.

In the 1970s, 'Ali Shari'ati, the prominent Shi'i intellectual and peda-
gogue, sometimes dubbed as the ideological father of the 1979 revolution
in Iran coined the term "Safavi Shi'ism" as the archetype of a degenerated
Shi'ism in contrast to "'Ali's Shi'ism" representing the ideal Shi'ism
of Imam 'Ali. To Shari'ati, "Safavi Shi'ism" represented an official "state
religion" stemming from the political and economic alliance of the official
clerical institution, which to him was an aberration of true Shi'ism,
with authoritarian and corrupt monarchs. According to Shari'ati, the

sociopolitical role of "Safavi Shiʿism" was to legitimize religiously the exploitation and bondage of the people, subsequently guaranteeing the political survival and economic enrichment of the ruling religious, political and economic triad. To this end, Shariʿati believed that the Safavi clerics not only distracted, duped and stupefied the masses with their superstitious brand of Shiʿism, but also succeeded to keep them docile and servile. For Shariʾati, "Safavi Shiʿism" had elaborated and instituted a reactionary and repressive political philosophy, divinely justifying the people's blind obedience to the dictatorial political rule of monarchs and the stupefying dictates of the clerical institution. This brand of Shiʿism, he believed, operated on the basis of "polytheism, superstition and divisiveness".[16]

Shariʿati not only holds "Safavi Shiʿism" as socially and politically reactionary, despotic, repressive, exploiting and bankrupt, but also charges it with religious ignorance, misrepresentation, falsification, fabrication and superstition. To Shariʿati, the most prominent and outstanding figure of Safavi clerics (*rowhaniyyat Safavi*) is Majlesi, whom he also sarcastically refers to as the thirteenth Imam of the Shiʿi.[17] In an iconoclastic statement encapsulating his drive to expose the deviations of "Safavi Shiʿism" and dethrone it, Shariʿati says, "I consider Gandhi the fire worshipper more worthy of being a Shiʿi than ʿAllameh Majlesi".[18] To Shariʿati, who sought a Shiʿi reformation or protestant movement, Majlesi was the Pope and "Safavi Shiʿism" the Papacy.

There can be little doubt that Majlesi's discourse and religious outlook has extended into twentieth- and twenty-first-century Iran. It continues to be a living legacy. While Majlesi's writings and teachings have, on the one hand, played a key historical role in mentally and religiously rearing the common folk to accept phantasmical and superstitious notions as an integral part of their faith, his firm belief in the incapacity of the same common folk to reflect has made a solid case for the absolutist and unfettered rule of the clerics or the kings or a combination of both. According to Majlesi, such rulers obtain their political authority and religious legitimacy from some sort of connectedness to a Divine source.

Five hundred years of Iranian history since the rise of the Safavis has been punctuated by the creation of "superstitious sacred histories" by rulers seeking to present themselves as representatives of the Divine. As Maxime Rodinson has argued, "every ideological movement creates its own sacred

---

[16] A. Shariʿati, *Collected Works*, vol. 9 (Tehran, 1359), p. 198.
[17] Ibid., p. 124; A. Shariʿati, *Collected Works*, vol. 1 (Tehran, n.d), p. 9.
[18] A. Shariʿati, *Collected Works*, vol. 1, p. 12.

history".[19] This sacred history needs to present rival discourses and those who challenge its authority as the embodiment of evil and the discourse or ideology itself as the inevitable historically perfected antidote to all "the evils of the age".[20] The leader or founder of a superstitious ideological movement "is credited with extraordinary powers and is glorified occasionally to the point of deification".[21] Such a leader needs to be presented to the public as a superhuman, drawing his authority and legitimacy from the supernatural forces of the hidden world. Opposition to this ideological movement, its leaders and followers is demonized, castigated, damned and subsequently exorcized and purified by any means possible. To expose their evil nature, all that is sacred to them must be rendered diabolic, and all that may be diabolic about this ideological movement must be rendered sacred. A considerable part of post-Safavi Iranian sacred history has been constructed around common and prevalent themes of Majlesi's discourse.

Nearly two months after the disputed June 2009 presidential elections returned Ahmadinejad to office and plunged Iran into its first serious post-revolution crises, the new President was officially confirmed by Ayatollah Khameneh'i (the leader of the revolution) and sworn in at the parliament (*majles*). A few days after the new President's confirmation ceremony, Ayatollah Mesbah Yazdi, the religio-ideological mastermind behind Ahmadinejad's ascent to power, claimed that, "Once the President is appointed and confirmed by the leader and becomes his agent, he will be exposed to the rays emanating from this source of light [Khameneh'i]". Ayatollah Mesbah Yazdi added that "when the President receives his edict from the Guardian Jurist (*valiy-e faqih*) obedience to him [the President] is the same as or on par with obedience to God".[22]

This was the first time in the Islamic Republic that the religious as well as the political status of a mortal president and that of the mortal clerical leader who empowered him were placed on a par with God. The people were being asked to pay the same obedience to the Creator as to His creations on earth. As blasphemous and blunt as the statement may have been, it was not completely novel to Iranians of an older generation. It echoed the old monarchical saying in pre-revolutionary Iran: "Be it the command of God or the Shah [as they are the same]" (*cheh farman-e yazdan cheh farman-e shah*). Ayatollah Mesbah Yazdi's reiteration of the fact that Ayatollah Khameneh'i's endorsement of Ahmadinejad's

[19] M. Rodinson, *Europe and the Mystique of Islam* (London, 2006), pp. 10–11.
[20] Ibid.   [21] Ibid.   [22] *Etemad Melli* (22 Mordad 1388).

worldly political powers, in effect, placed obedience to his political office on a par with that of God, recalled similar exaggerated statements by Mohammad-Baqer Majlesi in relation to Safavi shahs.

Mesbah Yazdi and Majlesi are of the same lineage in terms of their perception and vision of Shi'ism. Both men believe that there is only one single rendition of Islam and that only one message and one project can be deduced from it. To them, their particular view of Shi'ism is the only righteous and True Shi'ism. Both men share in the belief that they are the embodiment of Shi'ism. Majlesi's political use of superstition and religion in the service of the ruling powers is replicated by Mesbah Yazdi. In Ayatollah Khameneh'i, Majlesi's twenty-first-century kindred has found a clerical ruler who has combined the politico-military sword of authority with a so-called divinely confirmed religious legitimacy to rule unquestionably over the people in the name of God, Shi'ism and the imams. Mesbah Yazdi shares Majlesi's disdain for the opinion, judgement and reasoning of anyone who dares to question, oppose or contradict the ruling Guardian Jurist, who is claimed to have been granted authority over the people by God. It will be argued that Majlesi had a holistic Islamic project to mould society in the image of what he believed was the True Shi'i Islam. His modern day legatee has a similar vision that he wishes to impose upon society, by force if need be. The propagation of superstition, with differences in degrees, plays an important role in their politico-social quest to mesmerize, stupefy and control the pious.

It would be absurd and ahistoric to suggest that Majlesism has survived unscathed and unchanged throughout the centuries and that those clerics championing his ideology and discourse today are concerned with the exact same time-bound issues with which he was engaged. Clearly, time and history have left their imprint on what constitutes the immediate brief of the faith and the threats to it. In the twenty-first century, Majlesi's disciples do not directly and openly engage in denouncing Sunnis as Majlesi did. Nor do they consider Majlesi's prohibition of training and flying pigeons or his edict to smash Esfahan's Indian idols as pressing religious concerns. Yet the principles, fundaments and major axes of Majlesi's discourse continue to weave through the discourse of his present-day followers. It is this persistent continuity of certain core beliefs popularized and propagated by Majlesi that raises the issue of legacy. This study will also try to demonstrate that the core of Majlesi's religious ideology and its sociopolitical consequences can partially explain the state of mind and behaviour of some of the key clerical and non-clerical figures operating in present-day Iran.

THE LIMITATIONS OF THE SUPERNATURAL
POLITICAL LEADER

He who is capable of convincing, deluding or forcing society or parts of it into believing that a mortal can be guided, supported and accompanied by God, his Prophet or the imams in order to carry out a worldly mission in their name is making a claim to the powers of God, without daring to say so. Tiptoeing between the blasphemy of claiming divinity or certain Divine attributes and the political temptation to present themselves as though they were endowed with extraordinary abilities creates a grey zone in which the people are supposed to accept the claimants' pretence to a "unique status" as part human and part superhuman. This grey zone sometimes led the devout followers of Shah Esmaʻil Safavi to think of him squarely as a reincarnation of Imam ʻAli and hence slip into infidelity. The daunting yet unverifiable metaphysical attributes and powers associated with connectedness to the hidden world significantly enhances the appeal of mundane politicians in the eyes of their stupefied constituency, as small as this may be, thus transforming the self-perceived superhuman leader into an unrivalled and supreme political, social and religious force.

Iranian political leaders have tried to establish causal relations between sandstorms and military victories, the dream of drinking a potion and immediate recovery from a deadly disease, being engulfed by a column of light and the power to mesmerize diplomats to listen attentively to a speech at the UN. In all these cases, it is explicitly or implicitly claimed that an imam or a manifestation of him interfered in order to produce the uncanny outcomes. The "superhuman status" derived from the claim that the superhuman is somehow divinely chosen or protected enables the pretender or claimant to have at his disposition both rational arguments ordinarily available to worldly politicians, as well as non-rationally comprehensible explanations rooted in the hidden world and unverifiable by human methods of scientific enquiry.

A superhuman ruler, supposedly capable of swiftly relieving insurmountable hardships and misfortunes, could explain away or justify difficult or rationally incomprehensive situations by evoking higher-order imperatives only known to those endowed with superhuman characteristics. Metaphysical and spiritual reasons may subsequently be evoked to account for their predicament. The superhuman ruler is not responsible and accountable to his subjects, as he can claim that his responsibility is only to God, the Prophet and the imams who have chosen him. He would demand that his subjects accept his decisions and their condition, as adverse as that may be, as though it were the will of God, the Prophet or the imams. The sum of these two – rational and supernatural – tools of persuasion and conviction provides an incredibly potent powerhouse, lusted for by any power-seeking individual who would dare make such a claim and succeed, only temporarily to walk through the minefield that it naturally creates.

For at least 500 years, if not more, certain Iranian rulers have made explicit and implicit claims to being "supernatural leaders", part human and part sacred, and some have believed them, followed them and staked their lives for them. What can be said about a modern state in which the social, psychological and political conditions lend themselves to and enable a leader to claim supernatural attributes as if it was 500 years ago? Furthermore, how can such pretenders earnestly believe that society or segments of it would come to believe in and accept such pretences as genuine? Just as Shah Esmaʿil Safavi claimed to be connected with the hidden world and benefit from heavenly grace and Divine support through the imams, Mohammad-Reza Pahlavi and Mahmud Ahmadinejad, through their phantasmical claims, continued to behave politically in the same old tradition centuries later. This reality makes the quest of understanding why far-fetched beliefs have proven so resilient, more pressing.

When Shah Esmaʿil Safavi's claim to supernaturalness and connectedness with the hidden world was pitted against the Ottoman Soltan Salim's superior canon power, the Complete Spiritual Guide (*morshed-e kamel*) and the perfect Shiʿi Shah drowned his despair and grief in alcohol. Once Mohammad-Reza Shah's self-proclaimed divinely entrusted mission was challenged by Ruhollah Khomeyni in the early 1960s, after some resistance, he reverted to a privatized spiritual Islam, implicitly withdrawing his claim to being divinely chosen and supported. When an end was put to his monarchy, the last Iranian Shiʿi Shah resorted to a meek and unsatisfactory defence of his previous claim to Divine protection. He insisted that those who had taken power in 1979 were not Shiʿi Muslims but a combination of "black reactionary forces" (the Shah's usual manner of reference to his clerical opponents) and atheist foot soldiers of International Communism, as if such forces would be stronger than the will of God, in the eyes of a true believer.[23]

Ahmadinejad's private moment of realization and clarity came in the landmark presidential elections of June 2009. The man who had given a strong public impression of being the Hidden Imam's chosen and protected

[23] M. R. Pahlavi, *Pasokh be Tarikh* (n.p., 1371), pp. 177–178, 300.

agent committed to preparing his imminent return was faced with what is widely believed to have been a blowing defeat at the polls. One day after some two million people in Tehran marched against what they believed to be the great fraud at the polls, Ahmadinejad organized a meeting of some fifty thousand of his supporters at which he called the throngs of his opponents the "dregs and scum of society" (*khas o khashak*). In the stark face of reality and on pay-back day of claims or intimations to connectedness with the hidden world, leaders who sow political super-stition are forced into the dark chamber of denial. Their reactions vary from taking to alcohol, blaming foreign powers to be and rejecting their own people who have seen through them. What was an electoral fraud to a seemingly large majority of Iranians was given a religious spin by those whose political and economic interests were threatened by the people's vote. This was another attempt at political superstition.

Morteza Moqtada'i, the director of the Qom Seminary School and one of the few clerics who came to Ahmadinejad's support immediately after the 2009 presidential election, claimed that "this election is approved or confirmed by the Hidden Imam and God and there are no problems surrounding it".[24] Hamid Rasa'i, a junior cleric, a member of the parlia-ment and a zealous proponent of Ahmadinejad, repeated Moqtada'i's claim that irrespective of what the people may think, religion, God and the Hidden Imam are on the side of Ahmadinejad. He informed the people that the leader of the revolution had announced the involvement of the Twelfth Imam's invisible hand in the elections.[25] Rasa'i's statement was in reference to Ayatollah Khameneh'i's first reaction to the official announce-ment of the 2009 presidential election results proclaiming Ahmadinejad's landslide victory. The Leader of the Islamic Revolution and the Islamic Republic of Iran, Ayatollah Khameneh'i had said, "Verily there was a Divine miraculous hand behind the elections . . .".[26]

The popular objection and resistance to the 2009 election results could be considered as an important shift in perceptions. It demonstrated that a meaningful majority of the common folk had become immune to the illogical and superstitious spin that certain religious voices, presenting themselves as representatives of the Twelfth Imam, were trying to put on mundane political wrongdoings. The aftermath of the elections demon-strated that the power of political superstition in stupefying and inculcat-ing blind obedience in the people had radically dwindled.

[24] http://www.bbc.co.uk/persian/1g/iran/2009/07/090707_mg_ir88_aft
[25] http://parlemannews.com/?n=1778   [26] *Etemad* (25 Khordad 1388).

THE GREEN MOVEMENT: TRANSITIONING FROM
TRADITIONAL TO MODERN?

In late spring and early summer of 2009, the media gave news of unfolding events in Iran. News flashes of the following sorts kept sweeping across the front pages of newspapers, television screens and websites. Would Iranians get excited about the tenth presidential election? As jockeying among presidential candidates continues, general enthusiasm among the people is bubbling. Musavi launches his Green Movement, actively supported by Khatami the reformist ex-president. The Green Movement is sweeping across the country and gaining momentum, while Ahmadinejad's popularity is ebbing. Musavi's victory at the polls seems imminent as voters flock to the poll booths on Election Day. Musavi claims victory in the early hours of Saturday, promising celebrations. The official Iranian News Agency IRNA announces the landslide victory of the incumbent President Ahmadinejad.

As a sense of shock, deception and frustration overwhelms the partisans of Musavi, the Leader, Ayatollah Khameneh'i, congratulates Ahmadinejad on his overwhelming victory even before he is officially recognized as the victor by the Guardian Council. Within twenty-four hours of the elections, prominent members of reformist organizations and parties are arrested, their offices ransacked and sealed, and their newspapers are closed. The urgency to nip any dissent in the bud becomes more palpable as journalists, campaign activists and advisers of Musavi and Karubi are rounded up en masse. On Sunday, one day after the announcement of the election results, in a spectacular show of force, some one to three million Musavi and Karubi supporters fill the streets of Tehran demanding that their vote be counted and their rights respected. "Where is my vote?" becomes the pacifist slogan of Iran's Green Movement against electoral fraud and for deep-rooted reform. Peaceful marches are repressed, and demonstrators are attacked, beaten up, arrested and imprisoned. The Green Movement mourns its first martyrs. The news of torture, death and sexual abuse in prisons brings stupor to a nation. The distant but much publicized prisons of Abu Gharib and Guantanamo are brought home to Iranians, and Kahrizak prison finds its place in the annals of shame. The national television broadcasts images of arrested political leaders, activists and unknown demonstrators confessing to the abominable crimes of conspiring to overthrow the Islamic Republic through a velvet revolution, plotting against state security, sedition, collaborating with foreigners and falsely accusing the Ahmadinejad government of electoral fraud.

Parliamentarians are forced to investigate mass burials and mass graves in the aftermath of the clampdowns.

Images, rumours and facts prance before the eyes of audiences and readers. They whip up strong emotional responses, yet they do not provide reasons and explanations for why events turned out the way they did. What were the long-term causes of this major social, political and religious eruption? What was brewing in this society, which had remained elusive to certain eyes, especially those of the foreign press, Middle East and Iran political analysts and pundits? How can the pre-election euphoria, the post-election deception and the post-demonstration tragedy be accounted for? Now, we can say that a lot was brewing: economic, political, social, psychological and religious. This study does not claim to deal with all those factors that were at work, but tracks the evolution of superstition and its political use as one such element. This analysis thus hopes to shed a different light on certain events that unexpectedly occurred and certain ideas that were suddenly floated around society during the first four years of President Ahmadinejad's office.

In hindsight, it could be posited that during these first four years, society was systematically injected with religio-political superstition, as if it were being prepared to absorb, digest and accept unrealistic and inexplicable events and occurrences. The unusual barrage of religious and political superstition, unprecedented in the history of the Islamic Republic, raises questions as to the why and for what purpose of this type of a campaign. Was there an attempt to vaccinate society by superstition in order to limit its potential adverse reaction to the shock of a political earthquake, or was it simply the policy outcome of a superstitious discourse and ideology in power? Many among Ahmadinejad's supporters in his second bid for presidency must have believed that the outcome of the election was a miracle and a proof of his support by the hidden world. The religious figures that were instrumental in reviving political superstition during Ahmadinejad's first term were seeped in the superstitious religious ideology of Mohammad-Baqer Majlesi.

Nine months after the June elections, 'Abdolkarim Sorush, the prominent Muslim intellectual, argued that "the actually hegemonic or governing Islam in Iran possesses two salient features: firstly it is despotic (*estebdadi*) and secondly it is superstitious (*khorafi*)". He declared that by cleansing Islam of despotism and superstition, society would move towards a "green interpretation" of Islam.[27] The Green Movement may

---

[27] http://www.rahesabz.net/print/11447/

be heralding an important shift in the consciousness, collective thought and perceptions of the Iranian people. It may be the sociopolitical manifestation of a society transitioning from the traditional to the modern. This historical transition, which started some 100 years ago with the Iranian Constitutional Revolution, may be coming to fruition.

PITFALLS

This study may lend itself to three misunderstandings. First, readers may feel that the emphasis on the existence and persistence of superstition and the pseudo-religious claim of Iranian kings to some Divine guidance is particular to Iranians, Muslims, the Shi'i and Majlesi. This is by no means the intention of this study. As interesting as it may be, a comparative analysis of superstition and political superstition in Sunni Islam, Christianity and Judaism is well beyond the brief of this work. The affirmation of the existence of superstition and political superstition in Shi'i Iran does not mean the denial of it in Sunni Islam, Christianity and Judaism elsewhere. Addressing and analyzing Majlesi's writings and his discourse does not imply that a study of the founders and practitioners of the Anabaptists in Munster, around the 1530s, would not prove more phantasmical and bizarre. Comparing and contrasting the thoughts and works of Majlesi with his contemporary European counterparts, as well as the state of superstition in Europe as compared to Iran, would probably demonstrate some similarities and might even show a greater degree of superstitiousness in Europe than in Iran.

A quick glance at Europe between the twelfth and fifteenth century demonstrates that the lives of saints as recounted in Catholic books is replete with "miraculous achievements".[28] Accounts of saints able to "prophesy the future, control the weather, provide protection against fire and flood, magically transport heavy objects, and bring relief to the sick" abounds.[29] Saint worshipping became "an integral part of the fabric of medieval society" and their shrines became "objects of pilgrimage" for the sick "in the confident expectation of obtaining a supernatural cure".[30] The Church is also said to have encouraged talismans and amulets, which were supposed to "serve against all miseries and all unhappy harms".[31] According to the book of a Church authority in the fifteenth century, the daily recitation of certain prayers in the process of worshipping "the length

---

[28] K. Thomas, *Religion and the Decline of Magic*, p. 28.   [29] Ibid.
[30] Ibid.   [31] Ibid., p. 33.

of the three nails of Our Lord Jesus Christ" was promised to procure seven
gifts. The worshipping person would not: be slain with a sword or a knife;
die of a sudden death; be overcome by his enemies; be grieved by fever or
false witness; or die without the sacraments of the Church. "He shall have
sufficient good and honest living" and will be protected "from all wicked
spirits, from pestilence and all evil things".[32]

The history of Europe and Christianity is replete with references to and
justifications of the "Divine Right of Kings", legitimizing monarchical
absolutism by claiming that kings derived their authority from God,
rendering them free of any accountability to their subjects. This doctrine,
similar to its Iranian counterpart, argued that the king, as well as his
authority, was sacred. As late as 1662, the French bishop and theologian,
Jacques-Benigne Boussuet, a contemporary of Majlesi, praised and
bestowed the Divine Right to rule on his own king, Louis XIV, in almost
the same manner and in the same spirit as Majlesi did with the late Safavi
kings. Boussuet was only repeating in a very eloquent manner the common
European belief in the medieval period that kings were chosen by God.
Medieval kings were considered as sacred and "the monarch was the
representative of the powers that govern the cosmos, an incarnation of
the moral law and Divine intention, a guarantor of the order and righteousness of the world".[33]

According to Boussuet, all established powers are ordained by God and
therefore legitimate and justified in His eyes. For Boussuet, when God
wishes kings to be victors, He orders His spirits of terror to march before
the king's army to sow fear into the hearts of those whom He wishes to be
vanquished.[34] The Catholic Boussuet's claim that the authority of kings is
derived from God and not the people found its almost exact echo in the
sermons and writings of Majlesi in Esfahan. While in the 1660s Europe
had its Boussuet, who was of the same ilk as Iran's Majlesi, it also had its
Spinoza who was very different from Majlesi. At this time, Europe had also
experienced some 150 years of Luther, Calvin and John Knox.

Second, readers may feel that since, in this study, superstition and
political superstition in Iran are traced back to Majlesi, the intention is to
place the sole responsibility of such developments on one man. Conducting
a study of superstition in Iran from the Achamenians to the present may
show how such ideas are linked and have evolved in time. Yet such an
undertaking is not a brief of this study. Starting with superstition in the

---

[32] Ibid., p. 48.   [33] N. Cohn, *The Pursuit of the Millennium* (London, 2004), p. 283.
[34] J.-B. Boussuet, *Sermons Choisis de Boussuet* (Paris, 1845), pp. 219–220.

Safavi dynasty does not mean to dismiss a whole pre-Safavi history of superstition or to acquit the Zoroastrians of superstitious beliefs. Did such a history affect and influence Majlesi's discourse? As this is not a topic of this study, one can only make a logical guess and say: it must have! Yet every study has a point of entry and this one is Majlesi.

Third, readers may feel that since a bridge is made between Majlesi's religious discourse and the religio-political predicaments of present-day Iran, all socio-economic and political facts and developments are assessed as a reflection of beliefs and religion. It is not the intention of this study to present a one-sided or single cause explanation of social realities based only on religious factors. Even though the major topic of enquiry here is the understanding and analysis of the role of superstition and political superstition as embodied in a particular Shi'i discourse, this study does not claim that such a discourse offers the only historical explanation for the state of present-day Iran's society and political economy. Majlesi's discourse may be considered as one influential or at best one explanatory factor. Yet it is by no means thought to be the only one. It is therefore important to point out that the central subject of a study is not necessarily assumed to be the ultimately defining or determining explanation of a complex social reality.

The absence of a review and analysis of socio-economic factors contributing to the present-day conditions in Iran does not imply ascribing to an approach that Maxime Rodinson has called theologocentrism. Theologocentrism explains all observable sociopolitical and psychological phenomena reflected in historical events and occurrences through the lens of religion. This school of thought inevitably fails to take account of the role of "history and social conditioning" in explaining events and developments.[35] This study is not impervious to the importance and impact of different socio-economic, political, legal and international conditions that prevailed and defined Shah Esma'il's reign as compared to Mohammad-Reza Shah's and finally President Ahmadinejad's. Yet it wishes to demonstrate that, despite such differences, superstitious ideas have continued to germinate and linger in the minds of some Iranians. Even though the focus of this study is superstition in Shi'i Iran, neither the fusion of superstition with religion nor the instrumental use of religion for despotic political ends are specific to Iranians, Muslims or the Shi'i.

Recent political statements in the West demonstrate that superstitious ideas have gained popularity and that certain politicians continue to claim some sort of connectedness with God to justify their political actions. On

---

[35] M. Rodinson, *Europe and the Mystique of Islam*, pp. 104–107.

the first day of his second term as the governor of Texas, George Bush is reported to have told a group of supporters, "I believe that God wants me to be President".[36] Subsequently, after his victory, which in his mind probably confirmed his insight into God's predisposition towards his presidency, President-elect Bush reaffirmed his belief in being guided by God. In his first inaugural speech on 20 January 2001, President Bush hinted at his relation with God and said, "... we are guided by a power larger than ourselves, who creates us equal, in His image".[37] On 23 December 2001, in reference to President Bush's election, Rudy Giuliani opined that, "... there was some Divine guidance in the President being elected".[38] It was not until 2005 that President Bush referred to his direct dialogue with God and explained his foreign-policy decision to invade Afghanistan and Iraq as missions conferred upon him by God. Bush claimed that God had told him, "George go and end the tyranny in Iraq".[39] And he complied.

The fact that in the present day and age, when life has become relatively less precarious and more secure than in medieval times, there exist segments of society that remain attentive and receptive to the superstitious claims of political leaders is perplexing and complex. The pretence to connectedness with the hidden world, irrespective of the level of social, economic and political development of societies in which such claims are made, continues to appeal to some, and that is why the Ahmadinejads, Bushes and Mugabes of this world evoke it. It may be argued that in the modern world, the degree, spread and extent of popular sympathy and support for such phantasmical ideas is on the decline. While superstition has always found a favourable breeding ground among the insecure poor and the wretched of this earth, the modern world's capacity to generate inadvertently new types of insecurity has changed the classic profile of the superstitious. It has also made predictions about the growing or shrinking pool of possible adherents to superstition difficult.

In comparison to the medieval period, today individuals are confronted with a new set of uncertainties and fears: the hazards of the world market economy and its consequences on the livelihood of individuals; the anxieties of personal self-esteem in a world where "acceptable" standards of beauty, intelligence, success and life are constantly being readjusted and

---

[36] *PBS, Frontline*, The Jesus Factor.

[37] http://www.whitehouse.gov/news/inaugural-address.html

[38] J. Conason, 'Is George W. Bush God's President', *The New York Observer* (13 January 2002).

[39] *The Guardian* (7 October 2005).

upgraded; the collateral damage of others' decisions, pursuing their personal satisfactions; and the perils and unknowns of personal, social and human relations and interactions in an ever more complex social and psychological environment. This new array of possible sources of insecurity add to the variety of those who feel alienated, estranged, impotent, conflicted, crisis-ridden, marginalized, disaffected and spiritually wanting.

The vulnerable and disempowered of all sorts searching for serenity and security succumb more easily to the false claims of those who pretend to have connections with the hidden world. As long as the world system generates vulnerability and insecurity, it may be creating the bases for new superstitious backlashes not necessarily interlinked or intertwined with the Abrahamic religions. The main focus of this study is on a religious discourse that influenced superstition in Iran. However, as religion becomes purified and cleansed of superstitious ideas or Iranians distance themselves from such ideas, superstition as a social and political problem in Iran may become less pressing. Those countries, with a high or low income, exposed to increasing vulnerabilities and insecurities, may be faced with a rising wave of superstition, cultural and political, as their people come to grips with anxieties resulting from different kinds and mutations of precariousness.

If inadequacy, impotence, insecurity and ignorance generate fear, and one way to assuage fear is to turn to superstition, and if the superstitious need intermediaries to mediate with supernatural forces and negotiate desirable outcomes, then waves of insecurity – psychological, social, economic or political – may be accompanied by a rise in the fortune of so-called men of religion. In certain cases and certain societies, fears could be fanned to generate the need for superstition and in turn the need for the administrators of superstition. David Hume, writing in the eighteenth century, addresses two species of "false religion" opposite to one another: superstition and enthusiasm.[40] Enthusiasm, he argues is a state of rapture resulting from "hope, pride, presumption, a warm imagination, together with ignorance", where the inspired enthusiast thinks of himself so highly that he comes to believe that he is a "distinguished favourite of the Divinity" and inspired by above.[41] Superstition, he argues, results from "weakness, fear, melancholy, together with ignorance" and is "favourable to priestly power".[42] He maintains that "almost all religions" possess a

---

[40] D. Hume, 'Of Superstition and Enthusiasm' in *Essays, Moral, Political, and Literary* (Indianapolis, 1987), p. 73.
[41] Ibid., p. 74.   [42] Ibid., pp. 74–75.

"considerable ingredient" of superstition, and posits that there exists a direct relationship between the share of superstition in a religion and the weight and authority of the priesthood in that religion.[43] Hume defines priests as "pretenders to power and dominion, and to a superior sanctity of character". He considers them as "an invention" of superstition and distinguishes them from clergymen, to whom he pays the utmost respect for their "care of sacred matters".[44] Demonstrating the process by which fear and precariousness foster superstitious ideas, and such ideas play into the hands of priests who seek to strengthen their social and political hold, Hume explains that the superstitious person afflicted by "fear, sorrow and depression of spirit" becomes needy of another person "whose sanctity of life, or, perhaps, impudence and cunning, have made him be supposed more favoured by the Divinity".[45] To the priest, "the superstitious entrust their devotions: To his care they recommend their prayers, petitions, and sacrifices".[46] Hume argues that superstition "renders men tame and submissive", and while it "seems inoffensive to the people", in time, the priest firmly establishes his authority, "becomes the tyrant and disturber of human society by his endless contentions, persecutions and religious wars".[47] Hume concludes that "superstition is an enemy to civil liberty", as it renders men fit for slavery.[48] What Hume categorizes as enthusiasm and superstition can be considered as two species of superstition, since both refer to a state of mind in which the individual ascribes the cause of worldly events to the hidden world. Hume's enthusiast is the superstitious at the height of his success, pride and glory. He is Alexander the Great and Shah Esmaʻil after their victories, and the superstitious is the washed up, once again both men after their defeats. Hume's "enthusiast" is the megalomaniac on his winning streak, seeing his success as the design of God, and himself as the instrument of God. Hume's superstitious person in contrast to the enthusiast is the common man confronted with all conceivable worldly problems, afraid and dejected. Rather than two distinct categories, as Hume assumes, the two states of superstition can swiftly change positions; the enthusiast could readily become the superstitious or vice versa as his fortune changes radically. Both categories believe that God has or will intervene in the natural order of the world for their particular case.

---

[43] Ibid., p. 75.   [44] Ibid., p. 75, 617.   [45] Ibid., p. 76.   [46] Ibid., p. 75.
[47] Ibid., p. 78.   [48] Ibid.

PART ONE

POLITICIZING OCCULT ISLAM

I

Ahmadinejad

A Touch of Light

Some three months after his unexpected and contested victory in Iran's Presidential elections, Mahmud Ahmadinejad travelled to the United States to attend the 60th session of the General Assembly of the United Nations. On 17 September 2005, Ahmadinejad addressed the General Assembly. He concluded his political speech with a call for the return of the Twelfth Shi'i Imam. He told the world community:

Dear friends and colleagues, from the beginning of time, humanity has longed for the day when justice, peace, equality and compassion would envelop the world. All of us can contribute to the establishment of such a world. When that day comes, the ultimate promise of all Divine religions will be fulfilled with the emergence of a perfect human being who is heir to all prophets and pious men. He will lead the world to justice and absolute peace. "O mighty Lord, I pray to you to hasten the emergence of your last repository, the promised one, that perfect and pure human being, the one that will fill this world with justice and peace. O Lord, include us among his companions, followers and those who serve his cause".[1]

As unconventional and curious as the last few lines of Ahmadinejad's speech may have sounded to his audience in New York, to a large number of Iranians back home his appeal for the return of the Twelfth Imam was far from unusual. Faced with a predicament or a crisis, fervent Shi'i beseech God to hasten the return of the hidden Twelfth Imam to reign in the promised era of justice, thereby resolving all problems. According to Shi'i teachings, in the absence of the Twelfth Imam, the world becomes the theatre of spiralling and spawning evil and vice. This abominable vicious circle of impiety and injustice, believed to have started with the occultation

---

[1] *IRNA – Islamic Republic News Agency* (17 September 2005).

of the Twelfth Imam in 874 CE and exasperated by the rule of fallible
unjust leaders, will come to an end with his reappearance at an unknown
time.

To the Iranian President and his ardent supporters back home, the
speech at the UN and especially the reference to the Hidden Imam reawak-
ened and reinvigorated the honour and authority of Shiʿism in the world.
Some gloated at the idea that by calling on the international community to
recognize the Twelfth Imam, Ahmadinejad was in effect countering the
Western bogy or "straw text of human rights", the pride of the reformists
and the ex-president Khatami, with the true Shiʿi heritage of messianic
Mahdiism.[2]

This first worldwide appearance of Ahmadinejad, a political personality
of a different intellectual calibre, erudition, Islamic conviction and world
outlook from Khatami, was an important event, both internationally and
in Iran. In his encounter with world leaders, Iran's newly elected President
presented ideas drawn from a curiously mixed bag. At times, he used
Khatami's inclusivist discourse, reaching out to the international community, and at other times, he relied on an exclusivist discourse.

Instantaneously, images and sounds of Ahmadinejad walking to the
podium, addressing the delegates and leaving the podium were transmitted
to the four corners of the world. Events would later reveal that what the
world saw on that Wednesday was different from what Ahmadinejad and
at least one of his close aides had seen and experienced. The Western media
reported on Ahmadinejad's visit to New York and commented on his
speeches, his political remarks on the West, the international community,
the United States and Iran's nuclear program. Even though Ahmadinejad's
prayer for the return of the promised Messiah at the General Assembly was
very much appreciated by his supporter in Iran, it went largely ignored in
the West.

President Ahmadinejad's speech in New York and the unnatural
circumstances that he later claimed to have surrounded it proved to be
the prelude to the first wave of superstitious observations and ideas
widely disseminated during his administration. As much as his predecessor, Seyyed Mohammad Khatami, a cleric, employed and propagated a
rational, balanced and modern Islamic discourse blending the ethical and
spiritual message of Islam with enlightenment, humanism and universal-
ism, the lay Mahmud Ahmadinejad ushered in a new era of supernatural, inexplicable and abnormal ideas, befogging the minds of Iranians.

[2] F. Rajabi, *Ahmadinejad, Moʿjezeh Hezareh Sevom* (Tehran, 1385), pp. 300–301.

Ahmadinejad's promotion of unreasonable notions in the name of religion created a wave of incidents and behaviours demonstrating that a selective group of individuals believed or at least pretended to believe that some sort of external or exogenous force, logically inexplicable and often related to the hidden world, impacted the course of worldly events and determined its outcome. If, during the Khatami administration, a conscious effort was made to empower the much-cherished Shiʻi concept of *aql* or reason, Ahmadinejad's administration seemed openly intent on obfuscating reason. During his tenure, superstition begot phantasmical claims and practices, plunging a small cross-section of Iranians into an alarming frenzy of irrationality. The promotion of superstition during Ahmadinejad's tenure was carried out in the name of serving the fundaments and principles of Shiʻism. Politically, Ahmadinejad called himself a Principlist (*usulgara*) to distinguish his religion and politics from Khatami and his allies, whose Islamic discourse he viewed as an aberration of the true "principles" of the Islamic revolution.

A HOLY VISITATION IN A NOT-SO-HOLY CITY

Some seventy days after his speech to the General Assembly, Iranians learned that their president had undergone a special experience in New York. On 27 November 2005, Ahmadinejad's own personal account of the supernatural circumstances surrounding his 17 September speech at the UN became public. The details surfaced during a routine meeting of the President and a close circle of his followers with Ayatollah Javadi Amoli. During the first few months of his Presidency, Ahmadinejad was intent on regularly meeting with the leading traditional clerical dignitaries, to solicit their guidance and brief them on the affairs of the state. On his return from the United States, Ahmadinejad travelled to Qom.

In his report to Ayatollah Javadi Amoli and a small circle of confidants, the President carefully prepared the stage for his breathtaking scoop. Exuding with self-confidence, he sought to weave a uniquely mysterious if not transcendental plot. Ahmadinejad reported that, from the moment the Iranian delegation landed in New York, it suddenly became the focus of attention. The understandable fixation of the press and the public on the Iranian delegation must have given Ahmadinejad the feeling that there must have been something special and unusual about him and his entourage. The presence of the Iranian team seems to have overshadowed the presence of delegates from other countries. To conjure a paranormal image of the special occurrence during his speech at the UN General Assembly,

Ahmadinejad first relied on the observations of an assistant and then added his own sense of what had actually taken place. Relying on the eyewitness report of his aid, Ahmadinejad asserted that, from the moment he began his speech with the words "In the name of God" until he finished, he had been enveloped in a ray, column or halo of light. The President told Ayatollah Javadi Amoli that, throughout his speech, he felt enshrouded in a beam of light. Referring to the experience, Ahmadinejad used the expression of entering into an enclosed or bounded (*hesar*) space of light.

Elaborating on the supernatural circumstances of his experience, Ahmadinejad confirmed that, all of a sudden, he felt an inexplicable change in the atmosphere of the General Assembly lasting throughout his twenty-seven- or twenty-eight-minute speech. The metaphysical aura was perceptible in the particular state and gaze of his audience. Ahmadinejad was adamant that every single delegate seated in the General Assembly had his eyes fixated on him and seemed incapable of blinking. Perhaps feeling as though Javadi Amoli's comment of "God be thanked" (*Alhamdollelah*) at the end of his story implied a sense of disbelief or doubt about his account, the President reassured the Ayatollah that he was not exaggerating. Hoping to shed a more supernatural light on his audience's state of hypnosis, Ahmadinejad volunteered yet another revealing detail. He said that it seemed as though, during his speech, a hand was holding the delegates motionless and immobile. The identity of the mysterious invisible hand that had pushed the world leaders firmly back into their seats and placed them in a state of trance motionlessly staring at Ahmadinejad's face was left to the imagination of the audience at Javadi Amoli's home.

The "column of light" or "halo of light" episode, as the press referred to it, was first reported on the Iranian website *Baztab*, which was closed down in 2007 by the authorities. *Baztab* was affiliated with Mohsen Reza'i, the influential ex-commander of the Guardian Corps of the Islamic Revolution during the Iran–Iraq war, turned civilian. Reza'i was a presidential candidate during the 2005 elections and a rival of Ahmadinejad, as well as the spokesman of the Expediency Council, headed by Ayatollah Hashemi Rafsanjani.[3] *Baztab*'s report on the content of the meeting between Ahmadinejad and Javadi Amoli on 27 November (6 Azar) received considerable coverage in the reformist Iranian press and websites. What came to be a highly controversial meeting was filmed and widely distributed, confirming that the President had spoken about what he believed to have been his

---

[3] In the 2009 presidential elections, which turned into a fiasco, Reza'i challenged Ahmadinejad as a dissident Principlist.

supernatural experience with a "halo of light". The full account of
Ahmadinejad's explanation of his experience with the halo of light, including the expressive use of his hands depicting the column of light that
engulfed him, was placed on other websites and widely viewed by curious
Iranians.[4]

Some four years later, during the televised debates of the 2009 presidential election, Mehdi Karubi questioned Ahmadinejad on the topic of his
exceptional experience. Ahmadinejad denied the halo episode all together.
His disavowal prompted two important reactions, settling the issue once
and for all. Ayatollah Javadi Amoli's office confirmed that Ahmadinejad
had in fact made the claims that had been attributed to him.[5] Hojjatoleslam
Mohammad-Taqi Sobhani, a member of the Board of Trustees of the Qom
Seminary School's Islamic Propagation Office who had accompanied
Ahmadinejad to Javadi Amoli's house and was present at the meeting,
also confirmed that Ahmadinejad had indeed spoken about his supernatural
experience.[6] According to Sobhani, in reaction to Ahmadinejad's story,
Javadi Amoli had retorted, "Do not deceive the people". According to
Sobhani, the event at Ayatollah Javadi Amoli's residence was being filmed
by two cameras, one belonging to Javadi Amoli's office and the other to the
IRIB or the Islamic Republic's national television. The fact that two official
cameras were present at the meeting undermines the scenario of a secret
recording and confirms the hypothesis that Ahmadinejad knew full well
that what he was saying was being recorded and may be viewed by the
public.

As the controversy over the "halo of light" became more sensational,
some members of Ahmadinejad's administration attempted to defuse the
affair by shedding doubt on the content of the President's report to Javadi
Amoli. On 13 December 2005, during his first press conference as the
President's spokesman, Mr. Gholamhoseyn Elham was questioned on the
details of the "halo of light". Mr. Elham responded that the film had been
doctored, yet he did not specify what had been edited, changed or added.
He emphasized certain non-controversial issues such as the fact that the
meeting was a private one, that he had been there (he is seen in the footage)
and that he was surprised to see a video of the meeting. After an account of

---

[4] http://www.Peiknet.com (7 Azar 1384, 29 November 2005). This film was once again
placed on numerous websites during the 2009 presidential election, especially after
Ahmadinejad denied having spoken about his halo of light experience.
[5] http://emruz.net/print.aspx?ID=23037. Daftar-e Ayatollah Javadi Amoli 'haleh nur' ra
taeed mikonad (19 Khordad 1388).
[6] http://www.ayandenews.com/fa/pages/?cid=8629. *Ayandenews* (18 Khordad 1388).

Ahmadinejad's scientific attributes and the long hours – "16, 17, 18 even
20 hours a day" – that he puts into serving the nation, Elham added that
the accusation of "appealing to Divine-natured circumstances [*omour-e
malakouti*] to legitimize or justify his governmental responsibilities, did
not at all correspond to the President's style". However, Elham asserted
that "it was undeniable that an interested hand extended from the world of
angels [*'alam-e malakut*] was focused on [concerned with the lot of] our
people".[7] Elham's ambiguous comment did not dissipate the paranormal
aura that had come to reign.

Ahmadinejad engaged in an astute stratagem. He indirectly advanced
the idea of his connectedness with the hidden world, allowed the idea to
seep into and sweep through society and instructed his political followers
to fan the idea indirectly. Concomitantly, he sent signals through his
political and clerical associates denying that he had made such claims,
while not disavowing his connectedness. By giving vent to his own special
position without taking direct responsibility for it, he intentionally fudged
his supernatural image. Ahmadinejad must have believed that by publicizing his connectedness, he could attract the zealous common folk and gain
their trust and respect. He must have also believed that by distancing
himself from his own phantasmical claims, through the disclaimers of his
associates, he would be able to ward off criticism of his illogical and
outrageous claims by claiming that he had been misunderstood or misrep-
resented. The fogginess of the circumstances surrounding Ahmadinejad's
claim to connectedness provided him with an excellent opportunity to
attain a politico-religious following while remaining poised to deny it
when the absurdity of such a notion was criticized by both rationalist
reformers and traditional clerics.

An article by Qasem Ravanbakhsh in the weekly *Partov-e Sokhan*
addressed the topic of the meeting between Ahmadinejad and Amoli.
The significance of this article lies in the fact that *Partov-e Sokhan* is
officially published by the "Emam (Imam) Khomeyni Educational and
Research Institute". This institute was founded by Ayatollah Mesbah
Yazdi in 1995 and, from its inception, benefited from the "material and
spiritual support" of Ayatollah Khameneh'i.[8] In both the 2005 and
2009 presidential elections, Mesbah Yazdi supported Ahmadinejad
with all the means available to him. Ravanbakhsh argued that parts
of Ahmadinejad's report had been distorted or tampered with and

---

[7] *Sharq* (23 Azar 1384).   [8] R. San'ati, *Goftoman Mesbah* (Tehran, 1387), p. 191.

proceeded to explain what the President must have meant by the statement that the audience at the General Assembly were fixated on him and did not blink throughout his speech. Ravanbakhsh, however, avoided any reference to or discussion of the "halo of light", as though from his perception there were no anomalies or inconsistencies in that part of the President's account.[9]

Despite the fact that the film in which Ahmadinejad clearly refers to the "halo of light" had been widely distributed and seen by the public, Hojjatoleslam Ka'bi, another proponent of Ahmadinejad, categorically denied that the President had spoken such words during his meeting with Javadi Amoli. Ka'bi who was the representative of Khuzestan to the Assembly of Experts (*Majles Khebregan*), a jurist in the powerful Guardian Council (*Showray-e Negahban*) and a member of Mesbah Yazdi's office was present at the meeting.[10] He claimed that the reports attributed to Ahmadinejad on the halo of light incident were "an organized psychological war with the object of weakening Ahmadinejad's government".[11]

In view of the fact that Ahmadinejad had consciously chosen to discuss his paranormal experience in New York as the main subject of his meeting with Javadi Amoli and then, once his story had been made public, he sheepishly dodged acknowledging it, gives rise to all kinds of speculation, leaving the episode in a halo of mystery and ambiguity. Why would he recount this far-fetched tale in the first place, and why would he subsequently shy away from it? Was Ahmadinejad initially caught off guard by the rapid spread of the news of his supernatural experiences and the negative reactions to it? Was he concerned about the premature timing of its leak? Was he worried that his political rivals would capitalize on it and give it an unfavourable political spin? Did he wish to inform Iranians that he was connected with the hidden world, thereby allowing the imagination of his devout followers to think of him as a divinely ordained person, without directly and officially making such a claim and inviting the criticism that such an assertion may instigate? Did the ambitious new President feel that his claim to some sort of connection with the hidden world would effectively enable him to declare his "independence" from the

---

[9]   *Partov-e Sokhan* (16 Azar 1384).
[10]   H. Ahadi, 'Haleh Nour, Shayeat va Jang Ravani ast', *Rooz Online* (6 December 2005 or 15 Azar 1384).
[11]   *Ya Lesarat* (16 Azar 1384) and http://www.emrouz.info/archives/print/2005/12/002686.php

clergy and their guiding role in the affairs of the government, which he had very much sought during his election campaign?

If Ahmadinejad believed or wished to make believe that he was somehow connected with the hidden world, subsequent to his New York experience, he could claim that his mystical and transcendental credentials were more impressive than those influential clerics who lacked such spiritual histories and therefore powers. A relation may exist between Ahmadinejad's claim to some sort of connection with the hidden world and the gradual rift that occurred between him and an increasing number of high-ranking clerics. As time went by, a growing number of traditional clerics either moved away from supporting the President to a more neutral position or became outspoken critics of certain policies and positions of his. Yet a small, politically powerful and militarily backed hard core of influential clerics continued to support the President. It may be hypothesized that it was the political will and associated magical skills of this very same small circle of clerics that was capable of restoring the incumbent President in the 2009 elections.

It is said that one million copies of the recording in which Ahmadinejad describes the halo of light event in New York circulated in Iran.[12] It is also reported that, in certain Iranian villages, the President's meeting with Javadi Amoli was given a public screening in the presence of local Friday Congregational Prayer leaders to demonstrate Ahmadinejad's deeply felt allegiance to the Twelfth Imam and belief in his miracles.[13] Assuming the authenticity of this report and based on the fact that Friday Congregational Prayer leaders work within a centralized, hierarchical and well-disciplined organizational structure, it can be surmised that the dissemination of the far-fetched contents of Ahmadinejad's meeting with Javadi Amoli was a conscious politico-religious act. During his first term of office, Ahmadinejad continued to make similar supernatural, paranormal and otherworldly insinuations and assertions.

THE SIGNIFICANCE OF LIGHT IN SHI'I LITERATURE

By alluding to a halo of light, the President must have wished to evoke the presence of something supernatural and holy. Its function could have been

---

[12] O. Memarian, 'Vakoneshhay Tond Aleyh Tarvij Khorafeh va Oham', *Rooz Online* (14 December 2005).
[13] H. Ahadi, '*Haleh Nour, Shayeat va Jang Ravani ast*', Rooz Online (6 December 2005). http://roozonline.com/o1newsstory/o12280.shtml

to assist him in his diplomatic campaign of inviting the world leaders to the cause of Shi'i Islam and its messianic saviour, the Hidden Imam. The image that Ahmadinejad may have wished to portray was that, since he had politically and religiously taken up the banner of the Twelfth Imam, militated for and was paving the way for his return, the Hidden Imam had in turn directly intervened on his side. It can be speculated that by recounting the New York episode, Ahmadinejad was sending a simple yet clear message to his compatriots: I am a servant of the Twelfth Imam and he has acknowledged his support for my politico-social cause and endorsed me by coming to my aid in New York. To avoid the possible criticism of his learned religious compatriots, lay and cleric, the President seems to have coated his newly found conviction in the ambiguous notion of the halo of light, which meant different things to different people.

To understand the significance of the halo of light among the Shi'i and the conceptional associations it provokes, it is necessary to delve into Shi'i sources. My intention is to speculate on what was or may have been imparted to the common folk through the President's account of the halo of light. According to Koleyni, the prominent Shi'i compiler of reports (*ahadith*), the imams represented and symbolized the light sent by God to humankind, referred to in the Qur'an (64:8). Under the title of "On the fact that the imams are the lights of God", Koleyni cites six reports attributed to Shi'i imams. On the basis of these reports, it can be deduced that the imams are God-sent lights in the sky and on earth.[14] For a more fertile and prolific account of the meaning and significance of the concept of light in Shi'ism, one needs to turn to Mohammad-Baqer Majlesi's works. In his popular Shi'i texts, the column or cylinder of light, referred to as *ostovaneh nur* or *amud nur* is a particular feature or attribute of Shi'i imams. Imams are said to possess a column of light. This is one of their salient features, signs and signifiers. The column of light is said to have been sent by God to the imams while they were on earth so that they could maintain their connection and communication with the heavens or the hidden world. The angel Gabriel is said to have been made responsible for communicating God's messages to the imams, just as he had been assigned to do so with the Prophet.[15] The column of light is also the conduit of knowledge through which God makes available to the imams whatever it is that they wish to know.[16] It serves as a

[14] Koleyni, *Usul-e Kafi*, vol. 1 (Tehran, 1375), pp. 276–278.
[15] M. B. Majlesi, *Bahar al-Anvar*, vol. 7, Book 3, 'On Imamat', (tr.) M. Khosravi (Tehran, 1363), pp. 34, 83.
[16] M. B. Majlesi, *Bahar al-Anvar*, vol. 7, Book 4, 'On Imamat', (tr.) M. Khosravi (Tehran, 1364, p. 96.

medium through which imams can observe people and have knowledge of all their activities.[17] Possessing the column of light shields the imams from erring, rendering them infallible and omniscient. According to other Shi'i reports, the Prophet Mohammad and the imams have been described as a source of light for believers.[18] It is said that when the Twelfth Imam was born a ray of light emanated from him, rose high and then spread out into the skies.[19]

In contemporary writings of religious authorities, the light is usually associated with the Twelfth Imam. It is suggested that there is a single "sun of truth" in this world and that is the Twelfth Imam.[20] According to Ayatollah Mesbah Yazdi, one of the qualities of the Twelfth Imam is that he is luminous.[21] Mesbah Yazdi writes: "The light emanating from the Twelfth Imam is eternal and everlasting. What is important is that we should prepare our hearts, removing all rust so that the Twelfth Imam's light may shine on our hearts and his everlasting grace may rain upon us".[22] A literal and textual interpretation of Mesbah Yazdi's writing, which Ahmadinejad may have read, given his politico-religious loyalty to Mesbah Yazdi, gives the impression that the President's claim to the existence of a ray of light in New York may have been in reference to the physical presence of the Twelfth Imam in the form of a luminous body. It seems as if Ahmadinejad's report on his experience at the General Assembly was a reference to his belief that he had been in contact with the Hidden Imam throughout his speech. Using the symbolism of being enshrouded in light seemed like a clear public message to believers that the President was blessed and among the selected friends of God and the Hidden Imam. In his meeting with Javadi Amoli, was the President boasting about his newly acquired status of a person protected by and in contact with the Twelfth Imam? Is this why the President claimed to have been cloaked in a ray of light?

It could be argued that, during the four years of his first term in office, Ahmadinejad's statements and comments, as well as those of his cabinet members and staff, demonstrate that he is either convinced and/or wishes to make believe that: he has a sacred mission to speed up the reappearance of the Twelfth Imam; this goal constitutes the primary objective of his

---

[17] M. B. Majlesi, *Bahar al-Anvar*, vol. 7, Book 3, 'On Imamat' (1363), pp. 32–34.
[18] M. B. Majlesi, *Hayat al Qolub*, vol. 5, 'Emamshenasi' (Qom, 1376) p. 255; M. B. Majlesi, *'Eyn al-Hayat* (Tehran, n.d), p. 138.
[19] M. B. Majlesi, *Jala'al-'Oyun* (Qom, 1373), p. 1009.
[20] M. T. Mesbah Yazdi, *Aftab Velayat* (Qom, 1384), p. 18.
[21] Ibid., p. 38.   [22] Ibid., p. 44.

government; in his holy quest, he benefits from the direct help of the Hidden Imam; and that his objective and that of the hidden world overlap.

AHMADINEJAD'S MESSIANIC OCCULTISM

Either, in September 2005, Ahmadinejad had a supernatural experience at the General Assembly, or he was dragging the whole nation into his politico-religious fantasies. The ethically worst-case scenario is that the whole story was a hoax fabricated by the President to dupe the common folk for political purposes. Even though the images beamed from the General Assembly to the world did not demonstrate the veracity of Ahmadinejad's claim of being engulfed in a column of light, Ahmadinejad may have "felt" or "assumed" some sort of intervention from the hidden world. The President seems to have been seeped in Mesbah Yazdi's politico-religious school of thought. Even before the halo of light incident, some of the high-ranking clerics close to Mesbah Yazdi interpreted and heralded Ahmadinejad's contested victory in the 2005 Presidential elections as a miracle.

Circumstantial evidence points to a concerted politico-religious effort by a hard nucleus of clerics to present the Ahmadinejad presidency as the outcome of a new wave of intense supernaturalism sweeping over the country. This new "spiritual" mood is presented as the salient feature of an evolved and matured society, radically different from the "degenerated era" that came to reign between the death of Ayatollah Khomeyni and the 2005 election of Ahmadinejad. In this supposed new phase of religious and moral regeneration, culminating in the reappearance of the Twelfth Imam, the heightened and overimposing sense of mass religiosity, asceticism and spirituality forces a qualitative transformation upon society. The new community is expected to rise above the mundane debates between the political right and left, progressive and conservative, principlist and reformist and ushers in an almost metaphysical and homogenous state transcending worldly political ideologies and organizations. To prove that a totally different, superior and transcendental aura has come to reign over the country, Ahmadinejad's presidency is described by certain influential clergy as a Divine gift (*tohfeh elahi*), Divine plan or design (*tadbir elahi*) and full of miracles (*mashhun be keramat va mo'jezat*).[23] The President, too, seemingly convinced of the supernatural ambiance surrounding his election, talks about the beginning of a radically different phase in the

---

[23] *Partov-e Sokhan* (15 Tir 1384; 23 Tir 1384).

country. This new historical stage of regeneration has its own specific socio-economic theories and policies, but most importantly, it is distinguished by what Ahmadinejad calls its prevailing wave of spirituality (*mowj ma'naviyat*).[24] This phase is presented as a higher and a more advanced stage in the religious development of the Islamic Republic.

The advent of this new historical stage is based on the following argument. First, society comes to believe that the Hidden Imam regularly intervenes in the affairs of the material world through the agency of a few chosen individuals. Second, only the chosen few who have the gift of establishing contact with the hidden world are considered as capable of leading society and effectuating change in the manner and direction that is argued to be willed by the Hidden Imam. Third, faced with the unfathomable power of the Hidden Imam, society would come to realize that any human attempt or initiative unsynchronised with the will of the Hidden Imam, as identified by those in contact with him, is ineffectual and futile. Fourth, total reliance on the will of the Hidden Imam interpreted by the chosen few will set into motion a virtuous cycle of greater intervention by him prompting greater number of believers to pray for his return. This accelerating process will eventually expedite the return of the Hidden Imam.

The Idyllic War Fronts

The mastermind behind Ahmadinejad's religio-political discourse believed that the new spiritual era, ending in the return of the Hidden Imam, the stated goal of the President, had a momentary precedence in the history of the Islamic Republic. To him, it seemed as though, during the Iran–Iraq war, the conditions at the fronts were almost ready to trigger the process that would bring back the Hidden Imam. This opportunity, he believed, was aborted after the end of the war. During the eight-year war, the young, zealous and pious volunteers who rushed to the fronts established a self-sacrificing and selfless behavioural pattern in which egotistic and selfish impulses were downplayed and repressed if not mortified. A strong sense of religious puritanism, mysticism, fraternity and collective compassion for the sake of a higher religious ideal was promoted. Exalted and selfless religious values based on asceticism and sacrificing all one's possessions, including one's life, for the cause of God, the Islamic Republic, the charismatic Guardian Jurist and the motherland moved and mobilized the

---

[24] *Partov-e Sokhan* (12 Mordad 1384).

pious youth. The lofty status of attaining martyrdom became the engine of military success.

For eight years, some one million young warriors, the majority of whom were composed of the religiously motivated voluntary forces of the *basij-e mostazefan* or the mass mobilization militia of the disinherited and the *sepah-e pasdaran enqelab-e Eslami* or the Guardians Corps of the Islamic Revolution, went to the war fronts. For the majority of the volunteers who fought in the Iran–Iraq war, their experience was a unique religious happening in which they felt an inexplicable mystical proximity to their creator and the Shi'i imams. They would call the war fronts, "the land of light" where the scent of love and God filled the air and every warrior had buried his worldly desires only yearning for ascension to the hereafter and meeting the Beloved.[25] For many of them, the war was an opportunity in which they could demonstrate their unrequited love for God and honour their amorous covenant with Him and the imams. At the war fronts, numerous accounts circulated about the presence of the Twelfth Imam and other holy Shi'i figures.[26] The memoirs of those warriors writing about their experiences at the front are replete with accounts of exceptional spiritual experiences, miracles, visitations and supernatural occurrences.[27] These occurrences were believed to be the outcome of the interventions of the hidden world in the affairs of the material world. To these selfless, humble, ascetic soldiers, their deep-felt religious beliefs and spirituality was the guarantor of their victory. Remembrance of the imams by reciting their names under their breaths and the thought of martyrdom, meeting the imams and entering paradise emboldened these warriors to face all dangers and defeat the enemy. At the fronts, the stench of mutilated, burned and dead bodies was attenuated with the sweet scent of spiritualism and supernatural occurrences.

For the duration of their stay at the fronts, these warriors interacted with and obeyed their commanders who were their selfless role models, as well as their brothers in arms. These warriors also cultivated a fraternal relationship based on reverence and obeisance with the clergy and the preacher-performers (*maddahan*) who came to the fronts. Their role was to uplift the morale of the troops by reminding them of their religious role and responsibility and re-creating for them the trials and tribulations of the

---

[25] B. Podaat, *Safar be Sarzamin Nur* (Tehran, 1385), pp. 11, 27.
[26] H. Ghanipour, *Jebhe'y Jonoub* (Tehran, 1386), p. 16.
[27] H. Ghanipour, *Jebhe'y Jonoub*, pp. 281, 301; S. Akef, *Khakhaye Narm Kushk* (Mashhad, 1387), pp. 107–115, 118, 165, 187; M. Asgharizadeh, *Arefan Vesal* (Qom, 1386), pp. 24–25, 44, 64.

Shi'i imams. The moving speeches and sermons by the clergy and the preachers provided these young men with a religiously based mental and psychological mind frame and road map. The clerical speakers and preachers at the fronts explained to the young warriors the purpose of their sacrifices and the spiritual rewards that awaited them. They made sense of the hardships they were enduring, comforting, exciting and energizing them by recounting the long and glorious history of Shi'i martyrs.

When the war came to an end, the warriors went back to their homes. Some were sad and felt inadequate because they had not been worthy of martyrdom; some longed for the scent of God and love that they could only experience at the fronts; some missed the spiritualism, mysticism, fraternity and solidarity that they had cherished in the face of death; and some must have been happy to have survived the war and wished to forget the violence, hardship, anxiety and austerity that they had experienced. In the postwar period, the genie of worldliness and selfishness had escaped the bottle. The pursuit of private financial gain and political power and domination gradually became the yardstick of success and virtue, eclipsing the lofty ethical values of spiritualism, asceticism, humbleness and selflessness. The spirit of the front and the *basiji* mentality and behaviour was out of vogue and a vestige of the past. Those who had prided themselves in being *basijis* found themselves isolated, disoriented and estranged in a society intent on moving on. With the marginalization of the *basiji* spirit, the conditions for the return of the Hidden Imam seemed to have dissipated.

A Contrived Repetition of the War Front Experiences

Some five months before the 2005 presidential election, Mesbah Yazdi hammered at the idea that "Islam was in real danger" and that "a clear danger threatened Islam in the Islamic Republic". His solution to this pressing danger was the "election of a supporter of Islam", one who "pained for the faith and wished to implement the real Islam".[28] Rallying the pious believers behind Ahmadinejad, Mesbah Yazdi would rhetorically ask a group of his students and devotees, "If the Twelfth Imam wished to bestow his favours, to which coalition or group [competing in the elections] would he look favourably upon and for whom would he pray?"[29] To Mesbah Yazdi, Ahmadinejad seemed a suitable candidate

---

[28] *Partov-e Sokhan* (7 Bahman 1383).   [29] R. San'ati, *Goftoman Mesbah*, p. 860.

who could be presented to the zealous as the symbol and representative of the selfless, Imam-seeking *basiji* spirit during the eight years' war.

Once the 2005 election results were officially announced, Mesbah Yazdi claimed that Ahmadinejad was foreordained to become president and that his election was a miracle willed by the Twelfth Imam. In effect, Mesbah Yazdi prepared the grounds for the common folk to rally behind a president whose religious mission of establishing an "Islamic government" was aided by miracles and the blessing of the Hidden Imam.[30] It could be surmised that Mesbah Yazdi identified two religio-political goals for the President. First, he was charged with propagating the idea that he was expediting the reappearance of the Hidden Imam, and second, he was to popularize the notion that the Hidden Imam interacted with the material world on a permanent and regular basis. The "Islamic government" and, through it, the whole Iranian society was to become imbued with the Hidden Imam and his worldly interventions.

By supporting Ahmadinejad and launching a Hidden Imam-based discourse, Mesbah Yazdi, deeply concerned with the eclipse of the popularity and power of change-resistant clerics and the surge of various reformist platforms, sought to inculcate the common folk with the idea that respect for the Hidden Imam and the spirit of the war fronts was concomitant with anti-reformism. The novelty of this anti-reformist position was that it claimed to have the active support of the Hidden Imam. Referring to the miraculous nature of the liberation of Khoramshahr during the Iran–Iraq war, Mesbah Yazdi argued that "our minds should gradually become accustomed to these things".[31] It seemed as though Mesbah Yazdi's vague reference to "these things" was an open attempt at promoting the belief in the role and veracity of unnatural events.

This supposedly new historical stage of religious awareness launched by Ahmadinejad's election and masterminded by Mesbah Yazdi seems to have functioned under one equally vague single objective: the completion of history as we know it, and the attainment of human perfection through the reappearance of the Hidden Imam. Ahmadinejad's claim to a supernatural experience may have been intended as a signal to the Iranian society that the Hidden Imam approved of his policies, as he was among those who had been charged with expediting his return. The ideologue of Ahmadinejad's discourse seemed to hope that, once the common folk were convinced that the reappearance of the Hidden Imam was imminent and that their government was actively committed to it, they would wholeheartedly

---

[30] *Partov-e Sokhan* (8 Tir 1384).   [31] R. San'ati, *Goftoman Mesbah*, p. 845.

defend their leaders as the *basijis* had done during the war. To a vast number of Iranians, Ahmadinejad failed to win the 2009 presidential elections. His political defeat could also be construed as a public referendum in which Iranians rejected the manipulation of religion for worldly political ends.

MISAPPROPRIATION OF AYATOLLAH BEHJAT'S SPIRITUALITY

Mesbah Yazdi's view of an ever-present Hidden Imam impacting and interacting with the material world can be traced to the influence of the Grand Ayatollah Mohammad-Taqi Behjat, who passed away in 2009. According to one report, for fifteen years, Mesbah Yazdi studied Islamic jurisprudence (*feqh*), ethics (*akhlaq*) and mysticism (*'erfan*) with Ayatollah Behjat.[32] According to Mesbah Yazdi, he became acquainted with Ayatollah Behjat in 1952 and subsequently remained close to him.[33] Ayatollah Behjat has been hailed as one the greatest mystics of modern times. Referring to Ayatollah Behjat's "supernaturalness", Mesbah Yazdi believes that those who were close to the Ayatollah sometimes came across events and occurrences that were "certain signs" of the fact that he "possessed powers superior to others".[34]

On the basis of a statement attributed to Ayatollah Behjat, the position of the Hidden Imam is almost comparable to that of God. The Ayatollah says the Hidden Imam is the seeing eyes, hearing ears, speaking tongue and giving hand of God.[35] Ayatollah Behjat was also a fervent believer in the ability of pious Shi'i with purified souls to meet the Hidden Imam. He told his students that even though the Imam was hidden behind a veil and our eyes were incapable of seeing him, "there have been and are those who see and if they do not see him, they are connected with the Hidden Imam".[36] He was of the opinion that during the occultation of the Hidden Imam there is ample evidence of his favour, kindness and patronage towards the Shi'i and those who love him.[37]

When a devout believer craving to encounter the Hidden Imam asked Behjat to pray for him so that he may realize his quest, Behjat informed him that in order for his wish to be granted, he needed to "send many blessings

---

[32] Ibid., pp. 43–45.   [33] Ibid., pp. 51–52.   [34] Ibid., p. 52.

[35] Ayatollah Behjat's official website: 'Dar rastay-e 'Eshq be Emam Zaman'. The information in this section, unless indicated, is based on Ayatollah Behjat's official website: http://www. bahjat.org/fa/index.php. To facilitate the task of checking references, the subtitles from which the information is cited will be provided.

[36] Ayatollah Behjat's official website, 'Dar rastay-e 'Eshq be Emam Zaman'.   [37] Ibid.

(*salavat*) to the Hidden Imam concurrently with the recitation of the prayer hastening his reappearance [*du'ay-e fajr*] and regularly frequent the Jamkaran mosque performing the necessary prayers".[38] Yet according to Behjat, even though people went to the Jamkaran mosque to realize their needs – as the Hidden Imam is said to be present there – they failed to understand that the Hidden Imam was also in need of the people's prayers so that he may reappear. Behjat intimated that there is a reciprocal dependence between the Hidden Imam and believers. The Hidden Imam needs the people to pray for his return, and the people will not see an improvement in their conditions until they reinforce and concretize their relation with the Hidden Imam.[39]

There exists a whole series of reports pertaining to supernatural and occult events involving Ayatollah Behjat. It is said that one night at the Sahleh mosque in Iraq, which he regularly visited in his youth, he needed to renew his ablutions. As he walked out of the mosque and into the dark, "he became slightly scared". Immediately a light appeared in front of him, illuminating his path. The mysterious light accompanied him during his ablution and his return into the mosque. Once Behjat returned to his place of worship inside the mosque, the light disappeared.[40] In this account, no attempt is made at explaining the source or origin of the light. Yet the fact that the Sahleh mosque is associated with the Twelfth Imam, and is believed to be one of those holy shrines at which he appears and one could encounter him there, could shed light on the origin of the light.[41] Ayatollah Behjat is also said to have had knowledge of the unknown. Mesbah Yazdi believes that the Ayatollah often witnessed scenes from the unknown, and, in order to prevent himself from having these visions of supposedly the future, he often repeated the term *ya setar* or "O veil". By using the expression "O veil", Ayatollah Behjat is said to have pleaded with God to hide from him what he could see.[42]

Many other extraordinary capacities and gifts are attributed to Ayatollah Behjat. He is said to have been an oracle, a clairvoyant, a medium and a psychic capable of foretelling the future and reading people's minds. Mesbah Yazdi cites three particular cases and calls them thaumaturgic (*keramat*) or miraculous acts.[43] According to Mesbah Yazdi, the elevated

[38] Ayatollah Behjat's official website, 'Hazrate valiye 'Asr'.
[39] Ayatollah Behjat's official website, 'Dar rastay-e 'Eshq be Emam Zaman'.
[40] Ayatollah Behjat's official website, 'Vijegiha; Ziyarat va Tavasol'.
[41] M. B. Faqih Imani, *Foze Akbar* (Qom, 1382), pp. 228–229.
[42] Ayatollah Behjat's official website, 'Vijegiha; Etela az Gheyb va Zohure Keramat'.
[43] Ibid.

spiritual status reached by Ayatollah Behjat proves that through the grace of the Hidden Imam, there is still hope for the perfection of human beings. Mesbah Yazdi believes that spiritual beings such as the Ayatollah help strengthen the faith of believers. Intent on convincing his readers of the veracity of his comments about Ayatollah Behjat, Mesbah Yazdi ascertains that his accounts are "solid truths and not a joke".[44] It is even said that Ayatollah Behjat was capable of seeing behind him, if he wished to do so.[45]

While Ayatollah Behjat may have believed in the possibility of mortals encountering the Hidden Imam in this material world and even becoming connected with him through cleansing their souls and dutifully performing devotional rites and rituals, he was also known for two other special features. First, he was famous for his insistence on being silent about his personal and private spiritual experiences. His students are unanimous on the fact that Behjat concealed his supernatural encounters, abilities and experiences from the public. Even those who knew about the Ayatollah's supernatural characteristics were under oath not to publicize or divulge his spiritual secrets.[46]

Second, Ayatollah Behjat was equally well known for his non-political if not anti-political behaviour and disposition. For Behjat, "the solution to all problems is limited to supplications [by individuals] in private for the reappearance of the Twelfth Imam".[47] The Ayatollah is remembered as being intolerant towards meddling in political affairs.[48] Deeply involved in his spiritual and devotional practices and sensitive to the possibility of political consequences, manipulations and fallouts, Behjat was sceptical of even getting mixed up with the organizational and administrative affairs of the clerics in Qom. In 1995, the Association of Qom Seminary School Teachers suggested a list of seven well-known and high-ranking clerics as members of the High Council in charge of running the affairs of the Qom Seminary School. The list of seven appointees was subsequently sent to the six Grand Ayatollahs who were officially confirmed as Sources of Imitation (*maraj'e taqlid*) in 1993, for their final approval and signature. Ayatollah Behjat, one of the six official Sources of Imitation, was the only one who refused to sign. In his typically cautious mannerism, worried about getting caught up in what may have had worldly political

[44] Ibid.   [45] Ibid.

[46] Ayatollah Behjat's official website, 'Vijegiha; Taqva va Khodsazi and Seyro Soluk va Maqam ma'navi'.

[47] Ayatollah Behjat's official website, 'Dar Rastaye 'Eshq be Emam Zaman'.

[48] M. Yazdi, *Khaterat Ayatollah Mohammad Yazdi* (Tehran, 1380), p. 223.

implications, Behjat sent word that he would not oppose the activities of the seven members of the High Council, yet he said, "signing is difficult for me and I will not sign".[49]

Mesbah Yazdi may have appropriated and adopted certain beliefs of Ayatollah Behjat such as his conviction in: the possibility of establishing contact with the Hidden Imam; asking questions and receiving appropriate responses from the hidden world; possessing the power of foreknowledge and predicting the events of the future, as well as other powers derived from connectedness to the Twelfth Imam and the hidden world. He may have also borrowed from Ayatollah Behjat his deeply felt belief in the Twelfth Imam's imminent reappearance. Based on the testimony of a friend, who was said to be in contact with the Hidden Imam, in September 2008, Ayatollah Behjat declared that the coming of the Imam was imminent.[50] In a public sermon, Ayatollah Naseri referred to an account by Ayatollah Behjat based on the Ayatollah's conversation with a sixty-two-year-old friend who was said to be in contact with the Hidden Imam. According to Ayatollah Behjat, the Imam had told his friend that not only was his appearance imminent but that even people older than Ayatollah Behjat's friend would be able to witness his coming. Assuming that the life expectancy of Ayatollah Behjat's friend is ninety years, this account implies that the Twelfth Imam would appear within a maximum of twenty-eight years.

In order to pursue and attain his own political objectives, Mesbah Yazdi seems to have freed himself from the two major prohibitions of Ayatollah Behjat. To shield himself from the trappings of material and political temptations, Behjat had placed upon himself two major prohibitive rules. He kept silent about his own supernatural experiences, refusing to publicize or politicize them and he abided by a code of abstention from political activity. Behjat believed that, "If the rulers (*salatin*) of the world only knew about the pleasures of worship they would never pursue such mundane objectives".[51] He is said to have despised fame and did not even seek to be considered as a Source of Imitation (*marja' taqlid*).[52] For the spiritual and mystic Behjat, seeking true proximity to God could not be combined with the manipulation of spirituality for political and economic power and hegemony. For Mesbah Yazdi, however, the two objectives seem quite compatible. Contrary to all accounts of Ayatollah Behjat's dislike for

---

[49] M. Saleh, *Jame'eh-e Modaresine Howzeh 'Elmiyeh Qom az Aghaz ta Aknoun*, vol. 2 (Tehran, 1385), pp. 542–543.

[50] Yan.net/index.aspx?pid=76777, 'Aya zohour nazdik ast' (25 July 1387).

[51] *Etemad Melli* (28 Ordibehesht 1388).   [52] Ibid.

political involvement, Mesbah Yazdi insists that, despite his reputation, the Ayatollah was the main person who encouraged him to engage in politics.[53]

It would be safe to assume that when Mesbah Yazdi promotes Ayatollah Behjat as an ideal role model for believers, he is referring to his own construction of the Ayatollah, namely one who does bring the spiritual world into politics and one who does publicize his personal experiences.[54] Ayatollah Behjat seems to play an important role in the genealogy of Ahmadinejad and Mesbah Yazdi's discourse. Yet it is important to note that it is through distorting and politicizing Behjat's belief system that a new political discourse based on Messianism is constructed. A rumour was circulated by Ahmadinejad's proponents that in order to protect the President from dangers during his trip to New York, it was Ayatollah Behjat who was somehow responsible for the appearance of the famous halo of light. After the death of Behjat, this rumour was strongly denied by the Ayatollah's office as an utter fabrication.[55]

THEORIZING THE WORLDLY INTERVENTIONS OF THE
TWELFTH IMAM

In 2007, two years after Ahmadinejad's presidency, Hojjatoleslam Morteza Aqatehrani, a student and a very close associate of Mesbah Yazdi, published a book on the Twelfth Imam, a clumsy translation of which would be "The Desire to see the Friend's face". The subtitle of the book, "The practical ways of meeting the Twelfth Imam", disclosed the purpose of the author. From the outset, Aqatehrani candidly informs his readers that during the Twelfth Imam's occultation it is possible to visit him. He subsequently sets out to show how such encounters are made possible and enumerates them.[56] In this book, we are told about the supernatural experiences of individuals who have come into contact with the Twelfth Imam in the past and present. Personal accounts describe the sighting of the Twelfth Imam: with his "face hidden in a halo of light"; residing in a "fully luminous tent" and in the form of "an exceptionally bright and luminous light" travelling through the sky.[57] The author does associate the Twelfth Imam with light and luminousness. He also gives the

---

[53] H. A. 'Arabi, *Haqiqat Sharq* (Qom, 1381), pp. 35–36.   [54] Ibid., p. 29.
[55] http://www.noandish.com/print.php?id=29215
[56] M. Aqatehrani, *Soday-e Ruy-e Dust* (Qom, 1386), p. 10.
[57] Ibid., pp. 118, 154, 177.

impression that the Twelfth Imam may be the source of light. In his book, Aqatehrani refers to a report according to which a believer (perhaps Ayatollah Ansari Hamadani) waking up in the middle of the night to do his prayers perceives a ray of light emanating from a point and jetting all the way to the heavens. The believer receives an inspiration that at the point from which the light emanates, the Twelfth Imam is saying his prayers.[58]

Aqatehrani's book is a manual and guide written for the zealous to realize their dream of meeting with the Twelfth Imam here on earth and before his official reappearance. In his book, Aqatehrani provides a list of obligations and duties, the successful performance of which would first guarantee the readers of a meeting with the Imam and subsequently ensure the realization of their demands. Aqatehrani's list of duties include: the prayers that need to be recited and their specific number; the rites and rituals that ought to be observed; the holy shrines, such as the Jamkaran mosque, that should be visited; and the text, content and modality of writing the petition that has to be presented to the Hidden Imam.[59] Aqatehrani concludes his guidebook by producing a lengthy list of those factors that may prevent a meeting with the Hidden Imam.

During Ahmadinejad's time in office, Aqatehrani's work is but one of the many books written and published on this topic. Aqatehrani's proposition that the Hidden Imam has a continuous physical presence in this material world mentally prepares believers to expect supernatural experiences not explicable by reason.[60] Aqatehrani asserts that "there is no doubt that visiting the Imam [physically] is possible and practical".[61] This meeting cannot be a "normal" one according to earthy laws, as the Imam who must belong to the hidden world after his occultation in the ninth century is argued to be physically present in this material world. In emphasizing the possibility of a physical meeting with the Hidden Imam, Aqatehrani follows the official position of his teacher, Mesbah Yazdi. Mesbah Yazdi maintains that "establishing contact with the Imam is not forbidden". Even though he mentions that "we do not see him [the Imam], but he sees us", Mesbah Yazdi reiterates that "we can establish contact with him [the Hidden Imam]".[62] In a textbook intended for mid-level students of religious schools, Mesbah Yazdi argues that during the occultation period, people can benefit from the Twelfth Imam's "light" as though it was the sun hidden behind clouds. He informs his readers that

---

[58] Ibid., p. 64. [59] Ibid., pp. 19, 60, 67, 76, 104, 110.
[60] Ibid., p. 36. [61] Ibid., p. 34. [62] M. T. Mesbah Yazdi, *Aftab Velayat*, pp. 154–155.

many have been successful in visiting the Imam and he has assisted them by resolving their material and spiritual problems.[63] According to Mesbah Yazdi, once believers enter into a covenant with the Hidden Imam and respect the terms of the pledge, they will become the recipients of the Hidden Imam's help and special attention. Mesbah Yazdi councils that those who wish to receive such special attention should first proclaim: "Master [*aqa*] I would like to be your servant and of service to you" and should subsequently commit themselves to behaving in a manner acceptable to the Hidden Imam.[64] What is acceptable to the Hidden Imam will supposedly be known only to a selected few who implicitly or explicitly claim to be in contact with him, and the common folk come to accept their claim. In this manner, the "selected few" can abuse the Hidden Imam for their own political objectives.

Mesbah Yazdi is vague on the modality of the contact, even though he does confirm its possibility. Aqatehrani, his student, is quite explicit and candid on not only the details of how physical contact can be made, but also the importance of it. Aqatehrani's book encourages the pious and devout Shiʿi in love with their imams to set the task of meeting with the Hidden Imam as their prime objective in life. An important political outcome of this seemingly innocuous religious message is to prod and spur the common folk to forget their pressing material needs and conditions until they first succeed in meeting the Hidden Imam in this world.

Aqatehrani was not only Mesbah Yazdi's student, but he was subsequently handpicked and sent to the "Grand Islamic Centre" of New York by the Ayatollah.[65] Aqatehrani obtained his PhD in philosophy and mysticism from the State University of New York at Binghamton.[66] On his return to Iran, he collaborated with Mesbah Yazdi and was a vocal partisan of Ahmadinejad during the 2005 presidential election.[67] Aqatehrani's book on the "The practical ways of meeting with the Twelfth Imam" was published by the Emam Khomeyni Educational and Research Institute founded and headed by Mesbah Yazdi. After Ahmadinejad's presidency, Morteza Aqatehrani was invited by the President to attend the weekly cabinet meetings and lecture the ministers on Islamic ethics. In March 2008, Aqatehrani who had by then become known as the "teacher of ethics" of Ahmadinejad's government stood for election to the eighth

[63] M. T. Mesbah Yazdi, *Amuzesh 'Aqayed* (Tehran, 1385), p. 335.
[64] M. T. Yazdi, *Aftab Velayat*, p. 34.
[65] *Emrouz*, from *Etemad* (24 November 1385).   [66] *Ya Lesarat* (22 Esfand 1386).
[67] H. A. 'Arabi, *Haqiqat Sharq*, p. 101; *Partov-e Sokhan* (18 Khordad 1384).

Majles (parliament). Aqatehrani's name appeared second on a list of 30 candidates for Tehran, supported by Ahmadinejad's political group called the United Front of the Principlists (*Jebheh Motahed Usulgarayan*). He received the second highest vote in Tehran and entered the parliament. Ever since, he has been one of the staunchest supporters of Ahmadinejad in the *majles*. Anxiously campaigning for Ahmadinejad during the 2009 elections, Aqatehrani believed that Ahmadinejad had no real challenger and that all those who thought that someone other than him should become president were simply sick.[68]

THE MESBAH YAZDI–AHMADINEJAD AXIS: POLITICS AND THE HIDDEN WORLD

Well before the presidential elections of 2005, Ahmadinejad had close ties with Mesbah Yazdi and his students. According to Mesbah Yazdi, he knew Ahmadinejad when he was a professor at Iran's University of Science and Technology (IUST), better known as Science and Industry (*'Elm va Sanat*). At the time, Ahmadinejad was a member of the university branch of the mass mobilization militia organization, or the *basij*, and attended Mesbah Yazdi's gatherings.[69] Ahmadinejad was at IUST during 1989–1993 and then between 1997 and 2003. Therefore, Mesbah Yazdi could have known him since 1989. Mesbah Yazdi also mentions that he knew Ahmadinejad when he was the Governor General of the province of Ardebil.[70] Ahmadinejad held this position between 1993 and 1997. Therefore, it could be safely suggested that the two men knew one another at least some twelve to sixteen years before Ahmadinejad's presidency. It is also suggested that Ahmadinejad studied under Mesbah Yazdi, who taught him the pre-conditions of the appearance of the Hidden Imam, told him about the imminent appearance of the Twelfth Imam and informed him before the 2005 elections that the Imam had selected him as the future president.[71]

Ayatollah Mesbah Yazdi seems to be one of Ahmadinejad's very few politico-religious role models and religious sources of inspiration and imitation. Even though the President's official source of imitation is Ayatollah Khameneh'i, he seems to regard Mesbah Yazdi as an approachable source

---

[68] Yarinews.com/print.aspx/n/3280/%D%A2%D9%82 (8 Bahman 1387).
[69] *Partov-e Sokhan* (8 Tir 1384).   [70] Ibid.
[71] *Etemad*, Zamimeh Roozaneh (8 Mordad 1388).

of counsel and guidance on issues that Ayatollah Khameneh'i, given the constraints of his leadership position, may not have wished to personally and publicly commit himself. With the 2009 presidential elections, however, Ayatollah Khameneh'i set aside all semblances of neutrality and impartiality. After the 2005 presidential election, some of Mesbah Yazdi's loyal clerical students such as Morteza Aqatehrani, Mohammad-Naser Saqay-e Biriya and Manuchehr Mohammadi were appointed to key positions in Ahmadinejad's administration.[72]

By recounting his supernatural experience, which may well be construed as a contact between him and the Hidden Imam, Ahmadinejad may have wished to convince the common folk that, in addition to his political leadership role, he enjoyed the "special status" of a person chosen by the hidden world to fulfil a mission. Sliding between two separate spaces, with their respective laws and conditions, namely that of the material world and the hidden world, provided Ahmadinejad with great political manoeuvrability and flexibility. Whenever, as a political leader, he could not rationally explain events or unfortunate situations resulting from his policies, he could claim that the outcomes were the consequence of inexplicable forces of the hidden world. According to the rules of the material world, Ahmadinejad was accountable to the people who had elected him. Yet if he could convince his supporters that, at the General Assembly, he was accompanied by the Hidden Imam or some sort of power from the hidden world, then he could relieve himself of being accountable to his electors. By evoking some degree of proximity with the members of the hidden world, Ahmadinejad was hoping to obtain a carte blanche from his electors. One of the politico-religious messages of Ahmadinejad's discourse was that, irrespective of the tangible and prevailing social and economic predicaments, Iran was blessed because the country was being indirectly managed according to the Hidden Imam's will. Ahmadinejad gave the impression that the Hidden Imam's rule by proxy was temporary and that he would be the person who would usher in the Imam's appearance.

For the pious zealots, however, Ahmadinejad did not necessarily possess the qualifications and prerequisites of a person connected with the hidden world. He neither was a person known for his spirituality with a long history of stoicism and devotion nor was he a cleric. In order to convince the pious common folk, for whom he wished to pose as a politico-religious figure with supernatural powers, Ahmadinejad needed the support of and blessing of a religious figure or figures. The supernatural and

---

[72] *Emrouz*, from *Etemad* (24 Bahman 1385).

the hidden world had to be brought directly into politics by those who had some sort of religious credentials. The task of theorizing and propagating messianic occultism with Ahmadinejad as one of its flag bearers and chosen agents was effectively carried out by Mesbah Yazdi and the partisans of his school of thought.

Mesbah Yazdi's school of thought promoted and made banal the possibility of the Hidden Imam's regular intervention in all affairs eventually ascribing to him the management of state. Ahmadinejad was presented to the common folk as a trusted instrument of the Hidden Imam charged with carrying out his will while preparing the grounds for his imminent return. In books published after Ahmadinejad's election in 2005, the President is referred to as the commander of the Hidden Imam's army when he appears and the Guardian Corps of the Islamic Revolution, the *basij* and the security apparatus are presented as members of the Twelfth Imam's army.[73] Before and after the 2005 presidential elections, Mesbah Yazdi's promotion of Ahmadinejad as a political figure with special spiritual features and somehow connected with the hidden world could be deduced from his speeches and writings. Mesbah Yazdi's campaign gave the general impression that this man's presidency would effectively be a duet performed by a representative of this world and one from the hidden world.

Once Ahmadinejad became president, he was able to repay his debt partially to Mesbah Yazdi by not only following his macro politico-religious directives, but also by allocating more government funds to his research institute. The decision by Ahmadinejad's administration to increase the funding of Mesbah Yazdi's Emam Khomeyni Educational and Research Institute sheds some light on the symbiotic relationship between the two men. At the end of Khatami's presidency, the Institute received 350 million tomans or some $350 thousand from the government's budget. During the first year of Ahmadinejad's presidency, this budget allocation was increased tenfold to 3.5 billion tomans or $3.5 million. The government's hand-out to Mesbah Yazdi's Institute has been increasing exponentially over the years. Despite the decrease in the price of oil and the recession, the budget allocated by the government to Mesbah Yazdi's research institute in 1388 (2009–2010) increased by forty-nine per cent. This figure now stands at 7 billion tomans or $7 million.[74]

---

[73] *Etemad*, Zamimeh Roozaneh (8 Mordad 1388).
[74] *Entekhab News* (20 Bahman 1387); see http://www.tiknews.net/print/?ID=75935 and Alborz Mohammadi, 'Mesbah Yazdi Afzayesh, Tashkis Maslahat Kahesh' (21 Bahman 1387) in Rooz. http://www.roozonline.com/archives/2009/02/post_11508.php

THE UNUSUAL CONSEQUENCES OF A PHANTASMICAL
SOCIAL ATMOSPHERE

Since the formation of Ahmadinejad's government in 2005, there had been
talk of the new administration's firm belief in the imminent return of the
Twelfth Imam and the necessity of facilitating his reappearance. Soon after
his return from New York, Ahmadinejad told the Foreign Minister of a
non-aligned nation who had commented on Iran's troublesome situation
that "These are signs of the re-appearance of Imam Mahdi who will appear
within the next two years".[75] Early into his presidential term, it is reported
that, during one of his regular provincial trips, Ahmadinejad told the
people of Sistan and Baluchestan, one of the least-developed regions in
Iran, "Do not worry, the Twelfth Imam [*Imam Zaman*] will appear in two
years and will solve all the problems".[76] The President seemed intent on
presenting himself as an oracle and a facilitator of the Twelfth Imam's
appearance. The project of convincing a considerable proportion of the
population of such ideas may have been plausible some 500 years before.
In the twenty-first century, however, its success seemed implausible.

It could be argued that, by revealing his "supernatural" experience at
the UN and prophesying about the return of the Twelfth Imam, the
President sought to legitimize his claims and policies as sacred. By claiming supernatural capacities, the President not only sought to solicit political and religious support for himself, but he may have also wished to
warn his detractors that criticizing him, his cabinet and his policies was
akin to confronting a divinely commissioned person and hindering the
Twelfth Imam's reappearance. Acceptance of Ahmadinejad's claim
to connectedness could place believers in a delicate religious position.
Dissatisfaction with his worldly policies of managing the Iranian society
and economy could imply doubting the wisdom of the hidden world,
exposing believers to the charge of unbelief and apostasy. Once worldly
obedience due to otherworldly connections was established a relation
of politico-religious dominance and dependence between those who
believed such assertions and the person who pretended to have supernatural links ensued. By making such insinuations, implicitly the road
was being paved to introduce a quasi-substitution process: the chosen
person shrouded in a "halo of light" was sacred, since God or one of the
imams had identified him as such. In the register of those who were

---

[75] *Aftab News* (16 November 2005).   [76] *Etemad Melli* (11 Tir 1387 and 1 July 2008).

receptive to such ideas, it made perfect sense to accept, trust and therefore obey fully the politics of the politician-saint.

As such, the religious justification for a single political voice legitimized by the claim to some sort of connectedness to the hidden world was in place. Based on such a discourse, irrational claims and assertions could be advanced as a miracle or a work of Divine providence governed by rules incomprehensible by the scientific rules and laws of the material world. Once this reasoning process based on the "rules and conditions" of the hidden world, unknowable to human beings, was applied to the politics of the material world, all "seemingly" incompatibilities and paradoxes could be explained away. It could even explain how Ahmadinejad won the tenth presidential elections, even though his main opponent, Musavi, was poised to and, according to non-official sources, did obtain a much higher number of votes!

The general impression of connectedness to the hidden world that Ahmadinejad imparted to the public was unprecedented in the history of the Islamic Republic. No religious or political public figure had dared to enter this sensitive religious domain. Ayatollah Khomeyni had consistently stayed off this path and had sharply warned against this type of religious demagogy. Politicizing mystical connections with the hidden world was an exercise in deluding the people into believing that supernatural forces could support and legitimize the policies of a selected few politicians. The President's supernatural evocations were not private or personal accounts such as those of the reclusive Sufis or that of Ayatollah Behjat, who intentionally avoided the public sphere. In the name of Islam, the Prophet of which made no claims to miracles except the recitation of the words of God, the Qur'an, Ahmadinejad and his clerical supporters were once again opening a Pandora's box, which had been opened and shut several times in the past 500 years of Iranian history.

The frenzied and phantasmical so-called religious culture that came to reign during Ahmadinejad's presidency ushered a flurry of bizarre and occult happenings. Regular reports of unusual events mirrored a state of hysteria among certain segments of the population. The Congregational Prayer leader of one of Tehran's mosques, Mohammad-Reza Hojjati, wrote that he was prepared to be put to death if, after comprehensive prayers for the return of the Twelfth Imam at all mosques and especially at the Jamkaran mosque, the Twelfth Imam failed to reappear.[77] The claim, at odds with Shi'i religious culture, implied that the reappearance of the

---

[77] *Baztab* (27 Shahrivar 1384); see http://www.baztab.com/news/29142.php

Hidden Imam was in the power of human beings rather than God. According to another report, a dog had entered Imam Reza's mosque in Mashhad, paid its respects and then left the mosque in tears![78] Even a so-called visual recording of this event was said to have been widely circulated. Was the fabricated account supposed to prove that the exalted spiritual and religious aura that had come to reign in Iran during Ahmadinejad's presidency had transformed even dogs, traditionally believed to be impure (*najes*) animals, into pious creatures, performing the required and routine rituals of their devout human counterparts?

About two weeks after the "dog fable", a man by the name of Seyyed Hasani who was actively recruiting followers in Karaj, claimed that he was in contact with the Twelfth Imam and was his representative during the Imam's occultation.[79] Hasani's followers, dressed in black gowns and green shawls, chanted slogans in his support during the Friday Congregational Prayers in cities such as Qom and Qazvin.[80] The news of this very odd claim was soon followed by an even more outlandish declaration. In Shazand, a place near the city of Arak, a woman, known by her initials F.A., who had apparently published several books on the Twelfth Imam, contended that she had received a letter from the Twelfth Imam in which he had requested the people to pray for his appearance. In the same letter, the Twelfth Imam had promised to appear very soon. Ms. F.A. believed that the responsibility of disseminating the Hidden Imam's message was bestowed upon her by the hidden world.[81]

It suddenly seemed as though the floodgates of unfounded and occult claims of a religious nature had opened. A new climax was reached when a handwritten letter in Farsi and not Arabic, attributed to the Twelfth Imam, was published in a religious weekly called *Khorshid*. The same letter was reported to have been widely distributed at mosques in Tehran and at the Jamkaran mosque.[82] While a letter falsely attributed to the Hidden Imam was being published and distributed as proof of his interaction and correspondence with the material world, a phoney ka'beh (ka'ba) was constructed near the city of Karaj by another entrepreneurial charlatan.

---

[78] *Emrouz* (15 September 1984); see http://www.emrouz.info/archives/print/2005/12/002724.php
[79] *Baztab* (27 Azar 1384).   [80] *Shahrvand Emrooz* (22 Mehr 1386).
[81] *Baztab* (30 Azar 1384); see http://www.baztab.ir/news/32334.php
[82] H. Bastani, 'Moda'iyan Ertebat ba Emam Zaman' in *Rooz Online* (14 Azar 1384); see http//roozonline.com/o2article/o12247.shtml and also see http://www.Peiknet.com/1384/hafteh/04azar/hafteh_page/64khorafat.htm (15 December 2005).

Taking advantage of the heightened atmosphere of superstitious religious sensitivities whipped up among the pious common folk, the constructor of the fake ka'beh even duped a group of believers to circumambulate it and pursued his hoax to the point of calling the participants *haji* or those that had performed the religious pilgrimage of *haj*.[83] A thorough substitution process of replacing the basic principles and rites of the faith with bizarre and superstitious practices was under way.

The superstition frenzy permeating through the country during Ahmadinejad's office even affected the world of sports. In an interview with the newspaper *Iran*, 'Ali Da'i, one of Asia's star football players, a long-time captain of the Iranian football team and the head coach of both SAIPA, a first league Iranian football team and Iran's national football team, divulged an incredible secret about the misfortune of his team, SAIPA. Da'i claimed that he had proof of the fact that the entire SAIPA team was put under a spell by a sorcerer and that it was a talisman that had caused the consecutive losses of his team.[84] Da'i explained that the exact details of how his team was going to play against and lose to another team, Pegah, was already foretold and revealed to him before the match by the son of the sorcerer who had put the original spell on SAIPA. According to Da'i, two factors were instrumental in neutralizing the spell: first, appropriate prayers and supplications, and second, the intervention and special assistance of Ayatollah Behjat. The occult misfortunes of SAIPA came to an end and the team apparently resumed its winning streak through the inter-mediary of so-called religious solutions.[85]

The stories of the weeping dog at a holy shrine, a President who was engulfed in a halo of light, people receiving visitations from the Hidden Imam, the appearance of the Hidden Imam's handwriting in Farsi, the appearance of ka'beh in Iran, people in contact with the Hidden Imam declaring with certitude that he intended to appear in two years or less and a whole football team placed under a spell seemed to convey a social and psychological atmosphere of intense paranormal activities. To some, this state of strangeness characterized by the prevalence of bizarre occurrences and unusual events represented signs of the immi-nent return of the Hidden Imam.

---

[83] *Shahrvand Emrooz* (22 Mehr 1386).
[84] *Noandish* (10 Farvardin 1387); see http://www.noandish.com/com.php?id=14929
[85] *Noandish* (10 Farvardin 1387); see http://www.noandish.com/com.php?id=14929

In fact, there were also those who spoke passionately about the imminent reappearance of the Twelfth Imam years before the presidency of Ahmadinejad and found comfort and representation in the new President's discourse. The famous Iranian religious preacher-performer, *haj* Mansur Arzi, was one of those who had long claimed to have encountered the Hidden Imam after having secluded and cloistered himself at the Ark mosque.[86] Arzi is probably Iran's leading *maddah* or one who praises the imams in his lectures, sermons and chants. Arzi's emotionally charged religious sermons moved throngs of devout believers, who gathered at Tehran's Ark mosque to long spells of wailing, sobbing, chest-beating and agonizing ecstasy. He would remind his audience of the tragic accounts of Imam Hoseyn and his followers at Karbala. Then he would draw a parallel between that gruesome event and the fate of the selfless Iranian warriors seeking martyrdom against Saddam Hoseyn's well-equipped invading army during the Iran–Iraq war. Arzi was one of the many preachers who had frequented the war fronts, sensed and breathed in its spiritual aura, provided comfort and encouragement to the young warriors and was admired by them. Arzi now stands at the apex of a powerful organization of religious preachers and performers whose job is to move their pious audience to a state of exalted frenzy and are naturally in opposition to any political platform promoting reason, rationality and reform. Mahmud Ahmadinejad had a close affinity with this group of religious preacher-performers. He was one of them and had preached in the Turk's mosque at Tehran's central bazaar.[87]

Once Ahmadinejad became the mayor of Tehran, he supported the preacher-performers financially, and effectively organized them as his political and propaganda arm. Engaging the pious common folk and interacting with them at the mosques, the preacher-performers (*maddahan*) gradually replaced the clergy as the contact points and bridges with the common people. The task of this politicized and highly energetic group of lay preachers was to move the pious to a state of rapture by throwing them back into a distant historical episode and locking them in the rage and fury of the injustice of that moment, to be tapped into and manipulated in the present. The preacher-performer guild became instrumental in promoting and disseminating the Ahmadinejad–Mesbah Yazdi discourse.

[86] *Shahrvand Emrooz* (9 Day 1386).
[87] S. Rafizadeh, 'Hemayat Maddahan az Hamkar Sabeq Khod' in Rooz Online (27 Shahrivar 1384); see http://roozonline.com/o1newsstory/010188.shtml

Arzi's fellow colleagues and students fan out across Iran, mesmerising the zealots throughout the land. It is said that, during the 2005 presidential election, Arzi requested the preacher-performers to "uplift Ahmadinejad" or support him.[88] The President could depend on the favours of his preacher friends who were in turn supported by him to propagate the messianic occult discourse that kept segments of the population in a permanent state of feverish excitement and anticipation.

COMMODIFICATION OF THE FAITH: THE PHENOMENON OF THE JAMKARAN MOSQUES

The Jamkaran mosque and the supernatural events that are said to occur there have placed this revived holy shrine under the spotlight. During the presidency of Ahmadinejad, the attention paid to the development of the Jamkaran mosque and the propaganda surrounding its sanctity has catapulted the status of Jamkaran even beyond that of the traditional Iranian shrines of Imam Reza in Mashhad and Hazrat Ma'sumeh (Imam Reza's sister) in Qom. Parallel to Ahmadinejad–Mesbah Yazdi's articulation of a political and religious discourse based on the earthly interventions of the Hidden Imam and the possibility of inexplicable supernatural events, there seems to have been a need to promote a holy shrine associated with the Hidden Imam. Just as the Ahmadinejad–Mesbah Yazdi discourse had appropriated the Hidden Imam as its contact with the hidden world, it also needed a specific and distinct sacred space associated with the Hidden Imam for the followers of their own discourse. The popularity of Jamkaran, the centre that pilgrims from all corners of the country would converge upon, came to symbolize the success and appeal of Ahmadinejad and Mesbah Yazdi's Hidden Imam-based discourse.

According to Mesbah Yazdi, Behjat and Aqatehrani, the Jamkaran mosque was the most unique Shi'i shrine in Iran, which believers needed to visit regularly. In a chapter called "Jamkaran the pole of attraction of *velayat* [the devotees of the imams]", Mesbah Yazdi refers to the Jamkaran mosque as a prime example of the Hidden Imam's favours to Iranians.[89] To Mesbah Yazdi, Jamkaran's sudden popularity among the people and the mosque's rapid transformation from a relatively neglected mosque to a magnificent and splendid shrine was a miracle. He argues that it must have been due to the Hidden Imam's magnetic attraction that this holy mosque

---

[88] *Shahrvand Rooz* (9 Day 1386).   [89] M. T. Mesbah Yazdi, *Aftab Velayat*, p. 115.

developed into a pole of attraction for believers from all around the country and even abroad.[90] According to Mesbah Yazdi, the Jamkaran mosque is also important to all those who wish to establish contact with the Hidden Imam. He encourages and invites believers to visit Jamkaran. For the purpose of successfully contacting the Hidden Imam, believers are told to recite those prayers and supplications that are specifically designed for this purpose and which "are regularly read at the Jamkaran mosque".[91] Aqatehrani's promotion of the Jamkaran mosque as the only venue or shrine in Iran where a meeting with the Hidden Imam can occur is much more transparent and clear. According to Aqatehrani, along with other factors facilitating a meeting with the Hidden Imam, the importance of particular times, such as Friday nights and the birthday of the Hidden Imam (*nimeh sha'ban*) and special places such as Mecca, Medina and the Jamkaran mosque – the only mosque in Iran that he mentions – should not be overlooked.[92]

Mesbah Yazdi praises the people of Qom for their efforts to revive the Jamkaran mosque and tries to prove that the renaissance of Jamkaran was long ago foretold by the imams. In an attempt to demonstrate that the religio-historic mission of the people of Qom to rebuild the Jamkaran mosque is a prelude to the coming of the Hidden Imam, Mesbah Yazdi refers to a report attributed to Imam Sadeq and cited in Mohammad-Baqer Majlesi's *Bahar al-Anvar*. According to this report, around the time of the reappearance of the Twelfth Imam, Qom will become the world's centre and fountain of knowledge and virtue. Knowledge will radiate from Qom to the East and the West until the Shi'i faith reigns over everyone on earth. Only at that time will the *Qa'em* (Hidden Imam) appear.[93] By arguing that the people of Qom were destined to become the source of virtue and knowledge, Mesbah Yazdi intimates that the revival of the Jamkaran mosque was religiously preordained and that its popularity is the preamble to the return of the Hidden Imam.

The present-day Jamkaran mosque situated some six kilometres to the east of Qom is very different from the couple of humble rooms that were known as the old Jamkaran mosque. The new mosque and its minarets are built on a site claimed to have been selected by the Hidden Imam during one of his appearances in the eleventh century. According to Sheykh Hasan ebn Mosleh, a meeting took place between him and the Twelfth Imam, who seemed about thirty years of age and was accompanied by the ageless prophet Khezr at the site where today stands the Jamkaran mosque. The

[90] Ibid.   [91] Ibid., p. 155.   [92] M. Aqatehrani, *Soday-e Ruy-e Dust*, p. 39.
[93] M.T. Mesbah Yazdi, *Aftab Velayat*, p. 116.

Imam is reported to have informed him that God had designated this particular site as the land on which the Jamkaran mosque should be built. Subsequently, the Imam ordered the Sheykh to inform the peasant who worked on this land that he should stop cultivating it so that the mosque could be built upon it. It is claimed that the Twelfth Imam himself requested the Shi'i to visit this mosque.[94] The Hidden Imam is reported to frequent the Jamkaran mosque, where he is said to meet with people, engage in discussions with them and grant the pilgrims their wishes.[95] Many accounts of miracles, such as healing the paralyzed and patients with incurable diseases, through the personal intervention of the Hidden Imam, are attributed to the Jamkaran mosque.[96]

Today, in the courtyard of the Jamkaran mosque stand two separate elevations built on what is said to be the mouth of two wells, one for men and another for women. The elevations are covered with parallel metallic bars between which pilgrims may drop their letters or petitions to the Twelfth Imam. Instructions on how to write such letters are posted on the wall, sheltering the wells. The notion of petitioning the Twelfth Imam for favours and the guarantee of its realization constitutes an important aspect of the supernatural notion that the Hidden Imam intervenes in the affairs of the material world, resolving the problems and relieving the pains of those who petition him. The idea that if the Imam were petitioned according to proper rites and rituals then satisfaction would be obtained almost automatically is attributed to the works of Mohammad-Baqer Majlesi. Mohammad-Baqer Majlesi provides a detailed account of how a petition to the Twelfth Imam should be written, sealed, wrapped and left in a stream or thrown into a well in order for it to reach the Hidden Imam. It is argued that once the Hidden Imam receives the petition, he will become responsible for responding to it favourably. The directives of Majlesi appear in almost all the books that have recently proliferated on the topic of communicating with the Twelfth Imam.[97]

The development and expansion of the Jamkaran mosque, which is now receiving ever greater attention and a growing share of government funds, is of particular importance to both Ahmadinejad and Mesbah Yazdi. The popularity of the mosque is viewed as a gauge of the spread and growing influence of the Ahmadinejad–Mesbah Yazdi politico-religious discourse. In state reports and the official pro-government mass media, the status and

---

[94] J. Mir'azimi, *Masjed-e Moqadas-e Jamkaran Tajaligah Saheb Zaman* (Qom, 1385), pp. 27–28.

[95] Ibid., pp. 73, 74, 85.   [96] Ibid., pp. 91, 93, 105, 106, 108, 110, 118, 126, 128, 137.

[97] M. Aqatehrani, *Soday-e Ruy-e Dust*, p. 110; J. Mir'azimi, *Masjed-e Moqadas-e Jamkaran Tajaligah Saheb Zaman*, pp. 207–209; M. Faqih Imani, *Foze Akbar*, p. 133.

sacredness of Jamkaran is raised to such heights that it overshadows the importance of other traditionally sacred mosques both in Iran and abroad. Mesbah Yazdi refers to the growing numbers of young people, both female and male, who visit Jamkaran as an indicator of the growing piety and religiosity of Iranians.[98]

For Mesbah Yazdi, the traditional shrines in Mashhad and Qom are probably indicative of a traditional Shi'ism, while that of Jamkaran is directly associated with his newly revived particular discourse of the Twelfth Imam. Mesbah Yazdi maintains that he never dreamed that Jamkaran would reach the distinguished position that it has recently attained in the mind of the believers. He marvels at the fact that even though pilgrims can park their cars along several kilometres of parking space built around the shrine, there would still be a shortage of parking space for all the eager pilgrims.[99] According to official reports, on the evening and following morning of the Hidden Imam's birthday, some three million people visit Jamkaran.[100] If visiting the Jamkaran mosque is the believers' manner of paying respect and attention to the Twelfth Imam, then according to Mesbah Yazdi, they are choosing the best and closest way to be attentive to God.[101]

After Ahmadinejad's presidency in 2005, his ministers are said to have signed a pledge of allegiance, subservience and commitment to the Hidden Imam during one of their first cabinet meetings. The Minister of Culture and Islamic Guidance, Saffar Harandi, is said to have travelled to the Jamkaran mosque and dropped the pledge in the well designated for men.[102] Once in power, Ahmadinejad's government allocated some 10 billion tomans or the equivalent of $10 million to the expansion and renovation of the Jamkaran mosque, which is now advertised as a particularly holy place.[103] A budget of 20 billion tomans ($20 million) was also allocated by Ahmadinejad's government to building roads around the Jamkaran shrine.[104]

During a speech in September 2008 at the Emam (Imam) Khomeyni shrine, Nateq Nuri, an influential clergy and politician, lashed out at the building of a new shrine, which he dubbed as the "second Jamkaran", and

[98] R. San'ati, *Goftoman Mesbah*, p. 499.   [99] Ibid.
[100] *Kargozaran* (22 September 2008).   [101] M. T. Mesbah Yazdi, *Aftab Velayat*, p. 143.
[102] *Entekhab News* (24 Mehr 1384).
[103] O. Memarian, 'Vakoneshhay Tond Aleyh Tarvij Khorafeh va Oham' in Rooz Online (23 Azar 1384).
[104] *Kargozaran* (22 September 2008).

demanded that an end be put to these practices, which he called "harmful
to the people's beliefs".[105] A few days after Nateq Nuri's speech, the
newspaper *Jomhuriye Eslami* speculated that the "second Jamkaran"
was the revived and rebuilt version of an old mosque called Masjed
Mohaddethin in the city of Babol, located in the northern province of
Mazandaran.[106] The "second Jamkaran" resembles its older brother in that
it is said to have been built by the direct order of the Hidden Imam. The
Hidden Imam is said to have appeared to Molla Nasira and instructed him
to build the mosque. The name of the mosque is also said to have been
chosen by the Hidden Imam himself. There is disagreement on whether the
Twelfth Imam appeared to Molla Nasira in his dream or whether it was a
visitation. Molla Nasira was a staunch follower of Mohammad-Baqer
Majlesi and is reported to have built the Mohaddethin mosque in the
eighteenth century. The old mosque was renovated and rebuilt in 1964.[107]
The "second Jamkaran" is also believed to be the abode of miracles and
special experiences. In a book entitled "The miraculous acts of the holy
Mohaddethin mosque", all the miracles and supernatural events that have
occurred in the "second Jamkaran" have been compiled and recorded.[108]
According to the Congregational Prayer leader or imam of the "second
Jamkaran", Asgar Nasiriya'i, the popularity of the mosque, however,
began in 2005 and, ever since, it has been attracting more pilgrims. On
special religious occasions, the mosque is said to attract some 4,000 to 5,000
people.

According to Asgar Nasiriya'i, the "second Jamkaran" that Nateq Nuri
referred to in his speech was not the Mohaddethin mosque, even though
the newspaper *Jomhuriy-e Eslami* had claimed so. Nasiriya'i argues that,
in the village of Lamudeh in Qa'emshahr, a relatively uneducated woman
claims that the Hidden Imam has ordered her to build a Hoseyniyyeh.[109] A
Hoseyniyyeh does not have the appearance of a mosque, yet it is an equally
sacred space where usually the trials and tribulations of Imam Hoseyn are
remembered and mourned. Once the Hoseyniyyeh is built in Lamudeh, its
benefactor decides to call it the "second Jamkaran", as this building,
similar to that of the original Jamkaran, was also reportedly built on the
order of the Twelfth Imam. This "second Jamkaran" or "third Jamkaran"
flourishes as the woman who constructed it collects the sums of money that
believers pay in the hope that their wishes would come true or after their
wishes are fulfilled. The common folk's conviction that this site is blessed
by the Twelfth Imam and is therefore capable of performing miracles

---

[105] Ibid.   [106] *Shahrvand Rooz* (14 Mehr 1387).   [107] Ibid.   [108] Ibid.   [109] Ibid.

induces them to make solemn religious vows (*nazr*), which, once again if realized, would generate revenues.

The Hidden-Imam-based political and religious discourse of Ahmadinejad–Mesbah Yazdi has given rise to a predictable wave of eco-nomic entrepreneurship in the name of religion. By dragging the hidden world and its members, with its particular features and laws not necessarily discernible to human reasoning, into the mundane and material world, the sacred is materialized and commoditized. The market incorporates the sacred and packages it for sale at a market-determined price. The promotion of superstition in a religious guise can become a most demanded and exciting commodity, part fiction and fantasy and part real. If superstition-based religio-economic activities have a market, then superstition and occultism must be responding to a real social and psychological need. The role of state-supported propaganda and advertisement for the promotion of superstition as a commodity cannot be overlooked as an explanatory factor for the rise in interest in occultism during Ahmadinejad's presidency. Clearly, Ahmadinejad's concern for and attention to the original Jamkaran is very different from that of the two other Jamkarans. Since the first or original Jamkaran is the symbol of the Mesbah Yazdi–Ahmadinejad administration, financial support for it is therefore state-driven, while the other two seem to be market-driven religious enterprises. The blossoming and success of the two other Jamkarans, however, demonstrates that the government's partic-ular messianic discourse is finding resonance among some devout believers. If politicizing religion pulled a heavenly and spiritual belief down to earth by tying its fate to the fortunes and misfortunes, virtues and vices of humans and politicians, its commercialization by marketing superstition seems to be the *coup de grâce* to a once-comforting noble and uncorrupted belief system.

THE CLERICAL REACTION TO MESSIANIC OCCULTISM: SHIʿISM VERSUS SHIʿISM

The President's attempt at playing with and manipulating the religious sentiments of the common folk, followed by the stream of reports on far-fetched and highly unusual occurrences, met with different reactions among the clergy. Clerical reactions at first, except those of Ayatollah Makarem Shirazi and Hojjatoleslam ʿAli Zadsar, demonstrated a corre-spondence between the political tendency of the commentators and their preoccupation with or position on superstitious and obscurantist ideas. Ahmadinejad's political opponents criticized his instrumentalization of the religious sentiments and beliefs of the masses, while his political proponents hailed him for his reawakening and revival of certain Shi'i beliefs. Sceptical of Ahmadinejad and Mesbah Yazdi's politico-religious project for the country, the enlightened and reformist clerics rallied around Hojjatoleslam Majid Ansari warning about the "Jamkaranization of Shi'ism", which was an allusion to the state-led policy of presenting Shi'ism in an ever greater occult and mystified light.[110]

As Ahmadinejad's supernatural and unusual statements increased throughout his tenure, the little consensus and concordance that remained among the traditional clergy came under further strain. Sensitive to the charge of irrationalism, superstition and occultism levied against them, the traditional clergy suddenly found themselves in opposition to a relatively small nucleus of their cohorts who increasingly relied on evoking the Twelfth Imam to justify and legitimize the Ahmadinejad government and its policies. Shortly after Ahmadinejad's meeting with Javadi Amoli was made public, Ayatollah Musavi Ardebili, a one-time head of the judiciary during Khomeyni's era who had subsequently become a Source of Imitation (*marja' taqlid*) in Qom, reacted to the new assault of superstitious Islam. He told the personnel of the ILNA news agency that "unfortunately advocating and promoting superstitious ideas will drag our youth backwards". He warned that such "baseless ideas are harmful to Islam and its consequences would not be easily eradicated". Musavi Ardebili concluded that "abusing sanctities is very dangerous and such thoughts will push us backwards and the least that it can do is to damage our reputation abroad. It is best to leave religion in its state of sanctity".[111] Musavi Ardebili's comments were in the general spirit of enjoining good and forbidding evil. Identifying and warning of an impending danger, his recommendations were addressed to the whole community. He intentionally refrained from pointing an accusing finger at any particular person, group or politico-religious tendency. Musavi Ardebili's position was in accordance with the main brief of the traditional Sources of Imitation in times of internal socio-political "deviation", which could lead to a strife or conflict. He tried to stay above the political fray in order to advise and subsequently heal and reconcile by acting in an objective and non-partisan fashion.

Ayatollah Yusef Sane'i, an outspoken, iconoclastic and reformist-minded Source of Imitation, who has long been the *bete noire* of the

---

[110] O. Memarian, 'Vakoneshhay Tond Aleyh Tarvij Khorafeh va Oham' in Rooz Online (23 Azar 1384).

[111] http://www.emrouz.info/archives/print/2005/12/002612.hph

conservative clerics and their Principlist allies, warned against the rise of superstitious and obscurantist ideas in his regular interviews. Sane'i argued that "the spreading of superstition is a premeditated project that certain people are implementing in a goal-oriented manner". He pointed out that such superstitious ideas were contrary to Islam and had to be combatted, just as Khomeyni had engaged in battling them up to his last days.[112] In a politically charged statement, Sane'i argued that "when people are restrained from seeking science, engaging in reflection and thought and are unable to or prevented from benefiting from the real religion and the true Islam it is natural that instead of moving towards reason, science and religion, they will tend to regress towards the opposite direction of super-stition and obscurantism".[113] Sane'i's comments demonstrated how clearly the lines were drawn between the custodians of Shi'ism. For Sane'i, throughout history, the proponents of a Shi'ism grounded in reflec-tion and reason had been confronted by those whose interests required them to keep the people in darkness, irrationality and obscurity. The Ahmadinejad–Mesbah Yazdi discourse had triggered off not only another historical episode of Shi'ism versus Shi'ism, but also one of clerics versus clerics, while for the most part, the laymen were sitting on the sidelines watching. This alignment of religious voices and forces was a prelude to what would occur much more forcefully and intensively in the aftermath of the 2009 presidential election.

Ayatollah Makarem Shirazi, an independently minded, highly distin-guished and influential mainstream Source of Imitation, usually supportive of the political status quo and Ahmadinejad's government, especially during the first year of the President's tenure, proved that he was not willing to tow any political line when it came to religious principles. A personality very different from Sane'i in his approach to politics, Makarem Shirazi lamented that, throughout history, superstition and those who fabricate such ideas have harmed and impaired the faith. He equated the damage done to the faith by the fabricators of superstitions with the sworn enemies of the faith. In his assessment of "the issues related to the Twelfth Imam" and their origins, Makarem Shirazi suggested that the culprits were either ignorant, pursuing financial objectives or perhaps incited by foreign powers.[114]

[112] Meeting with the personnel of ISNA (20 Azar 1384), posted on Saane'i's personal website http://www.saaneie.org/
[113] Meeting with the personnel of Rooz Online (17 Dey 1384), posted on Saane'i's personal website http://www.saaneie.org/
[114] *Shargh* (5 Dey 1384).

A few months after Ahmadinejad's election, 'Ali Zadsar, the conservative clerical member of the Seventh Parliament from Jiroft and Anbarabad, wrote an important letter to him. In this letter, Zadsar referred to five issues constantly raised on various websites in relation to the President. Zadsar requested the President to clarify his position on the following rumours: first, "Ahmadinejad considers himself as a chosen person [*montakhab*] by Imam Zaman" (the Twelfth Imam); second, "Ahmadinejad receives his orders from Mesbah Yazdi"; third, "Ahmadinejad is a proponent and supporter of the Hojjatiyyeh Society"; fourth, "Ahmadinejad is favourable towards the hidebound"; fifth, "Ahmadinejad has assisted and encouraged the superstition-spreading preacher-performers".[115] Pursuing his policy of ambiguity and probably hoping that those whom he wished to move would deduce from Zadsar's letter that he really did think that he was the Twelfth Imam's chosen representative, Ahmadinejad never responded to Zadsar's poignant questions, which remained fresh and troubling in the mind of those many Iranians who did not ascribe to the President's outlandish claims.

Sane'i's implicit remarks about those guilty of immersing society into superstition were made explicit and clear by another candid and highly politicized cleric, who firmly believed that he had been cheated out of entering the second round of the 2005 presidential elections by those forces supporting Ahmadinejad. Mehdi Karubi, known to his followers and sympathizers as "the Sheykh of the reformist movement", accused "persons with governmental responsibilities" and "the members of the government" for spreading superstition and obscurantism. He criticized the authorities for "dragging the Hidden Imam into every-day trivial affairs". According to Karubi, those who spread such far-fetched ideas intended to "keep the people in ignorance and lead the intellectuals to conclude that Islam was useless and incapable of providing solutions". Karubi called this, "a plot against progressive and dynamic Islam".[116] If Karubi's comments are read in sequence to Sane'i's, it seems as if the reformist clerics believed that Ahmadinejad's government was intentionally and consciously spreading religio-phantasmical ideas in the public sphere to keep the people occupied with metaphysical concerns over which they had no

---

[115] *Entekhab News* (28 Mehr 1384); see http/www.entekhab.ir/display/?ID=6816&page=1. For information on the Messianic Hojjatiyyeh group, see: A. Baqi, *Dar Shenakht Hezb-e Qaedin-e Zaman* (Qom, 1362); A. Rahnema and F. Nomani, *The Secular Miracle, Religion, Politics and Economic Policy in Iran* (London, 1990), pp. 211–213.

[116] *Shargh* (17 Dey 1384).

real control, so that they would become resigned to their fate as that which is willed by the Twelfth Imam.

Talk about the imminent return of the Twelfth Imam, whose reappearance in Shi'i belief implied cataclysmic changes, left believers in a state of mental limbo, as all worldly concerns became insignificant before the magnitude and importance of the awaited Imam's return. To the Shi'i, the impending appearance of the Twelfth Imam is blissful news. Yet it puts an end to the notion of a futurity in terms of everyday life and routine. Planning for any material future, concern about day-to-day issues, interest in social, political and cultural topics and following domestic and international events suddenly become trivial and peripheral. Worldly and material life and preoccupations dim before the magnanimity of the promised return of the Messiah. How could a believer convinced of the imminent end of the world and history as we know it keep interest in daily and mundane affairs if the end was so clearly in sight?

Another group of reformist clerics focused on a different aspect of the problem. They sought to control the damage done to the faith by distinguishing between Shi'i beliefs and those ideas falsely attributed to the Shi'i. They tried to disprove the religious credibility of superstitious ideas in the hope of preventing the youth from becoming permanently alienated from religion. In an interview with the *Guardian Weekly*, Ayatollah Hoseyn'ali Montazeri, Khomeyni's deposed heir, probably the most learned of Iran's Sources of Imitation at the time and an untiring critic of the Islamic Republic's abuses of human rights, political freedoms and civil liberties, argued that "the Hidden Imam is a part of our beliefs, but our belief in him does not mean that some should abuse his name for political reasons. We are opposed to such misappropriations. Manipulating and exploiting the names of religious sanctities will lead the people and the younger generation to become disgusted with religion".[117]

Ayatollah Mohammad-Reza Tavasoli, a highly respected religious figure known for his close collaboration and friendship with Ayatollah Khomeyni, said, "Today the problem of obscurantism has become so widespread that [all sorts of] accounts are being attributed to the pure imams. [People talk about] visiting the Hidden Imam, seeing the Hidden Imam and assigning a specific time for his return ... In our [Shi'i] reports it is stated that those who assign a specific date to the return of the Hidden Imam are liars and falsifiers ... Today, the petrified, narrow-minded and reactionary forces are at the juncture of setting a time for the return of the

---

[117] Montazeri's website; see http://www.amontazeri.com/farsi/payamha/90.htm

Hidden Imam. They have masked their worldly concerns with the sanctities of Islam".[118]

While Tavasoli indirectly chastised the President as a liar and a falsifier for having set a date for the return of the Hidden Imam and having claimed some sort of a metaphysical visitation, Hojjatoleslam Rasul Montajabnia, yet another reformist cleric, chose a different route to demonstrate that Ahmadinejad's claims were in contradiction with the teachings of Shi'ism. Montajabnia, a close associate of Karubi, attributed certain practices to Ahmadinejad and his government and told reporters that "publicizing issues such as the reappearance of the Twelfth Imam in the next few years, identifying the place where he is to re-appear, building a road for him to travel along from his supposed point of appearance and rumours about constituting a welcoming committee for the Hidden Imam is contrary to the method and procedure of the prominent *'olama* [*ulema*] of Shi'ism". He opined that such ideas were rejected and rebuffed by Shi'i imams.[119]

Fully aware of the consequences of religious manipulation, Ayatollah Bayat warned against vulgar superstitious ideas and its threat to reason, religion, emamat (*imamate*) and ejtehad (*ijtihad*). In a direct reference to the President's experience with the "halo of light", and those who elevated him to supernatural stations, Bayat sarcastically noted that "sometimes, one mistakes the rays emanating from a flashlight for a Divine source".[120] Bayat sought to dispel the haze, undo the spin and delink the mundane realities of material life and the public sphere from the spiritual and personal beliefs of the Shi'i.

Despite the strong criticism of a relatively heterodox group of influential Shi'i clerics against the propagation of superstition and closed-mindedness, a small nucleus of powerful clergy, politically aligned with Ayatollah Khameneh'i, were instrumental in disseminating and transmitting such superstitious ideas. Ahmadinejad's clerical supporters had begun the process of instrumentalizing popular Shi'i beliefs for political ends before the President embarked on such a course. After Ahmadinejad's presidency in 2005, Ayatollah Mesbah Yazdi opined on the reason for his success and told a group of pious female visitors that "this election can not be accounted for by any external factors except that it was a Divine favour and the real reason for this happening [Ahmadinejad's election] was the prayers of the Guardian

[118] *Shargh* (20 Dey 1384).
[119] *Iranema Online* (4 Dey 1384). [120] *Emrouz* (23 Azar 1384).

of the Age, [the Twelfth Imam] the esteemed leader, [Ayatollah Khameneh'i] the family of the martyrs and the anxious".[121]

To demonstrate Ahmadinejad's supernatural credentials and present him as a political person chosen and appointed by the hidden world, Mesbah Yazdi narrated a story he had heard from an unnamed Islamic jurist (*'alem*) from Ahwaz. Apparently, during the 2005 presidential election campaign, the learned Islamic jurist from Ahwaz, whom one assumes to be a cleric, hears a voice in his dream commanding him "to awaken and pray for Ahmadinejad since the Hidden Imam was also praying for him".[122] Mesbah Yazdi adds more mystification and perplexity to Ahmadinejad's success in the 2005 elections by insinuating that the President-to-be had foreknowledge of events, which barring fraud would imply an unusual intuition or a connection with the hidden world. Mesbah Yazdi ascertains that Ahmadinejad was absolutely certain of his victory some six months before the elections! Enigmatically, Mesbah Yazdi adds, "I do not know whether he had dreamt of this or someone had told him so!"[123] In either case, Mesbah Yazdi strongly intimates that the person who could have told Ahmadinejad in his dream or spoken to him while he was awake had to be someone who knew of the future and may well have been the Hidden Imam.

In his first official meeting with Ahmadinejad, after his 2005 presidential victory, Mesbah Yazdi announced that the President-elect was different from others, and implied that his victory was willed and engineered by heavenly forces. He told the new President that "the future generations will arrive at the conclusion that this election was replete with miracles and thaumaturgic gifts [*keramat*]".[124] Mesbah Yazdi described the 2005 election as a miracle and a Divine exaltation. He hailed its results as the proof of the Hidden Imam's favour towards Iranians, called it a step in the unfolding process of "that same thing" that happened during the time of the Prophet and hoped that its final stage would be realized with the reappearance of the Twelfth Imam.[125] Dizzy with the success of Ahmadinejad's presidency, Mesbah Yazdi was overtly comparing Ahmadinejad's mission and import with that of the Prophet.

The President concurred with Mesbah Yazdi that the election results were the outcome of a "favour and a special kind of attention" (*yek lotf va*

---

[121] F. Rajabi, *Ahmadinejad, Mo'jezeh Hezareh Sevom*, p. 294.
[122] *Partov-e Sokhan* (8 Tir 1384).
[123] Ibid.   [124] *Partov-e Sokhan* (15 Tir 1384).   [125] Ibid.

'enayat vijeh) and added that, in this process, he himself probably played
no role at all. Ahmadinejad gave the impression that he considered himself
as an instrument in the unfolding of "grand transformations of a worldly
scale".[126] Ahmadinejad then candidly thanked Mesbah Yazdi for "intelli-
gently and graciously entering into this scene [election campaign] and
managing it [the election campaign].[127] The report on this meeting,
which appeared in Mesbah Yazdi's newspaper, *Partov-e Sokhan*, omitted
the term managing (*modiriyat*) and replaced it by the innocuous phrase
"putting in a lot of effort" (*zahamat ziyadi keshidid*).[128] Clearly, Mesbah
Yazdi did not wish the public to hear Ahmadinejad's candid appreciation
of the Ayatollah's management of his election victory.

Ayatollah 'Ali Meshkini, the powerful head of the Assembly of Experts at
the time, was in agreement with Mesbah Yazdi's assessment of the extraordinary and supernatural conditions surrounding Ahmadinejad's election.
Meshkini, too, told the members of the Qom branch of the Coordinating
Council for Islamic Propaganda that "in my opinion the ascent to power
of the ninth government [the government formed by Ahmadinejad] was
akin to a miracle".[129] Two days after *Baztab* revealed the contents of the
meeting between Ahmadinejad and Javadi Amoli, Ahmadinejad's Minister of
Education met with Ayatollah 'Ali Meshkini. At this meeting, Ayatollah
Meshkini first spoke about his state of anxiety during the sixth *majles* (parliament) in which the Islamic reformists had an overwhelming majority. He
recalled how very dissatisfied he was with that *majles*. Every time he listened
to their deliberations, he recalled, he would feel nervous about what the
reformists were about to ratify. Referring to the newly constituted seventh
majles controlled by Ahmadinejad and his Principlist political supporters,
Meshkini thanked God for the changes in the composition of the parliament,
which he qualified as a Divine gift. Seemingly intent on justifying his contention, Meshkini asserted that "the activities of the government and the
majles is supported and endorsed by those who are concerned with the state
of the country and the revolution . . . I believe that when the report of all that
has been done [by the government] was presented to Hazrat Mahdi [the
Twelfth Imam], especially the roster of the members of the seventh parliament, he endorsed it".[130]

---

[126] *Partov-e Sokhan* (12 Mordad 1384).   [127] R. San'ati, *Goftoman Mesbah*, p. 862.

[128] *Partov-e Sokhan* (12 Mordad 1384).

[129] F. Rajabi, Ahmadinejad, *Mo'jezeh Hezareh Sevom*, p. 296.

[130] *Iranema Online* (12 January 2005); ILNA (8 Azar 1384) quoted in H. Bastani,
'Moda'iyan Ertebat ba Imam Zaman', Rooz Online; see http://roozonline.com/
02article/012247.shtml

The claim that the worldly affairs of Ahmadinejad's government and the equally mundane issue of the Principlists gaining a majority in the Parliament had the support of the Twelfth Imam was a clear attempt at giving a special paranormal aura to the President and his newly elected political affiliates in the *majles*. Meshkini's statement was a novelty, since it effectively suggested that specific individuals with a particular political tendency such as the Principlists had the blessing and approval of the Hidden Imam. Here, the Hidden Imam was represented as having already taken sides with the neo-conservatives and against the reformists.

Particularly during his first year of office, Ahmadinejad's clerical supporters justified the President's policies and initiatives by publicly announcing that they were spurred, aided and approved by the hidden world. In May 2005, Ahmadinejad wrote his first unanswered eighteen-page letter to George W. Bush, the President of the United States. At home, Ahmadinejad's decision encountered mounting criticism especially among the reformists. During the Friday Congregational Prayers, Ayatollah Ahmad Jannati, the powerful chairman of the Guardian Council and a close ally of Ahmadinejad, defended the President's initiative. Jannati compared Ahmadinejad's initiative to Ayatollah Khomeyni's letter to Gorbachev, in which he had warned about the coming demise of the Soviet Union. Jannati recommended that Ahmadinejad's letter be put on the syllabus of all schools and universities in the country. To cap his adulation for Ahmadinejad and his letter, Jannati said, "As I have mentioned, this letter is a revelation. God is kind and wishes to increase the power of this country and this is how revelation happens".[131] What were the pious attendants of the Friday congregational prayers and those who were to hear it on the radio, see it on the national television and read it the next day in the newspapers to make of this statement? On face value at least, Jannati's message to the faithful seemed clear: Ahmadinejad's letter was a revelation or a quasi-revelation from God. If the President's letter were a revelation, his worldly policies would also be directed by God and ipso facto utterly undisputable. Jannati was wrapping the earthly president along with his mundane interests in the sublime mysteries of the spiritual hidden world, thereby rendering him attractive to naive pious believers.

The politically driven and instrumental use of the Hidden Imam by high-ranking clerical figures for the purpose of establishing credibility and coveting support for Ahmadinejad's particular politico-religious tendency and his policies heralded a new interface between religion and

[131] *Shargh* (23 Ordibehesht 1385).

politics. The Hidden Imam, one of the most salient features of Shiʻism, was being appropriated and manipulated by one Shiʻi discourse against the other. A hard core of political clerics were capitalizing on the emotional ties of the Shiʻi to the Hidden Imam to present themselves as his spokesmen and representatives on earth. Only two weeks after his September 2005 speech at the General Assembly, Ahmadinejad explained that an "Islamic government" needed to be attentive to religious matters and promised to allocate government funds to the restoration and expansion of the approximately 60,000 mosques in the country. Ahmadinejad continued, "the Islamic government which is today wearing the garb of an Islamic Republic has no other responsibility but that of preparing for the reappearance of the Twelfth Imam".[132]

In this important statement, Ahmadinejad clearly expresses the antirepublican feeling of his clerical supporters, as well as that of his own. He confirms that, in his view, the Islamic "Republic" is only a garment, which will hopefully be shed and replaced by an Islamic "Government". He then emphasizes that his government has no other responsibility than to prepare the conditions for the return of the Hidden Imam and suggests that the country should move towards "the propagation of justice, a state of material and spiritual exaltation and a Mahdiite [*mahdavi*] society".[133] Some two months after Ahmadinejad asserted that his government's only charge was to prepare for the coming of the Hidden Imam, Saffar Harandi, the Minister of Culture and Islamic Guidance, reminded the Iranian public that the government's hegemonic discourse was a Mahdiite one (*goftoman mahdaviyat*). According to Saffar Harandi, this Mahdiite discourse was the most important message that Iran could send to the world community.[134]

A SECOND ROUND OF SUPERNATURAL CLAIMS

Three years after what seemed like the performance of the first act of his supernatural politico-religious play, Ahmadinejad followed up with what may be considered as a second act. As the 2009 presidential elections approached, he seemed pressed to demonstrate that the Imam's interventions in the affairs of the state on his behalf remained uninterrupted and

[132] *Emrouz* (29 September 2005); see http://www.emrouz.info/archives/print/2005/09/000644.php
[133] Ibid.
[134] *Emrouz* (15 September 2005); see http://www.emrouz.info/archives/print/2005/12/002706.php

that he continued to benefit from the Hidden Imam's support. On 24 September 2007, Ahmadinejad had spoken at Columbia University. In the early spring days of 2008, addressing the seminary students of Mashhad, Ahmadinejad returned to the Columbia episode to make an important politico-religious point based on his old messianic and occult reading of Shi'ism.

Ahmadinejad rhetorically asked, "Do not the events at Columbia University demonstrate the management of the Twelfth Imam? They wanted me to lose my nerves and leave the auditorium, yet I smiled, delivered my speech and it was said that 500 million people watched the event. Is this anything other than the management of Aqa Imam Zaman [the Twelfth Imam]?" Ahmadinejad then reiterated that "The Twelfth Imam is managing the whole world and we are witnessing the fact that the Imam Zaman's guiding hand is visible in all the affairs of our country".[135] Ahmadinejad seemed to suggest that he was not directly responsible for the political, economic and cultural outcomes of his policies during his presidency, since the real master of the realm was the Hidden Imam, and the president was only an instrument in the hands of the Imam. To Ahmadinejad, it was the guiding hand of the Hidden Imam that was responsible for the events at Columbia University, as well as all the President's decisions as the chief executive officer.

Ahmadinejad's comments on the Hidden Imam's management of Iran were surprising to most Iranians. Yet the President was simply repeating what Mesbah Yazdi had clearly articulated years before. Mesbah Yazdi had argued that, through loving God and the imams, the youth could attain a stage where God and the imams would manage and control them. He wrote, "How good it would be if our master and beloved [the Hidden Imam] would take the management of our affairs into his own hand and decide upon it in the way that he wished. If you [the youth] would put your fate in his hands, he too would do this [manage your affairs] and would accept your special guardianship [*velayat khass*]".[136] Ahmadinejad's proclamation that the Hidden Imam had taken over the realms of Iran was probably after discussions with or approval of Mesbah Yazdi.

About three months after his speech on the Hidden Imam's management of Iran, Ahmadinejad relaunched the debate on his very special 2005 experience with the halo of light at the General Assembly. In his private

---

[135] *Etemad* (29 Khordad 1387).   [136] M. T. Yazdi, *Aftab Velayat*, p. 154.

weblog, he referred to the expression of a "halo of light" at least seven times, revisited the story of the General Assembly and apparently confirmed the veracity of the content of his meeting with Javadi Amoli. He wrote, "For the generation who witnessed the revolution and those who have been reared in the unitarian [*towhidi*] culture of Emam Khomeyni it is not unusual to see the light of God in world politics and [particularly] in the successive victories of revolutionary and Islamic values obtained in Lebanon, Palestine, Iraq, Iran and even in New York. On the contrary, that which is unusual is not to see these halos of light".[137] The Iranian President's comments placed in the context of his speech about the Hidden Imam's management of Iranian affairs seem to confirm his belief that all aspects of his policies were the reflection of God's will. To the President, God's will seems to be implemented through the intermediary of the Hidden Imam and Mahmud Ahmadinejad, one of the so-called instruments and representatives of the Hidden Imam in the material world.

By the summer of 2008, phantasmical ideas and reports springing from the views and cavalier comments of Ahmadinejad and his associates reached an alarming level. Once again, it seemed as if certain segments of the Iranian society were living in an unreal, irrational and fictitious fantasy wrapped in religion. Rasul Montajabnia renewed his criticism and challenged Ahmadinejad to address publicly the rumours circulating on certain abnormal statements and practices attributed to him. Montajabnia referred to Ahmadinejad's statement about the reappearance of the Twelfth Imam within two years, and referred to a highly controversial exchange between Ayatollah Khameneh'i, the Leader of the Revolution, and Ahmadinejad. According to Montajabnia, Ayatollah Khameneh'i had chided the President for his comment on setting a time for the Twelfth Imam's return. Explaining the reason for his statement on the return of the Imam within two years, Ahmadinejad is reported to have told Khameneh'i that "those who are in contact with the Twelfth Imam had said so [told me so]". It is reported that as Ahmadinejad was about to leave Ayatollah Khameneh'i's office, he had quipped, "he [Ayatollah Khameneh'i] thinks that I am his President, but I am the Twelfth Imam's President".[138]

Somewhat similar to Zadsar's unanswered letter to the President, Montajabnia requested Ahmadinejad to confirm or deny the veracity of his supernatural experience at the General Assembly in 2005. He then referred to a couple of new rumours. At meals, Ahmadinejad and or people associated with him would lay out an empty plate, spoon and fork and claim that it

---

[137] *Etemad* (29 Khordad 1387).   [138] *Etemad Melli* (11 Tir 1378).

was reserved for the Twelfth Imam. Ahmadinejad's colleagues would invite people to congregational prayers led by *aqa* (leader or master). Assuming that *aqa* referred to Ayatollah Khameneh'i, those attending would be surprised to find that a prayer mat was spread out on the floor without anyone standing behind it. When they inquired as to when Ayatollah Khameneh'i would arrive to lead the prayers, they were told to be quiet, as it was the Twelfth Imam who was already leading the prayers. Montajabnia finally referred to Ahmadinejad's comment that his government was managed by the Twelfth Imam, and asked the President to comment on and provide clear and direct responses to these troubling rumours permeating society.[139] Ahmadinejad never replied to Montajabnia's queries.

Ayatollah Tavasoli's sudden death on 16 February 2008 while delivering an impassioned speech at the Expediency Council and Ahmadinejad's comments about the Twelfth Imam's management of the affairs of the country triggered off another round of harsh criticism against the politically induced atmosphere of superstition. Moments before his death, Tavasoli who had started his speech by defending Ayatollah Khomeyni's grandson, Seyyed Hasan, against his Principlist detractors, embarked on the topic of Khomeyni's categorical disdain for superstition. Tavasoli recalled that, after the revolution, when a religious figure who visited Khomeyni daily had publicly said something about Khomeyni being in contact with the Hidden Imam, Khomeyni had become furious and had refused to see him again.[140]

At a ceremony commemorating Tavasoli, Hasan Rowhani, a powerful pragmatic cleric close to Hashemi Rafsanjani, argued that Tavasoli's heart stopped beating while he was lashing out against superstition and those who are in the business of duping and deceiving the people. Rowhani argued that Tavasoli died while he was defending the Twelfth Imam against the charlatans who were playing with the people's beliefs.[141] Rowhani warned against the proliferation and propagation of superstitious ideas and doctrines. He referred to a rumour according to which certain decision makers in the government deferred important meetings to Fridays arguing that, since *aqa* or the Twelfth Imam would be there on that day, he, too, would be able to participate in the deliberations. Indirectly referring to Ahmadinejad's claim during

---

[139] *Etemad Melli* (11 Tir 1378).

[140] 'Notq Natamam Ayatollah Tavasoli dar Majma Tashkis Maslahat' in *Emrouz* (22 Bahman 1387).

[141] ISNA quoted in *Noandish* (20 February 2008); see http://www.noandish.com/print.php?id=14186

the first year of his presidency, Rowhani asserted that those who claim to see the Imam are liars and falsifiers. He reminded his audience that today it has become evident that those who spoke about building a tribune for the Hidden Imam, in preparation for his reappearance in two years, were liars.[142]

In early spring of 2008, one of the most prominent members of the traditional clergy, Ayatollah Mahdavi Kani, a member of the Revolutionary Council in 1979 and Prime Minister in 1981, was forced to enter the fray. Mahdavi Kani supported Nateq Nuri against Khatami in 1997 and was opposed to the reformists. Yet as the spiritual leader of the Association of the Militant Clergy, the most influential clerical organization in Iran, Mahdavi Kani felt obliged to distance himself and his organization from Ahmadinejad and Mesbah Yazdi's messianic-occult brand of Shi'ism. Mahdavi Kani's criticism of Ahmadinejad's comments on the management of the country by the Hidden Imam demonstrated the real magnitude of the traditional clergy's discontent and anxiety about Mesbah Yazdi and Ahmadinejad's superstitious and Hidden-Imam-based discourse.

In response to a student's question, Mahdavi Kani said, "Mr. Ahmadinejad should not say these kinds of things as it would adversely affect the people's perception of the Twelfth Imam". He then went on to ask, "If the Hidden Imam was managing the affairs [of the state], would he not be able to rid the country of the mafia [of power and wealth]? Is the increase in the price of rice to five thousand tomans per kilo a result of the Hidden Imam's management?"[143] Mahdavi Kani added that not once had Emam Khomeyni said such things concerning the Hidden Imam. Before and after his presidential campaign, Ahmadinejad had tried to endear himself to Iranians by promising them that he would expose and free the country from what he called the mafia of power and wealth. Madhavi Kani's reference to this mafia was simply to remind the President that his inability to curtail or end the activities of this so-called mafia was proof of the simple fact that the Hidden Imam was not managing the affairs of the state, nor did he intervene in worldly affairs on behalf of the President. In his own diplomatic way, Mahdavi Kani, the patriarch of the conservative political clerics, was accusing Ahmadinejad of falsity and warning him against playing with a fire that could burn down the

---

[142] Ibid.
[143] *Tabnak* (21 Ordibehesht 1387); see http://tabnak.ir/pages/print.php?cid=1048

castle of beliefs of which Mahdavi Kani and other concerned clergy were
supposed to be the custodians.

On the heels of Mahdavi Kani's open criticism of Ahmadinejad's superstitious politico-religious discourse, Gholam-Reza Mesbahi Moqaddam, the
spokesman of the Association of the Militant Clergy (*Jameʻeh Rowhaniyyat
Mobarez*), at the time, issued an acerbic rebuttal to Ahmadinejad. Even
though the Association of the Militant Clergy represented the more conservative political clergy, it was far from a homogeneous religio-political
body. While one significant group within the Association allied itself
with Mahdavi Kani and Hashemi Rafsanjani, another group supported
Ayatollah Mohammad Yazdi who was among the small circle of
Ahmadinejad's clerical proponents. Mesbahi Moqaddam's open criticism
of Ahmadinejad signalled the general discontent of the conservative political
clerics with the President's manipulation of the Twelfth Imam for his
own political ends. Mesbahi Moqaddam told Ahmadinejad that if he
thought that the Hidden Imam supported the policies of his government,
he was wrong. He added that the Twelfth Imam most certainly did not
approve of a twenty per cent rate of inflation and that he could not be
supportive of it.[144]

To ʻAli Asgari, a clerical member of the parliament and Hojjatoleslam Doʻagu, the Friday congregational prayer leader of Shemiranat,
Ahmadinejad's attribution of the management of Iran's affairs to
the Twelfth Imam was an unacceptable excuse. Ahmadinejad's statement was assessed as a ruse to shift the responsibility and burden of his
own executive mismanagements and incompetence to the Hidden
Imam.[145] Asgari warned Ahmadinejad that he needed to "be accountable for the problems confronting society such as inflation", he "should
not fall back on the hidden world" and that he "should think in terms
of this material world and busy himself with the practical management
of the state".[146] The belief that Ahmadinejad was using the Hidden
Imam to hide his failures and that such a practice was detrimental to
the faith resonated with a large majority of the clerics cutting across
various politico-religious shades. In this period, Nateq Nuri once
again branded those who were engaged in propagating such superstitious notions, without naming them, as impostors, charlatans and
swindlers. He warned that attributing one's own acts and behaviours

to the Hidden Imam was a very dangerous practice, since once things went wrong, people would see the shortcomings as a reflection of the Imam. Nateq Nuri called on decision makers to take responsibility for their own acts.[147]

THE HIDDEN IMAM KIDNAPPED BY THE PRINICIPLISTS

Before Ahmadinejad's rise to power, Mesbah Yazdi had argued that one way for believers to materialize and sustain their love and admiration for the Twelfth Imam was to respect and honor whatever was associated with or attributed to the Hidden Imam. Clerics and the clerical robe, according to Mesbah Yazdi, revived the memory of God, the Prophet and the Twelfth Imam.[148] In an attempt to create an emotional link between the present-day clergy, the Twelfth Imam and the Prophet, Mesbah Yazdi suggested that "the garb of the clergy was that of the Prophet".[149] The common garb seemed to insinuate an association or correspondence in terms of qualities, attributes and virtues between modern day clerics and holy figures of Islam. The analogy may have been intended to claim for the clergy the submissiveness, deference and compliance that would be due to the Prophet and the Hidden Imam. Mesbah Yazdi's assertion that irreverence towards the clerical garb is the prelude to the erosion of faith demonstrates that he wishes to place the reverential status and authority of the clergy in modern Iran on the same plane as that of the Prophet and the Hidden Imam.[150]

Mesbah Yazdi intertwines respect for the clergy and their rule with piety and faith. He leaves his audience to conclude that any disrespect towards the clergy, including criticism, would imply faithlessness and infidelity. He argues that from a Shi'i point of view, in the absence of the Twelfth Imam, a jurist with all the necessary qualifications (*jame' al-sharayet*) who establishes his rule or government on the basis of Islamic edicts and Shi'i jurisprudence should be obeyed in exactly the same way as God, the Prophet and the infallible imams. Mesbah Yazdi emphasizes that, just as submission to this fully qualified cleric is obligatory (*vajeb*), opposition to him is forbidden (*haram*). Mesbah Yazdi reiterates that the jurist with all the necessary qualifications has to be appointed and selected by God and "there cannot be any other way".[151]

---

[147] *Kargozaran*; see http://kargozaran.com/ShowNews.php?3181
[148] M. T. Mesbah Yazdi, *Aftab Velayat*, pp. 45–46.
[149] Ibid., p. 46.   [150] Ibid., p. 46.
[151] M. T. Mesbah Yazdi, 'Velayat Faqih va Khebregan' (24 Esfand 1384); see http://www.mesbahyazdi.org/farsi/speeches/lectures/lectures21.htm

In time, the clerical alignment of forces for and against the messianic-occult discourse popularized by Ahmadinejad and Mesbah Yazdi effectively pitted the clergy against one another. In the absence of unanimity among those wearing the religious garb, the public, who were supposed to associate the clerical garb with the Twelfth Imam and the Prophet, were left in disarray and confusion. This state of confusion was exasperated after the 2009 presidential election when a growing number of prominent clerics questioned and rejected not only Ahmadinejad's presidency, but also Khameneh'i's credentials and qualifications for occupying the position of leadership. To confront and silence the dissenting voices among the clergy, the Ahmadinejad–Mesbah Yazdi camp needed to present itself as the true representative of the Twelfth Imam. By uniting behind Khameneh'i, the Guardian Jurist whom Mesbah Yazdi had already argued to have all the necessary religious qualifications and who, according to him, must have been directly or indirectly appointed by God, the Ahmadinejad–Mesbah Yazdi camp legitimized its claim of speaking on behalf of the Twelfth Imam. According to Mesbah Yazdi, in the absence of the Twelfth Imam, the Shi'i 'olama as his inheritors, possessed the same responsibilities as he, yet on a more limited scale.[152] Consequently, the Ahmadinejad–Mesbah Yazdi camp could posit that anyone who dared to criticize the Guardian Jurist or the circles close to him was an adversary and enemy of Shi'ism.

Mesbah Yazdi argued that the clergy were the servants of the Hidden Imam and their task was to "identify and carry out that which was demanded by the Twelfth Imam".[153] Mesbah Yazdi clearly intimated that he, as a clergy, could discern or intuit the wishes and demands of the Twelfth Imam.[154] Once he had identified the Hidden Imam's will, he was subsequently obliged to act according to them, irrespective of their popularity or unpopularity.[155] As such, Mesbah Yazdi could shield his words and actions from public criticism by claiming that he was acting according to the will of the Hidden Imam. Even though, according to Mesbah Yazdi, it was officially the Guardian Jurist or Ayatollah Khameneh'i who was the successor of the Twelfth Imam and by definition his spokesperson, Mesbah Yazdi effectively created a theoretical space for positing that a clergy such as himself and those whom he approved of were also acting according to the will and demand of the Hidden Imam.[156] So once Mesbah Yazdi

---

[152] M. T. Mesbah Yazdi, *Aftab Velayat*, p. 209.
[153] H. A. 'Arabi, *Haqiqat Sharq*, pp. 125, 133.
[154] Ibid., p. 125.   [155] Ibid., p. 125.
[156] M. T. Mesbah Yazdi, *Kavoshha va Chaleshha*, vol. 2. (Qom, 1382), p. 115.

"identifies" support for Ahmadinejad as the Hidden Imam's will, first
the pious would have to accept it as such, and second, by definition,
Ahmadinejad's political opponents would come to be viewed as the enemies of the Hidden Imam.

As the cleric who had focused his politico-religious discourse on the
person of the Hidden Imam, Mesbah Yazdi made a veiled case for himself
as the unofficial deputy of the Hidden Imam, while he acknowledged
Ayatollah Khameneh'i as the Hidden Imam's official deputy. It was
Mesbah Yazdi who had formulated and widely propagated the manner
in which people should augment their knowledge about the Hidden Imam
and manifest their active love for him. He argued that in order to "feel the
holy existence" of the Hidden Imam and to "establish connection with
him", the people needed to remind themselves of him constantly, place his
name on their desks or between books, pray for him so that he may appear,
refer to him during regular prayers and religious celebrations and mourning occasions.[157] Mesbah Yazdi's message to the devout was that those
clerics, who revived the messianic discourse of the Hidden Imam by speaking about him and his interventions in the material world furthering the
cause of his supporters, were the chosen men of the garb. Having established himself as the unofficial successor and representative of the Hidden
Imam, faced with Khameneh'i's silence and tacit approval, Mesbah Yazdi
could easily act as the detector, interpreter and translator of the Hidden
Imam's will in all domains.

Before the 2005 presidential elections, Mesbah Yazdi passionately argued
that the clergy were supposed to guide the people in their political decisions
and show them the correct path. He called on his followers and students
not to accept passively the people's preferences as indicated by the pre-
election opinion polls.[158] Mesbah Yazdi and Ahmadinejad conducted a
two-pronged campaign. First, they tried to demonize the policies of the
Rafsanjani and Khatami administration as un-Islamic and deviationist.
Rafsanjani's economic liberalization was argued to have led to the emergence
of social polarization, glaring schisms of wealth and poverty, corruption and
the emergence of a small, up-and-coming technocratic-entrepreneurial class,
which they dubbed as the "mafia of wealth and power". Khatami's political
liberalization was assailed as an attempt to change the constitution and do
away with the Guardianship of the Islamic Jurist, usher in the unconstrained

[157] M. T. Mesbah Yazdi, *Aftab Velayat*, pp. 44–45.
[158] *Partov-e Sokhan* (18 Khordad 1384).

rule of people and provide unrestrained Western-style individual liberties. Second, they appealed to the pious by presenting their vision of the ideal Islamic society as a Mahdavi or Mahdiite system, one belonging to the Hidden Imam. Attempts at conceptualizing a Mahdiite doctrine proliferated during the last two years of Ahmadinejad's first term in office. The Mahdiite doctrine is argued to be a global belief theory based on a "Mahdavi culture" and promised to be the singular route to human salvation.[159] The social function of the Mahdiite doctrine is argued to expedite the return of the Hidden Imam by creating a need and want among the people for the return of the Imam and the establishment of his government.[160] So, according to this doctrine, the pious need to think of and actively await the Hidden Imam by preparing their families and society for his reappearance. The government of the Hidden Imam after his return is argued to be a world government for all mankind.[161]

The appropriation and monopolization of the Hidden Imam by Mesbah Yazdi and Ahmadinejad in terms of speaking for him, claiming to have identified his desires, as well as his political preferences, and subsequently attributing the running of the affairs of the state to him takes a new turn when Mohammad-Naser Saqqa-ye Biriya, one of Mesbah Yazdi's students and Ahmadinejad's adviser on religious affairs, publicly asks the rhetorical question, "Even if the Hidden Imam was to re-appear would he not say the same things as Ahmadinejad is saying?"[162] The identification of Ahmadinejad's discourse with that of the Hidden Imam makes a political case for the pious to rally in support of Ahmadinejad "as if" he represented the Hidden Imam's will. The insinuation of such a close correspondence between the Hidden Imam and a mortal, especially by a cleric, was a reminder of the positions and statements of the extremist "exaggerators" (*ghaliyan*) throughout Shi'i history. During the presidency of Ahmadinejad, implicit and explicit references to such parallels and resemblances between the President and the Hidden Imam increased and effectively dulled the sensitivities of the people to the implications of drawing such comparisons.

---

[159] R. Musavi Gilani, *Doctrine Mahdaviyat* (Qom, 1387), p. 14.
[160] R. Musavi Gilani, *Doctrine Mahdaviyat*, p. 91.
[161] R. Musavi Gilani, *Doctrine Mahdaviyat*, p. 132.
[162] *Jomhoriyat* (12 Esfand 1387); see http://www.jomhoriyat.com/tag/page/news-776.html

THE HIDDEN IMAM: HOSTAGE TO THE PRINCIPLISTS'
POLITICAL AMBITIONS

The relative autonomy of the executive during the Rafsanjani and Khatami administrations, as well as that of the legislative during the sixth parliament from Khameneh'i, the Leader of the Revolution, confronted the Principlists with the reality that effective political power was slipping out of their hands. The popular inclination to the reformists' socio-political platform caused anxiety and panic among the Principlists. Khatami's Presidency proved that in open and free elections, the reformists were poised to take over the executive and legislative branches of the government. For Mesbah Yazdi, the reformists' control of the elected branches was a political threat to the power of the Principlists. Furthermore, the empowerment of the elected branches acting almost independently of the Guardian Jurist constituted a setback to Mesbah Yazdi's ideal model of an Islamic government based on the absolute power and authority of the successor and representative of the Twelfth Imam. The slightest departure or deviation from the Guardian Jurist's perceptions and even unsaid convictions would be construed as a deviation from the will of the Twelfth Imam and God.

In practical political terms, Mesbah Yazdi firmly believes that the foundation and sustenance of Islam depends only on the person who rules over the Islamic society. He argues that the success or failure of an Islamic state, society and economy is solely a function of the person of the ruler.[163] In Mesbah Yazdi's politico-religious discourse, the role and function of a constitution, the legislative, executive and judiciary are merely formalistic, decorous and ceremonial. He argues that when one person – the Islamic Leader or Guardian Jurist – is capable of performing all three functions of the legislative, executive and judiciary better than others, there would be no need for the separation of branches. Mesbah Yazdi claims that, according to Shiʻi jurisprudence or *feqh* (*fiqh*), it is necessary that all three branches of the executive, judiciary and the legislative be concentrated in the hands of the Guardian Jurist.[164]

To prevent the so-called sixteen-year "backslide" or "deviation" of the Rafsanjani and Khatami era, Mesbah Yazdi is intent on bringing the executive and legislative "in line with" or subservient to the will of Khameneh'i.

---

[163] M. T. Mesbah Yazdi, 'Velayat Faqih va Khebregan' (24 Esfand 1384); see http://www.mesbahyazdi.org/farsi/speeches/lectures/lectures21.htm
[164] M. T. Mesbah Yazdi, *Pasokh Ostad be Javanan Porseshgar* (Qom, 1385), pp. 49–50.

The effective elimination of the executive and legislative branches of the government is, however, unconstitutional. Yet, the task of converting the Islamic Republic into an Islamic government controlled and ruled by one person can in part be facilitated by the role of the Guardian Council and its chief Ayatollah Ahmad Jannati who has been a close associate of Mesbah Yazdi since 1966 when the two collaborated in administering the Haqani School.[165] An overtly biased sifting process of the candidates for all elective positions by the Guardian Council could assure the election of a trusting and obedient president, as well as a submissive parliament. The parliamentary elections in 2000 and the presidential elections from 1997 to 2009 demonstrated that in order to prevent the running and possible election of "undesirable candidates", the Guardian Council would have to set aside all superficial claims to political impartiality and categorically apply the wishes of the Guardian Jurist.

Faced with a constitutional obstacle, Mesbah Yazdi prefers to implement his perception of the Islamic government without officially dismantling and undermining the Republic. Ideally, the two elective branches of the executive and legislative would be filled with dependable subjects loyal to the Guardian Jurist, thereby eliminating a possible confrontation between the "illegitimate" position of the elected representatives and the divinely ordained responsibility of the Guardian Jurist. To Mesbah Yazdi, in an Islamic government, the contradiction between appointment by the Guardian Jurist and election by the people has to be resolved in favour of appointment. He insists that the legitimacy of the Islamic government or system (*nezam*) is not based on the will of the people but is accorded by God.[166] Mesbah Yazdi does not explain how human beings would ever come to know to whom God has actually accorded His legitimacy. Implicitly, he argues that since Ayatollah Khameneh'i is the Leader, the Guardian Jurist and the successor to the Twelfth Imam, God has endowed him with the right to legislate edicts and laws that are necessary for the everyday running of society.[167] He intimates that, since Ayatollah Khameneh'i is the jurist who is "closest to and most resembles the infallible imams", the pious are obliged to consider him as a model to be emulated and obeyed.[168] Mesbah Yazdi needs to blur the key distinction between an

[165] B. Sha'banzadeh, *Tarikh Shafah'ie Madreseh Haqani* (Tehran, 1384), p. 53–54.
[166] M. T. Mesbah Yazdi, *Pasokh Ostad be Javanan Porseshgar*, pp. 160–161.
[167] M. T. Mesbah Yazdi, *Kavoshha va Chaleshha*, vol. 2, p. 96; M. T. Mesbah Yazdi, *Naqsh Taqlid dar Zendegh'i-ye Ensan* (Qom, 1384) p. 102; M. T. Mesbah Yazdi, *Azarakhsh Karbala* (Qom, 1384), p. 167.
[168] M. T. Mesbah Yazdi, *Naqsh Taqlid dar Zendegh'i-ye Ensan*, pp. 102–103.

infallible imam and a fallible human being, in order to theorize and legitimize the absolutist and unfettered rule of a twenty-first-century religious leader.

The need to empower the Guardian Jurist with extra-constitutional absolutist powers is rooted in Mesbah Yazdi's pragmatic assessment of Ayatollah Khameneh'i's faltering power base, popularity and authority. To convince the pious common folk of the necessity to bring all branches of the government under the direct patronage of the Guardian Jurist, Mesbah Yazdi needs to demonstrate that, in the absence of his absolutist rule, Islam would be endangered and the return of the Hidden Imam would be delayed. Consequently, Mesbah Yazdi argues that ever since Khomeyni passed away, Islamic values and ideas have been under siege and constantly diluted.[169] He points out to Ayatollah Khameneh'i's eroding authority and power, and argues that at some point, government officials ignored the orders and directives of the Guardian Jurist. Mesbah Yarzdi implies that during Rafsanjani and Khatami's administration Khameneh'i was not really in charge and therefore deviations began to appear.[170]

During this period of the Guardian Jurist's relative "powerlessness", dubious characters, "the hypocrites" *monafeqin*, are said to have infiltrated the decision-making centres of the Islamic Republic with the intention of diluting the Islamic principles of the revolution. The term hypocrite, which was referred to the members of the Organization of the Iranian Peoples' Mojahedin (*sazman-e mojahedin-e khalq-e Iran*), is now used in reference to the reformists who, according to Mesbah Yazdi, intend to eliminate Islam and erase the concept of the Guardian Jurist from the constitution.[171] In order to pave the way for discrediting and eliminating the old guards of the revolution who disagreed with his concept of Islamic government and continued to believe in the republican feature of the Islamic Republic, Mesbah Yazdi declares that the mere fact that certain individuals possess revolutionary credentials and were close associates of Khomeyni in the past does not necessarily prevent them from becoming renegades.[172]

To justify and legitimize his open political opposition to the reformists, Mesbah Yazdi presents a religious-based argument demonstrating that the world outlook and policies of reformists presents a grave danger to Islam and is an affront to the Islamic values of pious believers. To him, the

---

[169] M. T. Mesbah Yazdi, *Kavoshha va Chaleshha*, vol. 1 (Qom, 1379), pp. 38–39.
[170] M. T. Mesbah Yazdi, *Azarakhsh Karbala*, p. 234.
[171] M. T. Mesbah Yazdi, *Azarakhsh Karbala*, p. 141.
[172] M. T. Mesbah Yazdi, *Kavoshha va Chaleshha*, vol. 1, pp. 43–44.

threatened values of pious believers are those cherished and demonstrated by the mass mobilization forces (*basijis*) at the fronts during the Iran–Iraq war. Mesbah Yazdi seeks to push through his politico-religious agenda of empowering the Guardian Jurist and his supporters behind the smokescreen of yearning for and wishing to re-create what he eulogizes as the "passion and love of the first generation of the revolution, the *basijis* who were enamoured with martyrdom, the fronts and the war".[173] Mesbah Yazdi deplores the fact that, after the Iran–Iraq war, religious values were being gradually forgotten and vows to revive them.[174] To him, the most important of those lost values are the sense of honor and virtue that people felt in relation to dying for the cause of God, and did no longer.[175] Mesbah Yazdi longs for the spirit of martyrdom that permeated during Khomeyni's leadership in the war fronts and wishes to encourage, harness and employ it in his confrontation with the reformists.

According to Mesbah Yazdi, the same mass mobilization forces that had succeeded in defeating Iraq had the responsibility of battling and rolling back the cultural onslaught against Islamic values, which according to him were permitted and encouraged during the Rafsanjani and Khatami period.[176] To reconstitute and rally those forces that respected the *basiji* tradition, Mesbah Yazdi warns that a cultural war is being waged against Islamic and *basiji* values. By identifying the Hidden Imam as the embodiment of what Mesbah Yazdi considers as Islamic values, a so-called war against those same Islamic and *basiji* values becomes tantamount to waging war against the Hidden Imam. Mesbah Yazdi appeals to the mass mobilization forces to engage in this so-called determining battle imposed on the pious by "foreigners" and fought out by their "domestic intellectual lackeys". The war against the reformers is given the same significance as the war against Iraq, which threatened the Islamic Revolution.[177] The object of the cultural onslaught is argued to be the destruction of the *basiji* spirit.[178] Mesbah Yazdi argues for a return to and the imposition of the value system and state of mind prevailing in the war fronts characterized by a spiritual sense of selflessness, devotion and self-sacrifice.[179]

The revival of the values of the mass mobilization forces is presented as the religious victory of the spirit of Mahdiism. Politically, it represents

[173] M. T. Mesbah Yazdi, *Kavoshha va Chaleshha*, vol. 1, p. 51.
[174] H. A. 'Arabi, *Haqiqat Sharq*, p. 136.   [175] Ibid.
[176] M. T. Mesbah Yazdi, *Negahi Gozara be Basij va Basiji* (Qom, 1386), pp. 61–75.
[177] Ibid., pp. 74–75.   [178] Ibid., p. 68.   [179] Ibid., pp. 15–16.

returning the genie of open society back into its airtight bottle. Mesbah Yazdi warns that when watching movies and listening to music becomes prevalent and replaces early morning prayers, mourning and lamentations, the people's relation with God will weaken, society will become misguided and deprived of God's support and assistance.[180] Mesbah Yazdi was aware of the fact that society and its values had irreversibly changed since the end of the Iran–Iraq war and that the pursuit of material well-being had become a dominant objective among all social classes, including the greatest majority of the old *basijis*. Yet he needed to rally his foot soldiers by harking back at a nostalgic and dated glorious historic moment. By hammering at the sensitive notion of a beleaguered and endangered Islam, he called on the zealous to unite and follow the directives of the Guardian Jurist and his supporters in order to reinstate what he labelled as the Islamic values.[181]

The selfless religious spirit prevailing in war fronts during the eight years of the "holy defence" was anchored in the devotion to defend the Islamic Revolution and the motherland, Khomeyni's politico-religious charismatic leadership, a religio-nationalistic sense of solidarity and fervor, a righteous feeling of chasing out the unjust aggressor and finally a proud conviction of standing up to the arrogant powers of the world. The sense of community and fraternity in the fronts was matched by the frugality and austerity of economic life behind the fronts. This spiritual and exceptional spirit of the fronts was a lofty and spontaneous particular moment in Iranian history. Against a backdrop of surging individualism, ostentatious consumerism, relentless drive to make easy money and rampant corruption that came to prevail after the end of the war, the idea of whipping up support for an atmosphere of selflessness was at best anachronistic and utopian and at worst demagogic. It was purposefully calling to a state of mind and predisposition that could no longer be. Yet even the empty reference to it revived something pious and noble among those who had not experienced it, or who had and were now devoid of it. At the time when Mesbah Yazdi propagated the synthetic selfless *basiji* spirit, some among the once-upon-a-time selfless warriors of the Guardian Corps of the Islamic Revolution made headlines not for their selfless spiritualism but for their successful materialist entrepreneurship. Sadeq Mahsuli, a former Revolutionary Guard, was President Ahmadinejad's Minister of Interior during the tenth presidential election. Mahsuli's life trajectory represents a

---

[180] Ibid., pp. 29–30.   [181] Ibid., pp. 49–50.

trend among a good number of the old Revolutionary Guards. He is an
extremely successful businessman, rumoured to be a billionaire – in
dollars – and among Iran's richest individuals.[182] It seems as though the
Shi'i's and, in particular, the mass mobilization volunteers' love for the
Hidden Imam and Imam Hoseyn was being used and manipulated for
religiously coated political and economic objectives.

Mesbah Yazdi ties in the *basiji* spirit and the experience of the warriors
during the war with the Twelfth Imam. To him, the fact that the youth at
the war fronts came to "see many of the Twelfth Imam's hidden assistances
[*emdadha-ye gheybi*] with their own eyes" was a blessing of the war
years.[183] He argues that these precious experiences and memories should
be kept alive, and adds that the Hidden Imam's assistances and his interventions were in tune with the Divine will, since the Twelfth Imam wills
whatever God desires.[184] The fact that the warriors received the hidden
assistance of the Twelfth Imam must have been due to their piety, purity
and sense of sacrifice for the cause of the Hidden Imam and God. Mesbah
Yazdi seems to be arguing that a spiritual atmosphere of piety and purity
produces the proper conditions for the interventions and assistances of
the Hidden Imam. Was the so-called recurrence of supernatural events,
rumours of the Hidden Imam's presence at various functions or talk of his
imminent return some twenty years after the end of the war supposed to
imply that the pure spirit of the war fronts had finally returned to Iranian
society and the tide of reformist "deviation" and "hypocrisy" had been
turned back?

Based on Imam Hoseyn's experience in Karbala, Mesbah Yazdi reminds
the pious of their responsibility faced with what he labels as the deviation
of the hypocrites. He argues that confronting threats to the faith needs a
hardened belief in the readiness and willingness to die and accept martyrdom for the sake of defending one's religion. Comparing the reformists to
Mo'aviyeh (*Muawiya*) and Yazid, he argues that once the culture of
martyrdom is properly propagated as an ideal, religion would become
immune to dangers.[185] Imam Hoseyn's model of "struggle based on
martyrdom against a system of corruption, injustice and unbelief" is
arrogated by Mesbah Yazdi and presented as the strategy that his followers should pursue against the reformists.[186] Finding it difficult to justify

---

[182] See http://www.roozonline.com/english/news/newsitem/article/2008/november/10//
        billionaire-general-to-replace-kordan.html
[183] M. T. Mesbah Yazdi, *Aftab Velayat*, p. 166.   [184] Ibid.
[185] M. T. Mesbah Yazdi, *Azarakhsh Karbala*, pp. 122–124.   [186] Ibid., p. 154.

his analogy and his promotion of violence against fellow Shiʻi pursuing legal means in a country under the firm rule of the Guardian Jurist – Ayatollah Khameneh'i – whom he considers as the successor to the Twelfth Imam, Mesbah Yazdi postulates a new type of *jahad* (*jihad*). Waging *jahad* in defence of "religious and human values" is presented by Mesbah Yazdi as a fourth kind of Islamic war.[187] He explains his novel exegesis by claiming that "When the faith is threatened, the conditions for *jahad* do not have to be considered and if the threat is not removed by any other means than blood, then one has to offer it and feel proud about it".[188] This is a new concept of preventive *jahad*.

Mesbah Yazdi claims that in an Islamic state, when the government is incapable of preventing the practice of forbidden acts, religion will be endangered. In such cases, he believes, the people themselves have an obligation to revolt and wage *jahad* as Imam Hoseyn did.[189] Appropriating Imam Hoseyn's cause, out of context, to justify the violent imposition of a monolithic and authoritarian perception of Shiʻism, Mesbah Yazdi issues a religious edict, rendering permissible the killing of those who threaten what he defines as "religious values" and the faith. He argues that if one is unable to unmask the hypocrites and the conditions leave no other choice, then those deceiving the people should be killed.[190] Mesbah Yazdi facilitates the task of those who wish to assassinate arbitrarily any so-called hypocrite by adding that whenever the people feel that Islam is endangered and a conspiracy is in the making against the Islamic system and the Islamic government is incapable of defending Islam on its own, then violence against the "conspirators" is permitted.[191]

Mesbah Yazdi's name along with that of his like-minded old friend and close associate Ayatollah Ahmad Jannati has become embroiled with issuing a series of *fatvas* instructing the liquidation of critics, dissidents, intellectuals and even clerical figures.[192] It is reported that, according to the written confessions of Saʻid Emami, the person considered as directly responsible for the summary execution of a number of Iranian intellectuals and political activists, the religious edict to murder these individuals came from a group of clerics. This group is said to have been composed of Mesbah Yazdi, Ayatollah Khoshvaqt, Ayatollah Khazʻali, Ayatollah

---

[187] See http://www.emrouz.info/archives/print/2006/02/005033.php   [188] Ibid.
[189] M. T. Mesbah Yazdi, *Azarakhsh Karbala*, pp. 274–275.
[190] See http://www.emrouz.info/archives/print/2006/02/005033.php
[191] M. T. Mesbah Yazdi, *Pasokh Ostad be Javanan Porseshgar*, pp. 265–266.
[192] A. F. Ebrahimi; see http://www.goftaniha.org/2001_04_01_archive.html

Jannati and, sometimes, Hojjatoleslam Ejeh'i.[193] Sa'id Emami is said to have confessed that once he received the order to murder Ahmad Khomeyni, Ayatollah Khomeyni's son, he hesitated and visited Ayatollah Mesbah Yazdi to seek his opinion. At Mesbah Yazdi's house, in the presence of Ayatollah Khoshvaqt, Hojjatoleslam Fallahian, Badamchian and Hojjatoleslam Ejeh'i, a consensus was reached by all those present that "no mercy should be shown to those who are hostile towards the Ruling Guardian Jurist".[194]

In 1993, Mesbah encouraged the Tehran branch of the Hezbollah or the Party of God, a group of zealots, the majority of who had been involved in the Iran–Iraq war as members of the *basij* or the Guardian Corps of the Islamic Revolution to take radical action against the enemies of Islam on their own. He reminded the members of this semi-official paramilitary and vigilante group that they should not wait around and expect to receive formal instructions or heeding from military, political or religious dignitaries. Encouraging them to take the law into their own hands, Mesbah Yazdi argued that the authorities were not in a position to provide direct orders and therefore those who felt that an evil needed to be prohibited had to act independently and autonomously. He argued that, faced with the silence of the Guardian Jurist, Ayatollah Khemeneh'i, zealots had a responsibility.[195] During the first term of Khatami's presidency, Mesbah Yazdi is also said to have ordered the elimination of 'Abdollah Nuri, Khatami's clerical Minister of Interior, whom he accused of working against the system, the path of *velayat* or the office of Khameneh'i and the revolution. In his meeting with a group of zealots, Mesbah Yazdi is said to have presented the elimination of 'Abdollah Nuri as a religious obligation.[196]

In the name of the Hidden Imam and Imam Hoseyn, Mesbah Yazdi constructs a religious discourse and appeals to the selfless spirit of the *basijis* to confront those whom he labels as forces "threatening Islam" and "Islamic sanctities".[197] According to Mesbah Yazdi, the enemies of the faith were plotting to desensitize the pious to Islamic values, undermining their zeal (*ta'assob*) and gradually eradicating the sanctities of the faith.[198] He believes the primary axes of this "cultural onslaught" to be: the propagation of notions such as religious tolerance (*tasahol va tasamoh*)

---

[193] *Peiknet*; see http://www.peiknet.com/1388/06mehr/09/PAGE/36EMAMI.htm
[194] Ibid.
[195] A. F. Ebrahimi; see http://farshadebrahimi3.blogpot.com, p. 2.   [196] Ibid., p. 4.
[197] M. T. Mesbah Yazdi, *Naqshe Taqlid dar Zendegh'i-ye Ensan*, pp. 67, 70–73.
[198] Ibid., pp. 74–76.

and pluralism; raising doubt about the principle of imitating Islamic jurists (*taqlid*); advocating democracy, freedom and the use of reason and independent thought; and finally an attraction for liberalism and Western laws.[199]

Propagating the belief that the Hidden Imam is proactive in the everyday politics of the nation and intervenes to manage it according to God's will sent two important messages to the pious. First, even though the war of "holy defence" against Iraq was over, an even more important campaign against the soul and spirit of Shi'ism was being waged by foreigners and their reformist "fifth column". Fending off this new onslaught had necessitated the active intervention of the Hidden Imam in support of the "true defenders of the faith", the *basijis* and their religious, political and military leaders. Second, the representatives of the Twelfth Imam were responsible for constantly reminding the common folk of the Twelfth Imam, explaining how and when the Twelfth Imam intervened, in whose favour he would intervene, who he opposed and which were the values he supported.

After repressing the popular peaceful demonstrations challenging the results of the tenth presidential elections in June 2009, Major General Hasan Firuzabadi, the Armed Forces Chief of Staff, wrote an open letter to the Hidden Imam. His letter echoed Mesbah Yazdi's major concerns. Firuzabadi reported that Divine hidden assistance along with the palpable and tangible guidance and support of the Hidden Imam had assured the national sovereignty of Iran during the Iran–Iraq war. He lamented that, after the war, the *basij* and the *basiji* mentality was assailed and abused by the new hypocrites and the cultural onslaught that they unleashed. The *basij* found itself isolated and forsaken. According to Firuzabadi, it was only *aqa* or Ayatollah Khameneh'i who was attentive to their demands and condition, and with the election of Ahmadinejad, the *basij* regained its status. Firuzabadi wrote that "Our leader Seyyed 'Ali [Khameneh'i] was no longer alone. He was happy and elated with the revival of the discourse prevalent during the first years of the revolution".[200] Firuzabadi referred to the events after the tenth presidential elections and deplored how the rabble-rousers and mutineers had attacked the *basijis* and the security forces, wounding and killing them. Addressing

---

[199] Ibid., pp. 98, 104, 109, 111, 117, 128; M. T. Mesbah Yazdi, *Azarakhsh Karbala*, p. 121; M. T. Mesbah Yazdi, *Velayat Faqih, Porseshha va Pasokhha*, vols. 1 & 2 (Qom, 1379), pp. 40–41.
[200] See http://www.bbc.co.uk/persian/1g/iran/2009/07/090712_m_forozabad . . .

the Hidden Imam, he wrote, "Like the sun behind the clouds, you are guiding us and you have entrusted us to the care of the Guardian Jurist [Ayatollah Khameneh'i] who is warning us against the enemies of the people and the nation and we have learnt to be extremely severe with the unbelievers".[201] Addressing the Twelfth Imam, Firuzabadi reiterated that "We are standing firm with all our might and preparedness to assure the survival of the system [*nezam*] so that you [the Hidden Imam] would be satisfied with us and the tender heart of your representative [Khameneh'i] would be content with us".[202] Firuzabadi seems convinced that the Hidden Imam is on the side of Khameneh'i, Ahmadinejad, Mesbah Yazdi and himself, and that they all represent the Imam's interests and designs.

Deeply rooted in Mesbah Yazdi's discourse, General Firuzabadi presented his political and military campaign against the reformists as supported and implicitly dictated by the Hidden Imam. Similar to Mesbah Yazdi and the clerical circle around him, Firuzabadi appeals to the emotional feeling that the Twelfth Imam engenders among the pious to win their support. Mesbah Yazdi indicates how he proposes to mobilize the pious and inculcate in them the lost spirit of selflessness and devotion. He maintains that experience has proven that when people are reminded of the miracles and Divine values of the Prophet and the imams, the people's love, emotion and passion are awakened and whipped up.[203]

It seems as though the public unleashing of superstition with Ahmadinejad's first volley of the halo of light incident in New York followed by the discourse that the Hidden Imam was intervening in the affairs of the state and would imminently appear was intended to orchestrate an emotional surge of yearning for the Twelfth Imam, whom Mesbah Yazdi and his supporters intentionally presented as the symbol of the anti-reformist agenda. Just as the brief of the Hidden Imam had been redefined to suit immediate political objectives, the role and nature of the new *basijis* also needed redefinition. The religio-political responsibility of the so-called foot soldiers of the Hidden Imam was to follow orders, defend the political status quo and combat the reformists. Even though they were claimed to be the same pious and spiritually motivated individuals, the new artificial *basijis* were alien to the original *basiji* spirit. They were a different crop living in a different time with different values, ideals and objectives. The ersatz *basijis* were at best ideologically rather than religiously motivated

---

[201] Ibid.   [202] Ibid.   [203] M. T. Mesbah Yazdi, *Rahiyan Kuy-e Dust* (Qom, 1384), p. 50.

combatants and at worst materially driven soldiers fighting their own countrymen primarily for worldly reasons.

PROPAGATING SUPERSTITION: CONTINUATION OR BREAK WITH KHOMEYNI'S POLITICAL ISLAM?

Ayatollah Khomeyni's charismatic politico-religious status along with his popularity as the undisputed leader of the revolution provided him with the authority and legitimacy he needed to rule the country. He was a firm believer in political Islam and a fervent opponent of Muslims disengaging from worldly affairs while dedicating themselves solely to spiritual or pedagogical concerns. For him, Islam was a political religion. The object of Khomeyni's politico-religious project was worldly. To Khomeyni, Islam was a repository on the basis of which an ideal Islamic state, society and political economy could be constructed. His social and political concerns were primarily focused on founding an Islamic society in which the welfare of his compatriots, from his perception, would be guaranteed. To realize his goals, he utilized Islam's this-worldly mediums and instruments. The practical process of reconciling evolving political interests and priorities of the state with moral, ethical and juridical precepts of Shi'i Islam proved to be the greatest challenge of Khomeyni's experiment with political Islam. His nine years in power demonstrate that in the tug of war between the political imperatives imposed upon him as a revolutionary leader and a statesman on the one hand, and the existing religious dogmas constraining his decisions as a religious jurist and source of imitation on the other, at times, if not often, it was the political exigencies that overruled the religious dogmas. Faced with the difficult practical task of reconciling the religious with the political, Khomeyni's view of Islam prevented him from succumbing to the temptation of seeking to justify his difficult decisions and choices by publicly evoking some sort of guidance from the hidden world.

Even though Khomeyni was very well situated to capitalize on or abuse his political success as a religious miracle or act of God, he hardly ever embarked on that path or in any way signalled his approval of attributing his earthly political acts and decisions to the Divine will. If anything, his perception was one of broadly trusting the intuition and reasoning of the common folk who had removed the Shah and brought him to power. His insistence on an "Islamic Republic" as the ideal form of government and his emphasis on the importance of the popular vote

through elections for the executive and legislative branches of the government were novel innovations in Shi'i politics. After his death, Shi'i jurists
such as Mesbah Yazdi sought excuses to prove that Khomeyni could not
have really meant that in politics "the criteria or measure is the people's
vote".[204]

In Shi'i Islam, can worldly acts be attributed to a Divine mission or will?
A very general outline of Shi'ism's sources of worldly considerations in
contrast to the roots of its otherworldly notions may be helpful. The
forthcoming classification will at times show deviations from traditional
Shi'i formulations to highlight certain points. Yet it will remain faithful to
the essence of classical categorizations.

Shi'i Islam could be viewed and explained through four different angles.
First, it could be considered as a belief with five fundamental articles of
faith (*usul-e din or e'teqadat*). Second, it could be described through the
traditional Shari'at-based jurisprudential (*feqh*) angle. The Shi'i jurisprudential domain could be broken down either into two spheres composed of
devotional (*'ebadat*) and commercial law (*mo'amelat*) considerations or
into four spheres of devotional, commercial law, family law (*monakehat*)
and criminal law (*'oqubat*) considerations. Third, Shi'ism is characterized
by its vast domain of rites, rituals, practices and promoted behavioural
patterns at times associated with the individual spheres of the *feqh*
domains and at times separate from and going well beyond those spheres.
This domain, particularly rich in Shi'ism, ranges from standard regulations
of how to prepare and perform various prayers to the purification, burial
and prayer procedures and ordinances (*ahkam*) concerning the dead.
Mohammad-Baqer Majlesi's classic work *Heliyat al-Mottaqin* is a maximalist example of detailed and at times far-fetched Shi'i writings on rites,
rituals and ethical behaviours, extending the realm of juristic opinions not
only to the quality, colour and the mode of wearing and taking off clothing, but also to that of underclothing.[205]

The fourth angle through which Shi'ism can be explained is that of
imamology or *emamshenasi*, the domain of understanding Shi'i imams
from A to Z, according to the tradition of Shi'i Twelvers. This fourth
domain is usually categorized as a subset of *Imamate*, the belief in the
twelve infallible Shi'i imams, itself a key component of the five fundamental articles of faith and belief (*usul-e din* or e'teqadat). Traditionally, topics
dealing with the imams are placed under the rubric of beliefs or e'teqadat.

---

[204] M. T. Mesbah Yazdi, *Kavoshha va Chaleshha*, vol. 2, pp. 100–104.
[205] M. B. Majlesi, *Heliyatal-Mottaqin* (Tehran, 1373), pp. 5–11.

Our reason for its separate categorization is the important role that it and
its subaltern and associated secondary discussions have historically and
recently come to play in Shiʻi Iran. This fourth domain of imamology can
be subdivided into numerous conceivable branches or topics. An interesting branch of imamology could be that of the status and position of "those
who transmit the reports and sciences of the imams", namely the Shiʻi
clergy.[206]

In this domain, which has very much coloured the image of popular
Shiʻi Islam, there are elements and accounts that could be categorized as
esoteric or only understandable to those with a special insight or knowledge of the faith. To begin understanding the subject of imamology and
reconciling the rational and irrational information provided in the popular Shiʻi text of Mohammad-Baqer Majlesi may require the abandonment of logical reasoning and questioning in favour of adopting an
intuitive or mystical approach. Where personal intuition does not help,
then grasping may come through acceptance on "face value" or blind
imitation.

Whereas the hidden world (*'alam-e gheyb*) has its own inner consistency
and logic and can be accepted on faith as the realm of the sacred, the
material world is governed by rational natural laws of its own. In imamology, a connection between the two is intently made. The imams are the real
bridges between the hidden and the material world. They are human, yet
connected to the Divine. They have human physical features, yet they are
effectively endowed with quasi-Divine attributes. Imamology therefore
fuses the sacred, supernatural and mysterious with tangible human beings
and their activities in this world. Shiʻi imamology works simultaneously
with two different registers, the natural and the supernatural belonging to
two different worlds and using two different methods of cognition –
respectively, the rational and the irrational. This is a highly subtle exercise
that, when watered-down, popularized, simplified and made into clichés,
could result in fanning superstitions, as it confuses the laws of the spiritual
world with that of the material world.

The above classification will hopefully facilitate the understanding of
Khomeyni's analysis of the spiritual and material world. In the process of
articulating his political theory of an Islamic government, Khomeyni
establishes the purview, constraints and conditions of rule by fallible
human beings, in contrast to the rule of God, the Prophet and imams.
In his treaties on Islamic government, Khomeyni makes a case for the

---

[206] M. B. Majlesi, *Hayat al-Qolub*, vol. 5, pp. 245, 253, 264, 486.

necessity of establishing an Islamic government not just by anyone, but by the jurist or *faqih*. To justify his proposition, Khomeyni refers back to the tradition and practice of the Prophet, when he established his governance or authority in Medina.[207] Khomeyni argues that if a capable and just jurist, also knowledgeable of the law, rises and establishes a government, he will possess the same kind of authority as that of the Prophet in managing the affairs of society, and it would be incumbent upon all people to obey him.[208] In relation to the worldly responsibilities of governance, Khomeyni attributes to the *faqih* the same earthly purview and responsibilities as that of the Prophet, while demanding from the public the same degree of obedience to the *faqih* as that which is due to the Prophet. The brief and mission of the *faqih* or the jurist is modelled on that of the prophets. To identify their objective, Khomeyni evokes an important maxim, typifying his approach. He writes, "according to the command of reason and the necessity of religions ... the most important mission of the prophets was to establish a just social system through the application of laws and ordinances".[209] Khomeyni repeatedly argues that the case he makes for the necessity of establishing the government of the jurist is based on Islamic law (*shar'*) and reason (*'aql*).[210]

In two key passages, Khomeyni differentiates between two types of guardianship (*velayat*). We know that, according to the Qur'an, ultimate sovereignty rests with God. According to Shi'i reports, this Divine sovereignty with partial spiritual and Divine attributes is subsequently passed on to the Prophet and the imams. The concept of *velayat-e takvini* or creational guardianship refers to the real or *de jure* authority of God, the Prophet and the Twelve Imams. The reality and legitimacy of this chain of authority constitutes a necessity of Shi'i beliefs. Based on this concept, Khomeyni argues that the imams possess an unrivalled spiritual status that gives them a "general and Divine position of representation or Caliphate" (*maqam-e khelafat-e koli-ye elahi*).[211] Implying that this position and the spiritual powers accompanying it precedes the creation of the world and are in effect the concerns of the hidden world, Khomeyni points out that such spiritual powers belonged to the imams even before the concept of government came to be.[212] He concludes his account of *velayat-e takvini* or creational guardianship by adding that "we do not have anything to say on this issue now, since it deals with another science".[213]

---

[207] R. Khomeyni, *Hokumate Eslami* (n.p, n.d), p. 25.   [208] Ibid., p. 55.
[209] Ibid., p. 77.   [210] Ibid., p. 26.   [211] Ibid., p. 58.   [212] ibid., pp. 58–59.   [213] Ibid.

By avoiding a detailed discussion of creational guardianship or *velayat-e takvini* in "Islamic government", Khomeyni separates the workings of the hidden world from that of this world when dealing with the rule of capable, knowledgeable, just, yet fallible jurists. Khomeyni does not enter that aspect of the classical field of Shi'i beliefs (*e'teqadat*), which deals with imams or imamology, necessitating a review of Shi'i reports on how the universe and the imams were created in the hidden world. Perhaps Khomeyni felt that such a literature review was inappropriate for his argument on the worldly guardianship of the jurist. To delineate clearly between the two types of individuals, infallible and fallible, one linked to the hidden world and the other to this world in terms of their responsibility to govern, Khomeyni refers to the otherworldly status of the imams and Fatemeh-e Zahra, Imam 'Ali's wife, and writes, "These [spiritually unparalleled] stations are separate from the duty of government".[214] As a Shi'i jurist, Khomeyni seems obliged to touch on the Divine-based spiritual authority of the imams and separate it from the material responsibility of establishing government in the absence of the Hidden Imam. As a Shi'i political theorist interested in the conceptualization and realization of an Islamic government, Khomeyni saw no reason to evoke or rely on *velayat-e takvini* or creational guardianship, as it was inapplicable to the here and the now.

Ayatollah Montazeri points out that creational guardianship refers to the power of intervening in the realm of creation, the universe, existence (*kown*), as well as the natural order (*tabi'at*). The effectuation of such a guardianship is called miracle making.[215] Ayatollah Taheri talks about the creational guardianship of the Prophet and the imams and provides a useful example. If the Prophet or imams order a tree to be uprooted and move towards them and then order the tree to go back to its place, the tree will obey.[216] The above example demonstrates the use of powers originating in the hidden world on earth. Such powers, according to Taheri, are limited only to the Prophet and the imams. Montazeri concurs with Taheri that the principle of creational guardianship in relation to the prophets and the infallible imams is a certainty. He adds, however, that the extent and limits of it, is beyond our precise knowledge and awareness.[217] Taheri's emphasis on the fact that, aside from God, only the Prophet and the imams

---

[214] R. Khomeyni, *Hokumate Eslami*, p. 59.
[215] H. A. Montazeri, *Mabani-ye Feqhi-ye Hokumat-e Eslami*, vol. 1 (Tehran, 1367), p. 171.
[216] H. Taheri, *Velayat Faqih* (Qom, n.d), p. 31.
[217] H. A. Montazeri, *Mabani-ye Feqhi-ye Hokumat-e Eslami*, vol. 1, p. 174.

can hypothetically intervene and undo the laws governing the material world is an attempt at demonstrating that other fallible and mortal souls cannot claim such powers. It could be argued that, in the absence of the Prophet and imams, miracle making, therefore, is impossible in this material world. Only once the Hidden Imam returns can one argue that the preconditions for miracle making are available.

Khomeyni makes his real argument for the temporal guardianship of the jurist by relying on the concept of contractual or derived guardianship (*velayat-e e'tebari*). This concept of earthly domination is concerned with the political authority and power of the *'olama* only during the greater occultation. Since it is a temporary office held until the reappearance of the Twelfth Imam, it could be considered as de facto authority, hence *velayat-e e'tebari*.[218] In an abstract sense, the jurist claiming power has the actual right of exercising power as a grant or a concession from one who has an absolute title to this position. Governance based on contractual or de facto authority (*velayat-e e'tebari*) is a concept of derived temporal power, delinked from *velayat-e takvini* and the spiritual powers attached to it. The justification for establishing an Islamic government or a contractual guardianship is based on the necessity of upholding Islamic laws during the occultation of the Hidden Imam.[219]

Khomeyni writes, "when we say that after occultation, the just jurist possesses the guardianship belonging to the Prophet and the imams, no one should be deceived to think that the station of the Guardian Jurist is the same as that of the Prophet or the imams".[220] Khomeyni explains that the parallel he is drawing between the Prophet and the imams on the one hand and the Guardian Jurist on the other is not based on comparable stations, positions or relations with the hidden world, but on comparable responsibilities to govern and apply the sacred laws of the Shari'at on earth. Anxious about the possible supernatural exaggerations and overstatements that his formulation could cause, Khomeyni reiterates that the guardianship or the governance position that he is proposing does not ascribe or attribute an "unusual" status to any person "raising them above the station of a normal human being".[221]

In his analysis, Khomeyni delinks creational guardianship with its associated supernatural powers of intervention in the natural order and miracle making from the earthly contractual guardianship, with no

[218] I am grateful to Ahmad Ashraf for his useful distinction between *Velayat-e Haqiqi* and *E'tebari* as de jure and de facto authority.
[219] R. Khomeyni, *Hokumate Eslami*, pp. 26–27.   [220] Ibid., p. 55.   [221] Ibid., p. 56.

unusual or supernatural powers associated with the guardian. This categorization provides a useful insight into Khomeyni's desire to keep the earthly affair of the temporal world completely separate from the supernatural occurrences of the hidden world. In contrast to Khomeyni's clear distinction between the two worlds, the process of ascribing the Divine-based powers and qualities of prophets, imams and infallibles to fallible human beings opens the door to superstitions and occultism.

When it came to the social and political realm, especially that of governance, Khomeyni clearly privileged the use of logical and analogical reasoning based on concrete political imperatives and conditions over impalpable and metaphysical claims and associations. Khomeyni's public approval and popularity hinged upon his conduct, his attributes, his policy choices and reactions at various historical moments. Even though during the revolution and before his return, his zealous partisans in Iran spoke about having seen his face in the moon, Khomeyni avoided formulating and fabricating supernatural scenarios that would enable him to claim intimacy and connectedness with the Divine. In his worldly affairs, Khomeyni was not in need of claiming special relations with the world of angels and the hidden world (*'alam-e gheyb*). Certain about his popularity among the people, he did not need to convince them that he had to be respected because he had a special relation with the hidden world. He did not believe in publicizing and politicizing possible spiritual relations between worldly beings and the hidden world. Neither on the basis of religious principles nor for pragmatic reasons did Khomeyni find any use in superstitious demagogy.

In response to the eulogizing and extolling remarks of those of his followers who raised him to supernatural stations in the hope of flattering his ego and raising their own status in his eyes, Khomeyni demonstrated disdain and chiding. He reacted negatively to false claims and flattery that directly or indirectly attributed some sort of otherworldly stature to him. He did not mix his worldly politico-religious position with the sacred realm of the invisible world. From the accounts of Khomeyni's close followers, it is evident that he did not believe in superstitious occurrences or causal relations.

'Ali-Akbar Nateq Nuri recalls that around a week before the triumph of the Iranian revolution in February of 1979, two men, one of which was a Seyyed, approached him. They were very distraught and confided in him that they were knowledgeable about magic and witchcraft, and "were informed" that a spell had been cast on Khomeyni. They claimed to possess a special neutralizing prayer and warned that if the spell were left unchecked, it would make Khomeyni "melt away like a candle". Against his own better judgement, Nateq Nuri grew anxious about the so-called spell and its possible effects on Khomeyni and eventually its impact on the course of the revolution. Nateq Nuri finally decided to report to Khomeyni on his meeting with the two men and their discussion of the spell. Khomeyni's dismissive response to Nateq Nuri reflects his contemptuous view of such superstitious ideas. Khomeyni is reported to have said, "Go, tell them that I am myself the neutralizer of spells!"[222]

On another occasion, three individuals claiming to be in touch with the Hidden Imam request an appointment with Khomeyni. Having listened to them, Khomeyni poses three questions that they are supposed to ask the Hidden Imam and report back to him. As soon as they leave, Khomeyni asks his son Ahmad to tell them, "Charlatans, stop doing these things".[223] According to another account, a woman claiming to have been visited by the Hidden Imam tries to meet Khomeyni. She pretends to have an "order" from the Hidden Imam concerning the Iran–Iraq war, which she claims will put an immediate end to the war. Once again, Khomeyni poses three questions, which the woman is supposed to put to the Hidden Imam and report back to him with the correct answers. It is said that the woman never came back.[224]

A review of Khomeyni's speeches and declarations during the initial years after the revolution reveals his very limited use of references to the supernatural. The supernatural events he tangentially refers to in his speeches do not revolve around a far-fetched phantasmical account, but the spiritual belief that the Beloved will eventually return the love of the devotee. Khomeyni calls on all to reach for the source of light and become a servant of God on earth serving the ordinances of God and the Islamic Republic.[225] To Khomeyni, the Islamic Republic was the country of Islam, the Prophet and the Qur'an, and it was natural that the God of Mohammad and the Qur'an would protect those who for His love had established an Islamic Republic and who were defending it against the aggressors.[226] According to Khomeyni, the Islamic Republic is God's gift and left as a trust in the custody of the people, to be protected and safeguarded.[227] Khomeyni considered only God as a source of

[222] *Shahrvand Emrooz* (22 Mehr 1386).
[223] M. Sadr-e Ballaghi, 'Ekhtellaf Ayatollah Tavasoli va Mesbah Yazdi'; see http://roozon-line.com/05newspapers/009561.shtml (30 Tir 1384).
[224] *Shahrvand Emrooz* (22 Mehr 1386).
[225] R. Khomeyni, *Sahifeh Nur*, vol. 12 (Tehran, 1361), pp. 124–129.
[226] Ibid., pp. 47–49.   [227] Ibid., pp. 128–129.

supernatural powers with the ability to intervene in the affairs of this world, not on the account or behalf of individuals but communities and people. For Khomeyni, God's favour was not a private matter, directed at particular individuals who could claim a special status and put themselves apart from and above others as if they were some sort of chosen saints. God's supernatural attention was in the form of collective blessings applying to the entire Islamic community. The mystical private relation between the lover and the Beloved does not enter into this discussion, as it has no social or political connotations.

On 24 April 1980, operation Eagle Claw, which was supposed to rescue the U.S. hostages held in Iran, turned into an utter fiasco. On 25 April, by the time the White House announced the failure of the rescue operation in a desert region near Tabas, the wreckage of three U.S. Sea Stallion helicopters and a C-130 aircraft was already abandoned on Iranian soil. The severely burnt bodies of eight fallen U.S. servicemen were also left behind near the debris of what remained of the aborted mission. During this operation, not one bullet was shot by Iranians at the intruders. The surviving forces of the original U.S. assault fled to the aircraft carrier Nimitz in the Arabian Sea, from where the rescue operation was launched.[228] The failure of the operation due to technical problems but more importantly because of an unexpected sandstorm had all the appearances of a grandiose miracle. While Iranians slept, U.S. troops had crossed into Iranian territory, were ambushed by natural forces, had fallen into disarray, incurred substantial losses, were forced to abort their mission and had been compelled to retreat.

Khomeyni's first official reaction to the astonishing if not incredible turn of events at Tabas was almost entirely political rather than religious. Concerned about the imminent possibility of an all-out U.S. attack on Iran, he lashed out against what he called the U.S. intervention and threatened that an attack against Iran would be construed as an attack against all Muslim countries and that Muslims of the world would not remain indifferent to such hostile actions. He warned Carter that an attack against Iran would lead to a complete oil embargo against the U.S. Khomeyni lambasted Jimmy Carter's rescue operation as a "stupid manoeuvre" and chastised him for his reckless political thirst to win a second term in the White House. He then made a prediction, of which he was himself instrumental in its realization. He told Carter that because of his rescue mission, he would have no hope for a second-term re-election.

---

[228] A. Rahnema and F. Nomani, *The Secular Miracle*, p. 310.

Speaking as the commander of the armed forces, Khomeyni placed all Iranians capable of carrying arms on red alert and besieged the people to prepare themselves for the defence of their Islamic motherland. Having advised the people not to panic, he posited that "this stupid operation was defeated by the command of God, the omnipotent", and added, "our cause is just and God is the protector of the Muslim people".[229]

Given the peculiarity of the circumstances surrounding the Tabas rescue operation, Khomeyni could, if he so wished, place the emphasis of his discourse on the "miraculous" nature of the events. He could have argued that he, as the leader of the Islamic Republic, was blessed by God and that the foiling of the rescue operation was somehow related to his special connection with the hidden world. Khomeyni could have certainly used this ideal incident to shore up his already sacred image and great popularity with the common folk. He could have capitalized on the situation to whip up superstitious sentiments. To Khomeyni, however, based on the laws of the material world, Iranians had to become militarily prepared in the event of a U.S. military attack. In Khomeyni's world outlook, the management and administration of the Islamic Republic, a worldly construct, was the responsibility of God's vicegerents on earth and was not to be left to fate or the unknown design of the hidden world. Yet to Khomeyni, as well as to all believers, the ultimate decision maker is God, and hence the Persian proverb, "you take the initiative, God will provide the blessing" (*az to harekat, az khoda barekat*). The believer never forgets the true universal source of power, yet he or she accepts responsibility for his or her acts according to the rules of the material world. Khomeyni avoided attributing the decisions and naturally the outcomes of worldly political, social and economic issues to the hidden world and refused to indulge in superstitious propaganda.

Khomeyni's assertion that the rescue operation was "defeated by the command of God, the omnipotent", was a natural affirmation as would be expected of all believers that the eventual outcome of events is ultimately and at the cosmic and macro level the work of God. Yet Khomeyni introduces what could be construed as an important conditional clause. The assertion that "our cause is just and God is the protector of the Muslim people" runs against the interpretation that God supports the Islamic Republic automatically and unconditionally as a blessed special state. Khomeyni introduces the issue of espousing "a just cause" as a condition for God's support and blessing. Instead of playing with the emotional

---

[229] R. Khomeyni, *Sahifeh Nur*, vol. 12, p. 59.

concept of "miracle", Khomeyni implies that as long as the Iranian people champion a just cause, God would look favourably upon them and their situation.

In his speeches to various segments of the Iranian society after the rescue operation or the U.S. intervention, Khomeyni addressed various domestic and international political issues and did refer to the Tabas fiasco on a couple of occasions chiding Carter's operation and arguing that the U.S. had violated the sovereignty and the right of self-determination of the Iranian people.[230] Khomeyni prompted Iranians to prepare themselves for a confrontation with the superpowers and reassured them that they had nothing to fear from the potential aggressors as the Iranian people were "protected by God and all powers were doomed to destruction before His power".[231] Conscious of the blanket conclusion that could be drawn from his assertion that Iranians were protected by God, Khomeyni added, "I hope God would approve of our objective", which he identified as "standing up to injustice".[232]

As a God-fearing politico-religious leader, cautious of his words before the Almighty, Khomeyni could only hope that his decisions would be "correct" and meet with the approval of the Divine. Yet he could neither impute to God what he wished nor assume that his acts and decisions would be necessarily approved by the Divine. In Khomeyni's public speeches, there is usually a reference to his wish and hope to succeed in serving Islam and God.[233] Khomeyni's deep certitude about God's omniscience, omnipresence and omnipotence prevents him from being certain that his fallible decisions would be in accordance with the will of God. In his speeches, Khomeyni's anxiety about the possibility of incorrect decisions or actions leading God to deny His blessing is palpable.[234]

For Khomeyni, once an objective or a goal had been achieved through human effort, there were no guarantees that those achievements would become permanent, even if they were ushered by the forces in the hidden world, unless humans took the initiative and responsibility to preserve and protect those gains. Khomeyni's reliance on the responsibility and importance of the human agency, as expressed in his speeches after the revolution, prevents him from assuming that irrespective of human conduct, the hidden world could effect change and maintain the achievements of change. When Khomeyni attributes the victory of the revolution to God and refers to its triumph as a miracle, he is not referring to a direct and

---

[230] Ibid., pp. 60, 66–68, 134.   [231] Ibid., p. 92.   [232] Ibid.
[233] Ibid., pp. 100, 101, 120, 130.   [234] Ibid., pp. 118–120.

unmediated intervention of the hidden world in the material world. In explaining the process, Khomeyni writes about the transformative work of the hidden world on the hearts and minds of the people (*moqqaleb al-qolub*) and how this miraculous transformation of the people in turn ushers victory.[235] Khomeyni's argument is non-superstitious. He maintains that belief in and reliance on God and the hereafter emboldens the believers, relieves them of their fear, and endows them with a defiant courage that puts fear into the heart of their enemies, be they the *ancient regime* or foreign powers. Khomeyni believes that it is God who activates the awakening process. A non-believer could attribute it to an array of other material factors.

Five weeks after the Tabas fiasco, Khomeyni addresses a group of foreign visitors invited to attend an international conference on "the assessment of U.S. interventions in Iran". In his speech, Khomeyni explains why he believes that neither a U.S. economic embargo nor direct U.S. military intervention would destabilize the revolution and bring back to power the old monarchy.[236] Khomeyni reiterates that conditions in Iran are different from what they were in the past, as today the people rely on and trust in God (*etekal be Khoda*).[237] He then draws a parallel between the early days of Islam, when a small group of Muslims were able to overcome large armies and inquires: "Was it not that an invisible hand was at work?"[238] Khomeyni heeds that "those who do not believe in the spiritual realm and the hidden world should wake up" and asks, "who destroyed Mr. Carter's helicopters which were on their way to Iran? Did we? It was the sand, the sand is God's agents, the wind is God's agent ... They can try again".[239]

Is Khomeyni attributing the U.S. losses at Tabas to the hidden world or providence? As a believer, how could he not, since everything is in the hands of God, including the natural elements such as the wind. Yet Khomeyni considers this Divine intervention as a reward for the spiritual disposition that Iranians developed and warns that if their spiritual power and fervour wanes, God may withdraw his favour.[240] Contrary to Ahmadinejad's practice of placing the imminent return of the Hidden Imam and his intervention at the centre of his public discourse and then presenting himself as a chosen person connected with the Hidden Imam, confronted with a rather exceptional turn of events, Khomeyni tries to draw a material lesson, while concurrently confirming the Divine power. The Iranian people's newly developed reliance on and trust in God,

[235] Ibid., pp. 143–144.   [236] Ibid., p. 139.   [237] Ibid.   [238] Ibid.
[239] Ibid., p. 140.   [240] Ibid.

Khomeyni argues, yielded the collective fruit of the defeat of the U.S. forces while Iranians were asleep. In Khomeyni's construction, the people as a collectivity benefit from a special status. God's favour and grace is not unconditional due to the intercession or special office of a specially connected person and varies as the people's disposition or spiritual strength alters. Khomeyni cannot guarantee the continuation of God's grace, the people can. Here, the will of God and His invisible hand becomes inextricably connected with the religiosity and spirituality of Iranians. Khomeyni's explanation of the Divine intervention, once again, resembles the Persian proverb of, "you take the initiative God will provide the blessing" (*az to harekat, az khoda barekat*). Providence is part and parcel of the believers' thought and value system, but attributing all events to some sort of a miraculous intervention opens the door to superstition. Khomeyni was mindful not to promote superstitious beliefs that "de-responsiblized" the people and sanctified individuals.

Khomeyni's theoretical delineation between the worldly and contractual guardianship and the cosmic and creational guardianship concepts enable him to keep the two spheres apart. The Ahmadinejad–Mesbah Yazdi discourse eclectically fuses the two for political expediency. For Mesbah Yazdi, the *faqih* or the Guardian Jurist who rules over the Shi'i during the occultation of the Hidden Imam derives his legitimacy and authority to rule from the fact that he is introduced by the Hidden Imam as his deputy or vicegerent. According to Mesbah Yazdi, the right of the *faqih* to rule is validated by and derived from his appointment by the Hidden Imam.[241] For Mesbah Yazdi, the *faqih* has the right to rule and the people are obliged to follow him only because he is a designated successor of the Twelfth Imam. Khomeyni, on the other hand, does not legitimize the right of the Guardian Jurist to rule by arguing that he is appointed by the Hidden Imam. Mesbah Yazdi's notion that the *faqih* has a mandate from the Hidden Imam and that is why he can rule is absent in Khomeyni's book on "Islamic Government". In his book, Khomeyni relies on the Qur'an, Shi'i reports and reason to prove the necessity of the rulership of the *faqih*. The *faqih* is said to have the right to take political command just as the Prophet Mohammad did.[242] Mesbah Yazdi alters Khomeyni's theoretical construction by introducing the notion that the jurisconsult is an appointee of the Hidden Imam and, because of this connection, he should be followed by the Shi'i. Mesbah Yazdi thus opens

[241] M. T. Mesbah Yazdi, *Hokumate Eslami va Velayat Faqih* (Tehran, 1369), pp. 160–162.
[242] R. Khomeyni, *Hokomate Eslami*, pp. 26, 80.

the door to the possibility of the pious believing that it would make sense for the Hidden Imam to protect his own appointee and designated deputy by intervening on his behalf. Mesbah Yazdi does seem to mix the two spheres that Khomeyni had painstakingly separated to keep the occult out of Islamic worldly politics.

After the election of the Islamic Republic's first parliament (*majles*) on 25 May 1980 and almost a month after the Tabas fiasco, the elected deputies paid a visit to Khomeyni. Fakhreddin Hejazi, the deputy with the highest votes in Tehran, delivered a speech on behalf of the other members of the first post-revolution *majles*. A one-time zealous sympathizer of the *Fada'iyan-e Eslam* (Devotees of Islam) and later one of the most popular speakers at Hoseyniyyeh Ershad, before the arrival of 'Ali Shari'ati, Hejazi was a vibrant, moving and charismatic orator fond of creating an atmosphere of quasi-theatrical drama and passion play. To influence and mesmerize his audience successfully and find a way into Khomeyni's heart, Hejazi exaggerated, gesticulated and overstated to make a point. He told Khomeyni that the people had risen to obey his command, as they had seen "the light of God in the mirror of his long forehead". Hejazi addressed Khomeyni as the son of Imam 'Ali and the Prophet Mohammad, and went on to praise him as the heir to all prophets and imams. Hejazi stressed that "the illumination of your existence is the manifestation of the proof of God" and added that "We pledge to you to disseminate your sacred wishes across the horizon of times, you who are the bright light and the embodiment of God's light".[243]

Those who saw the footing of this meeting on television remember that Hejazi ended his speech by saying, "Say it as it is O Imam, say it as it is!" Hejazi pleaded with Khomeyni to divulge a secret. Less than 18 months after Khomeyni had taken power, Hejazi was openly prompting him, by his unabashed flattery, to claim a special spiritual and divinely linked position for himself. This was at best a highly emotional attempt at a sacred investiture of otherworldly religious authority and power to which Khomeyni was expected to concede or at least implicitly give credence to. Given the extraordinary events of the Tabas fiasco, Khomeyni could have been tempted to take some credit by alluding to a special relationship with the hidden world.

Khomeyni's response was lucid and clear, leaving no room for ambiguities. He said, "I fear that I would come to believe what Mr. Hejazi said about me. I am fearful that as a result of his words and that of other people

---

[243] *Ettela'at* (5 Khordad 1359).

similar to him, I would become proud and degenerated. I seek the protection of God the magnificent and great from pride. If I were to think of myself as superior to others, this would constitute an intellectual and spiritual demise or downfall".[244] Khomeyni praised Hejazi for his oratory skills yet chided him for raising issues before him "that he may come to believe!" This was Khomeyni's way of putting an abrupt end to any attempt by enthusiasts and flatterers to engage in dangerous exaggerations about him and eventually turn him into an icon or a godhead. In the exceptional or quasi-miraculous context of the Tabas fiasco, Khomeyni must have been anxious about the adverse consequences of exaggerations on the long-term faith and belief of the people. He probably dreaded that Hejazi's type of adulation could open the floodgates of Shi'i extremism (*gholov*) attributing supernatural attributes to mere fallible mortals.

To win the hearts of his followers, Khomeyni promoted a tangible, this-worldly Islam concerned with the livelihood of Muslims. This assertion does not imply that he did not exalt spiritualism in the sense of deeply believing in God and his powers. His acute sense of pragmatism and realism in the service of expediting the implementation of his ideal government did not prevent him from experiencing moments of mysticism in private. But Khomeyni's personal relation with the hidden world, whatever it may have been, belonged to his private domain. Khomeyni did not find it necessary nor did he believe in the long-run political viability and possibility of seeking metaphysical and heavenly justifications for the public exercise of his politico-religious power and authority.

The public claim of connectedness to the hidden world of metaphysics and intangibles for the sake of obtaining popularity, recognition, power, wealth and status, sometimes derogatorily referred to as setting up or opening a business or shop (*dokkan*), has had a long history in Iran. The history of the so-called "men of faith" who take advantage of the piety, simplicity and ignorance of the common folk and try to first impress and mesmerize them and then control them by falsely claiming a "special connection" is, however, regularly paralleled with those other "men of faith" who try to lift the haze of stupefaction and occultism by decrying and condemning such outlandish claims as charlatanry, obscurantism and illusory nonsense (*vahm*).

---

[244] R. Khomeyni, *Sahifeh Nour*, vol. 12, p. 115; *Ettela'at* (5 Khordad 1359).

2

Mohammad-Reza Shah Pahlavi's Supernatural Shi'ism and Its Political Implications

THE DIVINELY GRACED CHILD

It is said that one night in Gonbad Kavus, Colonel Reza (later Reza Shah), still a member of the Cossack brigade, had a dream. The next day, Reza asked his servant, Yadollah Ardel, if he was at all familiar with interpreting dreams and divination based on dreams, before describing his own. He had dreamt that two candles were lit in his room. While Yadollah opined that the dream signified a double promotion for his master, Reza disagreed in amusement. Two days later, Reza received a telegram. His second wife, Taj ol-Moluk, had given birth to twins. Reza named them Mohammad-Reza and Ashraf.[1] At the hands of his entourage, the dream about the two candles was later developed into a subtle, insinuated yet unsaid reference to a spiritual experience by Reza Shah. Despite Reza Shah's disinterest in spiritual matters, this incident has been implicitly referred to by some as proof of Reza Shah's spiritual dimension and supernatural agency. It seems as though, traditionally and historically, Iranian political leaders were required to have possessed some sort of supernatural power or force to separate them from the masses and infer upon them a particular status of leadership somehow connected with the hidden world.

On 17 December 1925, the new Shah and founder of the Pahlavi dynasty lost no time in officially designating his heir. In a royal edict (*farman*) of twelve lines, signifying the new Shah's allegiance to and respect for Twelver Shi'ism, Reza Pahlavi appointed Mohammad-Reza Pahlavi, his son, as the official heir to what he called his "eternal" rule. Reza Shah

---

[1] Q. Mirza Saleh, *Reza Shah: Khaterat Soleyman Behbudi, Shams Pahlavi, 'Ali Izadi* (Tehran, 1372), pp. 28–29.

referred to the fact that Mohammad-Reza's "natural capacities and abilities were already manifested in his face and behaviour". He implored God to help his son realize his mission of pursuing and securing the welfare and progress of the country, by inscribing his destiny with "the pen of predestination in the eternal book of fate".[2] Some four months later, on 25 April 1926, Reza Shah crowned himself as king at the Golestan Palace. Wearing a special military uniform, the almost seven-year-old Mohammad-Reza, the Crown Prince, participated in the coronation.[3]

Reza Shah was very fond of his heir and had great dreams and aspirations for him. When the young man was sent to Switzerland to pursue his education, the Shah, who had never been to Europe, would eagerly await his news every Tuesday afternoon. When news was delayed, the punctual and somewhat regimented Shah would grow restlessly irate. On such stormy occasions, the courtiers would gather around the Shah, chitchatting and trying hard to cheer him up while buying time for the special courier to appear at the palace gates. One such Tuesday, when the royal entourage began praising and extolling the educational achievements of the Crown Prince and the services that Reza Shah had rendered to the country, the Shah is reported to have said, "Yes I have served this country very well but my most important contribution has been to appoint a Crown Prince. It is not apparent or known to you now, but once the Crown Prince begins his work, it will then become evident who he truly is".[4] Once the Crown Prince became Shah, history provided him with a few decisive moments to demonstrate his true metal. It could be argued that on none of those key occasions did he rise to what one would have thought to be his father's expectations.

A short while after Reza Shah's coronation, the almost seven-year-old Mohammad-Reza fell ill with typhoid. The young boy's fever mounted over a few weeks, causing Reza Shah and the Queen Mother to despair. Mohammad-Reza's health continuously worsened as his alarmingly high temperature enfeebled the boy to the point of making him fall into unconsciousness. At times, the boy would sleep for the entire day. Soleyman Behbudi, a member of Reza Shah's court and a lifelong trusted aid, recollected many years later that one day, having sweated heavily in his sleep, the Crown Prince jumped out of his slumber and

[2] R. Niazmand, *Reza Shah* (London, 1996), p. 456.
[3] E. Safa'i, *Reza Shah Kabir dar Ai'eneh Khaterat* (Tehran, 1365), pp. 77–78.
[4] Q. Mirza Saleh, *Reza Shah: Khaterat Soleyman Behbudi, Shams Pahlavi, 'Ali Izadi*, p. 353.

exclaimed delightedly that "I have been cured, I saw the Imam in my dream".[5]

Behbudi recalls that he dashed off to give Reza Shah the good news of the Crown Prince's recovery and to report his dream, as if it was the proof or sign of Mohammad-Reza's "special status". Reza Shah did not seem convinced or relieved. To put the royal mind at ease, Behbudi drew a parallel between the young Mohammad-Reza's dream and that of the Shah in Gonbad Kavus. Behbudi tried to console Reza Shah by reminding him of his dream about the two candles and how it had come true. Just as Reza Shah's dream had foretold the future, Behbudi argued that Mohammad-Reza's dream, foreseeing his recovery, would also turn out to be true. Behbudi concluded that the Shah should not worry, as "Mighty God is the protector of the Crown Prince".[6]

MOHAMMAD-REZA'S CONNECTION WITH THE HIDDEN WORLD

In 1961, or some thirty-five years after the typhoid incident, Mohammad-Reza Pahlavi, the Shah of Iran, published a book called *Mission For My Country*. In this book, he reminisced about his childhood and youth. He recalled that while hovering between life and death during his bout of typhoid, he had "entered into a special spiritual or holy realm".[7] The sacred realm that Mohammad-Reza entered into was itself in the mysterious world of dreams, in which individuals have claimed encounters with holy figures. After more than three decades, Mohammad-Reza remembered the fine details of his exceptional childhood experience. At the height of his disease, he wrote, he had seen Imam 'Ali sitting next to him. To convince his audience that he was not mistaken about the identity of the person in his dream, thus emphasizing the spiritual significance and dimension of his experience, the Shah clearly remembered that the Imam had his famous two-pronged *Zolfaqar* sword on his lap. Among the Shi'i, the *Zolfaqar* is the particular and unique mark of only one person, and he who sees the *Zolfaqar* knows that he must have seen Imam 'Ali, its owner and master. Imam 'Ali, the Shah recalled, held a bowl in his hand as he sat at Mohammad-Reza's bedside and ordered him to drink the liquid in it. The young boy naturally obeyed, and the next day, his unusually high temperature dropped and he recovered rapidly.[8]

---

[5] Ibid., pp. 275–276.   [6] Ibid., p. 276.
[7] M. R. Pahlavi, *Ma'muriyat Baray-e Vatanam* (Paris, 1366), p. 116.   [8] Ibid., p. 117.

In this supernatural episode, Imam 'Ali, the most venerated Shi'i personality, is said to have intervened on behalf of the Shah. Imam 'Ali's appearance in Mohammad-Reza's dreamworld and his mediation through the provision of the potion is reported to have produced immediate results in the material world. The next day, Mohammad-Reza is on the road to recovery. The Shah apparently believed and expected his compatriots to accept the argument that his recovery was due to the intervention of none other than Imam 'Ali safeguarding him from dangers. The Shah's public announcement of this so-called holy and miraculous occurrence seems to imply that he believed that he was a chosen figure protected by the hidden world and that he sincerely expected his subjects to share in his conviction. After recounting his miraculous recovery, the Shah writes that, at the time it had occurred to him that there may have been no connection between his dream and his quick recovery. However, with hindsight, he reassures his compatriots that having experienced two other special experiences during that same year, he became deeply convinced of his "particular status" as a divinely chosen and protected person.

During the same year, 1926, Mohammad-Reza had a second supernatural "personal experience". This time the sacred intervention did not take place through a dream, but manifested itself by altering the outcome of a this-worldly tragic accident. Yet, the process and details of the intervention remained obviously hidden from the eyes of the "uninitiated" public. The Shah recalled the family's regular summer excursion to Emamzadeh Davud, a holy shrine situated behind the mountain ranges north of Tehran, and one of the few cool and refreshing spots not very far from Tehran during the hot summer days. At the time, access to the holy shrine, which stood at a relatively high elevation, was only possible on foot or on horseback. The narrow trail leading up the hill was steep and treacherous. As the royal entourage made its way towards Emamzadeh Davud, the seven-year-old Mohammad-Reza was safely mounted into the saddle of a relative. Suddenly, the horse slipped and lost its balance. Both riders plunged to the rocky surface beneath them. Mohammad-Reza remembered that, as his head hit a hard and sharp stone, he fainted. When he regained consciousness, he found himself under the anxious and nervous eyes of his retinue. They were perplexed and bewildered by the fact that, after the deadly fall, Mohammad-Reza was unscathed. Confronted by their state of shock, Mohammad-Reza divulged a secret.

He recounted that as he toppled from the saddle, Hazrat-e Abolfazl ('Abbas), the valiant and glorious son of Imam 'Ali, appeared to him and protected him from grave injury and mortal danger.[9] In this second case, Mohammad-Reza, who wishes his readers to believe that Hazrat-e 'Abbas must have shielded him from the danger that awaited him, forces his readers to speculate about the modality of the intervention. The Shah must have been made as light as a feather, the hard and jagged stones on which his head had landed must have been turned into a soft bed of foam, or Hazrat-e 'Abbas must have held Mohammad-Reza's head in his hands and gently placed it on the rough surface below. Whatever the many imaginary possibilities may be, Mohammad-Reza seeks to convince his subjects that he enjoys the special protection of Hazrat-e 'Abbas. Mohammad-Reza confides in his readers that even though he recounted this second experience to his father at the time, Reza Shah did not take it very seriously and that, aware of his father's sceptical disposition toward such experiences, he did not wish to enter into an argument with him. Mohammad-Reza Shah, however, assures his readers that despite his father's incredulity, he had absolutely no doubt about the veracity of the events and Hazrat-e Abolfazl's visitation and intercession.[10]

Mohammad-Reza's third supernatural episode during that same year involved a visitation or a physical encounter in the material world. Contrary to the context of the first two experiences, in this one, Mohammad-Reza was not threatened by any mortal danger. Mohammad-Reza recalled that as he was strolling around the Sa'dabad Palace with his special tutor, he suddenly noticed a man with an angelic appearance who had a halo around his face. Reflecting on his childhood experience, Mohammad-Reza observed that the halo seemed similar to that depicted by Western painters portraying the Virgin Mary.[11] At the time, the young Mohammad-Reza had what he later labels as an "inspiration of a celestial origin" (*elham*) that the man whom he had met was none other than the Twelfth Imam. His encounter or visitation lasted a few minutes before the Twelfth Imam disappeared. Left in a state of bewilderment, the young Mohammad-Reza asked his tutor whether he too had seen the holy person. His tutor responded, "Who was I to see? There is no one here". The young boy was so convinced of the truth and accuracy of what he had witnessed that the response of his tutor did not make a dent in his certitude.[12] Later perhaps, the incident helped Mohammad-Reza build a case for his uniqueness and superiority. What he could see and intuit in relation to members of the hidden world, other mortals could not. Belief in this extraordinary sense may have convinced the Shah that he was a

---

[9] Ibid.   [10] Ibid.   [11] Ibid., p. 118.   [12] Ibid.

member of the highly selected circle of friends or protégés of God (*owliya*). As much as he trusted the authenticity of his very special meeting with the Twelfth Imam, Mohammad-Reza never recounted this experience to his father.[13] Reza Shah had scoffed at his son after hearing his account of the "miraculous" experience at Emamzadeh Davud. Faced with yet another supernatural occurrence, the veracity of which could only be attested to by himself, Mohammad-Reza keeps his spiritual experience to himself, only to protect its sense of "sacredness" from the possible ridicule of his father.

Mohammad-Reza traces the roots of his faith and religious convictions to his three "special personal experiences" during 1926. He interprets his experiences as proof or a clear sign of the fact that he was an extraordinary individual in whom sacred Shi'i figures took a particular interest. Twice they had saved his life, strengthening his belief that he was a divinely protected person. Finally, to confirm his esteemed station in the eyes of the hidden world and his state of grace, the Twelfth Imam had personally appeared to him. Reflection over the self-reported supernatural encounters in his life leads Mohammad-Reza to pose the anxiety-ridden yet self-glorifying quintessential question of all great mystics: "Is my will independent or contingent upon an external element?"[14] This type of intense soul-searching inquiry is usually conducted by renowned Sufi sages after attaining proximity to and interacting with the hidden world. By posing this question, Mohammad-Reza seems to intimate that he is merely a tool in the hands of God through which God intends to realize His will on earth. Thus it seems as though Mohammad-Reza's birth, from his point of view, has a particular religio-political purpose incomparable to that of normal mortals, as God has entrusted him with a mission. To Mohammad-Reza since God's power and providence has protected him from dangers and perils, there must be a higher reason for these events and a Divine design in which he plays a central role.

In view of the fact that Mohammad-Reza publicly refers to a series of other supernatural events occurring in the later stages of his life as proof of his special religious status, it becomes evident that the monarch is gradually building a solid dossier on the basis of which he could solicit special treatment and respect from his people. By attributing to himself a God-willed spiritual and political calling, Mohammad-Reza seeks to insure all his everyday acts and decisions against any public doubt, questioning or criticism. He hopes that through publicizing his spiritual experiences, the people on the street would recognize his divinely appointed position,

[13] Ibid.   [14] Ibid., p. 119.

devoutly abide by his will, as, by following him, they would be following
some sort of a sacred being blessed by heavenly grace. Mohammad-Reza
seems to have been convinced that the masses would eventually come to
believe that he was an instrument of God and an executioner of His will.
Once the public accepted this, they could also readily accept the myth of
inerrancy and sacredness of the Shah, a status historically associated with
shahs, rendering them unaccountable to their subjects.

Mohammad-Reza Pahlavi and Mahmud Ahmadinejad both publicized
what may have been a personal experience with the hidden world. The act of
sharing this information with the public, given the stark power relation
between them as rulers and the people as the ruled, could not be simply
construed as confiding in others or building intimacy and trust. Based on
their common evaluation of what was endearing to the people and what
would induce them to trust and blindly follow a leader, both Mohammad-
Reza Pahlavi and Mahmud Ahmadinejad, each coming from very different
backgrounds and with different views of their mission, identified the love of
Iranians for their imams as the most certain path to the hearts of their people.

The legends of those claiming to be in connection with the imams and
acting as their implicit deputies provided space for the emergence of a new
agent during the Twelfth Imam's occultation. These new agents were sub-
imams who claimed links with the imams. In a new cosmic organizational
chart, the sub-imams usually stood below the imams but certainly above
the common folk. It is in view of this implicit organizational chart with its
clearly delineated and unquestionable hierarchical chain of command that
Mohammad-Reza Pahlavi and Mahmud Ahmadinejad embarked on
informing the Iranians of their respective encounters with the imams and
the hidden world. The revival of superstition as a sociopolitical tool to
command submission and allegiance and subsequently exercise control is
an efficient tool, as long as Iranians believe that worldly fallibles could
have access to and be guided and aided by the imams in the hidden world.
The so-called connected person in authority would thus pretend to possess
some superior wisdom and foreknowledge, of which the common folk
would always be deprived and in want.

THE HIDDEN WORLD INTERVENES IN HISTORY ON THE
SIDE OF THE SHAH

Mohammad-Reza refers to four other events, none of which involves a
visitation, but each seems to have a miraculous nature in his eyes. All cases
have one theme in common: the course of history has been willed by God

based on the fundamental principle of safeguarding the Shah and his throne, so that he would accomplish his calling. According to the Shah, the four special events that later occurred in his life strengthened his childhood belief in the True Origin of the universe or God.[15] Even though the Shah does not clearly spell out what he wishes his compatriots to deduce from these events, he continues to intimate a divinely willed design in which he is but a player with no real independent will, leading Iran to its grandeur. His politics subsequently becomes divinely willed as well.

The first of these events occur when Mohammad-Reza, as the monarch, is on a royal inspection tour of a newly constructed dam in Esfahan. Mohammad-Reza provides a detailed account of how the single engine of a small plane that he was piloting stalled after ten minutes of flight over a mountainous region.[16] After skilfully manoeuvring the plane to minimize the impact and harshness of the crash, the Shah's plane miraculously lands without the slightest injury to him and the officer assisting him on the flight. In a seemingly curious and innocent manner, Mohammad-Reza reflects on this event and poses a question to which he already seems to have an answer. Rhetorically he inquires, "was this event the outcome of good fortune and luck or did it occur the way it did because an invisible power caused the good fortune?" He leaves the obvious answer, which he seems to believe in, to his readers.[17] The Shah seems anxious to persuade others of his conviction that he is a "special person" and it is for this reason that God or the invisible power guarding him intervenes in worldly events to ensure that he would go on making history.

The second miraculous case evoked by the Shah concerns the postwar events in Azarbayjan. According to the Shah, had it not been for another Divine intervention in his favour, the province of Azarbayjan would have seceded, Iran would have been Balkanized and his throne would have been endangered. Mohammad-Reza presents the 1948 withdrawal of Soviet forces from Azarbayjan, the flight of Pishevari, the fall of the Azarbayjan Democratic Party, the narrow escape from the establishment of an autonomous Azarbayjan and finally the military reclaiming and regaining of the region, as his second piece of evidence proving his preferential status with the Divine. He sums up that the liberation of Azarbayjan was due to Divine assistance, as well as Iranian nationalism.[18]

The Shah refers to the assassination attempt on his life in 1949 as a "peculiar and bitter episode of his reign".[19] Escaping the bullets of the would-be assassin constitutes the third supernatural happening.

---

[15] Ibid. [16] Ibid., p. 120. [17] Ibid., p. 121. [18] Ibid. [19] Ibid.

Mohammad-Reza provides an elaborate description of the manner in which Naser Fakhrara'i, opens fire on him at Tehran University. It is said that, at close range, Fakhrara'i misses the Shah three times as his bullets riddle the Shah's military hat. Fakhrara'i's fourth bullet rips through the Shah's right cheek and pierces his upper lip, right below his nose. The fifth bullet injures the Shah's shoulder and the sixth bullet jams in the barrel. The Shah's account of the event creates a sensational atmosphere of drama and marvel and succeeds in imparting to the reader a strong sense of the inevitability of his death given the proximity of his executioner and the absence of any worldly protection or safeguard mechanism to shield him from the bullets. Mohammad-Reza wishes to convince his compatriots that had it not been for an invisible supernatural force deflecting the bullets and then jamming the revolver of his assailant, the Shah should have been killed. The message he wishes to reiterate is a simple and repetitive one. He was spared because he was protected by God to fulfil His divinely designed mission. The fact that the Shah escaped the assassination attempt "strengthened his faith in God and His aid, fortifying his everlasting relation with the Almighty".[20] The fact that Mohammad-Reza believes his relation with the Almighty to be direct and free from intermediaries plays an important role in allowing him to believe that his Shi'ism is different from and more genuine than that of the clergy or his political detractors who opposed him in the name of religion.

The Shah's fourth historical proof of a Divine intervention, redirecting the course of history in his favour, is generally known to Iranians as the foreign-hatched coup against Mosaddeq. Ominously and ironically, what is usually considered as a historical tragedy by the Iranian people is renamed and relabelled "the miracle of 28 Mordad" by the Shah. This is the historical date in August 1953, during which Dr. Mohammad Mosaddeq's nationalist government was overthrown by the CIA and MI6 with the participation of sections of the Iranian army and clergy, the court, royalists, an array of one-time nationalists who had gradually fallen out with Mosaddeq and the active involvement of the lumpenproletariat. A few days before the coup, Mohammad-Reza Shah had fled the country. After the fall of Mosaddeq's government, the Shah returned home as a "triumphant" and "popular" king.

Upon his arrival, Mohammad-Reza embarked on re-writing history so that the tragedy and betrayal of 28 Mordad would be remembered and nationally commemorated as a miraculous popular uprising against

---

[20] Ibid., pp. 122–123.

Mosaddeq. Completely ignoring or denying that his victory over Mosaddeq was engineered and executed by foreign powers, which had no particular sympathy for anything Iranian other than its oil, the Shah insisted on giving the impression that he had returned on the shoulders of a popular and national uprising against Mosaddeq. If that were true, which it was not, then he could make a case for God being on his side, the people's side, the just side. Throughout his reign, the Shah had a hard time convincing Iranians that the events on that day were simply the manifestation of God's will and therefore for the good of the people and the country.

The Shah summed up his position on the "miracle of 28 Mordad" thus: "It is my firm belief that the toppling of Mosaddeq's government was the work of the ordinary people of my country in whose hearts blazed the Divine providence".[21] The Shah needed to convince himself and his compatriots that it was Divine providence, and not the money, planning and management of the CIA and MI6, that had stirred his "people" to reclaim him and reject Mosaddeq. Just as the Shah had convinced himself of his "miraculous" return to power, he had convinced himself that it was the people who were the true catalysts of this event and not the actual hoodlums, thugs and ruffians. Neither the Shah's historical rewrite nor his claim to a Divine intervention ever made much of a dent in the deep-rooted beliefs of his subjects, leaving him in an awkward political and religious lurch.

MOHAMMAD-REZA: GOD'S INSTRUMENT OR NOT?

The name of the book in which the Shah recounts his mystical and spiritual experiences is aptly called *Mission For My Country*. This mission seems to have been conferred upon him by God and the hidden world. The four events that he evokes as further testimony to his divinely guided status represent an interesting transition in the Shah's mind in terms of his own status in the make-believe world he seems to create for himself. The Shah wishes to demonstrate that he has been sheltered from different kinds of threats and dangers for a higher and much more important purpose and objective. Following the Shah's line of argument, if the Shah had not miraculously escaped from the plane crash and from the bullets of a would-be-assassin, his mission would have been aborted and perhaps God's design would have remained unfulfilled. To assure the fulfilment of God's grand scheme, in which Mohammad-Reza plays a key role, seems to be the reason why the miracles occurred. The conviction of

[21] Ibid., p. 123.

connectedness with the hidden world played out in the public and political sphere invariably produces a delusion of grandeur and an unrealistic over-estimation of the individual's powers and potentials.

Mohammad-Reza's inclusion of three key political events – Azarbajan, the assassination attempt and 28 Mordad – in his long list of supernatural episodes is important, as it signifies his attempt to portray himself no longer as a blessed seven-year-old child, but a looming national and international figure for whom God intervenes in the material world to safeguard his political vision and leadership. In Mohammad-Reza's eyes, Iran was saved from Pishevari, Fakhrara'i and Mosaddeq not only because the person of the Shah was a "protected individual", but also because his rule was divinely warranted and guaranteed. The Shah, much like Ahmadinejad, felt as if he was graced and appointed to fulfil a sacred historical mission on the world scale.

In 1960, looking back on his experience as a statesman with "special spiritual qualities", Mohammad-Reza recapitulates his relation with God, Iran and what lies ahead and concludes that "It is certain to me that all that I have done during my reign has only been possible through the aid and support of an invisible power".[22] Consistent with his position of being a passive agent of the Divine, Mohammad-Reza gives credit to an invisible power for his achievements, but also hides behind the same external invisible power to dismiss what others would consider to be his short-comings, injustices, impieties, failures and excesses.

Perhaps realizing the grave consequences of his exaggerated insinua-tions or more probably feeling as though he has already convinced his subjects that he is the object of God's grace, the Shah tries to attenuate his claims by dismissing the notion that he should ever be considered as God-sent or as God's instrument of realizing His designs.[23] Mohammad-Reza's attempt at diluting the relation that he fosters in the mind of his readers forces him to enter into a somewhat confusing dissimulation exercise. Having disclaimed that he should ever be considered as God-sent, he writes, "From my childhood I realized that a predestined hand will appoint me to the position of the guardian of an ancient country ..." and adds that all the progress that has been experienced in this country would not have been possible without the support of God.[24] Was this statement of humility and modesty before God the acknowledgement of the fact that he was Crown Prince poised to become king, or was this a reiteration of the fact that all his achievements were in reality God's work through him?

[22] Ibid.   [23] Ibid.   [24] Ibid.

Born in and ruling over a country where the tradition of religious mysticism is as strong as institutionalized religion, the Shah was probably submitting his "personal and spiritual experiences" as evidence of his particular brand of religiosity. The Shah wished to present himself as a political leader who possessed the hidden world's direct and unmediated grace and support. He was not in need of clerical support or alliance, as the hidden world had rendered him independent of them. As a protégé of God, he sought to endear himself not only to the supporters of his Westernization drive, but also to the religiously inclined common folk. As the future unravelled, it became clear that Mohammad-Reza's attempt at posing as a mystical politico-religious leader was not very successful.

MOHAMMAD-REZA'S DIVINE MISSION CHALLENGED BY KHOMEYNI'S ISLAM

If all three of Mohammad-Reza's supernatural episodes were genuine and not concocted after the events, the recounting of the visitations could be construed as innocent personal testimonies of unusual experiences of a seven-year-old boy. But by 1961, when the experiences were written down, Mohammad-Reza was a king who ruled a geostrategically sensitive and populated oil-rich country. The supernatural events that Mohammad-Reza Shah chose to report in his book seem to have been intended for politico-religious purposes. On the basis of a childhood vision or fantasy, to which he was giving a religious and mystical spin, he was constructing a political argument legitimizing his uncontested and lifelong quasi-sacred rule.

Some two years after Mohammad-Reza's ideas about his divinely ordained kingship were made public, the Shah was confronted with a formidable adversary who derived his religious authority from the formal study of the corpus of Shi'i theology and jurisprudence. In terms of his religious training, Ayatollah Ruhollah Khomeyni was a product of the Qom Seminary School. His political outlook, however, reflected an important, yet minority trend in Qom for which Islam was inseparable from politics, and it was the duty of Islamic scholars or *'olama* to enter the social and political sphere, guiding the people. Khomeyni's claim to speaking for and defending the Islam that he expounded was not based on his "personal religious experiences". He spoke as a religious authority and jurist, passing judgement on Iran's sociopolitical ills and the Shah's mismanagement of the affairs of the state. Among an initially small but growing circle of believers, Khomeyni became the embodiment of Shi'i Islam. He derived his legitimacy to challenge the Shah's rule from his religious position and political audacity and was not in need of compiling a detailed folder demonstrating that he was divinely guided or protected by the imams.

On 3 June 1963, Tehran was in the throes of a violent political upheaval, engineered by Khomeyni's supporters. Asadollah 'Alam, the Prime Minister at the time, later characterized those turbulent days of rioting as a "revolution in Tehran and the provinces".[25] The religious uprising of June 1963 sent three clear messages. First, the Shah and his policies were unpopular among a vocal and readily mobilizable social group. Second, this same disgruntled population was rallying in support of an anti-Shah and anti-U.S. Islam, which Khomeyni was representing and speaking for. Third, to the rebellious religious crowds on the streets, the Shah was neither blessed nor his rule ordained by the hidden world. The uprising could have been a useful warning reminding the Shah that there were segments of the population that were violently opposed to his manner of kingship and his vision of a future Iran. However, the challenge to the Shah's power and authority by Khomeyni and his partisans first rendered him irate and sensitive to the clergy or *akhundha*, with whom his father and he had a long, awkward history. After the summer of 1963, the Shah added Khomeyni's name to that of Mosaddeq as his arch-rival. The Shah was disdainful towards both men, since caught in his delusion of grandeur resulting from the conviction that he had a supernatural status, he believed himself to be the symbol of both fervent Shi'ism and diehard nationalism. Mosaddeq's legacy, however, reminded the Shah that he was not a nationalist, and Khomeyni's movement reminded him that he was not a worthy Shi'i king in the eyes of the pious common folk. Incapable of understanding the reason for their popularity as it implied facing the painful issue of his own unpopularity, the Shah sought to demonize them and deal with Khomeyni's threat by the use of force. In those whom he trusted, Mohammad-Reza Shah confided that the squelching of the June revolt was a "watershed in the history of his monarchy".[26] The Shah probably felt that this was a second miracle after the 28 Mordad one, consoling himself that the defeat of the June uprising was further proof of his divinely blessed status, as well as his personal popularity among his people.

Given the predominantly religious nature of the June uprising, Mohammad-Reza Shah should have become somewhat suspicious of the

---

[25] A. 'Alikhani, *The Diaries of Asadollah 'Alam*, vol. 2 (1349–1351) (Bethesda, 1993), p. 60.
[26] A. 'Alikhani, *The Diaries of Asadollah 'Alam*, vol. 3 (1352) (Bethesda, 1995), p. 318.

effectiveness and force of his claim to being supported by the imams and possessing a Divine mission. At least for those who had come out on to the streets opposing the Shah, as well as their silent sympathizers, it was evident that the Shah's spiritual credentials and assertions were suspect. Why would the religiously inclined crowds have revolted against the Shah if they were convinced that the Shah's Shi'ism was the Shi'ism of the imams? Were they not revolting in the name of Islam and against impiety and political corruption and injustice? Why would pious believers rebel against a person whom they thought was divinely guided and protected by God and the imams? Even though the Shah could and did discount all evidence of the unpopularity of his rule by arguing that foreigners had manipulated the angry crowds, the magnitude and religious message of the protest could not be discarded. It could be argued that from 1963, the Shah employed two parallel approaches to defuse his powerful political challenger and to resolve the dilemma of who really represented Islam, Shi'ism and the imams: Mohammad-Reza or Ruhollah. First, even though the Shah never abandoned his claim to religiosity and at times took concrete steps to demonstrate and publicize certain aspects of it, he renounced his earlier policy of seeking legitimacy and authority by publicly making claims to a supernatural status. His discourse of being a chosen leader became a private one. Second, the Shah gradually embarked on differentiating between his spiritual religiosity and Khomeyni's political Islam.

The Shah seemed to promote an Islam based on direct contact with the spiritual world and without the necessity of an intermediary clerical layer. He associated Khomeyni's Shi'ism with clericalism. The Shah believed that the clerics were conservative, cautious and more concerned with their own private or guild interests than with that of the grandeur and development of Iran. According to the Shah, the clergy were always the source of harm and misfortune.[27] Furthermore, to the Shah, Khomeyni's political Shi'ism and the events of June 1963 were manipulated and even financed by foreign powers for their own interest.[28] The Shah was intent on presenting Khomeyni's Shi'ism as unpatriotic and opposed to national interests. In a private conversation with Asadollah 'Alam, his Minister of Court, he even went as far as calling the Shi'i clergy in general as *bi-mazhab va bi-vatan* or "without religion or nation".[29]

[27] A. 'Alikhani, *The Diaries of Asadollah 'Alam*, vol. 5 (1354) (Bethesda, n.d), pp. 254, 426.
[28] A. Baqeri, *Khaterat-e 15 Khordad* (Tehran, 1388), p. 136.
[29] A. 'Alikhani, *The Diaries of Asadollah 'Alam*, vol. 5 (1354) (Bethesda, n.d), p. 426.

In 1971, the Shah would privately reconfirm his conviction that he was a chosen person. Seemingly convinced of this "scientific fact", Mohammad-Reza posits that "I have tested this. Whoever has opposed me, inside or outside the country, has been destroyed". Providing examples of those who opposed him and perished, he cites the Kennedy Brothers, Naser, Khruschev, Mosaddeq, Gavam ol-Saltaneh and Razmara.[30] It is important to note that by 1971, the Shah did not even think of his clerical detractors as a potential political and religious danger. He was convinced that, after the June 1963 repression and the dispatching of Khomeyni into exile, he had once and for all eradicated the influence of the clergy and Khomeyni, their leader.[31] Only eight years after the religious June uprising, which shook the foundations of his power, the Shah is once again comfortable enough to present the idea of his invincible "chosen status" as a scientific theory based on empirical tests.

The belief that God had destroyed his opponents must have convinced Mohammad-Reza that the political Islam of Khomeyni and his supporters did not have the support of God and that the Shah's Islam was the true Islam. At this time, a new Islamic discourse, different from that of the Shah and Khomeyni, was being developed and popularized. Shari'ati's Islamic and revolutionary discourse, was gaining widespread support among Iranian high school and university students. As time went by, a different kind of display of religiosity in society increased. A growing number of young women covered their hair in universities and public places and students congregated for public prayers on university campuses. Faced with increasing signs of religiosity and religio-political consciousness among a radicalized youth, once again, the Shah took the easy way out and identified his defiant Muslim subjects as instruments in the hands of foreign powers.[32]

IF THE SHAH IS DIVINELY SUPPORTED, THEN WHO IS SUPPORTING HIS DISSIDENT SHI'I SUBJECTS?

Feeling the gap between his perception of Islam and its quietist political implications and that of an increasing radical Islam, particularly popular among the youth, the Shah gradually embarked on deriding and attacking

---

[30] A. 'Alikhani, *The Diaries of Asadollah 'Alam*, vol. 2, p. 168.

[31] A. 'Alikhani, *The Diaries of Asadollah 'Alam*, vol. 5, p. 252; A. 'Alikhani, *The Diaries of Asadollah 'Alam*, vol. 6 (1355–1356) (Bethesda, 2008), p. 64.

[32] A. 'Alikhani, *The Diaries of Asadollah 'Alam*, vol. 6, pp. 64, 441.

the Islamicness of his opponents rather than promoting and defending his personal Islam. By this time, the Shah faced a different kind of Islamic opposition in comparison to that of Khomeyni and his supporters. The Organization of the Iranian Peoples' Mojahedin was a guerrilla vanguard waging an armed struggle against the Shah's regime. The organization's ideology was founded upon an egalitarian and revolutionary reading of Islam. Yet greatly influenced by the anti-colonialist and anti-imperialist experience and success of Marxist–Leninist liberation movements throughout the world, the organization implicitly accepted Marxism as the science of revolutionary struggle. It could be safely suggested that from early 1971, Hoseyniyyeh Ershad became a major recruitment ground of the Mojahedin. The youth who packed into and often stood outside the main lecture hall at Ershad would come to listen to the passionate, consciousness raising and insurrectionary lectures of 'Ali Shari'ati. Having "graduated" from his theoretical classes on the responsibility of the Shi'i to struggle against absolutism, colonialism, exploitation and stupefaction, Shari'ati's students moved on and sought action by joining the Mojahedin. In November 1972, the Mojahedin producing factory of Ershad was encircled and shut down by government forces and Shari'ati was forced into hiding until he went to prison in September of 1973. Yet the Mojahedin went on about their guerrilla war against the Shah's regime. Less than two weeks after the closure of Hoseyniyyeh Ershad, Mohammad-Reza Shah insisted that the rising militant Islamic movement among university students had nothing to do with Islam but that these students were "definitely communists, pretending to be fanatical Muslims".[33] The Shah was convinced that the new Islamic forces challenging his rule were communists manipulated by foreign powers.[34]

During the last week of October 1973, as the Yom Kippur war was grinding to a surprising end and about a month after Shari'ati was imprisoned, the usual annual court festivities commemorating the important Islamic celebration of *'eyd-e fetr* marking the end of the fasting month of Ramezan was held at the Shah's Royal Palace. During these festivities, the Shah received representatives of various constituencies of the state and society, heard their short reports, usually including homages to the King, and sometimes responded to them with a short statement. In view of the mixed feeling of pride and anxiety that was bubbling in the hearts of Muslims and Middle Easterners over the outcome of the Sinai war between Egypt and Israel, the Speaker of the Iranian Parliament, 'Abdollah Riazi,

---

[33] A. 'Alikhani, *The Diaries of Asadollah 'Alam*, vol. 2, p. 347.   [34] Ibid.

supported the cause of Iran's "Muslim brothers" in their struggle against Israel. Riazi was an almost lifelong speaker of the Iranian Parliament and one of the permanent and trusted figures in the Iranian political establishment. As such, he was experienced and adept at "political correctness" in the Shah's presence. Riazi's sincere and heartfelt supportive statement of solidarity with the Arab cause and Iran's Muslim brothers did not go unnoticed by the Shah. Given the Shah's political preoccupations at home and his uneasy and awkward historical rapport with radical Arab leaders, Riazi's apt statement produced a mini tempest in the Shah's mind. After Riazi's statement, the Shah murmured in his ear that "you do not realize this, but 'these brothers' are our greatest enemies".[35]

Later that day, still upset at Riazi's comments, the Shah confided in Asadollah 'Alam that he did not appreciate this notion of "playing out to be a Muslim" (*mosalmanbazi*). He then added that "I am a Muslim, but this 'playing out to be Arabs' (*'arabbazi*) is dangerous. As you know I am a fanatical Muslim, but what has this got to do with identifying ourselves with the Arabs (*'arabbazi*)?"[36] The Shah's dislike for the Arab cause was probably rooted in his chauvinistic perception of Iran as a land of Aryans, his revulsion towards Naser's radical and popular legacy in the Arab world, his mistrust and fear of the Palestinian resistance movements and their relation with the Iranian guerrilla movements and finally his admiration for Israel.[37] Around the same time that Seyyed Qotb (Qutb) was hanged by Naser – August 1966 – allegedly for attempting to overthrow the Egyptian government by force and establishing an Islamic society, Khomeyni, too, exiled in Najaf, was thinking and probably writing about the establishment of an Islamic government based on Shi'i tenets, which he made public in early 1970. The Shah knew that his nemeses, Naser the secularist proponent of Arab nationalism and Khomeyni the anti-secularist Shi'i cleric, both shared a deep dislike for him. To both men, the Shah of Iran was a corrupt puppet of Western powers. It was therefore understandable that the Shah would loath both men and their Iranian supporters whom he accused of playing out to be Muslims or Arabs. Naser passed away in 1970, and by this time, Khomeyni's partisans were neutralized as well. In the early 1970s, the Shah's scolding remarks at those "playing out to be Muslims" were probably directed at the guerrilla fighters of the Iranian People's Mojahedin, their sympathizers and the students

[35] A. 'Alikhani, *The Diaries of Asadollah 'Alam*, vol. 3, p. 259.   [36] Ibid.
[37] A. 'Alikhani, *The Diaries of Asadollah 'Alam*, vol. 1 (1347–1348) (Bethesda, 1992), pp. 259–261.

and admirers of Shariʿati. These new spokesmen of Islam threatened the Shah and his Islam, as had Khomeyni. The Shah had also become increasingly sensitive to the Palestinian resistance movement and especially the PLO because Iranian guerrilla organizations, both Marxist and Islamic, not only closely identified with the Palestinain cause and resistance, but also sought and were given training at their camps and used their literature for training their members at home.

For the Shah, "playing out to be a Muslim" (*mosalmanbazi*) implied the demagogic use of Islam for political subversion and sedition. It also conveyed the idea of flirting or sympathizing with the various political Islams, which confronted and challenged the Shah's political authority and rule. The notion of "playing out to be Arabs" (*ʿarabbazi*) had a similar negative connotation for the Shah as it implied an affinity with the Palestinian cause and not only an anti-Israeli political stand, but also some sort of an attachment to Naser's radical anti-colonialism and Arab socialism. The pairing and derision of these two terms by the Shah reflected his preoccupation with radical Islam joining forces with radical regional leaders and liberation movements. From the Shah's point of view, the Iranian sympathizers of political Islam and the Palestinian cause were neither genuinely Muslims nor nationalists. By homogenizing and labelling his Muslim adversaries at home as unpatriotic and irreligious false-pretenders, the Shah hoped to isolate them while still laying claim to the title of the Shiʿi king.

In the early 1970s, the Shah firmly held on to his brand of religiosity as the divinely approved one. On the other side of the religio-political divide, the Islamic guerrilla movement stepped up its activities, and consequently the backlash of repression and suppression against it intensified. The literature discovered from the Mojahedin's captured hideouts and the confessions wrenched out their tortured militants provided the Iranian security apparatus with what they believed to be the ultimate religio-ideological weapon against the Mojahedin. The state could now officially respond to what seemed to be the complicated question of why the youth were challenging the Shah in the name of Islam. The simplistic official answer was that those anti-regime elements, who claimed to be Muslims, were Marxists hiding their identity behind an Islamic mask. From around the end of 1972, the regime employed and indiscriminately used its newly found label of "Islamic Marxists" as a tag for the Islamic guerrillas and militants. The tightly controlled news coverage given to the "destructive and terrorist activities" of the Muslim opposition in the Iranian radio, television and press consistently referred to them as "Islamic Marxists".

It was hoped that this "damning discovery", proving the hypocritical, anti-Islamic and ultimately atheistic nature of the Mojahedin, would dishonour the young revolutionaries in the eyes of the people and decrease the popular sympathy for their cause, while increasing the popularity of the Shah's Islam.

The notion of "Islamic Marxists" resolved the contradiction that haunted the Shah since the Islamic uprising of 1963 and continued to agitate him afterwards. The Islamic opposition to his rule, which had grown into a hardened revolutionary vanguard, could now be written off as a band of disbelievers acting out to be Muslims. The new concoction of "Islamic Marxists" allowed for the homogenization of all opposition Islamic forces, and their branding as internationalists and atheists who would naturally oppose the Shah's nationalist, Shiʻi and monarchical rule. The 1975 internal ideological shift in the Organization of the Iranian People's Mojahedin demonstrated that a segment of the Islamic opposition had switched to Marxism as an ideology. Although the split within the organization only proved that "Islamic Marxism" as a philosophical construct was an irreconcilable contradiction for both the Muslim and Marxists members of the organization, the new term proved to be of great propaganda value. The Shah used this formula "generously" to dismiss and deride his Islamic rivals as godless atheists and saboteurs in the pay of foreigners. In the Shah's mind, it was clear that whereas God supported his Islam, it was foreign atheists who supported the dissident Shiʻi opposing his rule.

Even though, by 1973, the Shah believed that he had theoretically undermined, if not undone, the legitimacy and appeal of militant Muslims, he continued to seem insecure and diffident about his own people. Unsure of the exact fault that he identified in his people, other than their intermittent disobedience, the Shah's intuitive and gut reaction once again demonstrated that at times he considered the difference between his Islam and that of his people as an unresolvable problem. Either in frustration with the Islamicness of one important branch of opposition to his rule or towing the line of those Iranian intellectuals who believed that all the country's problems resulted from the religious beliefs of the people, the Shah turned his disdain towards the overwhelming majority of his own compatriots, the Shiʻi. In a private, yet rather light-headed and crass comment to ʻAlam, the Shah assailed the Shiʻi for being spineless (*pofyuz*).[38] Mohammad-Reza Pahlavi seemed to forget both his official position, religion and the image that he wished

---

[38] A. ʻAlikhani, *The Diaries of Asadollah ʻAlam*, vol. 4 (1353) (Bethesda, n.d), p. 184.

to impart to his people as the Shiʿi King. Had he forgotten how hard he had tried to prove that he was supported and guarded by the Shiʿi imams? Did his comment reflect his frustration with the "unruliness" of his co-confessionalists? The Shah explained his irreverent attack on the Shiʿi by arguing that they had been politically ineffective in Iraq and Lebanon, and that, in Iran, all the communists and Tudeh Party members had been Shiʿi. Mohammad-Reza Pahlavi supported his comment by suggesting that there had been fewer Tudeh Party members or communists (*tudehi*) among the Sunnis and never one among the Zoroastrians or the Baha'is.[39] The Shah added that even though [Musa] Sadr was at first supported by his regime, he turned out to be a Red.

Irrespective of the statistical validity or the empirical merit of the Shah's assertion about communist sympathizers and their religious background in modern Iran, it seems evident that in the Shah's mind there existed a clear association between political opposition to his rule and Shiʿism. The Shah saw all those who fell under the broad rubric of "communist agitators" as his main enemy; yet he felt betrayed that Shiʿism did not act as a bulwark against such elements intent on destabilizing his regime. On the contrary, he even felt that Shiʿism lent itself to anti-regime agitation and sentiments. Therefore, the gap between his Shiʿism and that of the people opposing him widened. The Shah's quest for blind political allegiance and his growing authoritarianism led him to label as spineless (*pofyouz*) all those who were not his staunch supporters or enemies of his enemies. At this time, the Shah had not only become delinked from his people, but had also come to disdain them, simply because they failed to follow his lead unquestioningly. The Shah may have believed that he was supported by the imams and God, but his people were becoming ever more convinced that he was being supported by irreligious forces both domestic and foreign. Had his people accepted that he was graced and chosen by God and followed him unreservedly, he would not have accused them of being spineless.

In 1976, the Shah continued to be steadfast in his conviction that he was protected by God to fulfil his mission of serving the Iranian people.[40] Did the Shah believe that his Divine mission in 1976 was to protect his "spineless" people from the threat of "communism" through the application of an iron-fisted policy? His close circle of devotees never ceased to remind themselves and his Majesty that the Shah was divinely protected to fulfil his

[39] Ibid.   [40] A. ʿAlikhani, *The Diaries of Asadollah ʿAlam*, vol. 6, p. 174.

world-scale mission.[41] The danger of believing in connectedness with the hidden world and possessing a Divine mission is that one can never doubt one's decisions and actions. Even to the last days of his rule in Iran, Mohammad-Reza Shah continued to maintain, "I have always felt and continue to feel that a mysterious invisible hand directs me in a particular way".[42] His proclaimed categorical conviction may have been an excuse to justify his state of denial in the face of growing political opposition to his rule.

In 1976, the Shah was informed of growing signs of religious sensitivities among Iranian students. It was reported that at the "Westernized" and seemingly elitist Pahlavi University in Shiraz, an increasing number of girls were appearing with veils in classrooms and there had been incidents of such girls refusing to shake hands with Farhang Mehr, the Zoroastrian President of the University. On hearing these reports, the Shah first became surprised and then enraged. When reference was made to the influence of the clergy, the Shah's response, demonstrating a dangerous absence of understanding of the situation, was simply that "there are no more clergy (*akhund*) left".[43] Some two years before the mass movement that would put an end to his monarchy, Mohammad-Reza was convinced that Shi'ism as a political let alone revolutionary discourse was repressed, washed out and forgotten in his country. The Shah unabashedly maintained that the only language that the opposition understood and the only solution to his political problems was the use of force.[44] He must have been convinced that, in 1963, force had succeeded in "exorcising" political Shi'ism from Iranian society.

The Swiss-educated Shah, who also believed to be guided by a mysterious force, may have been well versed in French and English literature and language, as well as Western civilization, yet he was less steeped in Islam, Shi'ism and its popular culture. To him, his personal experiences with Shi'i Imams were enough to prove his religiosity and Shi'i credentials. After a discussion on the kind of headscarves the Iranian women were increasingly wearing in public, the Shah told 'Alam that women could wear headscarves (*rusary*) to schools and universities. But the Shah argued that it would be wrong for girls to wear the veil (*chador*) or the (*maqna*'), a headscarf covering all their hair and their ears, only revealing their face. Once the Minister of Court informed the Shah that the term his Majesty

[41] A. 'Alikhani, *The Diaries of Asadollah 'Alam*, vol. 2, p. 367.
[42] A. 'Alikhani, *The Diaries of Asadollah 'Alam*, vol. 6, p. 531.   [43] Ibid., p. 64.
[44] A. 'Alikhani, *The Diaries of Asadollah 'Alam*, vol. 5, pp. 128, 254, 286.

was referring to was a *maqna'eh* not a *maqna'* and that it was an Arabic word, the Shah simply responded by saying, "It is a good thing you pointed this out to me. In any case tell my Special Secretariat to inform the government that women can wear the headscarf".[45]

The Shah was a Westernized leader more interested in the symbols and manifestations of his modernist image than his traditional religion. It was in the West's economic, technological and military capabilities that he was interested and to which he looked with awe and desire. To fulfil his goal of "putting Iran on par with France and Germany", he counted on the post-1973 hike in oil revenues and became ever more interested in beefing up the military power and capacity of the Iranian army and security apparatus. To eradicate all opposition to his dream, he harnessed the Iranian political parties and imposed a single party state while moving ahead with his lofty construction plans. The Shah was neither interested in nor thought it worthwhile to think about, understand and analyze the various Shi'i discourses that were gnawing at his power.[46]

By 1977, the Shah had become seriously troubled with if not obsessed by the fact that both at home and abroad, references were regularly made to the religious opposition in Iran. At the time, they were primarily referring to Khomeyni's supporters, Shari'ati's followers, Mehdi Bazargan's sympathizers, scattered members of the Organization of the People's Mojahedin of Iran and numerous small independent and spontaneous Islamic groups. But for the Shah, once again these people were not Muslims. In reaction to William Sullivan, the U.S. ambassador to Iran's comment concerning the religious opposition in Iran, Mohammad-Reza Pahlavi became flustered and insisted that the opposition was nothing but Islamic Marxists, manipulated by the Soviets.[47]

By homogenizing those political dissidents who spoke for Shi'ism as rebellious clerics or Islamic Marxists and then essentializing and demonizing them as irreligious and treacherous enemies of the state and puppets in the service of foreigners, the Shah believed to have had successfully justified his disdain for a growing number of his compatriots. In the process of pinpointing "the other", the Shah found himself ever more isolated and alienated from the Shi'i of his country, while he continued to believe that his one-of-a-kind Shi'ism was the authentic one supported and ordained by the hidden world.

---

[45] A. 'Alikhani, *The Diaries of Asadollah 'Alam*, vol. 6, p. 442.
[46] A. 'Alikhani, *The Diaries of Asadollah 'Alam*, vol. 5, p. 397.
[47] A. 'Alikhani, *The Diaries of Asadollah 'Alam*, vol. 6, p. 440.

From 8 September 1978, when martial law was declared in numerous Iranian cities to quell the anti-Shah uprising, to 16 January 1979, when the Shah left Iran, the monarch may have reflected upon about his claim to being connected with and protected by the hidden world. He must have thought about his Divine mission. If the Shah was a tool in God's hands to realize His designs, then the only conclusion that he could have drawn was that God had wished him to bring about the demise of his own dynasty and bring to power what came to be the Islamic Republic under the leadership of Ayatollah Khomeyni. After the June 1963 uprising, the Shah had consistently thought that by God's will, he had completely quashed Khomeyni's influence. After his departure from Iran, as a believer in a direct relation with the hidden world, Mohammad-Reza's candid reflections on his relation with the Divine may have been far more hurtful to him than his ouster from Iran.

Tying the decisions and acts of mortal human beings with the designs of the hidden world and speaking on behalf of the Divine will in order to impress the common folk and attain an impregnable degree of legitimacy and authority among them is a double-edged sword. As long as pretenders to a special connection with the hidden world are in power, they can arrogantly pass off the outcome of their own acts and designs as divinely intended and supported. But as soon as their power and strength begins to wane and finally dissipate, they would have to reconcile themselves with the reality that they can no longer be favoured by the hidden world. In their candid reflections, they could reach any of the following disturbing conclusions about their presumed "special status". First, they were not in any way favoured by the hidden world to begin with, rendering them either childishly naive, delusional or at worst charlatans trying to capitalize on the popular and superstitious beliefs of the common folk. Second, they had fallen from favour and grace, forcing them to seek out what they had done to deserve such a fate. Third, they had not fallen from favour and their historical mission was to bring about their own destruction and facilitate the rise to power of their adversaries. Whichever of these conclusions is drawn by rulers who pretend to be connected with the hidden world, it would be a far from comforting one when out of power they find themselves alone with the Almighty.

3

Shah Esmaʿil Safavi

The Quintessentially Occult Shiʿi King

THE EXTREMIST LINEAGE OF SHAH ESMAʿIL

From the impressionable age of six, Shah Esmaʿil was steeped and indoctrinated in the exotic and extremist Shiʿism of his father, Sheykh Heydar. Sheykh Heydar was the son of Sheykh Joneyd and the founder of the Heydariyyeh sect.[1] Between the ages of six and nine, Esmaʿil found sanctuary in Lahijan, where Kar Kia Mirza ʿAli, the governor of Lahijan and a renowned devotee of the Heydariyyeh, protected the young Shah-to-be and taught him the esoteric knowledge and secrets of his father's sect.[2]

The Heydariyyeh, an extremist Shiʿi sect believed that a part of God's Divine attributes was incarnated and embodied in Imam ʿAli. They argued that Imam ʿAli had torn down the door of the Khybar fortress because of his possession of Divine powers.[3] The Heydariyyeh believed that this Divine power was transmitted from Imam ʿAli to his descendants, Hoseyn, Zeynolʿabedin, Mohammad-Baqer, Jaʿfar-Saddeq and Musa al-Kazem. After Imam Musa al-Kazem (the Seventh Imam), this hereditary Divine feature is no longer passed on to the direct lineage of Imam ʿAli, but dwells in the founders of the Safavi dynasty, finally residing within Sheykh Heydar, Shah Esmaʿil's father.[4]

The belief in the Divine nature of Esmaʿil's father and grandfather among their zealot followers was so strong and tenacious that even after

---

[1] Aref Arzerumi, *Enqelab al-Eslami Beyn al-Khass va al-ʿAm*, vol. 1 (Tehran, 1308), p. 22.
[2] Ibid., p. 40; A.-B. Khatunabadi, *Vaqayeʿ Alsanayen val Avam* (Tehran, 1352), pp. 436, 439, 454.
[3] Aref Arzerumi, *Enqelab al-Eslami Beyn al-Khass va al-ʿAm*, vol. 1, p. 32. [4] Ibid.

the death of Joneyd, Esma'il's grandfather, his followers continued to claim that since their master and leader was God, he must have been endowed with eternal life.[5] Joneyd's partisans considered their relationship with him as that of submissive subjects to God, since, to them, Joneyd was the incarnation of God and the living God.[6] It was therefore not surprising that Joneyd's son, Heydar, was also considered as God's son or a demi-god. Heydar purported to receive Divine guidance in his dreams and claimed divinity.[7] Both Heydar and Esma'il followed in the footsteps of Joneyd.

Sheykh Heydar and Shah Esma'il's adulation for Imam 'Ali, as an aspect of God, was concurrent with their hatred for Sunnis, whom they considered as the enemies of the house of 'Ali and referred to as "dogs". The Heydariyyeh believed that the spiritual recompense or Divine reward (*savab*) for killing a Sunni was the equivalent of slaying five disbelievers waging war against Islam (*kafar harbi*).[8] The unfortunate practice of referring to Sunnis as dogs continued throughout the Safavi period.[9] The Heydariyyeh did not regard marriage with Sunnis as permissible. Sunnis were not considered as members of the free Islamic community and, as such, it was permissible to purchase and sell them as slaves. The expropriation of Sunni property was viewed as permissible (*hallal*), and their blood was forfeit without any religious retributions.[10] Furthermore, the Heydariyyeh believed that it was obligatory (*vajeb*) to slit open the belly of pregnant Sunni women and pierce a spear through their male offspring.[11] In greeting one another, rising or sitting and entering or leaving a place, it was customary among the Heydariyyeh to say, "'Ali", just as it was customary to repeat 'Ali's name 110 times every morning. According to the Heydariyyeh, it was obligatory for the Shi'i to curse the Sunnis.[12]

The interlocking pair of Imam 'Ali worshipping and Sunni hating became the two pillars of Shi'i identity, which the Safavis sought to institutionalize. Neither of these two simple belief pillars of extremist Safavi Shi'ism could be traced or even linked to Imam 'Ali the person, his words, his deeds or his writings. The institutionalization of 'Ali

---

[5] M. Parsadust, *Shah Esma'il-e Aval* (Tehran, 1375), p. 139.
[6] Fazlullah ebn Roozbehan-e Khonji, *Tarikh 'Alamaray-e Amini*, corrected by John Woods (London, 1992), p. 272, cited in M. Tabataba'ifar, *Nezam-e Soltani* (Tehran, 1384), p. 152.
[7] M. Parsadust, *Shah Esma'il-e Aval*, pp. 145, 150, 701.
[8] Aref Arzeroumi, *Enqelab al-Eslami Beyn al-Khass va al-'Am*, vol. 1, p. 34.
[9] Anonymous, *'Alam Aray-e Safavi* (Tehran, 1363), pp. 481, 591.
[10] Aref Arzerumi, *Enqelab al-Eslami Beyn al-Khass va al-'Am*, vol. 1, p. 34.
[11] Ibid.   [12] Ibid., p. 35.

worshipping served an irreligious purpose for the Heydariyyeh and the pioneers of the Safavi state. Normalizing the worship of Imam 'Ali gradually paved the way for implicitly resurrecting, re-establishing and popularizing the unholy concept of reincarnation (*tanasokh*) or transmigration of 'Ali's soul into the worldly body of Safavi kings, rendering Safavi kings sacred and worthy of reverence as demigods. Just as Sheykh Heydar is said to have claimed divinity, Shah Esma'il seems to have followed suit and claimed supernatural powers as if he too possessed Divine attributes. The extremist (*ghollat*) Shi'i firmly believed in Esma'il's metaphysical powers.[13]

SHAH ESMA'IL IS SUPPORTED BY THE HIDDEN WORLD

In 907/1501–1502, the fifteen-year-old Shah Esma'il, founder of the Safavi dynasty, entered Tabriz, crowned himself and proclaimed Shi'ism the official religion of Iran. It is said that the majority in Azarbayjan, Gilan and Mazandaran and certain cities in Khorasan and Iraq were Shi'i of different persuasions. The Shi'i of Gilan and Mazandaran were Zeydi, while those in Azarbayjan and Khorasan were Esma'ili.[14] The rest of the population were predominantly Sunnis of the Shafi'i and Hanafi School.[15] The diversity and plurality of faiths in Iran at this time is said to have troubled and preoccupied Shah Esma'il, who sought a single and unified religion as an effective barrier to Ottoman penetration into the region.[16] At the time, the creeds and sects in Iran included Zoroastrians, Mazdakians and a large variety of Sufi orders, such as the Ne'matollahiyyeh in Kerman, the Jallaliyyeh in Shiraz, the Davaniyyeh in Tabarestan and Gilan, the Sohravardiyyeh in Ardebil, the Qaderiyyeh in Kurdistan and the Naqshbandiyyeh in Khorasan and Turkistan.[17]

At the time, Tabriz, which would become Shah Esma'il's capital city, had a population of some two to three hundred thousand, two-thirds of whom were Sunnis.[18] When the King's advisers cautioned against a precipitous declaration of Shi'ism as state religion in a predominantly Sunni land, Shah Esma'il resorted to a justification, which was common among his forefathers. The Shah claimed that, in his sleep, Imam 'Ali had appeared to him in the form of a "pure light", assuring him not to worry

---

[13] M. Parsadoust, *Shah Esmai-el Aval*, pp. 701–704.
[14] Aref Arzerumi, *Enqelab al-Eslami Beyn al-Khaas va al-'Am*, vol. 1, pp. 53–54.
[15] Ibid., p. 54.   [16] Ibid., pp. 54–55.   [17] Ibid., p. 54.
[18] Anonymous, *'Alam Aray-e Safavi*, p. 64.

about the Sunni majority and commanding him to kill those who opposed his decision.[19] By referring to the apparition and command of Imam ʿAli in his dream, Shah Esmaʿil intimated that he was receiving some sort of "revelation" or "message", rendering him an "exceptional person" and a "chosen leader" in communication with and guided by supernatural forces. The claim that it was Imam ʿAli who ordered the murder of those who may oppose his decisions further legitimized the Shah's claim to absolute authority, adding to his superhuman image and stature.

There are various accounts of Imam ʿAli's intervention in the material world in order to save, cure, protect, support, advise and further the cause of Shah Esmaʿil. It seems as if either the subjects of Shah Esmaʿil needed to establish supernatural credentials for their leader or the Shah himself intended to impose upon his subjects the idea that he was not an ordinary military leader, but one that was chosen and guided by the Shiʿi imams. The reports on Esmaʿil's extraordinary spiritual experiences seek to demonstrate and convince the reader that he was but an instrument in the hands of Shiʿi imams so that they could realize their dream of establishing a Shiʿi empire. By insinuating that Safavi kings were the protected yet humble servants of the imams and that their vocation was simply to carry out the holy will of the hidden world, a sacred aura was created around them, providing them with a status clearly superior to their subjects and almost imam-like.

The accounts of Shah Esmaʿil's various encounters with the imams, during which he benefitted from their knowledge and power, will be categorized according to the purpose of the interaction, the medium and space of communication and the manner in which imams intervened in the material world. Even though at first sight, the interventions of the hidden world seem to be primarily aimed at furthering the cause of Esmaʿil, there is a strong underlying insinuation that its broad target was that of securing the interest of Shiʿism.

IMAM ʿALIʾS APPARITIONS IN DREAMS TO FURTHER THE CAUSE OF SHAH ESMAʿIL

In the majority of cases, Imam ʿAli is said to appear to and communicate with Esmaʿil in his dreams. The purpose of the Imam's apparition differs on each occasion. Yet there is always an important piece of information about the future provided by the Imam in the form of an advice or a

---

[19] Ibid.

recommendation, which completely turns around the situation to Esma'il's benefit. To the extent that Imam 'Ali shares his infinite knowledge of the present and the future, unknown to normal human beings, with Esma'il, the young Shah becomes as omniscient as the Imam. Shah Esma'il's supposed power of being knowledgeable about present and future events, essentially in relation to military pursuits, endows the Shah with spiritual, military and political superiority among his followers. The Imam is even said to appear in the dream of a third party to influence that person's decision in favour of Esma'il's cause. The third party is advised by the Imam to use whatever means available to him to secure the well-being of Esma'il.

According to one account, Esma'il's encounter with and access to Imam 'Ali predates his coronation. Esma'il must have been around the age of twelve when he lived under the protection of Kia Amireh, a devout follower of his father. Kia Amireh was the semi-autonomous ruler of Gilan, a northern province of Iran. At the time, the ruler of Iran, Rostam Padshah, was intent on exterminating Esma'il and his brother Ebrahim, who, due to their lineage, posed a threat to his rule. It is reported that Rostam Padshah sends a threatening message to Kia Amireh warning him that if he were to harbor Esma'il and Ebrahim and refuse to hand them over, he would send a huge army and lay waste to Gilan. Concerned with the impending danger of Rostam Padshah's ultimatum, Kia Amireh seeks council with the elders. His advisers unanimously concur that in order to avoid death and destruction, Kia Amireh has no other option but to comply with Rostam Padshah's demand.

On the night that the council of elders delivers its decision, Kia Amireh has a dream. In it, Imam 'Ali appears to him and reprimands him for his unbecoming thoughts about turning in Esma'il, whom he addresses as "our son", to his would-be executioners. Imam 'Ali informs Kia Amireh that if he does not wish to be dishonoured on the day of resurrection, he should reconsider his plans.[20] Upon waking up, Kia Amireh rushes to Esma'il's house to seek his pardon, hoping that if Esma'il pardons his ill intentions, Imam 'Ali would also forgive him. On reaching Esma'il's room, he hears Prince Esma'il addressing someone. The prince ends his statement by asking the unidentifiable person, "O King has the time come for me to lead the uprising?" Kia Amireh finds no one in the prince's room and enquires about Esma'il's interlocutor. The prince responds that he had been conversing with Imam 'Ali. Kia Amireh then falls on Esma'il's feet,

[20] Ibid., p. 42–43.

begging for forgiveness. Kia Amireh promises Esmaʿil that, as Imam ʿAli had already instructed him in his dream, he would never hand over the prince to his mortal enemies.

Preoccupied and disturbed with Rostam Padshah's dire and bloody ultimatum in case Esmaʿil was not handed over to him, on the one hand, and the promise he had made to Imam ʿAli, on the other, Kia Amireh goes to sleep. Once again, it is reported that Imam ʿAli appears to Kia Amireh in his dream and clearly outlines for him what he should do to ward off Rostam Padshah's threat while saving Esmaʿil from death. Imam ʿAli is reported to have instructed Kia Amireh to resolve the problem by taking a false oath on the Qur'an, testifying that Esmaʿil was not to be found anywhere in Gilan.[21] The important element in this report is that Imam ʿAli, the model of honesty, piety and righteousness, is presented as a pragmatic personality who would enter someone's dreams from the hidden world and instruct that person not only to lie but also to take a false oath to save Esmaʿil's life. The reporter of this story is purposefully elevating the safety and well-being of Esmaʿil to a level superior to the religious and Divine requirement of piety, honesty and respect for the Qur'an. The instrumentalization of the sacred for immediate political ends is not seen as a threat to the basic ethos and principles that the faith seeks to promote and inculcate. This report may intend to show the exalted and sublime status of Esmaʿil in the eyes of Imam ʿAli.

After he reaches the age of fourteen, Esmaʿil is said to have been permitted by the Imam to lead the Shiʿi rebellion. Soon, Shah Esmaʿil's military victories confirm his superiority over other contenders for power in Iran. Having consolidated his military grip and reunited Iran by 1509, he sets out to expand his dominion in Ottoman-controlled territories. In one of his sensitive campaigns against the Ottomans, Shah Esmaʿil is reported to spend the night weeping, talking to and supplicating God to help and give him victory in his battle tomorrow. By sunrise, having spent a restless and sleepless night preoccupied with the difficult day ahead, it is reported that Esmaʿil eventually falls asleep. In his sleep, he suddenly sees the apparition of the "light" of the "lion of God". Imam ʿAli is known as the "lion of God", and his supernatural presence is associated with some form of light. Imam ʿAli addresses Esmaʿil as his son and informs him that the Twelve Imams will all be present at the battlefield and will fight on his side in the form of sandstorms. According to this report, Imam ʿAli assures

[21] Ibid., p. 44.

Esmaʿil that the sandstorms signify the presence of all the imams on horse-back and at his side.[22]

In Shah Esmaʿil's dream, Imam ʿAli pledges the help and assistance of all Twelve Imams to Esmaʿil and promises that, "If God so wishes" (*ensha'allah*), victory will be his and the enemy's soldiers will become his prisoners. Once Esmaʿil wakes up and recounts his dream to his Shiʿi warriors, they rejoice. According to this account, the imams are able to transform themselves into natural phenomena such as sandstorms to assist Esmaʿil's army. In a report on a different military campaign, there is another reference to sandstorms helping Esmaʿil's army at a very sensitive moment when his soldiers were completely outnumbered by the Uzbeks. As the sand takes off and approaches from the direction of Mashhad, the shrine of Imam Reza, Esmaʿil turns to his army and says, "Thank God that the imams have joined us".[23] The sandstorm is reported to have blinded the Uzbeks and enabled Esmaʿil's army to pile the battlefield with the corpses of sixty thousand Uzbeks.

Another report narrates the events that occur during Shah Esmaʿil's siege of the impenetrable fortress of Firuz Kuh. Differences of opinion among Shah Esmaʿil's commanders on the most time-efficient strategy to enter the fortress cripple the Shah's decision-making power. Frustrated and exhausted, he retreats into seclusion, talking with and supplicating God. In his conversation with God, Esmaʿil explains that he is incapable of identifying the right military plan for over-running the fortress and asks God for guidance.[24] Once again, when the Shah falls asleep, the "pure light" of Imam ʿAli appears to him, addresses him as usual as his son, and inquires about the reason for his anguish. Esmaʿil asks the Imam about the proper way to invade the fortress, and he provides the Shah with specific instructions on the manner in which his army should go about accomplishing this task. Imam ʿAli is said to have revealed to Esmaʿil the existence of a secret passage located behind the fortress, constructed as an emergency escape tunnel for the inhabitants of the fortress at times when they were subjected to long-term sieges. Imam ʿAli is reported to have told the Shah to invade the fortress by sending an expeditionary force through the secret passage. Imam ʿAli is said to have also instructed Esmaʿil to destroy the fortress, explaining that it was best if it were not to stand.[25] When Esmaʿil wakes up, he conveys the Imam's instructions to his commanders and, upon disclosing the source of his information, his commanders rejoice.

[22] Ibid., p. 80.   [23] Ibid., p. 443.   [24] Ibid., p. 94.   [25] Ibid.

Soon, the Firuz Kuh fortress falls to Esma'il's army, and is subsequently levelled to the ground.[26]

During another important military campaign aimed at absorbing the province of Khorasan, Shah Esma'il lays siege to another fortress. The siege against the fortress of Marv probably took place around 1510. Having surrounded the Marv fortress, suddenly news arrives at Esma'il's camp that a sixty-thousand-strong Uzbek army has crossed the Jeyhun (Amudrya or Oxus) river to battle against Esma'il's smaller army and break the siege. The Shah summons a council of his military commanders to draw a plan of action. The council is unable to reach a consensus, and Esma'il informs the commanders that, in view of their precarious military situation, he would have to consult his master Imam 'Ali and seek a proper solution.[27]

That same night, Esma'il falls asleep after his long prayers. During his sleep, the "pure light" of Imam 'Ali appears to him and puts his mind at rest about the impending military campaigns. In this report, Imam 'Ali is portrayed as an esoteric military adviser, tactician and strategist with perfect clairvoyance. The Imam outlines in detail the steps that Esma'il needs to take and discloses to him the perfect military plan that would guarantee his victory over the Uzbeks. In Esma'il's dream, Imam 'Ali shares with him the stratagems and diversions he needs to employ to draw the enemy into a trap, and the exact location at which he would need to engage the Uzbek army to slay Shahi Beyg, their leader, and seal the victory of the Shi'i. The next day, Esma'il relays the Imam's instructions to his military commanders and they all fall to their knees.[28]

According to this report, Esma'il does exactly as he is told by Imam 'Ali. Consequently, Shahi Beyg falls for the ruse, his army is massacred and he is beheaded by Esma'il. Finally, through the intervention of Imam 'Ali on behalf of Shah Esma'il, the Marv fortress, the key to the conquest of Khorasan, is taken by Esma'il. In this report, there is also one incidence during which the Shah is alerted to an impeding mortal danger by a voice from the hidden world. When Esma'il enters the river in pursuit of Shahi Beyg, he hears a voice warning him not to go any further, since, if he were to, he would fall into a deadly whirlpool. At the heeding, the Shah looks behind him to see where the voice is coming from and realizes that there is no one there.[29] This is a voice from the hidden world looking out for Esma'il's safety. Once again, in addition to the macro military plan and the

[26] Ibid., p. 95.   [27] Ibid., pp. 305–306.   [28] Ibid., p. 306.   [29] Ibid., p. 313.

particular manoeuvres, the imams are reported to extend a helping hand to Esma'il on micro issues when his mission or life is threatened.

The distinguishing features of the last two accounts are the precision and importance of the military information provided by Imam 'Ali and his rather unusual request that a particular worldly object, such as the fortress of Firuz Kuh, be destroyed. However, a number of recurring and regular trends characterizing Shah Esma'il's relation with the hidden world can be observed from these reports. First, whenever the Shah confronts an insurmountable problem or a dangerous situation, he appeals to God or Imam 'Ali for help and assistance. The Shah's requests and supplications receive an affirmative response from God and Imam 'Ali. Second, the hidden world's special intermediary and intercessor, charged with giving satisfaction to Shah Esma'il's demands is Imam 'Ali. Third, Imam 'Ali appears to Esma'il in the form of "pure light". Fourth, Imam 'Ali addresses Esma'il as "my son". Fifth, Imam 'Ali has plenipotentiary rights and powers from God. Sixth, at times, Esma'il attributes the destruction and massacres that follow his victories, secured by the intervention of the hidden world, to the instructions of Imam 'Ali.

In the minds of the formulator of these reports, there seems to be an almost complete overlap between God and Imam 'Ali. These reports all bear witness to Esma'il's special, if not sacred, status as a personality endowed with very special powers and supernatural gifts. As long as Esma'il has access to Imam 'Ali's counsel and his unlimited and eternal knowledge of the known and unknown, the Shah can make history on earth according to his own wish and design. These reports wish to demonstrate and prove that the hidden world through the agency of Imam 'Ali directly intervenes in the natural order of the material world and its historical course to further the cause of the Shi'i by securing Esma'il's military hegemony. The author of such phantasmical reports assumes that Imam 'Ali has an active religio-political interest in the material world and that Esma'il is but his obedient religious, military and political envoy, administrator and executor on earth.

The dissemination and popularization of such recurring phantasmical reports among the common folk provided an occult and superstitious explanation for the historical course of events during Shah Esma'il's rule. The success or failure of campaigns was explained by agents in the hidden world conjured by Esma'il in the material world. This approach intentionally ignored the explanatory power of palpable earthly factors such as the elements determining the military strength and weaknesses of each side. Privileging the material explanatory factors would have certainly rendered the campaigns less sacred and the Shah, as its commander, less holy. The use of material and palpable explanations for military successes would have provided Shah Esmaʿil with the image of a military genius but not that of a commander closely connected with and guided by the hidden world. The Safavi phantasmical accounts of Shah Esmaʿil's supernatural powers dulled the Iranian common folk's power to reason by providing them with easy and straightforward solutions, not really requiring much mental exercise or application. The difficult and challenging process of applying logic to understand causal relations and its underlying reasons and then searching for rational solutions is blunted by such farfetched stories. The methodology of these unreal and superstitious accounts prevents the development of the critical and scientific method of reflection.

IMAM ʿALI'S APPARITION IN ESMAʿIL'S DREAM TO PROTECT, HEAL AND CURE HIM

According to a report, one day when the Shah was outdoors hunting on his horse of fine Arab stock, the horse slipped and the two tumbled to the ground. Esmaʿil's horse was shattered to pieces and died. Shah Esmaʿil lost consciousness and the courtiers present carried him secretly to his encampment to prevent a general panic among his soldiers. For a few days, all conceivable treatments were administered, yet the Shah's health did not improve. Esmaʿil was probably in a coma, as he did not open his eyes or show any signs of consciousness.[30] After three days, Esmaʿil opened his eyes, jumped out of bed and said, "O ʿAli help" (*ya ʿAli madad*). Confronted with the astonishment and amazement of his entourage at his sudden recovery, the Shah recounted that Imam ʿAli had appeared to him in his dream, healed him and instructed him to join his army as they were becoming anxious. In his dream, Imam ʿAli is reported to have caressed his head, and, overwhelmed with joy, Esmaʿil had opened his eyes.[31] The similarity between the content, details and the message of this story that, if correctly reported, must have occurred sometime around 1510 and the one that Mohammad-Reza Shah Pahlavi reports sometime around 1960 is striking.

In contrast to those reports in which Esmaʿil seeks the help and guidance of God to secure the victory of his army, in this case the hidden world intervenes without having been petitioned to save and prolong the life of one person. According to this report, Imam ʿAli takes the autonomous

[30] Ibid., p. 425.   [31] Ibid., p. 426.

initiative to assure Esmaʿil's good health. Therefore, the hidden world alters the course of events in the material world in favour of one person because of the supposed religious and historical significance of that person. The fate of Esmaʿil as the Shiʿi Shah is made out to be closely interwoven with the Shiʿi cause, the Shiʿi mission and its future. From the perspective of those who conceived of this report, it seems as though Shah Esmaʿil personified and embodied Shiʿism. This preconception may explain why the Shah's survival is presented as such a crucial factor requiring the intervention of God and Imam ʿAli. This report makes a case for the particular and unique standing and importance of Esmaʿil to the hidden world.

In a second report, the intricacy and complexity of the supernatural interferences to guarantee Esmaʿil's well-being are fascinating. In Tabriz, the Shah falls ill and his health deteriorates daily. His doctors eventually give up all hope and prepare themselves for the fatal eventuality. The military commanders, courtiers and officials visit the Shah at his sickbed, and, as his eyes are closed, they pray for his recovery. In the middle of their invocations, the Shah opens his eyes and instructs his anxious subjects to go away and pray for him. He requests that they leave him alone with his master, Imam ʿAli.[32]

All leave except for one – Najm-e Zargar-e Rashti. The Shah inquires why he has stayed behind, and Najm-e Zargar-e Rashti says, "I wish to pray for you as you are our spiritual leader and the propagator of Twelver Shiʿism, but I need you to say Amen so that my supplication would be immediately accepted and put into effect". Najm-e Zargar-e Rashti had petitioned God to accept a bargain. If the Shah's life had reached its end and if he (Rashti) had any time left in this world, he pleaded with God to take whatever was left of his life and add it on to Esmaʿil's. If God accepted the bargain, Esmaʿil's life would be prolonged while Rashti's life would be ended. Assuming that Najm-e Zargar-e Rashti was simply praying for the restoration of his health, Esmaʿil whispers Amen. Immediately, life returns to the Shah's death-ridden face and unaware of Najm's secret bargain with God, Esmaʿil rejoices at the immediate consequence of his prayer. Najm thanks God for the affirmative response to his supplication and tells the Shah about his agreement with God. By the time the Shah roars with pain that "O Najm, you have rendered me fatherless", life and death were already starting to switch places between the two men. In three hours, the Complete Spiritual Guide (*Morshed-e Kamel*), as Esmaʿil was called by

[32] Ibid., p. 304.

his followers, regained his health, while Najm's body laid cold in Esmaʿil's bedchamber.[33]

This story is about Najm's selflessness and devotion to Esmaʿil, but it is also a tale of Esmaʿil's supernatural power and unique status in the hidden world. It narrates a superstitious perception of the relationship between Esmaʿil and God. According to this report, God's approval of Najm's wish is encumbent upon Esmaʿil's confirmation or blessing. God is the ultimate power, giving and taking away life, yet in this case, without Esmaʿil's intercession, God may not have responded favourably to Najm's supplication. Here, God grants Najm's unusual wish to effectively commit suicide, an act reprimanded in Islam, so that Esmaʿil may live longer. Esmaʿil's Amen or expression of approval of Najm's bargain triggers the passing of life from Najm to Esmaʿil. It seems as though, to the devout subjects of Esmaʿil, God automatically validates the Shah's wishes, irrespective of their degree of compatibility or incompatibility with religious edicts. It could even be argued that, in the eyes of the narrator, Esmaʿil's affirmation was equivalent to that of God, raising the status and supernatural powers of the Shah way above that of worldly human beings. This report exemplifies the extremist accounts of Esmaʿil's so-called special power, dangerously approaching the notion that, as a mortal, his will was almost the same as that of God.

ESMAʿIL'S CORRESPONDENCE WITH IMAM ʿALI

Other than dreams and voices guiding Esmaʿil throughout his campaigns, there is a report on his ability to contact Imam ʿAli through petitioning him in writing. During a three-day pilgrimage to Imam Reza's shrine in Mashhad, Esmaʿil decides to push ahead immediately and engage Shahi Beyg. The outcome of this campaign and the defeat and death of Shahi Beyg at the hands of Shah Esmaʿil has already been discussed. Hearing about the Shah's decision to engage Shahi Beyg, the various Qezelbash tribes constituting Esmaʿil's army confer and plead with the Shah to delay his campaign so that the soldiers and the horses may rest and provisions could be prepared and stored to launch an effective attack. Esmaʿil finds their suggestions reasonable and rational, yet he argues that he needs to consult with Imam ʿAli, his master, without whose permission he would not drink a sip of water.[34] The tribes welcome his initiative. Esmaʿil writes a petition, questioning Imam ʿAli on whether he should proceed immediately

[33] Ibid., p. 305.   [34] Ibid., p. 292.

with the military campaign against Shahi Beyg or wait until a later date. The letter is placed in Imam Reza's shrine overnight with the two doors to it locked, secured and sealed. Guards are placed at the doors barring people from approaching the shrine and thereby making the letter inaccessible to any worldly beings.[35] As soon as dawn breaks, Esmaʿil enters the shrine in the hope of having received his response and takes possession of his own petition. On the petition, he finds a comment written in green. The one line statement reads, "Victory and triumph will be yours".[36] As soon as the Qezelbash see the Imam's written response to Esmaʿil, they fall on their knees and begin to weep. Gratified and delighted with Imam ʿAli's response, which simply confirmed Esmaʿil's original plan, the Qezelbash ask Esmaʿil for forgiveness and inform the Shah that they have come to realize that they were in no position to question his decision or interfere with the Perfect Guide's will.[37]

This report adds more variety to the mediums of communication between Shah Esmaʿil and Imam ʿAli. According to this report, Esmaʿil is capable of corresponding from the material world of mortals with the spiritual hidden world of the imams. In the minds of those who reported this story, the comment on Esmaʿil's petition seems to be proof of the fact that Imam ʿAli descended from the hidden world exclusively to resolve Esmaʿil's military dilemma and guide him. Furthermore, Imam ʿAli wrote to him in green, the colour popularly ascribed to the Shiʿi and a language understandable to Esmaʿil. There is also another aspect to this report. The episode intends to convince Esmaʿil's subjects that their Shah is truly an exceptional, sacred and superhuman being whose will and command should not be questioned as it is that of the Imam. In this report, Esmaʿil is presented as an irreproachable guide who cannot err, as on every sensitive issue, the imams would come to his aid. Esmaʿil's political authority and legitimacy is deeply imbedded in his special status as a very close friend of Imam ʿAli.

A PHANTASMICAL ACCOUNT OF ESMAʿIL'S RITE OF PASSAGE

There is a phantasmical "eye-witness" account of an esoteric ceremony in which Esmaʿil is groomed to lead the Shiʿi revolution, recounted by a dervish who starts off in Constantinople and is on his way to Mecca on pilgrimage. Dadeh Mohammad, the clairvoyant guide of the dervish,

---

[35] Ibid.   [36] Ibid.   [37] Ibid., p. 293.

foretells what awaits him on his journey. The dervish is told that, after Mecca, he will decide to go to Karbala and Najaf on pilgrimage and from there he will go on to Tabriz. As he enters Tabriz, he will witness the coronation of a new young Shah from the lineage of the pure and virtuous, who has led the Shi'i revolt. The dervish is instructed to convey the greetings of Dadeh Mohammad to the Shah and to present him with a black-and-white feather, which the Shah should wear on his crown, and a bell, which he should fasten around his horse's neck.[38] The follower of Dadeh Mohammad takes the two items entrusted to him and sets on his voyage.

On the second leg of his trip, as his caravan leaves Medina heading towards Baghdad, the dervish falls behind and suddenly realizes that he is lost in the desert. For three days, the dervish is stranded under the burning heat of the desert sun without water or provisions. By high noon of the fourth day, when fatigue overcomes him and he gives up all hope, surrendering himself to the idea of death, he sees a young Arab horseman. As the young man grips the dervish's hand to lift him on to his horse, the dervish suddenly feels his drained spirit, energy and stamina replenished. From the moment their hands clasp, it seems as though the dervish can access different dimensions of time and reality. The dervish retains the memory of his earthly and mundane life as he enters into a magical parallel world, with elements of what humans would imagine to be of the hidden world.

As the horsemen reach the top of a mound, below him the dervish observes an endless green space of flowers and tulips with gold-woven and silk tents interspersed. Perplexed by the existence of such an unusual place in the midst of the barren Najd, the dervish inquires about the geographical location of the lush green space spread out before them.[39] The young Arab informs the dervish that the "Shah" wished to see him and promises that he would soon get answers to all his questions. After the dervish rides through the magnanimous encampment, he enters a beautiful, almost ethereal building. In the palace, he notices a young masked man occupying a majestic throne. The masked "Shah", encircled by his military leaders, bids the dervish to help himself to food and drink, the kind of which the dervish had never tasted before.

Once everyone has eaten, the dervish notices a few men accompanying a fourteen-year-old boy into the building.[40] The boy is fair, with red hair and hazel-coloured eyes. The "Shah" addresses the young boy and says, "Esma'il, the time has come for you to lead the Shi'i revolt (*khoruj koni*)".

---

[38] Ibid., p. 45.   [39] Ibid., p. 46.   [40] Ibid.

The "Shah" calls forth the boy, takes him by his hip and raises him off the ground thrice. He then ties Esma'il's belt with his own hands, places the crown on Esma'il's head and removes Esma'il's dagger, replacing it with a special sword. The masked "Shah" throws Esma'il's old dagger in front of the dervish and instructs him to take it and hand it, along with the black-and-white feather and the bell, to the man in Tabriz about whom Dadeh Mohammad has spoken to him. At this point, the past earthly experience of the dervish enmeshes with his present encounter in an otherwordly dimension, and also with a future occurrence that will happen in the material world. Here, the parallel worlds meet.

The "Shah" then recites the first Surah of the Qur'an and gives his blessings to Esma'il's mission.[41] After Esma'il departs with the few companions that he had entered, the masked man turns to the dervish, gives him his blessings and instructs the young Arab to take him back to his caravan. As the two horsemen approach the dervish's caravan, the dervish pleads with the young Arab to disclose the identity of that majestic master of the palace (the masked man) and the young boy. The young Arab responds that the first was, of course, *Saheb al-Zaman*, or the Twelfth Imam, and the young boy was the future Shah Esma'il.[42]

This report has a double significance. First, it insinuates through the vision of a dervish that the Twelfth Imam personally furnishes Esma'il with his belt, sword and crown, conveying the message that Shah Esma'il was a special appointee of the Twelfth Imam, obeying his orders and acting according to his authority and designs. Making a case for a "special and privileged relation" between Esma'il and the Twelfth Imam in effect obliges the common folk to obey Shah Esma'il who is portrayed as chosen, irreproachable and a saint. Esma'il's coronation is claimed to be approved of and enacted by the Hidden Imam in the hidden world, before his actual coronation in this material world. This unusual condition is presented as proof of the fact that Shah Esma'il cannot be a normal human being. The story of the dervish's odyssey is a witness to this truth. These supernatural accounts propagated and popularized the notion that Shah Esma'il was truly an instrument or medium of Imam 'Ali, the Twelfth Imam, and invariably God, preordained to realize their will and wish on earth. Due to the superstitious connections devised for him, Esma'il was presented as a divinely designated and ordained person, faultless in his decisions and acts.

The second and probably more significant message of this report may be that the Twelfth Imam's preparation of Esma'il for his special mission of

[41] Ibid., p. 47.   [42] Ibid.

establishing a Shi'i empire puts into motion the long-awaited process of Esma'il, the chosen one, paving the way for the Twelfth Imam's own reappearance. Once Esma'il's historical rise to power is presented as the design of the hidden world and subsequently passed off as the first hallowed happening in a domino chain of events that will bring back the promised Mahdi, then the common thread that weaves through all the superstitious accounts involving Shah Esma'il becomes clear. If this hypothesis is accepted, then Esma'il's historical and religious position becomes evident. Shah Esma'il is made out to be the one who is destined to work towards and put into motion the return of the Twelfth Imam. The Twelfth Imam confers this responsibility upon Esma'il when he personally fastens his belt, hands him his sword and crowns him in a different dimension of time and reality. According to this scenario, Esma'il is the divinely designated agent that will begin preparing the conditions for the return of the Twelfth Imam. If it is assumed that Shi'ism has been historically denied its right of propagating itself and establishing its just rule, Esma'il is groomed by this report as the special envoy of the Twelfth Imam. Esma'il needs to be protected by all twelve of the imams, as certain reports allude to, since he is destined to continue their quest and fulfil the long unfulfilled mission and promise of spreading Shi'ism on earth. The constantly evoked allusion by the reporters of accounts pertaining to the interrelation between the hidden world and the material world becomes less enigmatic if the propagation of these stories is seen as part of an attempt to convince and prepare the Shi'i that Esma'il's reign is in effect the prelude to the coming of the Mahdi.

Based on the reports that sketch Esma'il's supernatural profile, it seems as though once the Twelfth Imam prepares and sets Esma'il off on his sacred mission, he leaves the scene of interaction with Esma'il to Imam 'Ali. According to biographers and hagiographers of Shah Esma'il, it seems as if the hidden world places the responsibility of guiding and protecting the Shah on 'Ali, the First Imam, the truly popular archetype and symbol of virtue to the Shi'i. Esma'il's initiation, as depicted in the dervish's fictional account along with the other reports reviewed, demonstrate that, for his devout followers, Esma'il's legitimacy, authority and politico-religious mission had the seal of approval of the Twelfth Imam and were continuously reconfirmed by Imam 'Ali. The coronation ceremony in the dervish's account clearly demonstrates that the rise to power of Esma'il was not accidental but that it was an intricate part of an elaborate grand design to realize and expedite the return of the Mahdi. Subsequently, since the mission was blessed by the Imams, theoretically there could be no room

left for mishaps or errors in Esma'il's quest for victory, eventually leading
to the return of the Twelfth Imam.

CRISIS OF EXTREMISM: WHEN THE HIDDEN WORLD
WITHDRAWS ITS SUPPORT

Having concocted an impeccable dossier demonstrating the supernatural
qualities of Shah Esma'il, his historical defeat at Chalderan in 1514 by the
Sunni Soltan Salim created something of a confidence crisis. The defeat
rendered the veracity of Esma'il's connections with the hidden world and
Divine support for him and his cause suspect. The reports of Shah Esma'il's
military successes and triumphs before his defeat at Chalderan were
always provided as proof of his status as a sacred man with a sacred
mission. By attributing Esma'il's impressive military feats to the intervention of imams, the popular case was easily made that Esma'il's designs were
automatically approved by God and the imams. The hidden world's
unconditional support for Esma'il was presented as the reason for his
success in fulfilling his mission of spreading Shi'ism. At Chalderan, the
so-called harmonious co-operation between the hidden world and Esma'il
breaks down. Esma'il's usual expectation that the imams would eventually
come to his aid in the form of a sandstorm is not fulfilled.[43] Chalderan is a
significant historical moment when miracles dry up.

The psychological impact of this event on Esma'il is very powerful. The
Shah realizes that Chalderan signifies the imams' withdrawal of their
support from his cause. The imams abandoning Esma'il also meant the
loss of his supernatural powers obtained through his close contact with
them. For those who believed that Esma'il had a mission blessed by the
imams, Chalderan represented a temporary setback to the grand scheme of
paving the road for the reappearance of the Hidden Imam. At the end of
the Chalderan war, Shah Esma'il informs his soldiers that he is certain that
he will not be able to accomplish anything more, since the imams desisted
from coming to his help.[44]

It seems as though, around the time of his defeat, a good number of
hypotheses were put forward trying to explain why Shah Esma'il was
defeated by Soltan Salim. The first explanation is that Shah Esma'il
had grown too proud and arrogant, and therefore, when his military
commanders cautioned him against confronting Soltan Salim, he lashed
out saying, "If he is a man he should come and I will engage him in such a

---

[43] Ibid., p. 490.   [44] Ibid., p. 494.

battle that would become an example to the whole wide world".[45] It is
reported that Shah Esmaʿil had grown so haughty and lofty that he did not
use the customary expression of *ensha'allah* or "God willing". The second
explanation is based on the notion that the Qezelbash, Esmaʿil's devout
soldiers, were on the verge of being led astray and becoming heretics, as
they would refer to Shah Esmaʿil as Imam ʿAli. The Qezelbash argued that
Shah Esmaʿil was no other than Imam ʿAli, since Esmaʿil had never been
defeated or injured in war.[46] The third argument is based on Soltan Salim's
deep sense of anger and revenge in reaction to Esmaʿil's past anti-Sunni
acts. It is reported that when Esmaʿil captured Baghdad, intent on demonstrating his extremist Shiʿi leanings, he dug out the remains of Abu Hanifa,
the founder of the Hanafi Sunni sect, burned it and buried a dog in its
place.[47] Here, we are not concerned with the fact of what remained of Abu
Hanifa's corpse, since he had passed away in the second half of the eighth
century. Esmaʿil's act of desecration sparked such a sense of vindictiveness
in Soltan Salim that his burning drive to punish Esmaʿil became a pressing
religious obligation and question of honour for the Ottoman Soltan.

For whatever conceivable reason, real or imagined, the so-called sacred
covenant and alliance between Esmaʿil and the imams broke down.
Nowhere in the book where these accounts have been reported from,
ʿAlam Aray-e Safavi, do we find a thorough explanation of why the tides
changed so abruptly and why the chosen one fell so quickly from grace.
After Chalderan, those who firmly believed in the supernatural status and
religious mission of Esmaʿil must have contented themselves with inexplicable and predetermined reasons rooted, in their minds, in the works of the
hidden world. Even though Chalderan should have undermined, if not
undone, the sanctification of Esmaʿil, the myth of the blessed and imam-
like Shah and his glorification continued.

After Chalderan, once the connection and cooperation between the
spiritual and material world is severed and Esmaʿil falls from grace, one
would not expect reporters or storytellers to return to the topic of Imam
ʿAli re-establishing contact with him. There is, however, another report
about Imam ʿAli's apparitions in Esmaʿil's dreams. Those who appreciated
the exaggerated status of Shah Esmaʿil probably wished to keep his supernatural memory alive in the minds of the Shiʿi. This post-Chalderan report
is probably intended to salvage and keep alive the myth of Esmaʿil as
the sacred agent of the imams. It is reported that, having defeated Shah
Esmaʿil at Chalderan, Soltan Salim continued his offensive, attacking and

---

[45] Ibid., p. 477.   [46] Ibid., p. 492.   [47] Ibid., p. 477.

destroying the fortresses in league with Shah Esma'il. One such fortress was the Varsaq Fortress.

According to a post-Chalderan report, one night in his sleep, Esma'il receives a visitation from Imam 'Ali, who appears once again as a "pure light" in his dream and warns him that the Varsaq Fortress is on the verge of occupation, and, if he does not reach the fortress on time, all its inhabitants will be massacred.[48] In this dream, contrary to the previous ones, Imam 'Ali does not present a detailed plan of action nor does he reveal to Esma'il any unknown information that may be useful for the success of his campaign. In this report, Imam 'Ali seems to be taking some distance from Esma'il as he does not refer to him as "our son". Yet by referring to an apparition, the reporter wishes to demonstrate some sort of continuity in Esma'il's glorified and sacred relation with the hidden world, which somewhat lies at the heart of Shi'i extremism.

In spite of Shah Esma'il's defeat at Chalderan, his dynasty continued for another 200 years. The supernatural aura created around Esma'il, which he inherited from his father and grandfather, was passed on to his progeny. The idea that a Safavi Shah is an instrument of Shi'i imams, protected and guided by the hidden world to pave the way for the reappearance of the Hidden Imam, became a generally accepted notion. Based upon their need for popular support and legitimacy, as well as their personality, Safavi Shahs used or abused this concocted "politico-religious gift" to varying degrees. In view of the unIslamic behaviour and military failures of the Safavi Shahs, the popular notion of their privileged status with the hidden world became, at best, suspect. The popularization of the belief that Safavi rule was destined to continue until the reappearance of the Twelfth Imam, popularized by Mohammad-Baqer Majlesi, re-legitimized the rule of the Safavi Shahs. According to this manipulation of religious beliefs in the service of political power, in spite of their moral and religious flaws, the Safavi Shahs were assigned a grand historical mission. They were to prepare the conditions for the return of the Hidden Imam, eventually empowering the Shi'i and rendering Shi'i justice to the world.[49]

---

[48] Ibid., p. 510.
[49] M. B. Majlesi, *Haq al-Yaqin*, p. 2; M. H. Asef, *Rostam al-Tavarikh* (Tehran, 1352), p. 98.

PART TWO

POPULAR SHI'ISM

Majlesism

4

Milieu, Childhood, Sanctity and Fame

Mohammad-Baqer Majlesi was born in 1037/1627, about two years before the death of Shah 'Abbas I and four years after Mohammad-Amin Astarabadi passed away. Each of these highly influential personalities in their respective domains impacted Mohammad-Baqer. Mohammad-Amin Astarabadi, the founder of the *hadith*-based Akhbari School, privileged Shi'i reports and discarded the use and application of reason in religious arguments and deductions. His static school of thought that had a long-lasting influence on most clerics of Mohammad-Baqer's generation was highly averse to providing Shi'i jurists with any latitude to provide a different and fresh reading and analysis of the basic Shi'i texts.

Shah 'Abbas's military successes, diplomatic acumen and administrative know-how had united the country and raised Iran to the status of a powerful and respectable regional and international power. Yet Shah 'Abbas's religious behaviour was somewhat different from his predecessors. He shared with them the commitment to the propagation and support of the Shi'i faith and humbly referred to himself as the "dog of 'Ali". Yet he was also known for his hospitality and tolerance towards the religious minorities in Iran. The Shah considered himself the father and protector of the Christian Armenians and attended their religious festivities. He was committed to ensuring the well-being, as well as the religious rights, of minorities, including the Jews, and acted as a shield against those clerics who were anxious about the scope and activities of the non-Shi'i in Iran. Shah 'Abbas had also considerably reduced the influence of the clerical institution in the realm of government and political decision making. During the reign of Shah 'Abbas, the political influence of the clergy was on the wane. Mohammad-Baqer Majlesi inherited a rather mutable and fluctuating society in which greater religious tolerance and empathy towards Jews, Zoroastrians and different kinds of Christians, especially Armenians, was being institutionalized by Shah 'Abbas, while concomitantly the more dogmatic Akhbari school of Astarabadi was taking roots among the disenfranchised clergy.

Mohammad-Baqer was born into a clerical family, which migrated from the Jebal al-Amel region in Lebanon.[1] Mohammad-Taqi, his father, also known as Majlesi-e Aval (the first Majlesi), was named after the ninth Shi'i Imam and had in turn named his son after the fifth Imam. At the time, little did Mohammad-Taqi know how zealously and systematically his son Mohammad-Baqer would seek to systematize, reconstruct, reshape and promote what he believed to be the religious legacy and tradition of Imam Mohammad-Baqer.

Mohammad-Baqer's grandfather was Molla 'Ali, sometimes referred to as Molla Maqsud 'Ali. The story of how Molla 'Ali came to adopt the curious title of "Majlesi" remains enigmatic. Molla 'Ali is said to have recited his own poetry at gatherings and subsequently adopted the literary pseudonym of "Majlesi", meaning a person present at or animating social gatherings.[2] According to another account, Molla 'Ali was in charge of organizing some of Shah 'Abbas's social gatherings or banquets. In these functions, he is said to have narrated stories and told tales to entertain the Shah.[3] It has also been suggested that Molla 'Ali was called Majlesi because he organized mystical and gnostic gatherings for Safavi Kings.[4] Finally, it has been suggested that it was Shah Tahmasb, the pious Safavi King, who gave him the title. Irrespective of the origin of Molla 'Ali's title, he seems to have been more renowned for his social skills, conviviality, storytelling and poetry reading at royal gatherings and banquets than for his religious knowledge.

Molla 'Ali's son, Mohammad-Taqi, seems to have had little in common with his father, except perhaps his Sufi tendencies. According to Mohammad-Taqi Majlesi, he became interested and highly knowledgeable in religious studies very early in his life. In a self-biography, Mohammad-Taqi presents himself as a child prodigy whom, at the age of four, in addition to performing his regular prayers was familiar with the concepts of God, heaven and hell. It is intimated that from that very early

[1] M. B. Khonsari-Esfahani, *Rowzat al-Jennat*, vol. 2 (Tehran, 2535), p. 317.
[2] A. Davani, *Mafakher-e Eslam* (Tehran, 1375), p. 42.
[3] M. Mahdavi, *Zendeghinameh 'Allameh Majlesi*, vol. 1 (Tehran, 1378), p. 74.
[4] Ibid., p. 74.

age, Mohammad-Taqi taught the Qur'an and the Shi'i reports of the Prophet to children.[5]

Even though it is reported that, around the time of Shah Safi's ascension to the throne (1629), Mohammad-Taqi was hardly known as a leading clerical figure, he soon became the first regular Friday Prayer leader at two of the most prominent mosques in Esfahan.[6] It must have been during the last years of Shah Safi's reign or the beginning of Shah 'Abbas II's reign – in the 1640s – that Mohammad-Taqi was appointed to the highly prestigious religious position of Esfahan's Friday Prayer leader.[7] During the reign of Shah 'Abbas II (1642–1666), Mohammad-Taqi is considered as a well-established and highly respected cleric who holds official religious positions and teaches at Esfahan's prestigious Seminary School.[8] It is at this time that the Shah commissions Mohammad-Taqi to translate his Arabic commentary on Ebn Babawayh's book of reports, *Man la Yahzarah al-Faqih*, into Farsi.[9] As a token of his gratitude and loyalty, Mohammad-Taqi dedicates this work to Shah 'Abbas II.[10]

Mohammad-Taqi's treatise, called "Rulings on non-Muslim citizens of the Islamic Community", demonstrates the cleric's exclusivist backlash to Shah 'Abbas I's attempt at institutionalizing tolerance towards religious minorities in Iran. Non-Muslims of the Book or the *ahl-e zemmeh* refer to Jews, Christians and Zoroastrians. Based on a report attributed to Imam Ja'far Sadeq, Mohammad-Taqi argues that even though the Prophet provided non-Muslims with refuge and protection, they were no longer worthy of such protection, since their initial sheltering was conditional upon the fact that they would not raise their children as non-Muslims.[11] Mohammad-Taqi maintains that non-Muslims are prohibited from encouraging their own children to follow their own religion. He expects non-Muslims to raise their children as good Muslims. According to Mohammad-Taqi, non-Muslims are forbidden to propagate their religion among Muslims or build churches, synagogues or fire temples. In stark contrast to Shah 'Abbas I, who built churches in Iran and allowed

---

[5] Ibid., p. 82.
[6] M. Sefatgol, *Sakhtar va Andisheh Dini dar Iran asr Safavi*, p. 216; M.B. Khonsari-Esfahani, *Rowzat al-Jennat*, vol. 2, p. 324.
[7] It has been suggested that it was probably Shah 'Abbas II, who appointed Mohammad-Taqi to the position of the imam, leading the Friday Congregational Prayers in Esfahan. A. Davani, *Mafakher-e Eslam*, p. 233.
[8] S.H. Mirkhandan, *Mohammad-Taqi Majlesi bar Sahel Hadith* (Tehran, 1374), p. 55–56.
[9] Ibid., p. 108; M. Sefatgol, *Sakhtar va Andisheh Dini dar Iran asr Safavi*, p. 217.
[10] M. Sefatgol, *Sakhtar va Andisheh Dini dar Iran asr Safavi*, p. 217.
[11] Ibid., pp. 556–557.

Christian missionaries to pursue their religious activities, Mohammad-Taqi believed that if non-Muslims built their places of worship, it was incumbent on the rulers to destroy such places of worship or convert them into mosques.[12]

Mohammad-Taqi's religious writings and positions indicate a marked inflexibility and a persistent sense of religious over-zealousness towards almost all topics, including the treatment of non-Muslims. Intent on rolling back Shah 'Abbas I's policy of religious openness, Mohammad-Taqi's discourse aimed at radically narrowing and reducing the freedoms of non-Muslims. In response to rumours about a Christian in Esfahan propagating his religion and proselytizing, Mohammad-Taqi enquires why such a "damned person" has not yet been killed and opines that his slaying is a religious obligation (*vajeb al-qatl*). Having proclaimed a religious opinion, which has the weight of a legal death sentence, Mohammad-Taqi proposes ways to keep the non-Muslims separated from Muslims in order to minimize their interaction and subsequently "the danger" of Muslims becoming exposed to non-Muslim religious ideas. He suggests that non-Muslims should be differentiated and segregated from Muslims. Mohammad-Taqi rules that non-Muslims should be forbidden to ride on horses or saddled animals and should only be allowed to ride on donkeys. He maintains that they should be prohibited from leaving their homes during rainy days, as they would walk around in the markets and sully Muslims.[13] Mohammad-Taqi further calls on non-Muslims not to look or peep at the homes of Muslims, not to become business partners with Muslims, not to employ Muslims as servants or workers and not to dress like Muslims. To distinguish between Muslims and non-Muslims, he suggests that non-Muslim women should wear different coloured shoes on each foot: he recommends that they should either wear a red or yellow shoe on one foot and a shoe of another colour on the other foot. Mohammad-Taqi even proposes that while receiving the *jazyeh* or the obligatory head tax from non-Muslims, Muslims should mistreat and humiliate them by slapping them across the face.[14]

Mohammad-Taqi Majlesi is credited for spreading the reports of Shi'i imams throughout the land and enlightening many through his teachings and writings.[15] To reach the common folk incapable of reading Arabic, Mohammad-Taqi is one of the first scholars writing Shi'i books in Farsi.[16]

---

[12] Ibid., p. 557.   [13] Ibid., p. 558.   [14] Ibid., pp. 558–559.
[15] M. B. Khonsari-Esfahani, *Rowzat al-Jennat*, vol. 2, p. 322.
[16] S. H. Mirkhandan, *Mohammad-Taqi Majlesi bar Sahel Hadith*, p. 109.

These books are essentially Farsi translations of Shi'i reports, for which Mohammad-Taqi had a special admiration.[17] It is said that he refused to accept the text of the Qur'an as an independently sufficient legal proof. He argued that if the apparent text of the Qur'an could not be corroborated by a report, it would be most prudent to desist from acting according to the Qur'anic text.[18] Such a radical position places Mohammad-Taqi among those extremist *akhbari* traditionists who effectively considered the authority of the Qur'anic texts as contingent upon its validation by the reports attributed to the Shi'i Imams.

MOHAMMAD-BAQER MAJLESI'S EARLY YEARS

Mohammad-Baqer Majlesi's initial career advances in Safavi Persia may not have been so easily achieved had he not enjoyed the head start of being Mohammad-Taqi Majlesi's son. Mohammad-Baqer's entrance on the religious, social and ultimately political scene of late Safavi Iran may be partially explained in the context of his father's reputation, connections, influence and legacy. The exaggerated accounts and myths that circulated at the time about Mohammad-Taqi's superhuman attributes, his exalted religious and spiritual status and his official religious position effectively placed him in a saintlike religio-political category superior to ordinary humans. The tradition of hereditary official religious positions, very similar to the system of a hereditary monarchy, assured that sons of trusted, tested and loyal clerical luminaries be groomed to serve the kings of the same dynasty.

Little is known about Mohammad-Baqer's childhood, youth and the specifics of his education. According to Mohammad-Taqi Majlesi, Mohammad-Baqer had studied extensively with him and under his supervision. Mohammad-Baqer is said to have learned his "rational and traditional sciences, especially the Prophet's reports and traditions along with their meanings" under his father's patronage.[19] In his writings, Mohammad-Baqer confirms this fact and identifies his father as his single veritable teacher, especially in the traditional sciences, concerned with the study of reports.[20]

During the last years of his life, Mohammad-Taqi issued his son a permit or certificate (*ejazeh*), allowing him to report the Prophetic Traditions that

---

[17] M. B. Khonsari-Esfahani, *Rowzat al-Jennat*, vol. 2, pp. 317, 319.   [18] Ibid., p. 319.
[19] A. Davani, *Mafakher-e Eslam*, p. 91.
[20] H. Taremi, *'Allameh Majlesi* (Tehran, 1375), p. 12.

Mohammad-Baqer had heard and learnt from him.[21] The recipient of a permit to refer to and report Traditions is not required to have studied a specific amount of time or any time at all with the person issuing the certificate. The permit is rather an attestation or confirmation of the knowledge of the recipient, in various aspects of Shi'i jurisprudence. In the tradition of Shi'i education, this important rite of passage meant that Mohammad-Baqer as a knowledgeable authority and repository of reports could subsequently transmit reports. Mohammad-Baqer is said to have received between eighteen and twenty-one permits from different Islamic scholars of his times.[22]

A survey of those who confirmed Mohammad-Baqer's authority as a learned scholar of reports sheds some light on the importance of three factors in the promotion and legitimization of clerics in the Safavi religious establishment of Mohammad-Baqer's time. First, family networks and relations play an important role in the development of Mohammad-Baqer's career. In addition to his father conferring upon him the permission to transmit reports, two of Mohammad-Baqer's other permits are also issued by his brothers-in-law, Molla Mohammad-Saleh Mazandarani and Molla Mirza Shiravani.[23] In one of his later writings, Mohammad-Baqer acknowledges that, during his childhood, he had obtained a similar permit or certificate from Sheykh 'Abdollah ebn-Jaber Ameli, a relative of his father.[24] Second, the clergy engage in a process of issuing reciprocal permits to one another. This mutually beneficial and self-serving system of acknowledgment promotes a sense of cooperation based on reciprocity. Seyyed 'Alikhan Shirazi and Sheykh Horr-e Amoli issued permits for Mohammad-Baqer and were themselves the recipients of permits from Mohammad-Baqer.[25] The issuance of such reciprocal permits among jurists of similar rank and status also served the purpose of adding numerical strength and credibility to the group of reporters of a Tradition and thereby buttressing the authority of the tradition cited based on a multitude of transmitters. The third factor that plays an interesting role in the promotion process of clerics, as well as their future cooperation and bonding, is that of their common and shared religious outlook and tendency. A common Shi'i position or discourse over controversial issues leads to the development of religious, as well as political, affinities and ties.

---

[21] A. Davani, *Mafakher-e Eslam*, pp. 91, 94.   [22] Ibid., p. 90.

[23] Ibid., pp. 110–111.

[24] H. Taremi, '*Allameh Majlesi*, p. 12; A. Davani, *Mafakher-e Eslam*, pp. 122–123.

[25] A. Davani, *Mafakher-e Eslam*, p. 151.

Among the scholars who helped Mohammad-Baqer join the ranks of prominent Shiʿi transmitters by granting him permits were like-minded members and proponents of the report-based Akhbari School. These Akhbari scholars, emphasizing the seminal and essential role of reports and traditions in Islamic theory and practice, were disciples of Amin Astarabadi, whose book, *Favaed Madineh*, written in Mecca, had a deep impact on Iranian religious scholars once it arrived in Iran. Astarabadi's book, completed in the first months of 1622, appeared some five years before Mohammad-Baqer Majlesi's birth. One of the most influential of this group, Molla Mohsen Fayz-e Kashani, is famous for his dogmatic Akhbari insistence on the primacy of traditions and his opposition to the *mojtaheddin*, who applied their reasoning in the deduction of Islamic laws. Another prominent Akhbari figure among those who issued a permit for Mohammad-Baqer is Seyyed Mirza Jazayeri. In a debate at the Grand Mosque of Shiraz, Jazayeri had argued that even the proper comprehension of the famous line "say that there is but one God" is in need of reports.[26] A third member of this group, Horr-e Amoli, who had issued a permit to Mohammad-Baqer and had also received a permit from him, was a highly prominent and reputable report compiler, well known for his Akhbari and anti-Sufi stance.[27]

Certain members of this close group of scholars who shared a common Shiʿi perspective and actively assisted in the promotion of one another impacted the history of Iranian Shiʿism in two significant ways. First, four of them, known as the "later four Mohammads" – Mohammad Faiz-Kashani (Mohsen), Mohammad Mirza Jazayeri, Mohammad Horr-e Amoli and Mohammad-Baqer Majlesi – produced four highly revered and popular compilations of reports or *ahadith*. These four texts are known as the "Later Quartet Books" – to be distinguished from the "Earlier Quartet Books". These texts, especially Majlesi's, have had a long-lasting influence on Iranian Shiʿism. Second, during the reign of Shah Soleyman, certain members of this close circle of scholars attained sensitive religio-political positions. Mohammad-Baqer Majlesi became the *sheykholeslam* of Esfahan, and Horr-e Amoli became the *sheykholeslam* of Mashhad. Another Akhbari, Mohammad-Taher Qomi, who had also given a permit to Mohammad-Baqer Majlesi, became the *sheykholeslam* of Qom. These three men came to constitute a powerful religio-political triad. Sefatgol has cautiously suggested that at no other period in the Safavi dynasty

---

[26] Ibid., p. 140.   [27] M. Tonokaboni, *Qesas al-ʿOlama* (Tehran, n.d.), pp. 289, 293.

was the presence of such powerful *sheykholeslam*s so perceptible.[28] Only Mohammad-Baqer Majlesi and Horr-e Amoli, who had also incidentally issued permissions for one another, were members of both the religiously influential circle of report compilers and the politically powerful triad of *sheykholeslam*s.

SCHOLAR AND TEACHER

Mohammad-Baqer became widely recognized as a learned and knowl-edgeable scholar before his father's death.[29] Mohammad-Taqi passed away in 1660. At this time, Mohammad-Baqer was thirty-three and he was already a well-established cleric. The act of issuing a religious permit to another person to transmit reports presumes an advanced scholarly knowledge on the part of the person granting the certificate. Since the first certificates issued by Mohammad-Baqer date back to 1654, it follows that he was already giving some sort of "terminal degrees" at the age of twenty-seven.[30] This also implies that Mohammad-Baqer must have started teaching sometime before the age of twenty-seven. It has been suggested that from 1660 until the end of his life, Mohammad-Baqer Majlesi's classes constituted the most authoritative and learned scholarly circle in Esfahan.[31]

Seyyed Ne'matollah Jazayeri, one of Mohammad-Baqer Majlesi's star students and later his close collaborator, throws considerable light on Mohammad-Baqer's life and his activities. Jazayeri must have first met Majlesi when the latter was thirty-four.[32] Based on Jazayeri's testimony, by the mid 1660s, Majlesi, who was in his mid-thirties, was already more than an established scholar and jurist. He taught *hadith* to some 1,000 students, some of whom, including Jazayeri, received a regular monthly salary from Majlesi.[33] These students who subse-quently spread across the land, managing the religious affairs of the people, constituted important propagators and representatives of the Majlesi discourse.[34]

---

[28] M. Sefatgol, *Sakhtar va Andisheh Dini dar Iran asr Safavi*, p. 452.
[29] H. Taremi, *'Allameh Majlesi*, p. 12.   [30] A. Davani, *Mafakher-e Eslam*, p. 360.
[31] H. Taremi, *'Allameh Majlesi*, p. 133.
[32] A. Davani, *Mafakher-e Eslam*, p. 476.   [33] Ibid., pp. 390, 474.
[34] N. Ansari Qomi, 'Sharh Zendegiye 'Allameh Kabir Mohammad Baqer Majlesi' in M. Mohrizi and H. Rabbani (eds.), *Shenakhtnameh 'Allameh Majlesi*, vol. 1 (Tehran, 1378), p. 79.

It is reported that during one of his classes on the rational sciences, while Majlesi was lecturing on the materialist (*dahry*) school and explaining their arguments, one of his students interjected that the materialist school was a "rightful faith" and rose to leave his class. Majlesi beseeched his student to sit and hear the counter-arguments to the materialist position. His rebellious student retorted that the materialist school was upright and that there were no possible counter-arguments. It is maintained that after this incident, Majlesi stopped his classes on dialectical or speculative theology (*kalam*) and philosophy (*hekmat*).[35] This incident may provide one explanation for Majlesi's strong dislike for reasoning and his conviction that the common folk were unfit to use their rational capacities.

MAJLESI'S RESEARCH CENTRE AND ITS PRODUCTS

Jazyeri's account of his collaboration with Majlesi on *Bahar al-Anvar* (Sea of Lights), Majlesi's magnum opus suggests that Majlesi had already collected the majority of the texts he needed as his primary sources and had therefore assembled the library that was necessary for the realization of his project. Some of Majlesi's references were rare and great pain and costs were incurred to obtain them from faraway lands. By the end of the third/ninth century, some 4,000–6,000 compilations or notebooks of reports each known as an *asl*, or source/base attributed to Shi'i imams had been written. The reports attributed to the imams cited in these compilations were often in contradiction with one another. It is even suggested that the imams intentionally propagated contradictory reports so that the uniformity of the reports would not come to be identified with one particular faith, posing a threat to Shi'ites.[36] Due to the accumulation of contradictory and fabricated reports, Shi'i scholars embarked on an expurgating campaign. Close to the occultation of the Twelfth Imam, 400 well-established *hadith* compilations were agreed upon as acceptable due to either the report that the imams had seen, verified and corrected them or because they were written by trusted and reputable writers.[37] From these classical texts, Majlesi is said to have assembled 200 and used the reports found in them in the compilation of *Bahar al-Anvar*.[38] Therefore *Bahar al-Anvar* is hailed as a unique and exceptional work, since it includes *all* reports (*ahadith*) found in report compilations that Majlesi could find.[39]

---

[35] M. Tonokaboni, *Qesas al-'Olama*, p. 209.   [36] Ibid., p. 210.   [37] Ibid.   [38] Ibid.
[39] M. B. Khonsari-Esfahani, *Rowzat al-Jennat*, vol. 1 (Tehran, 2535), pp. 268, 270.

In the introduction to *Bahar al-Anvar*, Majlesi informs his readers that having studied and researched the prevalent and well-known books on reports, he began searching for unknown or neglected authoritative texts.[40] These, he argued, were texts that had been disregarded due to the rule of anti-Shi'i monarchs, the prevalence of false sciences among the ignorant pretenders to knowledge or because later jurists had paid scant attention to them. Once Majlesi obtained these derelict Shi'i compilations of reports that had been abandoned by later jurists, he wrote, "when I read them carefully I realized that they had great value and merit absent in the present well-known compilations of Shi'i reports. From amongst these reports I came across the sources of many religious edicts". Majlesi first encourages his religious brothers to accept and embrace what he has compiled in *Bahar al-Anvar*; he then warns against those who fail to acknowledge the "towering status" of his work, which he believes will "render people free from consulting any other book" and finally labels the uninitiated and unappreciative as "undoubtedly ignorant, deluded and strayed".[41] Considering the fact that Majlesi is said to have largely excluded those reports that had already been propagated in *Nahj al-Balageh* and the standard compilations of Koleyni, Ebn Babawayh and Tusi, it is certainly revolutionary on his part to label as strayed those Shi'i who would not wholeheartedly embrace his new compilation.[42] To his proponents, the standard and traditional compilations of reports are a drop compared to the sea of reports in Majlesi's *Bahar al-Anvar*.[43]

The Herculean task of safely collecting and sifting through the forgotten and abandoned early Shi'i compilations, some of which were the only existing volumes, required substantial financial means and a capable and qualified team of researchers. The scale and scope of *Bahar al-Anvar* is well beyond the capacities of one man. According to one testimony, Majlesi disposed of sufficient funds to lodge Jazayeri and provide other seminary students (*tollab*) with a regular and sufficient salary to work for him. There seems to be sufficient evidence to suggest that not only was the Safavi state actively involved with Majlesi's *Bahar al-Anvar* project, but also that it provided the necessary financial support to realize Majlesi's undertaking.[44]

[40] A. Davani, 'Sharh Hale 'Allameh Majlesi' in M. Mohrezi and H. Rabbani (eds.), *Shenakht nameh 'Allameh Majlesi*, vol. 1, pp. 62–63.

[41] N. Ansari Qomi in M. Mohrezi and H. Rabbani (eds.), *Shenakht nameh 'Allameh Majlesi*, vol. 1, pp. 64–65.

[42] M. B. Khonsari-Esfahani, *Rowzat al-Jennat*, vol. 2, p. 268.   [43] Ibid., p. 270.

[44] H. Taremi, 'Allameh Majlesi*, p. 145.

According to one report, once Majlesi was informed of the existence of a volume of *Madinat al-'elm* written by Sheykh Sadduq in a Yemeni city, he conveyed the exciting news to the Safavi King. The King, who may have been Shah 'Abbas II or Shah Soleyman, is said to have dispatched an emissary with considerable gifts and offerings to the King of Yemen in the hope of securing his assistance in finding the book.[45] It is said that Majlesi sent emissaries in search of books to the "East and West".[46] Clearly, such expeditions were in need of a financial patron or sponsor. The Safavi King is said to have placed several pieces of his personal estate into an endowment, the proceeds of which were spent on the realization of the *Bahar al-Anvar* project. The wages paid to scribes also came from this fund.[47] It has been suggested that a large majority of prominent sources of imitation (*maraj'*) and learned scholars (*mojtaheds*), received a regular salary from the Safavi kings, and at times the King even ordered a residential house to be purchased for them.[48] The special attention that was given to Majlesi's project seems to have well surpassed the normal court–clergy financial relations.

Having secured the financial requirements for his project, Majlesi also solved the manpower problem of carrying out his encyclopaedic quest, which lasted forty years. The testimony of a number of his students demonstrates that Majlesi had successfully implemented an efficient recruitment system. He would select the most gifted from the very large number of his students and invite them to collaborate with him as his research associates and assistants. Seyyed Ne'matollah Jazayeri recalls that when he was studying with Majlesi, he was given the "opportunity" by being selected from more than 1,000 students to assist Majlesi in his compilation of *Bahar al-Anvar*.[49] Molla 'Abdollah Afandi (Esfahani), the author of *Riaz al-'Olama*, another student and research assistant of Majlesi, also maintained that Majlesi had 1,000 students.[50]

Majlesi's organizational method in compiling the reports in *Bahar al-Anvar* was systematic, well-organized and based on an efficient division of labour. He not only directed and coordinated the research, but also culled, classified according to subject and finally edited the work. Depending on his topic of research, say "rainfall" or "thunder", Majlesi would assign one of his students to collect the entire Qur'anic verses pertaining to that subject. Another student was set to collect all the relevant reports (*ahadith*)

[45] Ibid. [46] Ibid., p. 139. [47] Ibid., p. 145.
[48] Z. Safa, *Tarikh Adabiyat Iran*, vol. 5, part 1 (Tehran, 1363).
[49] A. Davani, *Mafakher-e Eslam*, p. 474. [50] Ibid., pp. 359, 416.

on the same subject.[51] Upon the completion of their research and once each
student had identified, compiled and copied all the verses and reports on
the assigned topic, each would leave a white sheet of paper at the bottom of
their stack of notes. The white sheet was used by Majlesi to write his
comments on the topic after having studied the appropriate verses, as
well as the relevant reports. The regular observations that appear as
commentary (*bayan*) in *Bahar al-Anvar* are Majlesi's notes scribbled on
those blank sheets of paper left by his students for him to write on. At
times, it also happened that Majlesi felt no need for a commentary and
subsequently left the paper blank.[52]

There has been some controversy over the method of compilation of
Bahar al-Anvar. Some of Majlesi's zealous proponents have rejected the
hypothesis that the work may be the result of a collective effort. They seem
to worry that such an eventuality would undermine the importance of
Majlesi's colossal contribution.[53] On the basis of his examination of three
parts (*joz'*) of the original manuscript of *Bahar al-Anvar*, Seyyed
Mohammad-Hojat Kuh-Kamareh'i has concluded that the writers are
different people with different handwritings using different pens. In most
cases, these writings are not that of Majlesi. However, the commentaries at
the bottom of the reports are predominantly in Majlesi's handwriting. Kuh-
Kamareh'i argues that, in the volume on Virtuous Behaviour (*makarem
al-akhlaq*), the commentaries are in someone else's handwriting.[54] This
observation indicates that even the commentaries were not solely the work
of Majlesi and that what is considered as Majlesi's commentaries today may
have been the works of his assistants. Kuh-Kamareh'i concludes that Majlesi
must have divided the book among his students and assigned each part to a
particular student who would be responsible for the primary research and
writing of the reports and verses. There exist other testimonies to the role of
Majlesi's students in his works.[55]

The year 1659–1660 constitutes an important threshold in
Mohammad-Baqer Majlesi's scholarly life. In this year, Majlesi finished
the task of indexing ten Shi'i books of reports. In the absence of a systematic subject arrangement of reports, Majlesi provided a single subject index
for all ten texts. Such a presentation, he believed, would make the reports

[51] This paragraph is based on M. Tonokaboni, *Qesas al-'Olama*, p. 208.
[52] M. Tonokaboni, *Qesas al-'Olama*, p. 208.
[53] A. Davani in M. Mohrizi and H. Rabbani (eds.), *Shenakhtnameh 'Allameh Majlesi*, vol. 1,
pp. 39–43.
[54] Ibid., p. 45.   [55] M. B. Khonsari-Esfahani, *Rowzat al-Jennat*, vol. 2, p. 263.

in the texts, their references and proofs accessible to readers.[56] This index, *Fehrest Mosanafat al-Ashab* or *Fehrest Mo'alefat al-Ashab* (Index of the Books by the Companions) laid the groundwork for his encyclopaedic compilation of Shiʿi reports, *Bahar al-Anvar* or the Sea of Lights.[57] This work is also referred to as the index to *Bahar al-Anvar*, even though the latter work includes many more references.[58] Having successfully completed his indexation project in 1660, Majlesi lost no time and embarked on the compilation and writing of *Bahar al-Anvar* in the same year. He spent the last forty years of his life working on this monumental project.[59] At the time of his death in 1699–1700, *Bahar al-Anvar*, the modern print of which is 110 volumes and some forty thousand pages, remained unfinished.[60]

The *Fihrist Mu'alefat al-Ashab* (Index of the Books by the Companions), a preliminary study, as well as a pilot project for *Bahar al-Anvar*, is entirely in Majlesi's handwriting.[61] Therefore, while it could be claimed that the *Fihrist Mu'alefat al-Ashab* was entirely a one-man product, the same could not be said for *Bahar al-Anvar*. While writing the *Fihrist Mu'alefat al-Ashab*, it could be argued that Majlesi did not have available to him the support system that was in place after he had finished this work. This detail is indicative of a transformation in the scholarly, as well as the social and financial, status of Majlesi. It seems as if, after the death of his father in 1660, and probably during the last six years of Shah ʿAbbas II, Majlesi obtained the religio-academic prestige and status that enabled him to recruit and employ scribes and research assistants to realize his project. The financial support of Majlesi's research centre must have been provided by Shah ʿAbbas II and subsequently continued by Shah Soleyman and Shah Soltan Hoseyn. It may be hypothesized that it was Majlesi's scholarly and religious status, the important religio-political implications of his project and his personal capabilities, in addition to his official religious positions, that paved the way for his project to receive the consistent support of Safavi kings.

[56] H. Taremi, ʿAllameh Majlesi, pp. 139–140.
[57] A. Abedi, 'Naqd Bahar al-Anvar dar Dayeratolmaʿaref Tashayoʿ in M. Mohrizi and H. Rabbani (eds.), *Shenakhtnameh ʿAllameh Majlesi*, vol. 2. p. 111; S.M. Mahdavi, *Zendeginameh ʿAllameh Majlesi*, vol. 2, p. 201.
[58] S.M. Mahdavi, *Zendeginameh ʿAllameh Majlesi*, vol. 2, pp. 298–299.
[59] A. Abedi in M. Mohrizi and H. Rabbani (eds.), *Shenakhtnameh ʿAllameh Majlesi*, vol. 2, p. 111.
[60] B. Khoramshahi, 'Bahar al-Anvar dar Dayeratolmaʿaref' in M. Mohrizi and H. Rabbani (eds.), *Shenakhtnameh ʿAllameh Majlesi*, vol. 2, p. 82.
[61] S.M. Mahdavi, *Zendeginameh ʿAllameh Majlesi*, vol. 2, p. 299.

It could be surmised that between finishing his studies sometime in his mid-twenties and finalizing his subject index of ten texts at the age of thirty-three, Majlesi had conceptualized and laid the foundations of what could be considered as a modern research centre. This centre was mandated to produce the most comprehensive encyclopaedia of Shi'i *ahadith* or reports. The ongoing research at the centre provided Majlesi with the raw materials for his key works in Farsi. During this period, Majlesi seems to have developed a clear idea of his religio-scholarly objectives, which was to have an immense and long-standing religious, social, cultural and political affect on Iranians and Iran. Whereas the most tangible fruit of his project and his research centre was the monumental encyclopaedia of Shi'i reports, *Bahar al-Anvar* in Arabic, the impact and results of his collateral writings in Farsi were far more consequential, permanent and far-reaching.

There is disagreement on the total number of Majlesi's works. Two accounts mention thirteen books in Arabic, including *Bahar al-Anvar al-Jame'atol leder Akhbar al-Imamat al-Athar*, which is *Bahar al-Anvar*'s full name, and fifty-three books in Farsi.[62] According to a third account, Majlesi wrote ten books in Arabic and forty-nine in Farsi, and finally a fourth source suggests that he wrote nineteen books and treatise in Arabic and seventy books in Farsi.[63] According to one calculation, Majlesi wrote 1,402,700 lines during his life.[64] Dividing this number by seventy-three years, it has been suggested that he wrote an average of about fifty-three lines per day from the first day of his birth or sixty-seven lines of about fifty letters per line since puberty![65] Tonokaboni has ascribed to Majlesi the exaggerated figure of 1,000 lines per day from the day of his birth and has considered this capacity as one of Majlesi's thaumaturgical gifts.[66] Majlesi's Farsi books constitute one-sixth of the volume of his total writings.[67] Even though the number of Farsi books written by Majlesi is greater than the number of his Arabic books, the huge volume of *Bahar al-Anvar*, in terms of total number of pages, accounts for the relatively smaller percentage of his Farsi writings in relation to the total number of pages he has written.

[62] M. Mohrizi and H. Rabbani, *Shenakhtnameh 'Allameh Majlesi*, vol. 2, pp. 79, 106.
[63] Ibid., p. 106.   [64] M. B. Khonsari-Esfahani, *Rowzat al-Jennat*, vol. 2, p. 266.
[65] Ibid., p. 274; S. M. Mahdavi, *Zendeghinameh 'Allameh Majlesi*, vol. 2, p. 125; H. Taremi, *'Allameh Majlesi*, p. 120.
[66] M. Tonokaboni, *Qesas al-'Olama*, pp. 205–206.
[67] H. Taremi, *'Allameh Majlesi*, p. 122.

Sheykh 'Abbas Qomi is a key popularizer of Shi'i rituals, whose books *Montahi al-Amal* (the limits of yearning) and particularly *Mafateeh al-Jennan* (the keys to heaven) are widely read by Iranians. Qomi, who wrote a manual called *Safinat al-Bahar* (the Ship of the Seas) to navigate properly Majlesi's Sea of Lights, praises *Bahar al-Anvar* as a "faultless and complete compilation, of all religious sciences, knowledge and secrets".[68] Emphasizing the undisputable authority of *Bahar al-Anvar*, Qomi argues that Majlesi's work renders the search for any other report superfluous.[69] Qomi is a loyal disciple of Majlesi in the sense that he too believed that any report, almost irrespective of its degree of authenticity, attributed to the imams constituted the noblest and most important source of Islamic knowledge.[70]

THE SUPERNATURAL PROFILE OF THE TWO MAJLESIS

Both Majlesis, father and son, have an impressive supernatural dossier, which attempts to make a solid case for identifying and presenting them as unique, superhuman beings, blessed and privileged by God, the Prophet and the imams. Mohammad-Taqi is said to have had thaumaturgical gifts (*karamat*) and performed incredible miracles.[71] He is even said to have written a book on his own spiritual dreams and visions.[72] According to Mohammad-Taqi, once God blessed him by allowing him to experience a visitation by Imam 'Ali (*heydar-e karrar*). It was through Imam 'Ali's grace that he came to experience many explorations, discoveries and learnings that feeble minds would not be able to fathom or comprehend.[73]

While in Najaf, Mohammad-Taqi is said to have seen Imam 'Ali in a dream, in which the Imam had instructed him to return to Esfahan immediately, as his presence was much more beneficial in that city.[74] In his dream, Imam 'Ali had "shown much kindness" towards Mohammad-Taqi and had informed him that Shah 'Abbas would pass away and Shah Safi would succeed him. Imam 'Ali is said to have argued that, since Shah 'Abbas' death would result in disorder and turmoil, God willed Mohammad-Taqi to be in Esfahan so that his leadership would prevent

---

[68] A. Qomi, *Safinat al-Bahar*, (tr.) M. B. Saidi (Mashhad, n.d.), p. 16. [69] Ibid.
[70] Ibid., p. 15. [71] M. Tonokaboni, *Qisas al-'Olama*, pp. 231–232.
[72] M. B. Khonsari-Esfahani, *Rowzat al-Jennat*, vol. 2, p. 321.
[73] M. Tonokaboni, *Qisas al-'Olama*, p. 231.
[74] M. B. Khonsari-Esfahani, *Rowzat al-Jennat*, vol. 2, p. 322.

the masses from slipping into corruption, chaos and dissent.[75] On his return to Esfahan, Mohammad-Taqi recounted his dream to a friend and his friend recounted it to Prince Safi. At that time, Shah 'Abbas was in Mazandaran. Shortly afterwards, Shah 'Abbas passed away, and his heir, Safi, was crowned as Shah.[76]

Mohammad-Taqi probably believed that Imam 'Ali was the intermediary who had provided him with information about the future and that God had chosen him specifically for the mission of leading the people in times of crises. This type of a superstitious claim to visitations by imams in dreams, providing information about the future only known to the hidden world, thus establishing a special supernatural and divinely inspired profile for a mortal, corresponds to the stereotypical image of such superhumans dating back to Shah Esma'il and his forefathers. The propagation of accounts focused on the superhuman powers of both political rulers and religious figures enhanced their quasi-holy stature. Mohammad-Baqer Majlesi reported extensively on his father's numerous wonder works, exceptional experiences, thaumaturgical gifts and incredible dreams, the veracity of which were said to have been proven.[77]

It is said that, one night, after long hours of prayers and supplications, Mohammad-Taqi Majlesi attained a special spiritual state. At that particular moment, he felt that God would fulfil whatever wish or petition he may have. While in his mind he was mulling over the nature of his request, his newly born, Mohammad-Baqer, began crying in his crib. Subsequently, Mohammad-Taqi requested God to designate his son as the propagator of His faith and the popularizer of the Prophet's edicts.[78] He also asked God to confer His boundless favour and grace upon Mohammad-Baqer. According to this story, Mohammad-Baqer Majlesi's supernaturalness is established while he is in his crib, and his exceptional success story until his death is effectively predetermined, foretold and guaranteed.

A very telling fabulation about Mohammad-Taqi Majlesi puts into perspective his popularly perceived reputation of almost an idol, more sacred and holy than the imams, in the eyes of his followers and admirers. Mohammad Lowhi Hoseyni Musavi-Sabzevari, also known as Mir-Lowhi, a student of luminaries such as Sheykh Baha'i and Mirdamad and a contemporary of the Majlesis, was an avid critic of both father and son.[79] Explaining the difficult task of criticizing the Majlesis during their time,

---

[75] Ibid., p. 323.   [76] Ibid.   [77] Ibid.
[78] S. H. Mirkhandan, *Mohammad-Taqi Majlesi bar Sahel Hadith*, pp. 83–84.
[79] Z. Safa, *Tarikh Adabiyat Iran*, vol. 5, part 1, p. 206.

Mir-Lowhi maintains that fame to wisdom and erudition in the eyes of the common folk is not a function of knowledge and scholarship but of wealth and fortune. Mir-Lowhi insinuates that Mohammad-Baqer Majlesi's financial fortune fused with his religious and political power during the latter part of his life, rendered his stature and reputation immune to criticism and objection in the eyes of his supporters. Majlesi's financial and religious control over a significant network of seminary students enabled him to establish a patron–client relationship, effectively preventing those who were indebted to him from criticizing their benefactor. Mohammad-Baqer's financial, political and religious position earned him the reputation of generosity, as he was able to assist the needy either personally or through appealing to others.[80]

As a background story to Mohammad-Baqer's exaggerated fame, Mir-Lowhi reports a fable recounted by one 'Ali-Reza about Mohammad-Taqi Majlesi. It is said that when Mohammad-Taqi was returning from Karbala, two horsemen rode beside him, keeping him company and asking him religious questions, as was the tradition of seminary school students picking the brain of their masters. Whenever Mohammad-Taqi asked the two horsemen to speed ahead of him or slow down, so that they would not be obliged to keep him company, the two pleaded with him that it was an honour for them to ride with him as they would learn from the master solutions to problems that they could not resolve on their own. Once Mohammad-Taqi realized that they would not leave him alone, he asked them about their identity. One horseman replied that he was Hoseyn-ebn 'Ali and the other responded that he was the Hidden Imam (*Saheb al-Zaman*).[81]

The message of the fable is clear. Imam Hoseyn and the Twelfth Imam, each a different kind of Shi'i archetype and model revered by the Shi'i, need to learn about their Shi'ism from Mohamamd-Taqi Majlesi. Mir-Lowhi reports on the superstitions and exaggerations of his time and informs his readers that, after the death of Mohammad-Taqi, the common folk believed his spiritual position to be much higher than that of the Twelfth Imam. The common folk even believed that Mohammad-Taqi's horse was capable of miracle making. After Mohammad-Taqi's death, the people ripped apart the material in which his body laid and wore the pieces on their arms as good luck charms.[82] Mir-Lowhi's account of Mohammad-Taqi's exaggerated religious prestige and reputation opens a window to

---

[80] M. B. Khonsari-Esfahani, *Rowzat al-Jennat*, vol. 2, p. 274, 275.
[81] M. Lowhi Hoseyni Musavi Sabzevari, *Ketab Arba'eyn. Ketab Kefayat al-Mohtadi* (Handwritten Manuscript, Shomareh Daftar: 833), pp. 5–6.
[82] Ibid., p. 5.

the superstitious manner in which the common folk venerated and even worshipped a mortal being, substituting a cleric for their imams and slipping into idolatry in the name of Shi'ism.

Similar to his father, Mohammad-Baqer Majlesi was credited with numerous accounts of miracles and thaumaturgical gifts. Tonokaboni lists seven cases of his supernatural acts (*karamat*).[83] Listing five of his wonder workings suffices to demonstrate the kind of myths circulating at the time about Majlesi's superhuman capabilities. First, it is said that some of the *'olama* of the *jenn* or the invisible creatures from the hidden world attended Majlesi's classes. Second, a friend of Mohammad-Taqi Majlesi dreamt that he had entered a room where the Prophet and the twelve imams were sitting. He saw Mohammad-Taqi bringing into the room a newborn in his swaddling clothes. Mohammad-Taqi approached the holiest of Shi'i personalities in the room individually and pleaded with the Prophet, Imam 'Ali, and each of the remaining eleven imams, including the Twelfth, to pray so that God would make the child the propagator of the faith. Each one of them consented, took the child into their arms and prayed for him. Once the man woke up, he rushed to Mohammad-Taqi's house. There he saw a newly born. Before the man could recount his dream, Mohammad-Taqi asked him to pray to God so that his son Mohammad-Baqer would become a propagator of the faith. Third, it is said that during Mohammad-Baqer's time, two men showed enmity towards him and gossiped behind his back. On the night of Majlesi's death, they both saw the same dream. In their dream, they had gone to Majlesi's house, where he was sleeping. Suddenly they saw the Prophet and Imam 'Ali enter his house. While the Prophet took Majelsi's right arm and Imam 'Ali his left arm, they told Majlesi that he had to wake up and go with them. And so they accompanied Majlesi out of his house. Once Majlesi's antagonists woke up and realized that they had had the same dream, they guessed that Majlesi must have passed away as he was sick. When they reached his house, they heard people crying and wailing from inside the house, and when they were told that Majlesi had passed away, the two ill-wishers were astounded and remorseful.

Tonokaboni's remaining two accounts of Mohammad-Baqer Majlesi's superhuman condition are clear depictions of the superstitious aura that surrounded him. The first account demonstrates Majlesi's very intimate relation with the Prophet of Islam and the second with the hidden world. It is reported that a devout follower of Majlesi's creed from Bahrain

---

[83] M. Tonokaboni, *Qesas al-'Olama*, pp. 205–208.

journeyed to Esfahan to meet him. Once he was close to the city, he asked about Majlesi and was told that Majlesi had passed away. The man was immensely saddened and went to sleep. In his sleep, he saw a place where the Prophet sat on a highly elevated pulpit, and next to him on a lower elevation stood or sat Imam 'Ali. In front of the pulpit, he saw one row of prophets lined up, and behind them stood many more rows of different kinds of people. Between the many rows, he identified Majlesi. Suddenly the man from Bahrain heard the Prophet say, "Akhund Molla Mohammad-Baqer approach". The man from Bahrain saw someone leave the rows where the ordinary people stood and approach the row of the prophets. When the Prophet bade him to approach again, he left the row of the prophets. At that time, the Prophet instructed him to sit. Majlesi pleaded with the Prophet to allow him to stand as he felt embarrassed and ashamed to sit before all the standing prophets. The Prophet then turned to the prophets and said, "sit so that Molla Mohammad-Baqer may sit". Thus the prophets sat, and Majlesi sat close to the Prophet, Mohammad. This account implies that Majlesi was dearer to the Prophet than all other prophets, and leaves the key issue of whether he sat closer to the Prophet than Imam 'Ali ambiguous and unresolved. What may be construed from this and other accounts mentioned is that according to his followers, Majlesi occupied a very special position in the eyes of the Prophet.

The last account of Majlesi's supernatural qualities is based on a personal experience recounted by Majlesi himself. One Friday night, Majlesi found a short prayer that was very rich in meaning and he therefore decided to recite it. On the next Friday night when Majlesi decided to recite it again, suddenly he heard a voice from the ceiling of his house. The voice addressed him as the "Perfectly Knowledgeable" and said, "the two illustrious angels who record every individual's good and bad deeds (*keram al-katebin*) have yet to finish entering the reward (*savab*) for the prayer you found and here you are reciting it again".[84] Majlesi leaves his audience guessing at the identity of the mysterious voice giving him a progress report on the activities of the two angels in the hidden world. Majlesi's account of his personal experience implies that he was in contact with the hidden world and knew of things to which other mortal humans could not be privy. The theme weaving throughout all these reports on Majlesi's thaumaturgical gifts focuses on the idea that the Prophet and the twelve imams were particularly fond of and respectful towards him. These

---

[84] Ibid., p. 208.

myths must have elevated Majlesi's religious station, in the eyes of the common folk, to that of a beloved of the Prophet and imams.

Taking the common Shi'i folks' veneration of the Prophet and the imams as granted, producers and propagators of fictitious accounts, such as those ascribed to the two Majlesis, aim at duping the masses into believing that their holy objects of adoration in turn revere special persons who actually live among them. The process of projecting and thereby transforming the love of the physically absent Prophet and imams on to living beings by "demonstrating" that the object of love of the truly loved ones is a worldly creature can produce a convincing argument through a simple syllogism. The common folk love their imams. Their imams love a worldly person. Therefore, the common folk can pour their love on an actually existing proxy. Capitalizing on the common folks' love of the twelve imams, individuals such as the Majlesis are fashioned to become objects of Shi'i adulation with all the religious, political and economic powers and privileges appertaining to such positions.

Creating fictive scenarios, which probably fulfil some human need, and succeeding to establish them as facts through repetition provides for a powerful tool of social engineering. The continued political, religious and economic success of false claimants rests, however, on the acceptance of superstitious fables by the common folk as facts. The continuous feeding of the Shi'i community with so-called religious tales of sacred figures on earth could be construed as a deliberate act of propagating superstitious beliefs with the intention of keeping the masses in a state of religious trance, thereby guaranteeing the worldly interests of the false pretenders who control them.

Building a superhuman profile for a mortal by attributing to him powers reflecting connectedness to the hidden world attracted political and religious respect as long as the common folk continued to believe in such superstitions. Mohammad-Baqer Majlesi's account of his father's connectedness with the hidden world, his miracles and wonder working, in addition to all the supernatural reports that circulated about the two Majlesis, seems to demonstrate that they were not averse to the spreading of such exaggerations about them. On the contrary, we are told that Mohammad-Baqer Majlesi propagated the fables pertaining to his own father. It could be argued that individuals engage in fabricating and propagating phantasmical stories about themselves and their lineage to obtain respect, authority and legitimacy not through worldly meritocratic acts but through improvable claims to connectedness. Such false claims need to be either accepted on face value or drilled into the minds of the common folk. Were the Majlesis, father and son, trying to establish a supernatural and superhuman lineage and ancestry for themselves? If so, they must have believed that possessing a supernatural reputation enhanced their religio-political stature and widened their following, thereby consolidating and expanding their power base.

MOHAMMAD-BAQER MAJLESI'S RISING FORTUNES

From the age of fifty-three, Majlesi the scholar and expert of reports, the researcher and the propagator of a particular brand of Shi'ism, gradually moves into religio-political positions of prominence in the land. Under the reign of Shah Safi II, better known as Shah Soleyman, Majlesi's eminence and official rank within the Safavi administration begins to rise. Shah Soleyman, however, did not have much of a reputation as a paragon of Islamic piety and virtue. On the contrary, he was known for his incessant excessive drinking, which constantly placed him in a state of semi-consciousness, leading to paranoiac killings of the nobility, dignitaries of the court, and military leaders. Shah Soleyman was also notorious for his endless erotic drives, which took perverse turns, when his agents went out hunting for beautiful young girls, who were then abducted and brought to the Shah's palace.[85] During the rule of the same Shah Soleyman, the common folk are said to have considered their far-from-pious Shah as infallible, and his edicts were respected as though they were that of God.[86] Despite his unIslamic ethos, Shah Soleyman is said to have observed his religious obligations of praying, fasting and attending the Friday mosque while maintaining a warm and close relation with the clergy.[87] Shah Soleyman represented an eclectic brand of religiosity common among numerous Safavi Shahs that was tolerated by the chief Islamic jurists. The shahs performed their religious rites and rituals and even went to lengthy excesses to prove their devotion to the imams, yet they continued to live non-Islamic if not anti-Islamic lives in practice. For both the shahs and the jurists, the contradiction between internal impiety and external piety did not seem to pose a problem. It seemed as if Safavi Shahs with the approval of Shi'i jurists operated according to a different set of religious rules and obligations than that of their subjects.

[85] E. Kaempfer, (tr.) K. Jahandari, *Safarnameh Kaempfer* (Tehran, 1360), pp. 62, 225.
[86] E. Kaempfer, *Safarnameh Kaempfer*, pp. 15–16; Sanson, (tr.) T. Tafazoli, *Safarnameh Sanson*, (Tehran, 1346), pp. 168–169.
[87] M. I. Nasiri, *Dastur-e Shahriyaran*, (Tehran, 1373), pp. 23–24; E. Kaempfer, *Safarnameh Kaempfer*, pp. 69–70.

In 1090/1679, Majlesi was appointed to the highest judicial office in
Esfahan. The chief judge of Esfahan wielded considerable judicio-religious
power, and the position was reserved for high-ranking clerics, as it
required the application of Shari'at (shari'a) laws.[88] In the same year,
Shah Soleyman appointed Majlesi to the important office of Emam
Jom'eh or the Friday Congregational Prayer leader.[89] It is also during the
same period that Shah Soleyman confers upon Majlesi the responsibility of
conducting the "affairs of Muslims" and applying "Islamic laws".[90]
Kaempfer, who arrived in Esfahan in March 1684 or some five years
after Majlesi became the religious judge of Esfahan, writes about the
abduction of Armenian and foreign girls and their forced bedding with
Shah Soleyman.[91] In 1098/1687 or some eight years after occupying
the powerful dual positions of chief judge of Esfahan and the Friday
Congregational Prayer leader, Shah Soleyman appoints Majlesi to the
position of *sheykholeslam*, the highest religious office in the land.[92]
Majlesi maintained his position of *sheykholeslam* until the death of Shah
Soleyman in 1105. The twenty-six-year-old Shah Soltan Hoseyn, who
succeeded Shah Soleyman, reinstated Majlesi as the *sheykholeslam*, and
he retained this position until his death in 1110/1699–1700.[93]

Majlesi held the powerful title of *sheykholeslam* for twelve years.
During these years, he is described as the "absolutist or unrestrained
ruler" (*ra'is-e motlaq al-anan*) of Esfahan in both the worldly and spiritual
realms.[94] Majlesi's power and influence, however, went far beyond the
confines of Esfahan, for whoever swayed control over Esfahan almost
ruled over the Safavi empire. Even though Majlesi's influence and power
was on the rise during Shah Soleyman's reign, it was, however, under the
rule of the young, weak and impressionable Shah Soltan Hoseyn that his
role in effectively running the state became ever more pronounced. It is said
that during this period, the rule of the monarch was sustained by and
hinged upon the person of Majlesi.[95] The influential role of Majlesi during
the last four years of his life under Shah Soltan Hoseyn was such that it has
been suggested that it was Majlesi who managed and controlled the
state.[96] His sway and authority during this period is said to have been so

[88] A. Davani, *Mafakher-e Eslam*, pp. 245–246.   [89] Ibid., p. 234.
[90] M. B. Khonsari-Esfahani, *Rowzat al-Jennat*, vol. 2, p. 261.
[91] E. Kaempfer, *Safarnameh Kaempfer*, p. 62.
[92] A.-H. Khatunabadi, *Vaqaye' al-Sanein val-A'yyam*, pp. 508, 540.   [93] Ibid., p. 549.
[94] M. B. Khonsari-Esfahani, *Rowzat al-Jennat*, vol. 2, p. 261.
[95] Z. Safa, *Tarikh Adabiyat Iran*, vol. 5, part 1, p. 181.
[96] H. Taremi, *'Allameh Majlesi*, p. 114.

pivotal that Shah Soltan Hoseyn's kingdom and monarchy depended solely on him, and once Majlesi died, signs of weakness and disintegration began to appear.[97]

In view of Shah Soltan Hoseyn's gross mismanagement and incapacity to govern, the political survival of Persia is said to have been due to Majlesi's "thoughtfulness and wisdom".[98] Highlighting the central religio-political role of Majlesi, it has been opined that the subsequent downfall of the Safavi dynasty during the reign of Shah Soltan Hoseyn was the direct consequence of Majlesi's death.[99] Shah Soltan Hoseyn is said to have been an undisciplined ruler. Yet as long as Majlesi was alive, law and order prevailed and the King's country endured. However, after Majlesi's death, Qandahar was lost, the country was infiltrated by foreign forces and the Afghans entered Esfahan and killed the Shah.[100] Sheykh 'Abbas Qomi, Majlesi's admirer expresses the same opinion in a different way. Qomi opines that "due to Shah Soltan Hoseyn's ineptitude and effective absence, his government was weakened and Majlesi was effectively turning the wheels of [running] the state, therefore after Majlesi's death, the state fell apart and Qandahar fell".[101]

Majlesi's rising religious and political position was accompanied by his growing financial fortune. During the reign of Shah Soltan Hoseyn, the *sheykholeslam* received a very high salary along with benefits.[102] According to Sanson, the French missionary who lived in Iran during Shah Soleyman's reign, the *sheykholeslam* received 50,000 livres or some 1,100 tomans per year.[103] Other than his official remuneration, it may be imputed that he had access to and the right to dispose of the religious obligations and dues paid to him by the Shi'i. We are told that Shah Soltan Hoseyn used the public treasury to buy a house for the *sheykholeslam* succeeding Majlesi.[104] If Majlesi's successor received a house from the Shah, there is reason to believe that Majlesi must have also received a similar if not a much greater favour throughout his twelve years of tenure as *sheykholeslam*. The house bought by the Shah for the *sheykholeslam* succeeding Majlesi was 300 tomans. If the tomans quoted by Sanson are equivalent to those referred to by Khatunabadi, it could be argued that

---

[97] M. B. Khonsari-Esfahani, *Rowzat al-Jennat*, vol. 2, p. 261.   [98] Ibid.   [99] Ibid.
[100] M. Tonokaboni, *Qesas al-'Olama*, p. 205.
[101] E. Alavi, 'Majlesi az Didgah-e Mostashreghan va Iranshenasan' in M. Mohrizi and H. Rabbani (eds.), *Shenakhtnameh 'Allameh Majlesi*, vol. 2, p. 302.
[102] E. Kaempfer, *Safarnameh Kaempfer*, p. 59.
[103] Sanson, *Safarnameh Sanson*, p. 41.
[104] A. Khatunabadi, *Vaqaye' al-Sanein val-'Avam*, p. 549.

Majlesi's state salary alone was the equivalent of about three-and-a-half houses per year. In his will, Majlesi refers to his assets and lists them as the Korbokandi property (*melk*), his estate (*zaminha*) around Ashkavand and a house in Tal-e Asheghan. All three pieces of property were rented out and generated income. In his will, Majlesi explains what he wishes to be done with the income generated by his assets after he passes away.[105]

Ne'matollah Jazayeri, Majlesi's talented student who became his collaborator on the *Bahar al-Anvar* project and lived in his house for four years and to whom we have already referred, observed the transformation in his livelihood. Jazayeri reports on the ever-growing material prosperity of the Majlesi household, enabling the members of his family to benefit from a highly affluent lifestyle.[106] Jazayeri maintains that he was certain that even Majlesi's servants and young slaves were clad in expensive cashmere garments. It seems as if Majlesi's extravagant and conspicuously luxurious lifestyle began to disturb Jazayeri who was unable to reconcile the legendary account of the austere and simple lifestyles of the imams with the opulent living conditions of his master. According to Majlesi's own teachings, the pious were instructed to reach into their hearts and uproot worldly attachments such as "fortune and status", replacing it with the search for eternal salvation and proximity to God through worship.[107]

The stark contrast between Majlesi's teachings and his fortune must have perplexed the young Jazayeri, who subsequently raises some questions and reservations about his lifestyle. It seems as if Majlesi fails to justify convincingly the luxurious state of his household. To resolve the problem, Jazayeri suggests that whichever of the two passes away first should promise to appear in the dream of the one who was still alive and recount the truth of the matter on this issue, which could only be known in the hereafter. Majlesi is reported to have accepted the deal, and subsequently the debate over his reasoning and motives for possessing such an opulent lifestyle comes to an end.[108]

After Majlesi's death, Jazayeri visits his master's grave and, while praying for him, falls asleep. In his sleep, he sees Majlesi lushly and lavishly dressed and ornated. Majlesi speaks of the great pain he was enduring during his moment of death until suddenly a mysterious man dressed in

---

[105] M. B. Majlesi, *E'teqadat* (Qom, 1378), p. 84.
[106] M. B. Khonsari-Esfahani, *Rowzat al-Jennat*, vol. 2, p. 279.
[107] M. B. Majlesi, *'Eyn al-Hayat*, pp. 27, 29.
[108] M. B. Khonsari-Esfahani, *Rowzat al-Jennat*, vol. 2, p. 279.

luxurious clothes approaches him on his deathbed, sits at the foot of his bed and starts touching his body. Wherever he touched, the pain would be relieved until he touched his chest causing the pain to disappear altogether. At that moment, Majlesi told Jazayeri that he noticed his own motionless body in the corner of the room.[109] Majlesi does not identify or describe the man who was effectively the angel of death, except by stressing that he was opulently dressed. In Jazayeri's dream, Majlesi talks of his experience in the grave when he is asked to report on his righteous and pious acts during his lifetime. At first, the accounts of his good deeds do not meet the approval of the questioning voice, and Majlesi finds himself in a bind and cites one last accomplishment. It is this one singular act that eventually washes away all his sins, saves him and secures him eternal salvation and bliss. Majlesi recounts that the good deed, which he cited at the end of his list of accomplishments as he did not consider it important, was that one day he had saved an indebted man from the violent clutches of his angry creditors by repaying his debts and providing for him.

In Jazayeri's dream, Majlesi convincingly settles his dispute with his student over the vices and virtues of material gains and of Majlesi's own affluent lifestyle. Majlesi says, "If I did not possess the opulence and wealth that I had, how would I have been able to free that man from the clutches of those people, repay his debts and obtain the eternal ease that I now possess".[110] Once Jazayeri wakes up from his dream, he realizes that "whatever Majlesi had done during his life was in accordance with the expediencies of the faith and the well being of Islam and Muslims".[111] Jazayeri goes to great lengths to both bear witness and justify Majlesi's wealth and extravagant lifestyle in the name of expediency and the common good of Muslims.

---

[109] Ibid., p. 280.   [110] Ibid., p. 282.   [111] Ibid.

5

From Conceptualization to Officialization
of a Religio-political Ideology

To contextualize the significance of Majlesi's compilation of *Bahar al-Anvar*, it is necessary to grasp the significance of the transition from the early and abandoned texts to the later standard report compilations. Majlesi attached greater importance and merit to those long-abandoned reports, which he included in his compilation, than the reports found in the standard Shi'i *hadith* compilations of Koleyni, Ebn Babawayh and Tusi. In his important contribution to the study of early Shi'ism, Amir-Moezzi refers to a process of moving from "traditionalism" to "rationalism" starting in the fourth/tenth century. He explains that, in this process, pioneered by Sheykh Mofid (d. 413/1022) and Sharif Morteza (d. 436/1025), there is "a progressive silencing of a number of traditions". The traditions or reports silenced are those "with a quite original metaphysical and mystical (and thus 'heterodox') scope in Islam".[1]

Based on three themes in Imamate dogma – "(1) cosmogenic data; (2) information on the miraculous and occult aspects of the imams, particularly where these concern knowledge and their supernatural powers; and (3) those data pertaining to what the imams thought of the Qur'an" – Amir-Moezzi argues that from Saffar Qomi's (d. 290/903) oldest compilation of Imamite dogma to Koleyni (d. 329/940), Ebn Babawayh (d. 381/991) and finally to Mofid and Morteza, there is a process of culling, diluting and silencing the supernatural and occult reports. Amir-Moezi

---

[1] M. A. Amir-Moezzi, *The Divine Guide in Early Shi'ism* (New York, 1994), pp. 18–19.

identifies a movement from non-rational and esoteric traditions to the rational ones.[2]

To understand the significance and implications of Majlesi's incorporation of the neglected or abandoned early reports, it is imperative to comprehend the contours of the internal transformations and doctrinal rivalries within Shi'ism between the first/seventh and the fourth/tenth centuries. In his substantial contribution to unveiling the intra-Shi'i debates in its formative period, Modarressi argues that during the lifetime of the imams, "new opinions were put forward by a new extremist wing of the Imamate tradition, which had links to the now-vanished *Kaysanite* movement of the late first/seventh century". These extremist opinions "emphasized the supernatural qualities of the imam, maintaining that he was the centrepiece of the universe".[3] It seems as though from the early second/eighth century, another extremist notion based on the eternal life of certain key Islamic figures was revived.

At the same time, according to Modarressi, "numerous heretic persons and groups emerged who proclaimed one or another prominent figure of the House of Prophet as God".[4] This claim too had its roots in the period after the death of Imam 'Ali. Certain Shi'i groups attributed to the imams knowledge of the hidden world, as well as all that had happened was happening and will happen. It is suggested that Imamite jurists in Qom considered such attributions as exaggeration.[5] These types of ideas were labelled as *gholov* or exaggerations, and the people who ascribed to these extreme positions were called exaggerators or *ghollat*. In the first decade of the second/eighth century, there emerged another extremist group known as the *Mofavvazeh* (*mufawwida*) or the delegationists. This group held many beliefs in common with the *Kaysanites*. They believed in "the Divine nature of the imams, namely that the imams were supernatural beings, who possessed limitless knowledge, including that of the unseen and had power of disposal over the universe".[6] Even though they did not attribute the status of God to the Prophet and the imams, the *Mofavvazeh* believed that the imams performed "nearly all functions that God was supposed to do; the only difference was that His power was original and theirs subordinate".[7]

---

[2] Ibid., pp. 16–19.

[3] H. Modarressi, *Crisis and Consolidation in the Formative Period of Shi'ite Islam* (Princeton, 1993), pp. 9–10.

[4] Ibid., p. 20.   [5] N. Safari-e Forushani, *Ghallian* (Mashhad, 1999), p. 35.

[6] H. Modarressi, *Crisis and Consolidation in the Formative Period of Shi'ite Islam*, p. 21.

[7] Ibid.

After the death of Imam Reza in the third/ninth century, the belief that the imams "were superhuman beings possessed of a Divine light" was popularized, leading to the flourishing of "extremist literature in general and the *Mofavvazeh*'s in particular".[8] Reports quoted on the authority of imams and ascribed to them dealt with their Divine aspects, miracles performed by them and their relation with and connection to the antediluvian world.[9] According to Modarressi, a group of supporters of the *Mofavvazeh* believed that the imams were knowledgeable about all human, animal and bird languages, as well as whatever was happening in the world. They also believed that after the death of the Prophet, the imams continued to receive revelations "when they needed it".[10]

It would be logical to assume that the rationalist tendency intent on weeding out supernatural, non-rational and occult reports referred to by Amir-Moezzi was primarily concerned with the *hadith*s that were fabricated and spread by the exaggerators and the *Mofavvazeh*, who according to Modarressi were gradually gaining "some sort of recognition in Imamate scholarship".[11] Modarressi argues that even in Koleyni's *Usul-e Kafi*, one of the four major *hadith* compilations of the Shi'i, which Amir-Moezzi believes to contain far less non-rational *hadith*s than Saffar's *Basa'ir al-darajat*, there are some 9,485 "reports of doubtful and inauthentic origin".[12] This, as Modarressi argues, implies that some two-thirds of the 16,199 reports in Koleyni's *Usul-e Kafi* are suspect and unreliable. In what seems to be a barely veiled reference to Majlesi, Modarressi writes, "in more recent centuries the pre-occupation of some Shi'i authors with preserving whatever early Shi'i material has survived has spread to the material from the works of heretical authors".[13] By retrieving and reincorporating the supernatural and non-rational *hadith*s of the exaggerators, Majlesi played a key role in rolling back the attempts of those Shi'i scholars who wished to uproot such superstitions. His *Bahar al-Anvar* is said to include "most of the remains of the scholarship of the extremists of the early centuries that found their way into Imamite works".[14]

Therefore, it could be posited that Majlesi wished to undo and reverse the rationalization trend that, according to Amir-Moezzi, had started in the fourth/tenth century. By reinjecting Shi'i traditions with the supernatural, superstitious, occult, esoteric and non-rational reports that had been carefully and gradually winnowed and abandoned by the rationalist tendency, Majlesi was turning back the rational forward march of

---

[8] Ibid., p. 33–34.   [9] Ibid., p. 34.   [10] Ibid., p. 38.   [11] Ibid., p. 47.   [12] Ibid.
[13] Ibid., p. 48.   [14] Ibid.

Shi'ism. In this light, it may become less enigmatic to understand the contention of 'Abdol-'Aziz Dehlavi, a Sunni jurist and contemporary of Majlesi who argued that "it would be fair to call the Shi'i religion, Majlesi's religion".[15] Dehlavi's statement could make sense if it is assumed that, during his time, what had come to be known as the Shi'i religion as propagated by Majlesi had overshadowed all previous readings of Shi'ism and that Majlesi's variant was dramatically different from that of the Shi'i luminaries such as Mofid, Sharif Morteza and Tusi. By reintegrating and popularizing abandoned supernatural reports into the main body of Shi'i *hadith* literature, Majlesi promoted the resurfacing of extremist ideas in all domains of the faith.

Interest in ascribing godlike characteristics to the imams by the *ghollat* or exaggerators and the later repopularization of this concept by Majlesi may have had more worldly and material reasons than religious and spiritual ones. Modarressi maintains that, during the second/eighth century, the idea of proclaiming an imam to be God constituted "the first half of a two-part claim; the second half was that the claimant himself was that god's messenger".[16] If the false claim that an imam was God is accepted by the common folk, the claimant could automatically maneuver himself into the position of the dead imam's messenger, demanding respect and obedience from his followers. A new chain of authority between a falsifier and God, through the intermediary of imams as God, is therefore presented to the public. In this way, worldly status and prestige with its concomitant gains can be obtained by the lie of a falsifier if it appeals to popular religious sentiments. The problem with this rudimentary and rather convoluted ruse for appropriating worldly authority and power in the name of religion was that it was simply idolatrous, as it assigned human partners to God, let alone created many false messengers.

To avoid the charge of polytheism and belief in messengers after the Prophet Mohammad, it made more sense for the power-seeking worldly imposter to convince the masses that, after the imams, God actually chose and blessed certain people with special capacities and supernatural powers. These divinely selected individuals would be in contact with God and charged with carrying out His mission. Such superhumans, "sub-imams" endowed with the so-called ability and gift of being in touch with the hidden world, served the same purpose as those false

---

[15] 'A. A. Talafiy-e Daryani, 'Bahar al-Anvar, Dayeratolma'aref Shi'i' in M. Mohrezi and H. Rabbani (eds.), *Shenakht nameh 'Allameh Majlesi*, vol. 2 (Tehran, 1378), p. 147.

[16] H. Modarressi, *Crisis and Consolidation in the Formative Period of Shi'ite Islam*, p. 20.

pretenders who tried to pass themselves off as messengers of imams who had been raised to the status of God in the second/eight century. Furthermore, this superstitious construct deflected the threat of idolatry and heresy against the new pretenders.

Another parallel argument with the intention of justifying the existence of non-imam supernatural sacred individuals with almost godlike powers interfacing with the hidden world, while avoiding the accusation of idolatry, was developed in a roundabout way. It was argued that imams possessed certain attributes of God, yet they were not God. As such, the imams were human but they were different from ordinary people due to their Divine attributes. In the absence of the imams and until the reappearance of the Twelfth Imam, the world would be graced with certain "sacred" humans, who were blessed by the imams and God. These special sacred beings, sometimes referred to as the deputy of the Twelfth Imam, in turn came to be thought of as possessing certain attributes of the imams. As temporary substitutes for the Twelfth Imam, they became the shepherd of the common folk. During the Safavi period, these Shah-appointed "sacred individuals" were also considered as the most eligible to exercise in abstensia the political and/or religious authority and leadership of the imams in society. An idolatrous transmission line of exaggerations is automatically established as soon as any property or characteristic of God is claimed by or assigned to ordinary human beings. Claiming some sort of a special status accompanied by special powers based on a presumed connection with God, segregating the so-called superhuman from the human folk, is an invitation to exaggeration and superstition, easily abused by those possessing a great appetite for political, religious and economic power.

Well before Majlesi's efforts to revive the abandoned reports and incorporate the literature of exaggerators in his compilation of reports, the concept of normal individuals claiming supernatural powers did exist. Shah Esma'il and his forefathers had claimed supernatural powers; Joneyd was even considered as God and his disciples believed that after his death he was endowed with eternal life. It seems as though the step-by-step process of ascribing certain Divine powers to ordinary mortals was greatly facilitated by the attribution of all or some of God's characteristics to the imams. The veritable substitution process of the *Kaysanite* and *Mofavvazeh* had set a precedence that could be extended through history.

Majlesi's *Bahar al-Anvar* certainly provides a very rich and diverse treasure chest of phantasmical, non-rational and superstitious accounts that has throughout time been injected into the Shi'i community, keeping the common folk hypnotized with the mirage of seeing agents of the hidden world among themselves and performing acts particular to the hidden world in their own material world. To the common people, as well as a considerable segment of the clergy, *Bahar al-Anvar* has the semblance of being religiously correct and unchallengeable. The general and forceful claim that the content of this book is truly the word of the imams assures the common folk, unfamiliar with the manifold authentification issues of reports, that they do not need to ponder over its message by themselves. The common perception of sacredness and veracity attributed to Majlesi's compilation and the largely uncritical embrace of it by the clergy renders *Bahar al-Anvar* a dogmatic and an ideological text.

Acceptance of *Bahar al-Anvar* as a sacred and flawless religious text facilitates the reception and affirmation of the spiritual and political power structures and relations that it intimates and seeks to establish and normalize in society. *Bahar al-Anvar* articulates in minute detail the acceptable mode of reflection and action of the Shiʻi. Moreover, it maps out in great precision the plethora of acts and deeds that would define a person as a pious Shiʻi. The material in *Bahar al-Anvar* has become imbued with the belief system of the Shiʻi community. As long as the common folk continue to believe in those parts of *Bahar al-Anvar* that are superstitious and probably fabrications as religious truths, Majlesi's work will continue to have the same socio-political impact as any other lingering ideological dogma. As has been contended by ʻAli Shariʻati, *Bahar al-Anvar* is a highly effective medium and intermediary for the maintenance of the common folk in a state of unconscious, daze, stupefaction or incapacity to think.[17]

MAJLESI'S POPULARIZATION OF PERSIAN SHIʻISM

At the time of the Safavi's ascension to power, there were hardly any books available in Farsi on the Shiʻi creed and its jurisprudence to educate the public.[18] The scholars who were initially invited to and eventually settled in Persia came from Bahrain and the Jebal al-Amel in Lebanon. These scholars were Arabic speaking and wrote in Arabic, not in Farsi.[19] The Safavi kings, who considered themselves the "servants of the Twelver creed" and "dogs of ʻAli's abode", were keen to create a conducive environment for the study, research and teaching of Shiʻism, its principles, rites and rituals, history and jurisprudence. Once the faith was revived in

---

[17] A. Shariʻati, *Collected Works*, vol. 1 (Tehran, n.d.), p. 23.
[18] A. Davani, *Mafakher-e Eslam* (Tehran, 1375), pp. 465–466.
[19] M. Mirahmadi, *Din Va Mazhab dar ʻAsr Safavi* (Tehran, 1363), p. 80.

scholarly circles, it needed time for it to be propagated and popularized in
the language of the Persians. Majlesi was well aware of the fact that the
religious books written in Arabic by Shi'i scholars were incapable of
making inroads into the Persian community. The language barrier posed
a major communication problem. Even though during the time of Shah
'Abbas I, Sheykh Baha'i wrote a book on religiously forbidden and permissible acts in Persian, it was not until the time of Mohammad-Baqer
Majlesi that Shi'ism was widely propagated in simple Farsi.

Majlesi's Farsi writings have been a guiding torch, familiarizing the
popular masses with their religious obligations and the principles of their
creed. His style of writing is simple, fluent and accessible to the common
folk. He knew for whom he was writing and therefore targeted his works
to their level of understanding, state of mind, as well as their absorptive
and analytical capacities. Majlesi wrote in Farsi to show the way, and to
convince and strengthen Shi'i beliefs among the Persians. He sought to sow
religious and ideological certitudes through the selection, repetition, interpretation and affirmation of reports, which he thought constituted the
backbone of true Shi'ism. In return, Majlesi expected approval and compliance from the people. He did not wish his writings to generate intellectual debates, but on the contrary believed that they should put an end to
the controversies and scepticisms that had been generated by the Sufis and
the philosophers.

It can be strongly suggested that Persian Shi'i essentially learned their
Shi'ism from Majlesi and his popularized works. Hardly a Shi'i household
in Iran, Pakistan, Iraq, Afghanistan or Lebanon could be found without
one or more of Majlesi's works.[20] Mir Mohammad-Saleh Khatunabadi,
Majlesi's son-in-law, explains the impact of Majlesi's works in Farsi and
writes, "These [Farsi] works have directed and guided the majority of the
common folk (in contrast to the learned) and there is hardly a house in
populated Shi'i cities, where one of Majlesi's writings cannot be found".[21]
Some well-known jurists and staunch partisans of Majlesi have placed the
popularity, spread and acceptance of his works on a par with the Qur'an.
Mirza Hoseyn Nuri, better known as Mohaddeth-e Nuri or the "Second
Majlesi", is reported to have said that "'Allameh Majlesi's books on
the translation of reports (*akhbar*) are as popular and widespread as the
Qur'an among Farsi speaking people".[22] Mohaddeth-e Nuri is also the

---

[20] S. M. Mahdavi, *Zendeghinameh 'Allameh Majlesi*, vol. 2 (Tehran, 1378), p. 120.
[21] H. Taremi, *'Allameh Majlesi* (Tehran, 1375), p. 95.
[22] S. M. Mahdavi, *Zendeghinameh 'Allameh Majlesi*, vol. 2, p. 122.

author of a book called *Fasl al-Khatab*, which is said to be the most important modern source of reviving the concept of the incompleteness of the Qur'an.[23] This notion is understandably offensive to mainstream Muslims, both Shi'i and Sunni.

Majlesi's writings in Farsi, which were mainly based on translations of parts of *Bahar al-Anvar*, became a key medium through which Shi'ism was propagated in Persia. It is said that Majlesi tried to bridge the gap between the sophisticated religious language of the jurists and the crude mind of the masses.[24] Majlesi was intentionally writing for the lowest common denominator, using the common tools of generalization, stereotyping and essentialization to get his message across effectively and clearly. However, Majlesi has also been praised for his ability to write popular books appealing to a general public and reaching all social layers. It has been said that Majlesi's books were well received by "masters and students, the ignorant and commoners, women and children".[25] Having produced a simple and easy-to-grasp report-based Shi'i manual for the common folk, Majlesi is said to have used his religious position and power to propagate his writings in all Iranian cities.[26] Throughout the centuries, these books have become the people's handy tools, guides and references to proper Shi'i conduct and dogma. Tonokaboni maintains that Islam and Muslims owe a great deal to Majlesi, since the propagation of Shi'ism is due to his writings.[27]

Majlesi wrote six major Farsi books between 1073/1663 and 1110/1699. Like all other works of Majlesi, reports and *ahadith* attributed to the imams constitute the foundation, raw material and cornerstone of his writings. Majlesi relies on the vast base of *hadith* literature that he collected during his lifetime to address, discuss, interpret and communicate all conceivable issues and topics. Each book, a piece of a jigsaw puzzle, locks into others to form a monumental religio-ideological construct. Majlesi's Shi'i belief system covers just about every conceivable spiritual and material issue that may come to the mind of a believer. It is not surprising that his supporters consider him as a unique figure of Shi'i scholarship. He is not only considered as superior to the scholars of his own time,

[23] B. Khoramshahi, 'Tahrifnapaziri-e Qur'an' in Encyclopaedia of Shi'a, vol. 4 (Tehran, 1373), p. 145.

[24] M. Mohrizi and H. Rabbani, *Shenakhtnameh 'Allameh Majlesi*, vol. 1, p. 7.

[25] S. M. Mahdavi, *Zendeghinameh 'Allameh Majlesi*, vol. 2, p. 121.

[26] A. Davani, 'Sharhe Hale 'Allameh Majlesi' in M. Mohrizi and H. Rabbani (eds.), *Shenakhtnameh 'Allameh Majlesi*, vol. 1, p. 27.

[27] M. Tonokaboni, *Qesas al-'Olama*, p. 205.

but he is ranked far higher in status, knowledge and influence than the scholars (*'olama*) that came before and after him![28] In view of all the illustrious Shi'i scholars that preceded Majlesi, such a categorically lauda-tory statement is a significant and bold contention on the part of Majlesi's advocates. Praise and appreciation of his contribution is taken a step further when it is suggested that "the faith and the pious believers, even all human beings on earth are indebted to his services and it is evident that his works will be valid and authoritative until the day of resurrection".[29] Claiming eternal validity and authority for a book throughout time is a characteristic only attributed to the Qur'an by Muslims. The suggestion that "the faith" (*din*) is indefinitely indebted to Majlesi highlights his esteemed religious position for some and the pivotal role he has played in articulating and propagating popular Shi'ism.

MAJLESI AND THE SAFAVI COURT: A SYMBIOTIC RELATIONSHIP

The active politico-religious relationship between Majlesi and the Safavi Shahs begins with his appointment to the prestigious and high-profile religious position of *sheykholeslam* by Shah Soleyman. Until this time, Majlesi is the religious ideologue, drafting and propagating a manual on proper Shi'i conduct in all spheres of life. The rights, responsibilities, tasks, duties and powers of the *sheykholeslam*, however, went beyond publiciz-ing and preaching. His brief was well reflected in the edict given to him by the Shah. Shah Tahmasb had set an interesting precedent when he appointed 'Ali ebn 'Abdol'al Karaki as the first *sheykholeslam* of the Safavi dynasty. By proclaiming him as the deputy or vicegerent of the Hidden Imam, Shah Tahmasb in effect empowered Karaki with absolutist and unlimited powers.[30] To enhance the powerful position of his *sheykho-leslam*, Shah Tahmasb issued an edict outlining the consequences of contradicting or opposing the *sheykholeslam*'s views, positions or deci-sions. Shah Tahmasb ruled that "opposition to the rule of *mojtahed*s, who are the guardians of the faith is tantamount to polytheism (*shirk*)".[31] He decreed that whoever opposes or disobeys Karaki, "the Seal of the *mojta-heds*", would be damned, rejected, exiled and subjected to heavy and hard

---

[28] M. B. Khonsari-Esfahani, *Rowzat al-Jennat*, vol. 2 (Tehran, 2535), p. 270.
[29] Ibid., p. 274.
[30] M. B. Khonsari-Esfahani, *Rowzat al-Jennat*, vol. 5 (Tehran, 1360), p. 168.
[31] Ibid., pp. 169–170.

punishments.[32] As such, Karaki's religious opinions and rulings were raised to that of the letter of the faith. Shah Tahmasb's decree effectively placed the *sheykholeslam* in a quasi-Divine position. A special and "sacred" religious personality was born. The Shah seemed to believe, but most importantly wanted his subjects to believe, that Karaki was the deputy of the Hidden Imam. The deputy of the Twelfth Imam in the eyes of the people in the 1520s must have been somehow chosen by and connected to the Hidden Imam and the hidden world. It was not long before supernatural characteristics were attributed to the "deputies" of the Hidden Imam and even *mojtaheds* of a lower status.

In Shah Soltan Hoseyn's edict, Majlesi's sweeping powers as the *sheykholeslam* of Esfahan and all regions annexed to it are clearly enumerated. He is responsible for handling and managing all the religious needs, problems and requirements of the people. He is also charged with: enjoining good and forbidding evil; enforcing the *Shar'iat* and upholding the national customs; collecting the religious dues of *khoms* and *zakat* and distributing them among the needy; preventing and punishing vices and innovations; the construction and spread of schools, mosques and religious venues; and securing the rights of Muslims and countering injustices. Shah Soltan Hoseyn orders all social classes in the land, as well as all those holding governmental ranks and positions, be they ministers, judges, nobility, governors, bureaucrats or sheriffs to be obedient to whatever Majlesi enjoins or prohibits.[33] The exceptional religio-political status and power conferred upon Majlesi by the Shah rendered his ideas and edicts quasi-sacred among the common folk to whom Majlesi's writings were addressed. Not only did Majlesi promote his own writings as the absolute truth, the Shah too supported his claim religiously and politically. From the time of Shah Tahmasb, disagreeing with the *sheykholeslam* was tantamount to infidelity. Given the political and religious concentration of power, from which he drew his economic power, Majlesi's position became unassailable, particularly by the common folk.

In return, Majlesi supported the Safavi shahs who appointed him as *sheykholeslam* without qualification or reservation. Majlesi served, propped and praised irreligious and incompetent kings. Even though his religious duties and responsibilities towards the faith and the faithful could have conflicted with his allegiance towards the shahs, Majlesi privileged his alignment with the Safavi rulers. He sacrificed upholding ethical standards, promoting right and forbidding evil and defending the weak

---

[32] Ibid.   [33] R. Ja'fariyan, *Din va Siyasat dar Dowreh Safavi* (Qom, 1370), pp. 99–100.

and the wronged, as would be expected from a religious dignitary, if not the most important religious figure in the land, for the status and position that he held by the grace of the Safavi Shahs.

In the preface of his books, *Haq al-Yaqin*, *Jala᾽ al-'Oyun*, *Heliyat al-Mottaqin*, and *Zad al-Ma'ad*, Majlesi pays excessive tribute to Safavi shahs, flattering them to no end. Some ten years into Shah Soleyman's reign, he writes that as a consequence of the Shah's justice "sorrow has become a rarity in the people's mind".[34] Expressing his religious assessment of the general public's satisfaction with Shah Soleyman's reign, Majlesi writes that those who spend their time in the mosques only pray for the "perpetuity of his rule".[35] In view of the generally irreligious, weak and corrupt rule of Shah Soleyman, Majlesi's positive assessment of his reign could only be understood as unabashed and self-serving flattery. Shah Soleyman was an incompetent alcohol-consuming womanizer, who openly abducted young girls to replenish his harem.[36] Shah Soleyman's reign is depicted as one of the worst periods of the Safavi dynasty, characterized by crises, chaos, mismanagement, widespread corruption, popular discontent and opposition to the Shah's rule.[37] In the preface of *Haq al-Yaqin*, Majlesi's last book in Farsi, written one year before his death, Majlesi glorifies Shah Soltan Hoseyn as "the lord and master of all kings" and he who "commands an army of angels". Majlesi describes the Shah as "the embodiment of Divine grace", "the just Soltan" and "the shadow of God" and prays that his reign would last until the reappearance of the Hidden Imam.[38] The symbiotic relationship between Majlesi and the Safavi Shahs reflects the common interest shared by official state religion and political power in this period. One needed and depended on the other to assure its privileges and its sustained power.

SUPERSTITION AS THE DRIVING FORCE OF AN IDEOLOGY

In light of Majlesi's endeavour to retrieve, compile, produce and disseminate a vast reservoir of *hadith*-based literature, a thorough assessment of the topics covered in his writings would be well beyond the scope of this

[34] M. B. Majlesi, *Jala᾽ al-'Oyun*, p. 23.   [35] Ibid.
[36] J. Chardin, *Voyages de Monsieur le chevalier Chardin en Perse et autres liux d'Orient*, Tome 6, pp. 18, 226, 243.
[37] J. Chardin, *Voyages de Monsieur le chevalier Chardin en Perse et autres liux d'Orient*, Tome 4, p. 26 and Tome 6, p. 140.
[38] M. B. Majlesi, *Haq al-Yaqin*, p. 3.

work. The focus of this study is on the supernatural and occult content of his writings. In this study, it is hypothesized that a significant volume of Majlesi's works, commentaries and reproductions are phantasmical, bizarre and superstitious. Following Majlesi's thought process through his writings demonstrates the method by which he articulates an absolutist ideology based on the promotion of superstition and demotion of human reasoning. The enthroning of a superstitious discourse necessitates a simultaneous rejection of rational thought as a means of arriving at truths. Majlesi's emphasis on and widespread use of a *hadith*-based discourse constitutes the alchemy that enables him to turn ephemeral, fictive and supernatural accounts of entanglements with the hidden world into a tangible, this-worldly material ideology to manage society and polity. His emphasis on the primacy of *ahadith* attributed to the imams as the absolute source of truth on the one hand and the inability of human reason to arrive at any truth on the other enables him to argue that the Shi'i should not reflect on religious matters that lie beyond the grasp of their feeble minds.

Majlesi uses and abuses the popularly accepted religious authority of *ahadith* to convince the common folk to disengage from intellectual, social and political inquiries, leaving all aspects of their affairs to the connoisseurs of the *ahadith*, who in his esteem are the sole authorities, entitled to think for them. Majlesi's very strong religious recommendations in just about every conceivable human domain takes the shape of an ideology enjoining the Shi'i to abandon independent reasoning first in religious domains and then by analogy in politics. His call on the Shi'i to abandon the application of independent thought and embrace blind imitation of Shi'i jurists not only provides the intellectual justification for an absolutist ideology but also lays the grounds for the establishment of a superstition-based absolutist political system.

Majlesi grounds his superstitious ideology in his careful selection of Shi'i *hadith* literature. In the name of irreproachable religious truths, claimed to be backed by the authority of the imams and the Prophet, he continuously negates rationalism and independent thought. To him, the non-*hadith*-based system of truth finding is anchored in the defective and flawed apparatus of fallible human reasoning. Once a belief, an act or a ritual is broached and elaborated as religiously correct or necessary, Majlesi invites the Shi'i to obey blindly and accept unequivocally his interpretations, comments, enjoinments and prohibitions. To the extent that Majlesi's writings include illogical superstition, their popular acceptance accustoms people to internalize non-rational causal relations and become alien or averse to reason-based arguments and outcomes. In time, the common folk, reared and habituated in this mould of thought, could grow impervious to demanding reason and rationality for prescribed and proscribed acts, commands, rites and rituals. Individual as well as social behaviour and reaction becomes rooted in and a consequence of timeless and ahistorical prescribed pronouncements rather than a contextualized and synthesized assessment of goals and constraints. Majlesi's ideology, which educates people to trust and believe in the validity of superstitious ideas in the name of religious correctness, helps the acceptance of and sustains the longevity of absolutist regimes.

Superstition does not rely on logical or common-sense explanations, since it establishes bridges and relations between causes and effects in conflict with worldly natural laws. For example, Majlesi writes that "whoever cuts his nails on Thursday or Monday, will recover from toothaches or eye pains".[39] The relationship between cutting nails on Thursday and Monday and recovery from toothaches or eye pains may only be known to him and a very select few. The fact, however, remains that the validity of such a relationship cannot be scientifically or logically proven. The illogical relationship between cutting nails on a particular day of the week and recovering from a physical pain is expected to be taken as a fact on the authority of religious dignitaries to which Majlesi attributes such stories.

The devout follower of Majlesism is not only expected to believe in this bizarre causal relation but is supposed to accept that the promised outcome will be obtained only if the autonomous action (cutting nails) is conducted on Mondays and Thursdays. Majlesi's instruction to the common folk to abandon independent reasoning precludes any disputation of the illogism. The inability to seek a common-sense explanation for this indeterminable supposition through testing or challenging it renders the so-called relationship an arbitrary opinion or a dictate. This type of untenable relations, where the cause and the effect is occurring in this world and is subsequently supposed to follow the rules and laws of the material world, is different from the superstition based on conflating the hidden and material world and its distinct laws. Such superstitious relations, lacking proof, methods of verification or some degree of consistent predictability, rampant in Majlesi's writings, can be labelled as illogical or nonsensical relationships, to which Majlesi first adds a religious spin and then a political one.

---

[39] M. B. Majlesi, *Ekhtiyarat* (Tehran, n.d.), p. 25.

Superstition coated in religious justifications trains and steeps believers in arbitrariness at all levels of human relation and social organization, including the political domain. The replacement of reason and rationality with non-related, non-understandable, illogical or superstitious causal relations renders the notion of checks and balances in society and the polity futile and superfluous. Checks and balances can become meaningful only if individuals can be held responsible and accountable for their claims about causes and effects or actions and consequences. Holding leaders to task for their promises and actions requires questioning that is shunned in Majlesism. Superstition as a form of mental arbitrariness inculcates and promotes the acceptance of unaccountable or inexplicable autocratic relations. Rulers relying on superstition as a tool to exercise power base their demand for blind allegiance by the common folk on the following claims. First, whatever they say and do is the result of some sort of connectedness with the hidden world. Second, they have the power and gift of mediation between the Divine and the common folk. Third, they have the right and authority to understand and interpret the word of God, Prophet and the imams. Fourth, they possess and command a "truth" inaccessible to others.

Concepts such as checks and balances, accountability and transparency belong to domains where rational expectations and logical or reason-based relations are accepted as norms and respected. As such, checks, balances and accountability in the political, social or religious realm become incongruent with the world of inexplicable, arbitrary and obscure relations. Once superstition cloaked in religious or ideological discourses seeps into the mind-set and belief system of the common folk, it provides politicians, preachers, leaders and rulers with an ideal shield of ambiguity, mystery and opaqueness behind which to hide. When their promises, projections and prophesies do not materialize or when they wish to find refuge from reasonable questions about their shortcomings and failures, they can resort to superstitious or illogical explanations.

Three key elements are combined to give birth to Majlesism as a superstition-based comprehensive ideology. First, Majlesi positions himself as a unique legitimate intermediary between God and the people, since he claims to possess the authority to correctly understand and interpret the Qur'an and the reports of the Prophet and the imams, a task of which the common people are claimed to be incapable. Second, the Shah's absolute political support for Majlesi, the key religio-judiciary positions that he occupied and the implied sanction of infidelity in case of insubordination and disobedience towards Majlesi's religious positions render his judgements, rulings and dictates almost binding upon all believers. Third, Majlesi is the author and producer of the minutely detailed religio-social manuals that defined, engineered and coordinated correct personal and social behaviour for every member of society. While his books formulated proper Shi'i behaviour, his religio-political office not only gave authority to the importance of his formulations, but could also oversee their proper imposition as law.

This writing will attempt to explain Majlesism based on four fundaments derived from the body of his works in Farsi. First, that human reasoning is deficient. Second, that there is a pressing need for society and polity to be led and guided by Islamic jurists and/or kings if the community is to attain felicity. Third, that what is here considered as superstitious and irrational causal relations is made believe to be part and parcel of Shi'i traditions. Fourth, that a redefinition and alteration of the necessities of Shi'i belief and practice is a natural corollary of Majlesi's rereading of the faith.

It will be argued that the synergy and interconnection between these four key elements results in an ideology supporting any variety of an absolutist and autocratic religious and/or political system, be it a hierocracy, monarchy or an undemocratic republic. Majlesism as an ideology is founded on the belief that the common folk are afflicted with "deficient minds" and in need of guidance both in the spiritual and temporal realm by Shi'i jurists. The leadership role of the Shi'i jurist, as in the time of Majlesi himself, could be shared with an authoritarian ruler accepting and confirming the religio-legal right of the jurist to intervene and guide in sociopolitical matters of the state or it could be fused with it in the position of a ruling jurisconsult. Majlesi feeds and replenishes the assumed "deficient minds" of the common folk with two types of information. First, he provides the public with the necessary instructions on how to conduct their everyday activities and their general personal behaviour. Second, Majlesi informs the public of their correct religious beliefs, dogma, rites and rituals. This all-encompassing educational-cum-propaganda process enables Majlesi to practice individual and social engineering, as well as control. The body of literature pertaining to so-called religiously approved general behaviour establishes a private and social code of conduct for the community.

In the realm of religious beliefs, dogma, rites and rituals, Majlesi redefines the necessities of belief and Shi'i obligations with three objectives in mind. First, he seeks to provide the Shi'i with a distinct and exclusive religious identity. Second, he wishes to articulate a legally and politically binding official state religion. Third, he attempts to tighten the circle of the Shiʿi while branding and excluding those who refuse to comply with the new official religion as irreligious and impious "others". Majlesism needs to define the "us" tightly in order to segregate and reject the "them" naturally. This is a religious exercise with important political consequences.

6

Deficiency and Defectiveness of the Human Mind

The intellectual incapacity and feeble-mindedness of the common folk constituting the Muslim community (*ommat*) is a theme that permeates the writings of Majlesi. For Majlesi, in the final analysis, the human mind is defective and incapable of discerning the proper path to felicity and discovering the truth. Majlesi's repeated assertion that humans have a deficient mind needs to be understood in the context of his belief that the reports of the imams are the absolute repository of all knowledge and certitudes. As long as human reasoning confirms and validates such reports, be they on independent topics or pertaining to interpretations of Qur'anic verses and injunctions, Majlesi honours and respects the mental and rational capacity of humans. Once doubt creeps in, questions are raised and alternative explanations to the Majlesi-approved constructions and understandings are advanced, he unequivocally categorizes such exercises as futile outcomes of deficient minds. Majlesi refers to a report attributed to an imam to support his own position and demonstrate the deficiency of human reasoning. He argues that those who do not receive revelations and who God has not designated as leaders to whom obedience is compulsory are not in a position to speak on religious issues, for if they do, it would imply that they have considered themselves as partners to God.[1] Majlesi later includes the scholars of reports in the circle of those who are entitled to speak on religious issues. This may be because he believed that they or some of them were actually designated by God as leaders.

---

[1] M. B. Majlesi, *Hayat al-Qolub*, vol. 5, pp. 30–31.

BACKGROUND TO THE DEBATE ON REASON

Historically, the debate between the role and significance of reason-based truth, the outcome of human mind and *hadith*-based truth, the outcome of reports attributed to the imams well preceded Majlesi's time. It has been argued that Shi'i scholars regarded their imams and not "mere human reason" as the "ultimate source of knowledge".[2] This perception, which categorized reason as a means to, and not a source of, arriving at the truth, characterized the dominant Shi'i discourse "until the middle of the third/ninth century".[3] It seems as if the imams themselves had a dual approach to the topic of reason. While they endorsed the use of rational arguments employed by Shi'i theologians in the defence of Shi'ism against its opponents, they cautioned against the use of reason as a basis for constructing beliefs.[4]

On the one hand, the use of reasoning in arguments and polemics as a defensive weapon protecting Shi'ism was indispensable, giving rise to those who employed speculative theology or the *motakallemin*. The majority of Shi'i *motakallemin*, however, had an instrumentalist approach to reason. It has been suggested that they appreciated it as a tool and not an end in itself, since they did not consider reason as an independent source of discerning religious truths. For them, reasoning or argumentation could be employed only if "its attributes were based on revelation, the teachings of the Prophet and religious texts".[5] There were, however, highly distinguished scholars that took an interest in reason on its own merits. Going against the tide of Shi'i scholars intent on limiting if not totally negating the ambit of reason, Seyyed or Sharif Morteza, Sheykh Mofid's outstanding student, argued that "in fact, the yardstick and criteria of assessing ordinances is the command of reason and not the Imam".[6]

On the other hand, those Shi'i scholars who rejected any use of reason, instrumental or otherwise, fearing its corrupting and subversive effects on believers, rejected independent and unrestrained use of reason as reprehensible if not prohibited. These Shi'i scholars, the *mohaddethin*, became the proponents of the *hadith*-based creed. The meaning of reason among the *mohaddethin* was reduced to the capacity or power, assisting individuals to obtain a better understanding of religion. In this Shi'i paradigm, the

---

[2] H. Modarresi, *Crisis and Consolidation in the Formative Period of Shi'ite Islam*, p. 112.
[3] Ibid., pp. 112–113.   [4] Ibid., p. 115.
[5] M. T. Sobhani, 'Aqlgaraie va Nassgeraie dar Kalam Eslami' in *Naqd va Nazar*, Shomareh 3 va 4 (1374).
[6] Ibid.

use of reason was bound and restrained by reports. Exegesis and interpretations, inevitably using reasoning, were subsequently confined to the limitations set by the reports. Consequently, reason had to be either anchored in reports or was rejected as a means or path to infidelity. According to Sobhani, the text-based and, by definition, anti-rationalist School of Shi'ism, was later elaborated, propagated and ultimately perfected by Sheykh Horr-e Amoli and Mohammad-Baqer Majlesi.[7]

The *hadith*-based Akhbari school, which may be traced to the Buyid dynasty during the tenth century, was revived and crowned as the mainstream of Shi'i discourse by Molla Mohammad-Amin Astarabadi during the seventeenth century.[8] Aimed at reviving *hadith* literature while countering and rejecting recourse to *ejtehad* and independent personal judgement, the Akhbari school reversed the advances of the rational school of Shi'ism embodied in works of Sheykh Mufid, Sharif Morteza, Sheykh Tusi and 'Allameh Helli. Astarabadi's school is founded on the critique of 'Allameh Helli's method of deriving religious ordinances based on the four proofs of the Qur'an, the Sonnat (*Sunnah*), reason and consensus. Arguing that the formal and literal text of the Qur'an and the reports largely sufficed as a basis for the derivation and deduction of religious ordinances, Astarabadi concluded that the use or application of reason was utterly useless.

Chiding 'Allameh Helli (1280–1358) for introducing reason (*aql*), opinion or conjecture (*zann*) and consensus as sources for deriving ordinances, Astarabadi accused those who had accepted these two sources as being influenced by the Sunnis.[9] Astarabadi believed that 'Allameh Helli's novel method, which was in fact somewhat similar to al-Shafe'i's classification of Shari'at bases in his *al-Risala*, demonstrated his neglect of pursuing the path of traditional Shi'i scholars. Astarabadi maintained that Helli's formulation was rooted in his intellectual sympathy for Sunni texts.[10] In view of Astarabadi's rather harsh reaction towards 'Allemeh Helli, it is less surprising that faced with modernist challengers, later neo-Akhbaris resorted to the same intimidating tactic of denouncing their opponents as Sunnis and Wahhabis.

The *'olama* of the Akhbari school believed that the reports of Shi'i imams constituted the most important source of religious beliefs and ordinances, since in their eyes, other sources such as the Qur'an and

---

[7] Ibid.   [8] E. Kohlberg, *Belief and Law in Imami Shi'ism* (Hampshire, 1991), p. 133.
[9] A. Davani, *Mafakher-e Eslam*, p. 462.
[10] M. H. Mashayekh, 'Akhbariyeh' in *Encyclopaedia of Shi'a*, vol. 2 (Tehran, 1372), p. 8.

reasoning were justifiable and employable as religious proofs only if they had been approved by reports.[11] Astarabadi maintained that the *ahadith* attributed to the imams constituted "the single most important source of law".[12] Even the correct understanding of the Qur'an was believed by the Akhbaris to hinge upon reports.[13] In the absence of reports, the Akhbaris maintained that the content of the Qur'an would have remained ambiguous and ineffective as legal evidence. As will be shown, Majlesi ascribed to the same position.

The Akhbaris went to the extreme position of maintaining that reference to the Qur'an was permitted only if report-based interpretations of the Qur'anic verses were available.[14] Looking at the Qur'an only through the lens of reports and considering the *hadith* as the sole proof and source of religious knowledge, belief and ordinances justifies characterizing the Akhbaris as the proponents of "the *hadith*-only" Shi'i discourse.[15] In his scathing attack against reason and *ejtehad* as an anti-Shari'at innovation, Astarabadi is said to have believed that the sole binding obligation of Muslims was to follow the letter of reports attributed to the Prophet and the imams.[16]

On the sensitive issue of the authenticity and validity of reports, the Akhbaris maintained that all the *ahadith* in the four major Shi'i compilations of Koleyni, Ebn Babawayh and Sheykh Tusi (two works) were authentic, dependable and represented the exact words of the imams themselves.[17] Save for weak (*za'if*) reports to which Tusi had explicitly referred in his two works, *al-Tahzib* and *al-Estebsar*, the Akhbaris considered all other *ahadith*, irrespective of their degree of authenticity, as sound enough for believers to act upon.[18] One of Astarabadi's main criticisms of 'Allameh Helli was that he had tried to introduce a system of sifting through reports and classifying them according to their reliability, thus shedding doubt on the accuracy of all reports collected in Shi'i compilations. Astarabadi considered the examination and classification of the *ahadith* by Helli as evidence of Sunni practices.[19] Mohammad-Baqer Majlesi, who was born four years after the death of Astarabadi, was raised in a predominantly Akhbari environment and was

[11] Ibid. p. 7.   [12] E. Kohlberg, *Belief and Law in Imami Shi'ism*, p. 134.
[13] M. H. Mashayekh, 'Akhbariyeh' in *Encyclopaedia of Shi'a*, vol. 2, p. 7.   [14] Ibid., p. 10.
[15] Ibid.   [16] H. Anousheh, 'Astarabadi' in *Encyclopaedia of Shi'a*, vol. 2, p. 107.
[17] A. Davani, *Mafakher-e Eslam*, p. 462.
[18] M. H. Mashayekh, 'Akhbariyeh' in *Encyclopaedia of Shi'a*, vol. 2, p. 9.
[19] E. Kohlberg, *Belief and Law in Imami Shi'ism*, p. 134.

taught by Akhbari teachers, one of whom, Mohammad Mo'men Astarabadi, was Mohammad-Amin Astarabadi's son.

QUR'AN AND REASON CONSTRAINED BY HADITH: MAJLESI'S ASSESSMENT OF THE QUR'AN

Through an interesting process of elimination within the Shari'at sources, Majlesi crowns the reports attributed to the imams as the only authentic and dependable source of truth for the Shi'i. Both the Qur'an and reason are first constrained and subsequently trumped by reports. Consensus or *ejma'* (ijma) is not really appreciated as a Shari'at source by Majlesi. If Majlesi can demonstrate that the Qur'an, the word of God, the indisputable source of truth for Muslims only becomes meaningful and useful when it is interpreted, and made apparent by reports, rendering the authority of the Qur'an dependent on reports, then it becomes rather easy for him to prove that reason cannot stand a chance in competition with reports. Majlesi privileges the explanation attributed to the imams over the word of God in the same breath as privileging the words ascribed to the same imams over the reasoning capacities of mortal human beings. The end result of this important exercise by Majlesi is to show the usefulness, if not superiority, of the *hadith* over the Qur'an and ipso facto human reason.

According to Majlesi, reason (*aql*) is the power to differentiate between right and wrong and the capacity to distinguish between good and evil.[20] The power to reason, however, is subject to error. To prevent the human mind from erring, Majlesi argues for checking the products of reasoning against the Shari'at. The outcomes of the application of rational thought validated by the Shari'at are deemed acceptable and authorized. For Majlesi, reliance on reason without anchoring it in the Shari'at will inevitably lead to deviation and corruption. The key Shari'at source for Majlesi, however, is not really the Qur'an but the reports.

Making his case in favour of the primacy of reports in comparison to all other Shari'at sources, Majlesi argues that the extreme ambiguity of the Qur'an leads to different interpretations and understandings of it.[21] Arguing that the Qur'an is ambiguous (*mojmal*) and "multi-faceted" (*zuvujuh*) allowing for multi-interpretations and discourses, Majlesi

---

[20] M. Kadivar, 'Aql va Din az Didgah-e Mohaddes va Hakim' in M. Mohrizi and H. Rabbani (eds.), *Shenakhtnameh 'Allameh Majlesi*, vol. 1, p. 130.

[21] M. B. Majlesi, *Haq al-Yaqin*, p. 37.

identifies the major role of the imams and the reports ascribed to them as a clarifying, standardizing and homogenizing force, capable of providing an exclusive and correct interpretation, putting an end to the multiplicity of meanings and dissent. Without the reports attributed to the imams, the understanding of the Qur'an is said to be impossible, rendering the conduct of religious and worldly pursuits inconceivable and impracticable. Since the reports illuminate and explain (*tafsir*) the Qur'anic verses, the pious are expected to refer to such reports to grasp the meaning of the Book. If a verse is not explained by reports, individuals will be unable to understand the meaning of the Book.[22]

Aside from the ambiguity of the Qur'anic verses, Majlesi maintains that the majority of Islamic injunctions (*ahkam*) may not be discerned or derived from the apparent text of the Qur'an.[23] Elsewhere he maintains that only a few Islamic injunctions are revealed by the Qur'an and even those are highly ambiguous and allegorical.[24] This shortcoming, according to Majlesi, also necessitates an interpreter, the Imam, sent by God and capable of deriving injunctions from the Qur'an.[25] Majlesi openly declares that in the absence of an infallible interpreter who would explain the injunctions of the Book to the members of the community (*ommat*), the Book would be useless.[26] Based on Majlesi's view, the significance and importance of the Qur'an hinges upon the explanatory role of the interpreters and commentators, the imams.

In an interesting analysis of knowledge and its limitations, Majlesi argues that seeking knowledge is a religious obligation (*vajeb*). He posits that God loves those who seek knowledge and that the quest for it is the highest form of prayers. Yet Majlesi argues that not all knowledge would lead to eternal felicity.[27] The knowledge deemed useful, leading to salvation, according to Majlesi, is that which has reached the people through the reports of the *ahl-e beyt* or the imams. In these reports, he asserts, the certitudes (*mohkamat*) of the Qur'an are all interpreted and so are a good majority of the ambiguous texts (*moteshabehat*). Majlesi adds that those ambiguous Qur'anic texts for which an interpretation in the reports cannot be found should best be left alone, since it is neither advisable nor useful to think about them.[28]

---

[22] M. Kadivar, 'Aql va Din az Didgah-e Mohaddes va Hakim', p. 131.
[23] M. B. Majlesi, *Hayat al-Qolub*, vol. 5, p. 19.   [24] Ibid., p. 123.
[25] Ibid., p. 19.   [26] Ibid., pp. 22, 33.
[27] M. B. Majlesi, *'Eyn al-Hayat*, pp. 166, 170–171.   [28] Ibid., p. 171.

As for other types of knowledge, Majlesi argues that except for the interpretation of the imams, all other knowledge is either futile and its pursuit a waste of life or it would lead to doubt, which in turn usually leads to infidelity (*kofr*).[29] According to Majlesism, knowledge and science cannot go beyond the very closely defined ambit of the imams' attributed reports. Those who venture beyond the body of reports will become infidels without a chance of salvation. It is difficult to understand how, in this fundamentally anti-science atmosphere promoted by Majlesism, the Shiʻi would take a liking to the sciences. Majlesi's emphasis on report-based knowledge as the only source of knowledge may be based on his love for the attributed words of the imams. Yet it may also equally be motivated by self-interest and the protection of his own unique position as an interpreter or narrator of the imams' words.

Majlesi argues that if the Qur'an, on its own, were sufficient to guide the Muslims to felicity and salvation, there would not have been so much schism among Muslims.[30] The necessary appointment of the Imam, representing a single authoritative voice, Majlesi argues, prevents the community from falling into disorder and perversity.[31] In his writings, however, as would be expected, Majlesi does insist on the primary role of the Qur'an, but he attenuates and modifies his position by arguing that without an infallible interpreter capable of deducing the injunctions from the Qur'an, the Book will remain ineffective and unusable.[32] He maintains that, independently and alone, the Qur'an does not constitute a proof or source of truth. According to Majlesi, the Qur'an can attain the status of a source of truth or a proof only when it is accompanied by a knowledgeable and truthful interpreter, an imam.[33] Majlesi, therefore, concludes that there is a greater need for the interpreters than the Book.[34] He posits that the imams are the complete containers and possessors of the Qur'an.[35] The imams are said to know the wording and meaning of the Qur'an and it is even suggested that they are the only ones who can read the Qur'an, as they are aware of all its secrets.[36]

Having raised the status of the imams to one without which understanding the word of God and pursuing one's religion is made impossible, Majlesi subsequently projects the power, significance and importance of the imams onto their attributed reports. A *hadith* could be broken down into three distinct aspects: first, the Imam to whom a report is attributed;

---

[29] Ibid., p. 170.   [30] M. B. Majlesi, *Haq al-Yaqin*, p. 20.   [31] Ibid., p. 37.
[32] Ibid., p. 23.   [33] M. B. Majlesi, *Hayat al-Qolub*, vol. 5, p. 33.
[34] Ibid., p. 122.   [35] Ibid., p. 123.   [36] Ibid., pp. 148, 150.

second, the content of the report; and finally, the person of the recorder and reporter of the hadith. For Majlesi, it seems as if the transmitter, the content and the imams are but one unassailable holy unit. In this interesting transformation process, the attributed reports are elevated to a level of sanctity equal to the person of the Imam. Majlesi's methodology overlooks the fact that even though a *hadith* attributed to an imam may be the word of the Imam, it may also be a fabrication by a falsifier who wishes to denigrate the imams and the Shi'i or use the imams' name and authority for personal ends. Majlesi assumes that the transmitters of reports are as sacred and dependable as the imams. According to Majlesi, the religious duty of the common people incapable of understanding the Qur'an and endowed with defective minds subsequently becomes simple. They can only resign themselves to the reports left behind from the imams and collected in Shi'i compilations. In this ingenious transmission process, the sanctity of God is effectively passed on to the sanctity of reports attributed to the Imam. The last phase of this transmission process, as we shall see, passes on the sanctity of the reports to the scholars and experts on the reports.

In his writings on Shi'i beliefs, Majlesi brings his process of empowering the reports attributed to the imams to a logical conclusion and demonstrates that only recourse to and reliance on reports can guarantee felicity in this world and salvation in the other. Having emphasized that all wisdom and knowledge, well expounded and explained, are to be found in the reports, Majlesi writes, "the paths to well-being and salvation are clearly elucidated in the reports".[37] In this and many other references to the proper source of seeking worldly well-being and deliverance in the hereafter, Majlesi does not refer to the Qur'an as a repository, but substitutes the word of God with that of reports or what is attributed to the Prophet and the imams. To understand Majlesi's position in relation to the Qur'an, it may be helpful to know that, at times, Majlesi hints at the fact that the complete or true Qur'an is different from the one compiled during 'Osman's (Uthman's) Caliphate and remains in possession of the imams.[38]

MAJLESI'S REFUTATION OF REASON

Majlesi's refutation of the validity of human reasoning and rational thought is conducted along three major axes. First, for Majlesi, the human mind and

---

[37] M. B. Majlesi, *E'teqadat*, p. 48.
[38] M. B. Majlesi, *Majmu'eh-e Rasael-e E'teqadi* (Mashhad, 1368), p. 110.

the human capacity to reason is simply defective and thus incapable of attaining the truth. According to this line of argument, there is something fundamentally wrong or missing in human reasoning, rendering this tool incapable of discerning right from wrong and good from evil. Even though at times Majlesi recognizes the ability of humans to differentiate between right and wrong, the crux and bulk of his arguments demonstrate that he believes otherwise. Without some sort of help or guidance from the non-human world, there can be no possibility of felicity in this world and salvation in the next world for human beings.

For Majlesi, God appointed prophets in order to compensate for the defectiveness of human reasoning. Majlesi argues that if God believed that independent human reasoning sufficed to lead people in life, He would not have sent them the prophets. The appointment of prophets by God is presented as the proof of the fact that independent thought is deficient and needs to be abandoned as a source of arriving at the truth. Having accepted this axiom, human beings are required to resign themselves to the guidance of the prophets.[39] Does not the people's act of choosing to embrace and accept the prophets of God and their guidance require the application of human reasoning? Majlesi does not address the question at this point. Once reasoning is argued to be defective and therefore unreliable and incapable of resolving problems, Majlesi needs to convince human beings that a viable and non-depletable source of truth does exist as an alternative, which they need to rely on, if they do not wish to go astray. The task of convincing human beings that if they wish to be considered as pious they need to accept their eternal condition of mental incapacity (until the reappearance of the Twelfth Imam) and reject the use of independent judgement may have been easier as long as the Prophet and the imams were alive. With the death of the Prophet, the viable source of truth becomes the imams, and after their death, the source is transferred to the reports ascribed to them. The combination of defective human minds and the need to follow prophets, imams and subsequently their attributed reports leads to a very important religious and political corollary. Majlesi argues that once the infallible Imam goes into occultation, it becomes incumbent upon believers to refer to their reports and "those who report their *ahadith*", as well as the *'olama*.[40] Majlesi clearly assumes that the mind of the transmitters of the reports and the *'olama* cannot be defective.

---

[39] M. B. Majlesi, 'Resaleh-e Majlesi dar bareh Hokama, Ousouliyoun va Sufiyeh' in R. Ja'fariyan (ed.), *Din va Siyasat dar Dowreh Safavi*, p. 261.

[40] Ibid., pp. 261, 265.

The second axes of Majlesi's refutation of human reasoning revolves around his key argument that the human mind as compared to the innate and acquired faculties of the imams is deficient and inadequate. Whereas Majlesi's first axis of refuting human reasoning was based on the absolute deficiency of the human mind, this second axis puts forward a comparative argument. This line of thought suggests that the human mind cannot measure up to or compete with the knowledge of the imams expressed in the reports. It is based on the comparison between the human mind and the intellectual capacity of the imams that Majlesi rules against the use of human reasoning. Having condemned human reasoning to structural and fundamental failures and defects, Majlesi buttresses his refutation of reasoning and rules that in comparison to a superior source of wisdom – the reports – it would be best to desist from the use of a weaker force, human reason. This comparative disadvantage of the human mind is the main theme and argument found in Majlesi's works.

In his writings, Majlesi encourages the common folk to desist from reflection and reasoning (*ta'aqol*) on issues that he deems too complicated for them to grasp, such as the degree to which God subjects human beings to compulsion or choice (*jabr va ekhtiyar*) or the role of expediency (*maslahat*) and wisdom (*hekmat*) in God's acts.[41] Majlesi supports his calling on the common folk to abstain from reasoning by invoking the existence of many reports that prohibit reflection on certain issues.[42] To Majlesi, all that needs to be known by human beings and contains any value or truth has been comprehensively covered and stated by the imams in their attributed reports. Human reflection, therefore, in his mind, is incapable of shedding any new light on the realm of human knowledge and wisdom. It is not surprising that Majlesi calls for the cessation of human reflection after the imams, arguing that the imams have closed the door of reason after their own cognitive contributions, forbidding the people to rely on their own deficient reasoning and ordering them to follow the imams in all matters.[43] According to Majlesi, the words and deeds of the Prophet and imams are superior to human reasoning because they never use their independent judgement (*ra'y*, *ejtehad*) but they receive their knowledge from God and the Prophet, with each imam passing it on to the other.[44] Interestingly enough, Majlesi argues that with the return of the Twelfth Imam, the defectiveness of the human mind will be overcome, and

---

[41] M. B. Majlesi, *Haq al-Yaqin*, p. 18. [42] Ibid.

[43] M. Kadivar, 'Aql va Din az Didgah-e Mohaddes va Hakim', p. 130.

[44] M. B. Majlesi, *E'teqadat*, p. 29.

once again, their ability to reason will attain its complete capacity.[45] But until that time, Majlesi invites the common folk to inactivate their minds and accept the interpretations, formulations and explanations of the reporters of *ahadith* and the '*olama*.

Majlesi drives home his main point by arguing that according to numerous reports, the imams have reiterated that whatever they have said (has been attributed to them) needs to be accepted by the people. If the common folk cannot grasp the essential content of the reports based on their own understanding, they should accept them on face value. Majlesi warns people against denying or rejecting reports just because they are rationally incomprehensible. He presents two arguments for his position. First, he maintains that there is always the possibility that the imams may have said them.[46] Given that possibility, rejecting the reports would mean rejecting God.[47] In effect, Majlesi homogenizes all reports as the true and proven words and acts of imams and subsequently rules that rejecting them would imply apostasy. Second, Majlesi argues that the human mind is incapable of grasping the experience and the knowledge of the imams, since they are abnormal, incredible and fantastic.[48] He maintains that human reasoning cannot fathom the saying and behaviour of the imams, and therefore this domain is beyond the grasp of human beings. Understanding this inaccessible domain, beyond human mental capacity, obviously cannot result from the use of independent judgement or reasoning. Majlesi suggests that instead of denying those reports attributed to the imams that are incompatible with reason, people should accept them, as they may be correct.[49]

Based on his two arguments, he concludes that people are obliged to accept the reports ascribed to the imams, even though they may seem phantasmical and superstitious running against human common sense and rational judgement. The possibility of fabricated reports unrelated to the imams does not enter into Majlesi's discussion. To him, whatever is attributed to the imams is the veritable word of the imams, and therefore the Imam and his reports are the one and the same. According to Mohsen Kadivar, 'Allameh Tabataba'i, whose twenty-volume magnum opus, *Tafsir-e al-Mizan*, is one of the most authoritative contemporary commentaries on the Qur'an and whose scholarly credentials in the field are unquestionable, maintained that Majlesi's *Bahar al-Anvar* included

[45] M. B. Majlesi, *Majmu'eh-e Rasael-e E'teqadi*, p. 108.
[46] M. B. Majlesi, *E'teqadat*, p. 30.   [47] M. B. Majlesi, *Haq al-Yaqin*, pp. 368–369.
[48] M. B. Majlesi, *E'teqadat*, p. 31.   [49] M. B. Majlesi, *E'teqadat*, pp. 30–31.

certain reports in opposition to the Qur'an and reason that were undoubt-edly fabricated and forged.[50] Ayatollah Neʻmatollah Salehi-e Najafabadi also refers to reports in *Bahar al-Anvar* and certain of Majlesi's sources as unreliable.[51]

Majlesi's third axis of refuting reasoning is based on the argument that rational engagements could lead to doubt and the questioning of the faith. To Majlesi, reason is subversive and a major threat to religion. He brands this type of scepticism as apostasy. He refers to the philosophers, who had relied on their own "deficient reasoning and false thoughts" and "had gone astray" as the best examples of the fate of those who employed reasoning.[52] He advises the philosophers not to opine on the basis of their reasoning, especially on religious and issues, and reminds them that often what is evident according to reason is no less than an illusion. Majlesi finally warns the philosophers to measure and weigh their thoughts according to the scales of Islamic law and the confirmed reports of the imams in order to avoid perishing.[53] Majlesi consistently argues that the "deficient minds" of the people suffering from "a thousand defects" and "flooded by a hundred thousand lustful thoughts" if left to itself is bound to distort the faith.[54] So it is argued that in any religion, one should follow the report and teachings of the founder of that faith and strictly avoid the employment of one's own deficient reasoning, which would lead to inno-vations and bring about one's demise and delusion.[55]

In Majlesi's writings, the issue of human reasoning (*aql*), independent judgement or opinion (*ra'y*), and interpretation (*ta'vil*) are interrelated. His position against human reasoning should be understood in terms of how its unfettered application in the process of interpretation could impact, reconstitute and even subvert that which Majlesi wishes to establish as unassailable Shiʻi dogma. It is the fear of human reasoning's revolutionary impact on irrational dogma that compels Majlesi to rule that once the honest reporter has conveyed the message of the imams, "interpretation (*ta'vil*) in any and all domains should be desisted from, lest the person engaging in it would fall to apostasy and infidelity".[56] In Majlesi's static

---

[50] M. Kadivar, 'Aql va Din az Didgah-e Mohaddes va Hakim', p. 146.
[51] N. Salehi-e Najafabadi, *Asay-e Musa ya Darman-e Bimariy-e Quluw* (Tehran, 1380), pp. 79, 137.
[52] M. B. Majlesi, *Eʻteqadat*, p. 15.
[53] M. Kadivar, 'Aql va Din az Didgah-e Mohaddes va Hakim', p. 198.
[54] M. B. Majlesi, *ʻEyn al-Hayat*, pp. 202–203.   [55] M. B. Majlesi, *ʻEyn al-Hayat*, p. 202.
[56] M. B. Majlesi, *ʻEyn al-Hayat*, p. 153.

and uncontextualized construction, there exists a clear connection between human reasoning, reinterpretation, innovation in the faith (*bed'at*) and the natural end result of apostasy and infidelity.

Referring to a report attributed to one of the imams, Majlesi demonstrates how the use of reasoning would spark off a chain of reactions leading to unbelief and apostasy. He writes that whoever looks at religion through his own individual opinion or independent judgement (*ra'y*) will perish, and whoever neglects the teachings of the Prophet's Household (*ahl-e beyt*) will be misled and deceived, and whoever parts ways with God's book and the sayings of the Prophet is an infidel (*kafar*).[57] To Majlesi, God's book and all reports irrespective of their degree of authenticity is one single package. Therefore, infidelity, according to Majlesi, applies to those who deviate from the attributed reports of the imams or the Prophet. Majlesi argues that the major distinction between the Shi'i and the Sunni is that the former always act according to the edicts of their imams, whereas the Sunni manage their affairs based on their own deficient reasoning, leading to gross deviations.[58] Majlesi chooses not to acknowledge the fact that his Shi'i *hadith*-based discourse with its particular aversion to reasoning is very similar to the *hadith*-based school of the Sunnis, the only difference being that Shi'i reports transmit prophetic words and deeds through the imams or they can originate with the imams, while Sunni reports are transmitted by the companions of the Prophet. A close comparison between Ibn Hanbal and Majlesi, with eight centuries of difference between them, could demonstrate similarities in their view of the importance of reports and their rejection of the use of reasoning and opinion, while it could equally demonstrate great differences between the relation of the two men to power and worldly attachments. To Majlesi, interpretation is the product of human reasoning, the natural outcome of which would condemn the person practicing it to apostasy and eternal damnation. In his mind, reason is reprehensible, as it constitutes a subversive capacity in need of rigid control, while mental and intellectual resignation and obedience reflect desirable and beneficial conduct in the believers' pursuit of attaining belief and certitude.

What may seem inconsistent in Majlesi's writings is that, at times, he does concede to the fact that reason is a God-given gift.[59] In support of monotheism, for example, Majlesi appeals to the human mind and argues that the validity of monotheism is rationally evident and that "there exists

[57] Ibid., pp. 203–204.   [58] Ibid., p. 203.
[59] M. B. Majlesi, *Majmu'eh-e Rasel-e E'teqadi*, p. 46.

a rational consensus" on the matter, thus relying on human reasoning and consensus as a proof or a justifying source.[60] Majlesi's references to reason on issues such as monotheism, where the faith explicitly prohibits belief on the basis of blind obedience to someone else (*taqlid*), seems to be a pragmatic exercise. To buttress his own arguments, where it suits him, Majlesi invokes reason on a limited scale, as a decorative tool, but does not believe in it as an analytical, explanatory and problem-solving tool. In his book on imamology (*emamshenasi*), Majlesi refers to numerous rational arguments forwarded by Shi'i scholars supporting the indispensability of a God-appointed imam. Majlesi does makes use of rational proofs, but before presenting them, he warns his readers that he is interested in presenting proofs based on evidences from the Qur'an and reports.[61]

Elsewhere Majlesi engages in an interesting exercise. He appeals to what he calls reason-based arguments as evidence to prove that people are inept at appointing a leader or an imam.[62] Given the deficient minds of the people, Majlesi argues that, based on reason and reports, the task of appointment belongs to God. Here, Majlesi appeals to human reasoning to conclude that the human mind is deficient. Kadivar, however, argues that Majlesi accepts reason as a power that can differentiate between good and evil, right and wrong. Yet he adds that, for Majlesi, reason is incapable of understanding and rendering correct judgement. Therefore the only acceptable reasoning is one, which is in agreement with Shari'at. According to Kadivar, Majlesi seems to believe that the only domain in which reason has the right to express itself is that of identifying or knowing the Imam. Once reason serves the purpose of identifying the Imam, it would need to cease functioning, since people have no other alternative but to rely on the reports of the imams.[63] To Majlesi, human reasoning has to be refuted, since its outcome is at best suspect. Human reasoning is presented as a threat that cannot be neatly controlled and managed and therefore needs to be essentially muzzled by reports that are ultimately selected and interpreted by the connoisseurs of *ahadith*.

---

[60] M. B. Majlesi, *Haq al-Yaqin*, pp. 10, 11, 15, 16.
[61] M. B. Majlesi, *Hayat al-Qolub*, vol. 5, pp. 18–19.
[62] M. B. Majlesi, *Haq al-Yaqin*, pp. 36–37.
[63] M. Kadivar, 'Aql va Din az Didgah-e Mohaddes va Hakim' in M. Mohrizi and H. Rabbani (eds.), *Shenakhtnameh 'Allameh Majlesi*, vol. 1, pp. 130–131; M. Kadivar, 'Ayar Naqd dar Manzelat 'Aql' in M. Mohrizi and H. Rabbani (eds.), *Shenakhtnameh 'Allameh Majlesi*, vol. 1, pp. 212, 213, 219.

Throughout his writings, Majlesi warns against interpretation (*ta'vil*) and argues that such an exercise would undermine the certitudes of the faith and "trample upon the belief of believers".[64] Majlesi's opposition to interpretation is partly rooted in his textualist and literalist Akhbari tendencies and partly based on his unease with the consequences of such an endeavour by the "uninitiated", as it could lead to the modification and alteration of established dogma. Interpretation in "wrong" hands could undermine Majlesi's established truths and subvert his intricate method of social and individual engineering through religious formulations. Ironically, however, in his writings Majlesi engages in interpretation wherever and whenever he needs to make a point or support a position for which there are no clear and evident texts available in the Qur'an. In these instances, Majlesi the textualist and literalist transforms into a contextualist and an exegetist. He forbids everyone other than himself and presumably certain other reporters of *ahadith* to use their reasoning and power of interpretation. In his writings, he seems to be quite at ease working within a double-standard system. If the use of reason is reprobated and even prohibited for all, why should it become an accepted practice for some unless they are considered as the chosen "sacred" people? In effect, by giving the reporters of *ahadith* the exclusive right to reason and interpret, Majlesi empowers them to reason and prescribe for the rest of society. In this task, Majlesi seeks shelter from the accusation of applying his personal opinion by relying, selecting and employing reports attributed to the imams.

Majlesi is perfectly at ease with interpreting the Qur'an, based on the reports attributed to the imams that he selects. Majlesi reads Shiʻi reports attributed to the imams back into the Qur'an. He interprets the Book in such a way that his understanding and reading of the text ends up different from the original. Majlesi quotes verse 88 of the Surah *Al-Qasas* (28), "Everything [that exists] will perish except His own Face".[65] He subsequently refers to numerous reports attributed to the imams, such as one that is supposed to have said: "we [imams] are the faces from whom God's religion, the knowledge of God and His worship should be learnt". Majlesi then concludes that the "Face of God" mentioned in the Qur'an is a

---

[64] M. B. Majlesi, *Eʻteqadat*, p. 31.
[65] M. B. Majlesi, *Hayat al-Qolub*, vol. 5, p. 496; *The Holy Qur'an*, (tr.) A. Y. ʻAli, p. 328.

reference to Shiʻi imams.[66] In this case, when Majlesi the exegete seeks to prove that the imams are mentioned in the Qur'an, he is perfectly at ease with abandoning his literalist claims, as he can argue that the attributed reports explain the Qur'an.

Based on an arbitrary process of interpretation and association, Majlesi refers to attributed reports commenting on a Qur'anic text and subsequently presents a completely different meaning from the term used by the Qur'an. This process replaces the apparent and clear meaning of a Qur'anic verse with an esoteric interpretation. Majlesi arranges and systematically presents his creative exegesis to deduce from Qur'anic verses information favourable to the Shiʻi. In a telling case, Majlesi refers to verse 83 of the Surah *al-Nahl* (16), which reads: "they recognize the favour of God, yet they deny it and most of them are disbelievers".[67] He then quotes ʻAli ebn-Ebrahim as saying, "the favours of God are the imams" and proceeds to make a reference to a report attributed to one of the imams, at the end of which the Qur'anic verse "they recognize the favours of God" is retranslated by Majlesi into Farsi. Majlesi's new version of the same Qur'anic verse reads: "they recognize ʻAli's guardianship, yet they deny it and most of them are disbelievers in ʻAli's guardianship".[68] The term "favours" used in the Qur'an is interpreted, retranslated and passed on to Persian language readers by Majlesi as "ʻAli's guardianship", thus seeking to prove that there are references in the Qur'an to the imams and that the acceptance of Imam ʻAli's leadership is required of all Muslims, since it is stated in the Qur'an.

In another effort to interpret the Qur'an, Majlesi presents verse 143 of the Surah *al-Baqarah* (2). The translation of the first part of the verse reads: "Thus We have made of you a median (balanced) *ommat* – meaning just or the average between extremities, as has been referred to before or the best of communities – so that you might be witnesses over the people and the Prophet a witness over you".[69] In his own commentary under the subheading of "the translator says", Majlesi argues that "according to numerous reports those addressed in this verse as you and the *ommat* are the imams and they are the witnesses over the people".[70] Majlesi reads into the Qur'anic verse a notion that is not explicit in the text. He then supports

---

[66] M. B. Majlesi, *Hayat al-Qolub*, vol. 5, pp. 498–499.
[67] Ibid., p. 362; see also the English translation of *The Holy Qur'an*, (tr.) A. Y. ʻAli, p. 659.
[68] M. B. Majlesi, *Hayat al-Qolub*, vol. 5, p. 362.
[69] Ibid., pp. 266–267. This is my English translation of Majlesi's Farsi translation of the Qur'an 2:134.
[70] Ibid., p. 268.

his position by falling back on reports ascribed to the imams on this theme. According to reports attributed to them, they had stated, "We are the median community, the witnesses of God over the people and the proofs of God on Earth".[71] To Majlesi, who accepts reports as factual words of the imams, this is yet another case where the so-called ambiguity in the Qur'an is clarified and made plain by reports.

Majlesi's position on the deficiency of human reasoning leads one to assume that he would be averse to the use of reasoning as a tool for shedding light on religious truths. If human reasoning is assumed deficient, then all types of human interpretation, explanation or exegesis, should be shunned, as is the position of the mainstream Akhbaris or firm believers in the reports. However, Majlesi informs us that once he began his search for, study and analysis of the reports of the imams, he used and applied his "power to think" (*niruy-e tafakor*) to the task at hand.[72] This application of reasoning or reflective capacities could be construed as *ejtehad* if the explanation or interpretation offered by Majlesi turns out to be different from the apparent and literal meaning of the report. Even the process of choice and selection, accepting a *hadith* or privileging one over another, is the application of reason. Majlesi confirms the suspicion that he does use some form of quasi-*ejtehad* by positing that certain reports have to be "interpreted" (*ta'vil*).[73] In view of Majlesi's political and religious status, supported by the authority of the state to formulate and implement an ideology, his seemingly innocuous self-ascribed right of interpretation, while refusing to acknowledge such rights to others, takes on a political dimension and significance.

In two cases, Majlesi reconfigures reports to demonstrate that some 700 years before the ascension of Shah Esma'il to the throne, the rule of the Safavid dynasty was foretold by the imams. Majlesi not only sanctifies the Safavi dynasty and all its shahs by making the claim that the imams gave good tidings about the coming of the Safavis and therefore they must be blessed and divinely supported, but he also claims that the Safavis were the chosen forerunners of the Twelfth Imam. Here, the ascribed reports of the imams are reconfigured and interpreted by Majlesi to yield the desired political results. The claims made by President Ahmadinejad that his rule was in effect the prelude to the coming of the Hidden

---

[71] Ibid.
[72] A. Davani, 'Sharh-e hal'e "Allameh Majlesi' in M. Mohrizi and H. Rabbani (eds.), *Shenakhtnameh 'Allameh Majlesi*, vol. 1, p. 62.
[73] M. Kadivar, 'Aql va Din az Didgah-e Mohaddes va Hakim' in M. Mohrizi and H. Rabbani (eds.), *Shenakhtnameh 'Allameh Majlesi*, vol. 1, p. 139.

Imam implying that whoever opposed him obstructed the Imam's return was by no means original and had its roots in similar claims by Majlesi.

Majlesi refers to a report attributed to one of the imams predicting that a group will appear from the East inviting the people and waging *jahad* in the name of the True faith (Shi'i). This group is said to establish a dynasty, which will last until the time when they will hand over the realms of power to the Twelfth Imam. Having stated the report, Majlesi suggests that it is evident to the wise that this was the Safavi dynasty, which came from the East, invited the people and waged *jahad* in the name of the True faith. He leaves the conclusion to be drawn to his readers by saying that the meaning and implication of "good tidings" is evident to those who possess reason.[74]

Majlesi refers to another report attributed to another imam according to which in response to Imam Hoseyn's question from Imam 'Ali on when God will cleanse the earth from the oppressors and the unjust, Imam 'Ali is said to have provided a long chronological answer in terms of historical events, certain details of which, according to Majlesi, are omitted by the reporter of the *hadith*. Looking into the future, Imam 'Ali is said to have referred to "a King who is one of us (*az ma*)", implying that he would be a Shi'i and who would lead a successful rebellion in Gilan. Imam 'Ali is reported to have referred to this person as "my son".[75] According to this same report, Imam 'Ali refers to the reappearance of the Twelfth Imam, who is said to cleanse the world from infidels and oppressors.

Majlesi's interpretation of this attributed *hadith* is clearly in favour of the Safavis. He writes that it is apparent that Shah Esma'il was the person who Imam 'Ali had referred to as the one who will rebel from Gilan. To Majlesi, Imam 'Ali's reference to this person as "one of us" and "my son" was further proof of the fact that once again, the Safavi kings were blessed and, according to the *hadith*, they were designated to be the forerunners to the appearance and rule of the Twelfth Imam.[76] Majlesi's instrumental use of interpretation to further the cause of the Safavi kings by connecting them on the one hand to Imam 'Ali and on the other to the Twelfth Imam has a clear political objective. This is a useful if not opportunistic religio-political exercise in interpretation or *ta'vil*. Majlesi not only empowers the monarchy by connecting it to the hidden world and providing it with a mission, but also renders Majlesism into a potent ideological support system for the Safavi monarchy.

---

[74] M. B. Majlesi, *Raj'at* (Mashhad, n.d.), pp. 5–6.   [75] Ibid., p. 8.   [76] Ibid., p. 10.

It has been suggested that "on the issue of *ta'vil* or speculative interpretation of reports and the Qur'an, Majlesi rejected all explanations in
discordance with the apparent meaning [of the texts]".[77] It has also been
suggested that Majlesi resisted any attempt at *ta'vil*.[78] The above examples
tell a different story. Majlesi is perfectly at ease with the use of both
speculative and even manipulative reasoning, as well as rigid reference to
the apparent text, as long as it suits his objectives. Majlesi's use of speculative and arbitrary interpretation demonstrates that it is not the tool and
use of reasoning per se that is acceptable or unacceptable to him, but it is
the person who uses it and the purpose that it serves that defines whether it
is warranted or not. It may be suggested that *Bahar al-Anvar* provided
Majlesi with a wide collection of reports from which he could choose and
use those reports that helped him construct his ideology, and, when
necessary, he interpreted other reports to support and buttress his religio-
political objectives.

---

[77] H. Taremi, *'Allameh Majlesi*, p. 192.
[78] See Taremi's comment to this effect in his biography, H. Taremi, *'Allameh Majlesi*, p. 94.

7

Society Needs the Leadership of Jurists and/or Kings

Having argued that people should not rely on their own reasoning, as it is deficient and likely to lead them astray, Majlesi extends the logic of the argument from the private to the public sphere. If, due to the disfunctionality of reasoning, people cannot think and reason properly for their own individual good, then naturally those same people would be equally unequipped to either choose a leader or govern a society. For Majlesi, societies were in need of a guardian or a leader capable of properly guiding them and resolving their disagreements and conflicts.[1]

Majlesi wrote that God would never leave humans to their own doings and ways, since, in the absence of guidance, people would become perplexed and bewildered, walking like four-legged animals in the land of deception.[2] Majlesi is convinced that the Muslim community is incapable of proper decision making especially in the sensitive domain of politics. He rhetorically inquires: "Can the worldly and the spiritual leadership of masses be left to the reasoning of people?"[3] And he readily responds that human beings are incapable of electing leaders who are able and qualified to guarantee their felicity in this world and their salvation in the next.[4] Having claimed the people unfit to choose their own leaders, Majlesi turns to the hidden world as the ultimate source of appointing a leader.

The worldly and spiritual leader of the Muslim community or the Imam, he insists, cannot be elected by feeble-minded humans prone to erring, but has to be appointed by God. He argues that the Shi'i believed that it was incumbent upon God to appoint an imam just as He had appointed the

---

[1] M. B. Majlesi, *Haq al-Yaqin*, p. 36.   [2] M. B. Majlesi, *E'teqadat*, p. 15.
[3] M. B. Majlesi, *Haq al-Yaqin*, p. 38.   [4] Ibid., p. 37.

Prophet.[5] Therefore similar to the Prophet, the imams were appointed by
God and obtained their legitimacy from Him and not from human beings.[6]
As long as the Prophet and the imams were alive, Majlesi's political
formulation benefited from an internal logic.

To highlight the unique position of the Prophet and the imams in
relation to leadership, Majlesi refers to a report attributed to Imam
Ja'far-Sadeq. "He who speaks about religious issues and has neither been
the recipient of revelations nor has God imposed his leadership on the
people, speaks in vain and even worse, he has made himself a partner to
God".[7] The concept of leadership specific to the Prophet and imams leaves
this crucial topic in limbo during the occultation era. According to a strict
interpretation of the above report attributed to the Imam, since only the
prophets and imams can rightfully address religious issues, even Majlesi
may be categorized as a false pretender who has made himself a partner to
God, unless it is argued that his leadership has been imposed on the people
by God.

The main theoretical challenge therefore begins with the absence of the
Twelfth Imam, since, once again, the Shi'i community would need to
conceive of a new process or system of identifying a leader or guardian
for itself. With the Twelfth Imam in occultation, the link between God and
a worldly and spiritual leader is ruptured. This break would once again
create a vaccum. If, according to Majlesi, in the absence of infallible imams
the masses would be incapable of leading themselves, who would be
eligible to lead the community? Should religious leadership be abandoned
until the return of the Twelfth Imam if religious leaders are incapable of
receiving revelations and God does not directly impose their leadership on
the people? At this point, Majlesi engages in a theoretical somersault and
looks to the reporters of *ahadith* and those knowledgeable about reports as
a substitute for the Hidden Imam, without explicitly proving that God has
imposed their leadership on the people.

As the most reliable and knowledgeable repository of the wisdom of all
imams, the reporters of the words and deeds of the imams and the
Prophet also considered as religious scholars are argued to be the most fit
to rule. It will be argued that as much as this theoretical second-best
alternative may have seemed as the most suitable solution in the absence
of imams, the reality of effective power relations imposed by the might and
autocratic rule of the Safavi kings forced Majlesi to entertain and promote

---

[5] Ibid., p. 36.   [6] Ibid., p. 47.
[7] M. B. Majlesi, *Hayat al-Qolub*, vol. 1 (Qom, 1375), p. 30.

a different, yet more realistic, theory of leadership. One can argue that his theoretical analysis privileged the guardianship position of the reporters of *ahadith*, while his practical position consistently made a case for the rule and authority of the Shiʿi King.

CONTEXTUALIZING MAJLESI'S POSITION ON RELIGIO-POLITICAL LEADERSHIP

Etan Kohlberg argues that the Akhbari School, which relies fundamentally on the *ahadith* or the reports attributed to the words and deeds of the Prophet and the imams, is far from homogeneous and that two distinct positions on the issue of religious authority after the occultation of the Twelfth Imam coexists within it.[8] According to one school of thought, only the imams have the knowledge and insight to interpret correctly the Qurʾan. In the absence of the imams, religious scholars would not have any particular privileges or a unique religio-political function. They, too, would be similar to the common folk in their inability to make any special claims to accessibility to God or the Prophet. This position could be labelled as the purist Akhbari position. The Shiʿi had always argued that religious leadership required the unique Divine gift of obtaining and possessing knowledge, unavailable to others within the community. This gift and subsequently the position of authority of Shiʿi imams was bestowed upon them not by their fellow beings but by God and the Prophet. It was argued that only the imams could make a real claim to religious authority after the Prophet as they were connected to the fountain of knowledge, namely the Prophet and God. The imams were said to hear the words of the angels and receive inspirations (*elham*). They were believed to have inherited by birth the sayings and reports of their fathers and forefathers.

According to Kohlberg, proponents of this Akhbari current "often advocated a diminished role for the religious scholar and the more extreme among them held that he [the religious scholar] was superfluous altogether".[9] Based on the inherent logic of the purist Akhbari position, in the absence of the imams, all human beings are equal in terms of religious authority, as none among them is connected to the hidden world and therefore worthy of a special status or privilege. This anti-elitist and anti-hierarchical Shiʿi position, during the absence of imams, is essentially a leveller school in its view of religious authority and leadership. It does not

---

[8] E. Kohlberg, *Belief and Law in Imami Shiʿism*, p. 146.   [9] Ibid.

lend itself to any kind of justification for giving the religious scholars or clerics a position of social or political privilege. This current considers all believers, cleric and lay, as equal in their capability of discerning right from wrong through the study of the reports containing all necessary knowledge for humankind. The Muslim community, according to this non-stratified Akhabri current, is composed of a homogeneous body of followers, taking their lead from the reports of the imams and not a particular living religious scholar.

On the issue of religious authority in the absence of the imams, the position of the second current of thought within the Akhbaris "closely resembled those of the *mojtahedin* among the Usulis".[10] This eclectic Akhbari current, similar to the Usuli School who privileges the jurists' right to deduce laws, accepts some degree of human reasoning by those steeped in religious knowledge and believes in a religiously stratified community. Such a community is organized on the basis of the individual's degree of understanding Islamic jurisprudence and ability to exercise *ejtehad* or personal reasoning to infer religious laws from Shari'at-based evidences. Within this hierarchical scheme, the *mojtahedin*, *foqaha*, *'olama* or religious scholars capable of deducing laws are in a position of authority, standing at the apex of the religious power structure. Below them sits the general public. The religiously unlettered common folk are considered as followers. They are expected to emulate and comply obediently with the directives, interpretations and edicts of the religious sages, their leaders.

This hierarchical and stratified wing of the eclectic Akhbari School believed in the leadership or guiding role of religious scholars and clearly rejected the egalitarian notion of the first current. Kohlberg demonstrates that on the issue of religious authority, the hierarchically oriented current in the Akhbari School becomes undistinguishable from the Usuli School. Both tendencies seek to reproduce and institutionalize the stratified religious hierarchy that existed during the time of the imams. The logic that could justify the initial differentiation among believers was based on the notion that only the infallible imams possessed access to the real sources of knowledge, unavailable to others. During the period of occultation and in the absence of imams, however, this logical construct lost its raison d'être.

Majlesi claims to occupy an intermediate position between the Akhbari and Usuli Schools. Kohlberg posits that Majlesi "did not really belong to either group".[11] It could also be argued that Majlesi incorporated and

<hr>

[10] Ibid.   [11] Ibid., p. 152.

blended aspects of both. Majlesi lashes out at independent interpretation while concomitantly he interprets the Qur'an with the intention of glorifying and privileging the reports attributed to the imams. Furthermore, he interprets the reports and reads back into them unrelated information for the purpose of glorifying Safavi kings and sanctifying their rule. Majlesi inherited his dim view of human reasoning from the Akhbaris and his admiration for the elitist view of the leadership role of the *'olama* from the Usulis. The exercise of *ejtehad*, the lynchpin of the Usuli School, accepts the problem-solving capacity and efficiency of human reasoning. However, new religious edicts based on *ejtehad* may be different from the message of reports. Yet, according to the Usulis, interpretations and rulings based on the mental exertions of Shi'i scholars are equally if not at times more binding than attributed reports on pious followers. Majlesi's position can incorporate and accommodate all these seemingly contradictory elements, and he seems perfectly at ease with his eclectic Akhbari position.

It is the authoritative religious power of *ejtehad* that forces obedience and following on the common folk and provides the *mojtahed* or the person engaging in this exercise with a religious and consequently religio-political leadership position. Simultaneously believing in the deficiency of human reasoning and the authority of *ejtehad* based on human reasoning seems paradoxical. The contradiction dissipates in the context of a stratified and unequal social system based on a superior clerical class in all religious and therefore politico-religious domains and an inferior class of the rest of society. Majlesi expects the common folk to accept his opinions blindly, explicitly because he is a connoisseur of reports and implicitly because he is a knowledgeable clergy who effectively exercises *ejtehad*. Majlesi resolves the potential paradox by acting as though his reasoning cannot be deficient while that of the common folk is bound to be. In the final analysis, for Majlesi, mastery of the reports attributed to the imams seems to entitle and empower jurists to reason without going astray. Possessing both these qualities which applies in Majlesi's case, seems to provide a cleric with the right and authority to assume a leadership position.

Majlesism proves to be an interesting hybrid of the two tendencies within Shi'ism. While it is firmly based on the *hadith*-only principle of the Akhbaris, it gives practical freedom to the application of interpretation and reason. Furthermore, it purposefully dispenses with a most important theoretical corollary of the purist Akhbari School, namely the disbelief in a religiously determined leader/superior and follower/inferior dichotomy within the Shi'i community. To deduce correct religious practice on any

issue, the purist Akhbari jurists sought the precedence of the infallible
imams, as reported in the *ahadith*, and acted according to it. Jurists adher-
ing only to reports were neither compelled nor in need of applying personal
reasoning. Consequently, the purist Akhbaris considered *ejtehad* or the
application of reason in the process of arriving at judgements or discerning
correct practices as forbidden or *haram*.[12] The use of reason or opinion
(*zann*) and inference (*estenbat*), irrespective of the knowledge or status of
the person employing it, is dismissed by the purist Akhbaris, since it in effect
stands either parallel to or in opposition to the word of the Imam.
Astarabadi, the father of the Akhbari tendency, considered the use of
ejtehad as an innovation (*bed'at*) or a heresy, in contradiction with the
Shari'at. No one, he argued, could voice an opinion on the legacy of the
Prophet and the infallible imams.[13] Subsequently, the equal and subservient status of all believers in terms of their obedience to and compliance
with the *hadith* created a homogeneous mass. The members of this community would be followers of the imams, with no religious distinction
among them.

Astarabadi did not believe in the division of the Islamic community into
religious leaders (*mojtaheds*) and followers (*moqqaleds*).[14] Arguing that all
Shi'i were followers (*moqqaled*) of the imams, Astarabadi ruled that
believers could individually and directly deduce their obligations from the
hadith on the condition that they knew Arabic and had reviewed the
reports.[15] The purist Akhbari position rejected the necessity of an intermediary clerical caste in possession of the special knowledge of deducing
Islamic ordinances for the religiously ignorant masses. Dismissing the notion
that the common folk were in need of a *mojtahed*, as long as the *ahadith*
could be consulted, the Akhbaris refused to consider the *mojtahed* as the
legatee and vicegerent of the Twelfth Imam. By the grace of the *hadith*, the
mojtahed had no particular social or political status in the community and
was subsequently denied a privileged religio-political position of leadership.

This is exactly where Majlesi parted ways with the purist Akhbaris and
articulated a new and eclectic discourse, combining the *hadith*-based content of Akhbari *feqh* (jurisprudence) with the unlimited religio-political
power of the cleric over the common folk. Without abandoning Akhbari
feqh, Majlesi embraced the politically empowering and socially engineering aspects of the Usuli School. Even though, as a proponent of Akhbari

---

[12] M. H. Mashayekh, 'Akhbariyeh' in *Encyclopaedia of Shïa*, vol. 2, p. 9.
[13] H. Anousheh, 'Astarabadi' in *Encyclopaedia of Shïa*, vol. 2, p. 107.   [14] Ibid.
[15] M. H. Mashayekh, 'Akhbariyeh' in *Encyclopaedia of Shïa*, vol. 2, p. 9.

feqh, Majlesi should have been averse to interpretation, conjecture and the use of opinion, he made considerable use of personal interpretation when he needed to. The elevation of the religio-political position of the *mojtahed* to that of the deputy of the Twelfth Imam and the subsequent division of the community between religious followers and leaders, practiced during the Safavi period and bolstered by Majlesi, could not be derived from the tenets of the mainstream Akhbari School. Yet, it could be deduced from the teachings of the Usulis. Majlesism, promoted both the primacy of reports, borrowed from the Akhbaris and the religio-political leadership position of Shiʿi jurists, which could be deduced from the Usulis during the occultation of the Twelfth Imam.

LEADERSHIP OF THE ʿ*OLAMA* OR THE ISLAMIC JURISTS

Arguing for the perpetual necessity of an imam or a person in authority to guide the people in their religious and worldly affairs, Majlesi tries to shed light on the attributes and qualities of this person by delving into reports attributed to Imams Baqer, Sadeq and Reza. These reports essentially argue that, at all times, societies are in need of honest and just guardians or leaders from the house of the Prophet to guide the people, establish the Divine law of Shariʿat, defend the cause of the people and prevent the corruption and distortion of the faith.[16]

In his *Treatise on the Philosophers, Usuliyoun and the Sufis*, Majlesi refutes the position of the philosophers (*hokama*) and the independent use of reasoning as a tool for discovering the truth and distinguishing between good and evil. He argues that all matters, spiritual and worldly, according to the Qur'an have to be referred to the Prophet during his time. After the Prophet passes away, according to his own instructions, all worldly and spiritual matters have to be referred to the Qur'an and the members of his household or the imams, as they were knowledgeable about the Qur'an. Finally, Majlesi addresses the occultation period, during which the Twelfth Imam is absent. He argues that, based on the explicit instruction of the imams, people are to consult and use the reports of the imams by following the reporters of *ahadith*. So, in relation to a religio-political theory of governance and leadership, Majlesi believed that in the absence of infallible imams, truth and guidance had to be sought from reports and those knowledgeable about the reports.[17] Here, Majlesi is presenting the

---

[16] M. B. Majlesi, *Hayat al-Qolub*, vol. 5, pp. 43–44.
[17] R. Jaʿfariyan, *Din va Siyasat dar Dowreh Safavi*, p. 261.

reporters of *ahadith* as the deputies or successors of the imams. Starting from a purist Akhbari position of privileging the reports, Majlesi deduces an Usuli position entrusting religious leadership to a group of experts on the reports.

For Majlesi, the reporter takes over the functions of the Prophet and the imams simply because he is an expert on reports, not because he has an extraordinary power of obtaining knowledge, unavailable to others, as was assumed about the imams. While the purist current of the Akhbaris rejected the notion of religious leadership and ipso facto political leadership of fallible Islamic jurists or clerics, Majlesi makes such a case. His prescription that people should follow fallible reporters of *ahadith* undermines the strength of the Akhbari argument that imams had to be followed because they were infallible and therefore could not go wrong, make mistakes, sin, be biased or unjust.

There is a clear attempt by Majlesi to demonstrate that the reporters of *ahadith* and the *'olama* are a suboptimal yet unavoidable replacement for the imams and as such are the natural guardians, custodians and leaders of the common folk. An important verse in the Qur'an addresses the issue of guardianship and leadership of the people. It says, "O ye who believe! Obey Allah, and the Messenger, and those charged with authority among you".[18] Shi'i jurists agree that the reference to "those charged with authority among you" is a direct reference to the infallible imams. Yet the issue of obeying "those charged with authority among you" after the occultation of the Twelfth Imam leaves room for all kinds of inferences and interpretations about the exact qualifications of the leader, as well as the mode and process by which he attains that position of authority.

In the absence of imams, Majlesi argues that leadership is passed onto and becomes the prerogative of those who grasp the meaning of the reports and consult it directly when confronted with religious questions, ambiguities and problems. If reports attributed to the imams are the lighthouse to worldly felicity and eternal salvation, then the common folk who are incapable of directly understanding them need the guidance of those who do. To balance and attenuate his emphasis on the expertise aspect of the reporters of *ahadith* as the justification for their religious leadership, Majlesi maintains that the reporters are also highly spiritual individuals impervious to the attractions and temptations of the material world. The reason why reporters qualify for leadership is therefore both their expertise in the significant religious domain of reports and their piety and asceticism.

---

[18] A. Y. 'Ali (tr.), *The Holy Qur'an* (4:59), p. 67.

Majlesi argues that "God has provided them [the common folk] with a solution" and that is to consult "the reporters of the imams' *hadith*s, who are knowledgeable about the science of the imams and are not attached to this fraudulent world".[19] Majlesi does not cite the source of such an important contention. Usually careful to cite all his sources, Majlesi chooses to evoke the word or intention of God, without proof, to prove the key point that God has willed the community to seek guidance from the reporters of the imams' *ahadith*.

During occultation, therefore, Majlesi claims that God has endorsed the right of the reporters and the *'olama*, as "those charged with authority among you". God does not describe or expound on the profession or profile of "those charged with authority among you". Majlesi infers and speculates from unavailable evidence and ascribes to God what he thinks. Majlesi supports his argument in favour of the guardianship of the reporters by attributing a report to *Hazrat-e Saheb-ol-Amr* (the Twelfth Imam) who is reported to have said that "confronted with ambiguities or questions and new events, refer to those who report our *hadith*, who are my proofs (*hojjat*) among you as I am God's proof among you all".[20] Majlesi continues by arguing that according to numerous authoritative reports, which he does not give references to, in case of a disagreement among the people, they should seek guidance from and accept the verdict of those who have reported *ahadith* and are knowledgeable about the permitted and the prohibited in the faith.

Majlesi follows his inference and speculation by a threat. He declares that those who refuse to follow the reporters are in fact rejecting the command of the imams and invariably that of God. Majlesi posits that "if he [who reports the *ahadith* of imams and is familiar with their edicts or what they consider permissible and prohibited] passes a judgement and you [the people] do not obey, you would be belittling the judgement of God and rejecting the judgement of imams and he who rejects the imams has rejected God and stands as an idolater or a polytheist".[21] Majlesi makes a forceful argument for the reporters of *ahadith* and the clergy as the only deputies of the Twelfth Imam and God. In the absence of the imams, therefore, the clergy are presented as the best substitutes capable of leading the community.

Majlesi faced an insurmountable theoretical problem in his attempt to establish a clear and incontestable connection between the imams and the fallible worldly and spiritual leaders, which he designated as the

---

[19] M. B. Majlesi, *'Eyn al-Hayat*, p. 206.　　[20] Ibid.　　[21] Ibid.

custodians of the people. A key argument justifying the special position of imams as leaders of the community was that they were infallible and appointed by other infallibles. This key concept implied that no humanly possible mistake could be made in their selection to the position of leadership, and they in turn could not err in their choices, decisions and rulings. Majlesi's justification for calling on those who know the reports of the imams to lead the community did not fulfil this important requirement that he had set for such a leadership position.

Majlesi relies on another attributed report to provide further justification and proof for the transfer of authority and leadership from the imams to their deputies or the *'olama* during occultation. One of the imams is quoted as saying, "I swear to God that we are the face of God and will survive until the day of resurrection. God has commanded people to obey us and accept our guardianship. As each one of us passes away most certainly another one of us will rise to the position of Imam until the day of resurrection".[22] Majlesi relies on this report to infer that the Imam not only anticipated but even legitimized the guardianship and rule of the reporters of *ahadith* or the Islamic jurist. In view of the occultation of the Twelfth Imam, the continuation of the office of imams "until the day of resurrection" is suggested to occur through the transfer of power to the *'olama* as the deputies of the Imam.

According to Majlesi's formula, a simple transmission line of authority exists between God and the reporters of *ahadith*. The linkage originates from God, who appoints Mohammad as His Prophet. From Mohammad, through Fatemeh (Fatima), his daughter and 'Ali, his son-in-law and cousin, infallibility, authority and legitimacy flows to the eleven offspring of 'Ali and Fatemeh. 'Ali is Mohammad's deputy, appointed by him at *Qadir-e Khom*, and the imams continue to be the Prophet's deputies, each appointed by his predecessor. Once the Twelfth Imam goes into occultation, his authority is exercised through his special deputies (*novvab-e khass*). With the declaration of the fourth special deputy, that there will be no one following him as an intermediary between the people and the Imam, since the Twelfth Imam has embarked on his long absence, the line of directly designated authority comes to an end.

Majlesi had already laid the logical foundations for his future arguments. He had argued that the earth could not function without an Imam and that the inadequate minds of the common folk were incapable of proper guidance and decision making. With the end of the period when

---

[22] M. B. Majlesi, *Hayat al-Qolub*, vol. 5, p. 497.

the Twelfth Imam had a designated deputy, a pressing religio-political solution was needed for the Shiʻi community. The succession line had already been extended from the Hidden Imam to his special deputies. It seemed necessary that the line be extended from the Hidden Imam's special deputies (*novvab-e khass*) to his general deputies (*novvab-e 'amm*).

Whereas the special deputies were not considered as infallibles, they were at least in theory selected and designated by the Twelfth Imam. Majlesi's replacement for the special deputies were neither infallible nor could they be appointed by an infallible as were the special deputies of the Hidden Imam. Based on Shiʻi arguments against the Sunnis, the legitimate and just ruler worthy of emulation could only be the infallible imam who had access to all conceivable sources of knowledge, unavailable to others. Majlesi had argued that, at the time of death, each imam transmitted and communicated not only the sum total of their wisdom and knowledge to the next imam, but also handed over the three key texts of *Jameʻ*, *Jafr* and *Mosahaf-e Fatemeh* to their successors.[23] Armed with such an arsenal of knowledge, which even included "news of future events until the day of resurrection" and "every possible ruling and decision that the sons of Adam may need", the Shiʻi made a strong case for the guardianship of the imams.[24]

After the occultation of the Twelfth Imam, the succession line of the imams temporarily ended. The logic justifying and legitimizing the rule of the imams disappeared, confronting the Shiʻi community with a major predicament. In the absence of a candidate with clearly predefined qualifications and connections with the hidden world, two options seemed possible. First, the quest on the part of the religious establishment for worldly and spiritual leadership be abandoned until the reappearance of the Twelfth Imam. This scenario could naturally result in separating the worldly and spiritual realm and rendering unto Caesar what was Caesar's. Second, a deputy deprived of all the exceptional qualities and endowments of the imams and not directly designated by an imam be identified as a potential successor to the imams and the four special deputies of the Hidden Imam. To make the second option understandable and acceptable to the Shiʻi community, the reporter of the *hadith*, the *'alem* or the cleric had to be presented as a special deputy, whereas technically he could not qualify as such. In a community where an all-knowing Imam was not available, Majlesi made the argument for the leadership of a very distant second-best candidate. According to Majlesi's discourse, only the

[23] M. B. Majlesi, *Haq al-Yaqin*, pp. 43, 45.   [24] Ibid., p. 43.

second-hand knowledge of reports by the general deputies and the supposed asceticism of the clergy qualified them for leading the community.

LEADERSHIP OF KINGS

During the Safavi period, official religious positions such as that of the
sheykholeslam, Molla Bashi or *Sadr* were created by the state, and the
selection or appointment of such religious leaders became the right and
responsibility of the king. In appointing 'Ali ebn 'Abdol'al Karaki or
Mohaqqeq-e Karaki (d. 940/1562), as *sheykholeslam,* Shah Tahmasb
referred to him as "the deputy of Imam". Shah Tahmasb wrote, "it is
evident that opposition to the edicts and ordinances of the *mojtahed*s or
the jurist/religious leaders who are the defenders of the Prophet's law is
tantamount to *shirk* or polytheism".[25]

In the preface to the first volume of *Hayat al-Qolub* Majlesi's third
Farsi book, which is a translation of the fifth, sixth and seventh volume of
Bahar al-Anvar, he dedicates his book to the Safavi King, Shah
Soleyman.[26] The first volume of *Hayat al-Qolub* was completed in
1085/1674. In his dedication, Majlesi praises Shah Soleyman as the
"propagator of justice", "the benefactor of his subjects" and "the shadow
of God's grace".[27] The Shah is eulogized as "he for whom the speaking
hoopoe could not find words to praise and to whom the bird and fish were
loyal and obedient".[28] Majlesi lauds the Shah as "the founder of the rules
of the Shari'at", "the founder of the fundamentals of belief" and "the
uprooter of unbelief and rebellion".[29] He concludes his dedication by
wishing that God would prolong the Shah's rule until the reappearance
of the Twelfth Imam.[30] About a decade later, Shah Soleyman appointed
Majlesi as *sheykholeslam*, and, after his death, Majlesi was again
appointed to the position of *sheykholeslam* by Shah Soltan Hoseyn. The
Shah referred to Majlesi as "the *mojtahed* of his times" and "the most
knowledgeable about the Book and the Sonnat (Sunnah)" and gave him
plenipotentiary religious powers.

In practice, Majlesi's official and public stance on the issue of the person
charged with authority among the people or the designated leader of the

---

[25] R. Ja'fariyan, *Din va Siyasat dar Dowreh Safavi*, p. 96.; H. Taremi, *'Allameh Majlesi*, p. 51.
[26] S. M. Mahdavi, *Zendeghinameh 'Allameh Majlesi*, vol. 2, p. 179.
[27] M. B. Majlesi, *Hayat al-Qolub*, vol. 1, pp. 30–31.
[28] Hoopoe is the bird with which Soleyman the Prophet conversed. M. B. Majlesi, *Hayat al-Qolub*, vol. 2 (Qom, 1375), p. 991.
[29] M. B. Majlesi, *Hayat al-Qolub*, vol. 1, p. 31.   [30] Ibid., p. 32.

community was different from his theoretical position. While theoretically he believed that the reporters of *ahadith* deserved to be the deputy of the imams and therefore charged with authority, officially he proclaimed the king as the person charged with authority. Kings who were not steeped in the knowledge of reports and were therefore unable to guide the common folk in their everyday lives according to the Qur'an and reports seemed to be the least fit to be charged with authority among the people.

In addition to their shortcomings in the domain of *hadith* and religious knowledge, the Safavi kings who Majelsi praised were not known for their asceticism, but for their glaring moral, ethical and religious shortcomings. Majlesi's continuous glorification of the Safavi kings, whom he officially served, and their labelling as just deputies of God, the Prophet and the imams may seem enigmatic or pragmatic. He may have been engaging in religious dissimulation (*taqiyyeh*) or Machiavellian realpolitik. Majlesi was well aware of the fact that real power in terms of military might rest with the kings, irrespective of their moral shortcomings and irreligiosity. Irrespective of his inner convictions, beliefs and theoretical constructs on the deputyship of the reporters of *ahadith*, Majlesi officially endorsed the rule of kings as divinely willed and threw his spiritual weight behind them.

In his famous sermon delivered during Shah Soltan Hoseyn's coronation, Majlesi hammered out his practical theory of the deputyship of kings and effectively tabled his theory of the guardianship of the reporters of *ahadith*. The sermon, which could have only focused on the glorification and exaltation of the new King, began with a theoretical premise, which set the tone for Majlesi's call upon Shah Soltan Hoseyn's subjects to be thankful and appreciative of their God-chosen-and-sent King. Reproducing his classical approach in other writings, Majlesi started his speech by asserting that at no time has God left the world without a guide or a guardian to direct the misguided who had gone astray. Majlesi asserted that, after the Prophet passed away and the Twelfth Imam went into occultation, due to His finesse and grace (*lotf*) towards the community (*ommat*), God endowed the mighty (*falak eqtedar*) kings or soltans (*salatin, khavaghin*) with the keys of victory over nations and rulers.[31] According to Majlesi's theory of the deputyship of the kings, the third in line in terms of worldly leadership after the Prophet and the infallible imams are the mighty and powerful kings or soltans, under whose rule subjects would "lounge in security and safety", protected from "the oppression and enmity of the masters of tyranny and

---

[31] M. I. Nasiri, *Dastoor-e Shahriyaran*, p. 22.

rebellion".[32] Majlesi suggested that once God wills to provide welfare, well-being, security and betterment for a people, He will place the crown of mastery on the head of a ruler to reign over them.[33]

For Majlesi, not only does the guardianship of kings now replace that of reporters of *ahadith*, but the deputyship of kings is presented as the will and design of God. For Majlesi, the king with no particular spiritual attribute yet in possession of military force and power suddenly becomes the vicegerent of God on earth. In this very important substitution or turnabout, the knowledge of God's law, albeit incomplete and subject to error, by the fallible reporters of *ahadith*, which constituted the main element in Majlesi's argument in support of their guardianship, is discarded. By arguing that the king, rather than the reporter of the *ahadith*, had the right to rule, Majlesi was in effect confirming that military might, rather than knowledge of God's law, was the real prerequisite for leadership in the Shi'i community. To Majlesi, the fact that the king could or had conquered, overpowered and subjugated a people gave him not only the political but also the religious legitimacy to rule. As holder of the highest religious office in the land, Majlesi was subsequently obliged to prove that the king was appointed to this position by God. Here, Majlesi needed to provide a religious justification for giving to Caesar what was Caesar's and God's.

Whereas Majlesi largely relied on reports attributed to imams to explain and justify the deputyship of the reporters, in the construction of his purely politico-military theory of guardianship/rulership, he simply states that kings are chosen by God. This kind of categorical statement of an opinion with no attempt at some sort of grounding in reports is not unprecedented, but is rare in Majlesi's works. In view of the shift in his position, Majlesi's array of justifications demonstrating the necessity of leadership by someone steeped in and familiar with the reports of the imams becomes superfluous. According to Majlesi's new theory, kings seem to be charged with authority among the people by God because of their power to coerce, conquer and impose their rule. Here, Majlesi is providing a strong religious justification for the rule of whosoever is powerful enough to impose his might. Majlesi shifts his salient feature or requirement for guardianship of the society from religious knowledge to divinely sanctioned military might.

To support his theory on the deputyship of kings, in his coronation speech, Majlesi twice refers to the Qur'anic verse, which states, "Say 'Oh Allah! Lord of Power (and Rule), Thou givest Power to whom Thou

---

[32] Ibid.   [33] Ibid.

pleasest ...'".[34] Based on this verse, Majlesi argues that God chooses the Soltan and actually appoints him by clothing him in the royal garb. To Majlesi, whoever is in power becomes the appointee of God, since He gives power to whom He pleases. Using and interpreting this Qur'anic verse in a political context provides Majlesi with the justification he seeks to make a strong argument in favour of the political status quo. The verse is used to demonstrate and prove the divinely determined and blessed position of kings, as well as their very special connection with God. If the one "charged with authority" among the people is the divinely chosen and appointed king, then he deserves the unswerving obedience of the people.

Obedience to the king in power is thus transformed into a religious obligation. Expediency compelled Majlesi to ignore his own dictum. "He who is charged with authority among people should resemble the Prophet. He should not lie, sin or err".[35] Majlesi knew that none of the Safavi kings were comparable to the Prophet. Yet he needed to find and formulate some sort of religious-based legitimacy for their rule. In his haste to legitimize and condone religiously the right of rulership and governance of kings in power as God-willed, Majlesi probably overlooked the fact that his line of argument could also be used to condone and legitimize the rule and policies of all those dynasties and rulers who persecuted the imams and their Shi'i. The Majlesi argument implying that rulers as persons "charged with authority" have a God-given right to govern becomes a double-edged sword cutting both in favour of as well as against the Shi'i.

Believing that he had provided sufficient religious references and evidences to prove the right of kings to rule as deputies of God and the imams, Majlesi moves to make a particular case for the legitimacy of Safavi rule. According to Majlesi, the Safavi dynasty is a sound proof of God's will to empower a just and benevolent king ushering in the welfare and prosperity of the people.[36] In the second part of his coronation speech, Majlesi reiterates the important role of Safavi monarchs in protecting the faithful from engaging in dark deeds and slipping into unbelief. Majlesi urges the common folk to be thankful and appreciative of their kings. Considering the Safavi kings as God-given bounties and blessings, Majlesi rules that gratefulness towards each one of them is a pressing obligation. He glorifies the Safavi shahs and refers to them as unique personalities. So special are they, he argues, that it has been a very long time since the moon and the sun

[34] A. Y. 'Ali (tr.), *The Holy Qur'an* (3:26), p. 133.   [35] M. B. Majlesi, *Haq al-Yaqin*, p. 39.
[36] M. I. Nasiri, *Dastoor-e Shahriyaran*, p. 22.

laid eyes upon their kind! Majlesi justifies his exaggerated claims about the Safavi shahs by claiming that it is God who has made this radiant sun – the King – appear.[37] Ironically, Majlesi praises and credits the Safavi shahs for their religiosity, piety and devoutness. At the end of his speech, he prays that the Safavi rule would be prolonged until the reappearance of the Twelfth Imam.[38]

At first, it may seem as if Majlesi exalts the role of the reporters of the *ahadith* as the worthy deputies of the imams to demonstrate the significance and importance of their full support of the Safavi kings. The more successful Majlesi is in demonstrating the close link between God and the reporters of the *ahadith*, the more reliable and worthy would the Safavi shahs – supported by the same reporters of *ahadith* – appear in the eye of the common folk. However, in view of the absolute and unchallengeable military power of kings and the impossibility of replacing their power with that of the religious experts, Majlesi may have pursued a parallel argument supporting both the deputyship of the reporters of the *ahadith* and the kings. As long as the responsibilities of the two powers, one worldly and the other spiritual, were separated and did not clash, symbiotic mutual benefits could be gained. For Majlesi, if political reality did not allow for the rule of the religious scholars, a situation of separation of the religious realm from the political realm or dual leadership seemed stable and desirable. Historically, the Shiʿi imams, with the exception of Imam ʿAli, had exercised spiritual leadership without possessing political leadership. While, under Sunni rule, the Shiʿi imams, Shiʿi jurists and the Shiʿi were persecuted and victimized for the expression and propagation of their religious beliefs, at least under the rule of a Shiʿi King, in theory they would not face such persecutions.

Under the Shiʿi rule of the Safavi kings, Shiʿi religious experts were suddenly catapulted into a historically unprecedented position of power and respect. This position was bestowed upon them effectively by the grace of Shiʿi Safavi shahs who needed their religious support and endorsement. The dual-power situation allowed prolific and energetic Shiʿi figures such as Majlesi to write and speak for Shiʿism. Majlesi preached and popularized his discourse with the open support of the Shah. In exchange, he turned a blind eye to the personal and private impieties and irreligiosities of the Shah, as long as the Shah continued to officially pay lip service to Shiʿism and publicly act as its protector and upholder. In effect, the dual and parallel power of the Shah and the religious authority allowed each to

---

[37] Ibid., p. 23.   [38] Ibid., pp. 23–24.

pursue their own objectives separately. Majlesi could propagate Majlesism and hope to see the implementation of its personal, social, cultural and political aspects among the common folk and the Shah could follow his whims from waging war to engaging in his private debauchery with Majlesi's blessing.

In his first book in Farsi, *'Eyn al-Hayat*, finished in 1074/1663 or some three years after he had started *Bahar al-Anvar*, Majlesi had set the ground work for the unassailable position of the Shi'i Shah.[39] To demonstrate that it is religiously incumbent on the inhabitants of Persia as subjects of the Shi'i Shah to follow him and naturally desist from opposing him in any form, Majlesi sets forward three arguments. First, he refers to a report attributed to one of the imams, according to which, when the Prophet Abraham walked ahead of Nimrod the legendary King, he received a revelation from God instructing him to stop walking in front of the unjust King and reminding Abraham to be respectful to the King by walking behind him.[40] From this ascribed report, Majlesi infers that people are required to be respectful and courteous to kings, even though they may be non-Mulims, unbelievers and unjust.

Second, Majlesi conjures reports attributed to the Prophet to prove that unquestioning and absolute obedience to kings is not only God-willed and commanded, but such resigned behaviour would further secure one's personal safety and avoid the royal wrath. On the basis of these reports, Majlesi argues that people should not belittle their kings, oppose them or struggle against them. Antagonism and resistance towards kings, Majlesi maintains, will bring misfortune and hardship upon those who oppose them. In addition to worldly disincentives of opposing kings, Majlesi evokes religious retributions for contradicting or challenging them. He refers to a report attributed to the Prophet and rules, "whoever refuses to obey kings disobeys God".[41] Majlesi elevates quietism, submissiveness and compliance before kings to a quasi-religious obligation.

Based on his second argument, Majlesi sends a clear signal: whoever challenges an unjust king is entirely responsible for the consequences of his acts. Dissidents and opponents of kings, irrespective of their justice, should not expect any assistance, mercy or support from God. Majlesi writes that those who are harassed, pained or tormented as a result of their opposition

---

[39] H. Taremi, *'Allameh Majlesi*, p. 94. The finishing date of *'Eyn al-Hayat* is cited as 1074 in S. M. Mahdavi, *Zendeghinameh 'Allameh Majlesi*, vol. 2, p. 198.
[40] M. B. Majlesi, *'Eyn al-Hayat*, pp. 500–501.   [41] Ibid., p. 501.

to kings will receive no recompense from God, and He will not even endow
them with patience to ease their predicament.[42] In short, Majlesi articulates a politically conservative and pro status quo position and seeks to
ground it in his version of Shī'ism. From Majlesi's point of view, one who
rebels against kings of any kind is similar to he who defies the reporters of
the *ahadith*. In both cases, the defiant person will be rebelling against God
and should accept the wrathful consequences of his acts.

In his third set of arguments, Majlesi makes an attempt at effectively
demonstrating that what kings do is the will of God. He writes that God
has "tested" kings and then given them the "right to prevail over and rule"
as kings.[43] Majlesi bases his divinely willed kingship theory on a report
attributed to the Prophet, without citing the report's chain of transmission.
According to this report, kings are creations of God, and it is He who
controls their hearts. Whenever kings obey God, their hearts are softened
and made kind by God, and whenever they sin and offend God, their hearts
are enraged and angered by God. According to Majlesi's account of this
report, God orders people to refrain from damning and insulting kings.
God says if people were to repent their sins, I would soften the heart of
kings and make them kind towards their subjects.[44] Here, Majlesi is
arguing that, in effect, if kings are unjust or oppressive, this is because
God has willed it as the people's punishment for their sins and their
disobedience. Unjust kings therefore are tools of God, just as much as the
just ones. So society is obliged to accept passively whatever social and
political condition is imposed on it.

Majlesi backs up his contention by referring to another report according to which, when God wishes welfare and felicity for a people, He would
appoint a kind king to rule over them.[45] Majlesi argues that, according to
reports, people should pray for the longevity of the rule of just kings, and if
they happen to be unjust and oppressive kings, people should petition God
to reform them.[46] In either case, for Majlesi, kings are fathers and guardians, some of whom are kind and some unkind. According to Majlesi's
position, the kindness or unkindness of kings is ultimately a function
of God's will and the religious behaviour of the people. The people,
according to Majlesi, have no right to oppose kings, let alone rebel against
the oppressive ones.

As part of his official duty, Majlesi seeks to secure the people's absolute
obedience to kings, by making a religious case for the Divine right of kings
based on reports attributed to the Prophet and imams. For Majlesi, the

---

[42] Ibid.   [43] Ibid., p. 500.   [44] Ibid., p. 501.   [45] Ibid.   [46] Ibid.

legitimacy of the king's authority as a political leader lies not in his piety, justice, kindness, Islamicness or even Shi'ism, but simply in the fact that he possesses the military power to impose his supremacy and domination, which must have been willed by God. In simple terms, Majlesi believes that it would be best if kings were just, but injustice does not invalidate their right to rule, since effectively they are chosen and directed by God. Therefore, based on Majlesi's overall position that kings, irrespective of their behaviour towards their subjects, have to be obeyed, the issue of whether Majlesi really viewed Shah Soleyman or Soltan Hoseyn as pious, just and worthy of all the praise he bestowed upon on them becomes a non-issue.

8

Superstitious Education

Fogging Minds, Fostering Resignation

Stupefaction implies a state of insensibility and disconnection with reality. It refers to a condition in which a person's common sense and reason becomes distorted or blunt. Whatever distorts or desensitizes the faculty to reason, rationalize and establish logical causal relations could potentially stupefy and dupe. Inverted or false consciousness may have many roots. The power of superstition to warp the senses is no less potent than hallucinatory or intoxicant substances. Religion-based superstition can provide individuals with a sense of righteousness that normal intoxicants usually do not. Constructing rules and laws based on arbitrary and bizarre conjectures and raising them to the status of religious recommendations, injunctions and necessities of belief deforms the natural thought process of believers, blurring their power of distinction between the real and the unreal. It also harms the appeal of the faith to a growing rational population. This make-believe method of argumentation and explanation produces a false consciousness, which views reason as standing on its head while furnishing its own unpalpable and unrealistic theories. Faced with fiction and fantasy passed off as faith by those who promote it as religion, the pious intent on safeguarding their religiosity and beliefs are forced to distrust reason, as its employment would contradict and undermine the imaginary construction. In this process, reason is portrayed as the enemy of faith.

One of the major, if not defining, features of the common folk in Majlesi's mind is that their independent reflection is incapable of producing satisfactory results, be they material or spiritual. This incapacity opens the door to the necessity of guiding and leading the common folk in a language that they grasp. To Majlesi, the effective language and means of communicating with the people was storytelling, fabulation or fictive creative writing. Peppered with selective reports attributed to the Prophet and imams, Majlesi's dictates were draped in a religious authority convincing to the ordinary people who were never in the position to question the degree of authenticity or veracity of such reports. Even those renowned jurists such as Sharif Morteza and ʿAllameh Helli, who reasoned, were derided and discredited as deviants and accused of being Sunnis.

Superstitious thought could act as a mesmerizing agent capable of soothing the anxieties of the material world with the comforting thought that the hidden world would consistently play a role in the events, phenomena and occurrences of the material world and eventually come to the aid of its inhabitants. In this sense, superstition acts as a painkiller, distorting reality. The belief in the veracity of and evocation of illogical causal relations in stark contradiction with the established natural laws of the material world as an explanation of events can be considered as another category of superstitions. This type of superstitious belief in nonsensical causal relations or occurrences can provide the common folk with a simple yet false and obfuscating mental device, which can pretend to help them "understand" their predicament and consider possible solutions. Once superstitious arguments creep into the religious belief system, the pious common folk would become obliged to coordinate and manage their lives according to unreasonable rules of behaviour. Unchallenged use and application of irrationality as religiosity impairs the agility of collective and social wisdom, sapping its judgment and ingenuity.

Majlesi's selection, organization, systematization and propagation of superstitious precepts at odds with reason constitute a salient feature of Majlesism. This is a religious ideology developed and articulated to rule over and manage a society of pious Shiʿi. To guard against any deviation from superstition, the common folk are systematically warned against the danger of reflecting upon the dictates of the reporters of attributed *ahadith* and succumbing to doubt, lest they slip into apostasy. Majlesi instils a false sense of certainty and piety in the people by presenting unnatural causes and effects as religiously approved everyday possibilities and occurrences. He also infuses the common folk with the fear of relying on rational argumentation. Once, in the name of religiosity, the mind becomes prepared to replace reason with fantasies, accounts of abnormal events become acceptable as veritable explanations of the functioning of the material world and the people who live in it.

Political manipulation of the religious masses, already susceptible to superstitious thinking, is facilitated by dispensing with rational arguments believed to cause "doubt and devisiveness" among some in favour of appealing to a different and higher "religious" source of truth, resonating with a greater number. Majlesi's command and almost monopoly over producing and propagating religious and ideological literature enabled him to move and mould the pious public as he and his so-called divinely guided kings wished. His method of mass brainwashing through the dissemination and popularization of superstitious explanation or narration of events sought to foster an unquestioning and fatalistic community, which in turn facilitated the political domination and control of those who controlled and injected the phantasmical string of information.

The adoption of Majlesi's religio-political discourse with all its corollaries by the latter Safavi kings provided the state with a powerful, clearly defined and religiously based comprehensive national plan, legal structure and behavioural manual. Majlesism as an ideology possessed legal, philosophical, political, cultural and religious prescriptions recommended but often imposable and binding on society. In his written works, Majlesi clearly outlined the basic conventions and laws regulating and defining the comportment, of the "correct" Shi'i community. Aside from broad and general topics, he described the specifics of what he considered to be "acceptable" mannerism, etiquette, ethical conduct and mode of action and interaction of the Shi'i. Majlesism was far more encompassing and comprehensive than a political program. Majlesi's dictates permeated throughout all conceivable domains and spheres of personal, familial, communal and social relations. The implementation of his comprehensive ideology pre-empted the practice and institutionalization of speculation and reason-based argumentation, stunting the historical process of reason-based religious, cultural, social and political change and adjustment in the face of evolving times and conditions.

Majlesi's second Farsi book, *Heliyat al-Mottaqin* (The Ornament of Believers) completed in 1079/1668, during the first years of Shah Soleyman's reign, serves as the prime repository of his instructions on proper individual behaviour.[1] This is one of Majlesi's most famous Farsi books. In the introduction of his book, Majlesi argues that two essential features distinguish human beings from other animals: first, the human tendency and inclination to acquire proper morals and ethics; and second, the human desire to become embellished with good manners.[2] Basing his conclusion on an attributed report, Majlesi maintains that Islam possesses

---

[1] S. M. Mahdavi, *Zendeghinameh 'Allameh Majlesi*, vol. 2, pp. 177–178.
[2] M. B. Majlesi, *Heliyatal-Mottaqin*, p. 2.

the totality of desirable and commendable manners, decorum and etiquette, along with estimable and coveted morals and ethics.

Majlesi's quasi-binding instructions on proper Shi'i etiquette and behaviour covers the following fourteen topics: (1) dressing and wearing shoes; (2) use of cosmetics and ornaments; (3) eating and drinking; (4) marriage, sexual intercourse and educating children; (5) personal hygiene; (6) use of perfumes, ointments and smelling flowers; (7) bathing and bodily depilation; (8) sleeping, awakening and defecation; (9) cure of certain diseases and medicinal properties of spices; (10) social conduct and the rights of social groups; (11) social gatherings, greeting and sneezing; (12) entering and exiting the house; (13) mounting horses and donkeys; walking, shopping, trading and cultivating; and finally (14) travelling.[3] Each of these major headings is subsequently divided into further subheadings.

The headings and subheadings in *Heliyat al-Mottaqin* cover a vast array of subjects and practices in minute details. For example, part two of the first topic is called "On the custom of wearing ornaments and embellishments for men and women, darkening the eyelids, looking into the mirror and coloring hair, facial hair and the body". In each part and chapter, where necessary, Majlesi includes the particular prayer that accompanies a particular practice to assure the perfect results and the successful outcome of the ritual.[4]

Heliyat al-Mottaqin is a fully comprehensive code of proper Shi'i conduct based on reports attributed to the imams. It is a complete manual prescribing Shi'i orthopraxy. Majlesi's broad and all-inclusive selection of subjects and his detailed and exhaustive treatment of each topic indicate that he intends to codify and propagate his bill of conduct as an almost compulsory guide to "correct" Shi'i behaviour. Majlesi effectively transforms the personal and non-legally binding content of attributed reports into almost legally binding rules. The widespread adoption of Majlesi's guide would provide the Shi'i community with a common individual and social identity. The codification process of these so-called rules had two immediate consequences. First, it imposed a cultural straightjacket on the Shi'i, as it formulated a singular religiously acceptable and dominant behavioural pattern, encompassing very diverse sets of activities. Second, through the identification and labelling of what was recommended or legitimate Shi'i practice, Majlesi's codification movement automatically set into motion the process of excluding and chastising those who disagreed with him on the authenticity, appropriateness and

---

[3] Ibid., pp. 2–3.   [4] Ibid., pp. 3–11 in the table of contents.

therefore binding property of his "articulated and established" standard
of Shiʿi piety.

The purpose of *Heliyat al-Mottaqin* was to homogenize the individual
and social psychology of the Shiʿi community according to Majlesi's pro-
totype of the ideal Shiʿi value system. *Heliyat al-Mottaqin* is presented to
the Shiʿi as the ultimate manual guaranteeing worldly well-being, as well as
felicity in the hereafter. The Shiʿi observing Majlesi's code of conduct are
given the impression that their everyday choices in both the private and
public sphere would be in perfect accord with the tradition of the imams
and would therefore be blessed by them. Majlesi's concern with codifying
the finest details of personal and social life was so pervasive that it hardly
left any room for private initiative and reflection.

To demonstrate and highlight the manner in which Majlesi develops a
specific Shiʿi code of life based on irrational, whimsical and superstitious
ideas and subsequently presents them as identifiers and exemplifiers of
Shiʿism, five generic examples in his works will be examined. These examples demonstrate the extent to which his writings could be considered as
highly effective means of individual and social engineering, thought control and ultimately political domination. Through his extension and
expansion of the religiously correct standard of individual and social
practice, Majlesi moulded a Shiʿi identity through redefining the belief
system and world outlook of the common folk. These very selective and
far from exhaustive examples demonstrate Majlesi's bizarre generalizations
and rulings, which he forcefully expects the common folk to accept and
abide by. These examples have been classified on the basis of the so-called
causal relations Majlesi establishes between (1) believers and objects,
(2) believers and human activities, (3) believers and individuals of the
other world, (4) believers and dates and (5) believers and prayers.

BELIEVERS AND OBJECTS

Majlesi believes that certain objects such as amulets or talismans have
supernatural or magical powers. The primary function of such objects is
to protect their owners from a wide variety of misfortunes and procure for
them health, welfare and happiness. The assumption of power associated
with such objects is usually, but not always, linked to an experience
ascribed through a report to a Shiʿi imam or the Prophet with a given
object. Convinced of the supernatural effectiveness of such objects, Majlesi
holds that people would benefit from possessing them and therefore
strongly promotes their use.

In great detail, Majlesi elaborates a whole theory along with its own mode of operation on the topic of wearing rings. He states that men should wear rings made of silver, as golden rings are forbidden to them, and that they should be worn on the fingers of the right hand. Majlesi supports his recommendations by simply positing that according to "several valid reports", to which he does not refer in his book *Heliyat al-Mottaqin*, the Prophet wore his ring on the fingers of his right hand and that he told Imam 'Ali to do the same so that he would be one of the "close ones [to God]". Majlesi adds that the act of wearing rings on the fingers of the right hand is the "mark or sign of our Shi'i according to which they could be identi- fied".[5] Based on a suspect report establishing a causal relation between wearing a ring on the right hand and attaining proximity to God, Majlesi strongly recommends this practice to both Shi'i men and women as their creedal signifier. If Majlesi rules that wearing a ring on the right hand is the sign of being a Shi'i, the absence of a ring on the right hand of a Shi'i renders the person a non-Shi'i in spite of the person's beliefs and convic- tions in Shi'i Islam.

Based on a selection of attributed reports, Majlesi elaborates on the "virtues" of a ring with an agate stone and rules that such a ring would "dispel enemies and misfortunes", "shut out poverty", and prevent a person from being "robbed", "whipped" and "amputated".[6] Majlesi argues that according to ascribed reports, among the worshipping hands extended to the sky, God prefers those fingers wearing a ring with an agate stone. Having arbitrarily established God's preference for agate rings over other rings or no rings, Majlesi proceeds to make the wearing of an agate ring into a Shi'i quasi-necessity. In Majlesi's construction, which reflects anthropomorphism, God is assumed to have human taste and preference for different kinds of ornaments. He further argues that God would not torment in hellfire a hand that wears a ring with an agate stone.[7] Finally, Majlesi drives home the importance or almost religious necessity of wear- ing an agate ring by stating that "two sections (*rak'at*) of the regular daily prayer of Muslims recited with an agate mounted ring is better than the recitation of one thousand sections without one".[8]

Majlesi attributes an array of supernatural powers such as the dispelling of misfortune and prevention of poverty to an inanimate object – a stone. Such powers are usually believed to belong only to God, and their associ- ation with a stone can be considered as idolatry or taking a stone as a substitute for God. In his emphasis on the importance of an agate ring,

[5] Ibid., p. 15. [6] Ibid., pp. 16–17. [7] Ibid., p. 17. [8] Ibid., p. 18.

Majlesi effectively adds a creedal obligation to the standard and traditional Muslim ritual of prayers. The long list of quasi-creedal reasons, however, presented by Majlesi in support of wearing a ring with an agate stone on the fingers of the right hand is elaborate and forceful. For the common folk wishing to excel in their piety and seeking a guaranteed place in paradise, following Majlesi's recommendation without reflecting upon its rational merit becomes a de facto religious obligation. Majlesi's so-called religious justification of the supposed material and spiritual benefits of a stone and his subsequent codification of its use, based on a set of irrational causal relations, is a case of religious superstition.

Through the discussion of another detailed type of relation between believers and objects, Majlesi draws on attributed reports to address the topic of how the Shi'i should dress. After emphasizing that it is best for men to wear cotton and that it is reprehensible for them to wear woollen clothes regularly, Majlesi encourages the pious to wear specific colours and associates particular properties with those colors, promoting a Shi'i style or fashion of dressing.[9] He ranks the colour of garments according to a specific order of preference and writes that white is the best colour followed by yellow, green and pale shades of red. He suggests that dark red and black dresses are repugnant. Wearing black clerical gowns or turbans is considered as an exception to his rule. In Majlesi's opinion, it is even preferable not to wear black gowns and turbans.[10] Majlesi's colour preference for shoes and slippers is almost the same as for men's garments. He voices a preference for yellow and white shoes and slippers, but maintains that black is the best colour for boots.[11] Majlesi supports his recommendations for the Shi'i fashion he proposes by referring to an attributed report that claims that whoever wears yellow or white slippers will become prosperous and enjoy having many children, while whoever wears black slippers will be denied such pleasures.[12] Based on a report attributed to an imam, Majlesi encourages the pious to wear footwear or boots (*muzeh*), as their continuous use, he argues, improves eyesight and prevents tuberculosis and a painful death.[13]

The element of religious superstition underlying Majlesi's argument in support of wearing a particular colour of shoes becomes evident when he associates unrelated benefits to the use of one colour of footwear. If he were simply promoting and rooting for one colour or another, his claim could be considered as a personal statement of preference or an attempt at setting fashionable trends. Yet as soon as he posits that wearing yellow and

---

[9] Ibid., p. 6.   [10] Ibid., p. 7.   [11] Ibid., p. 12.   [12] Ibid., p. 13.   [13] Ibid.

white slippers would result in wealth and many children, he is engaging in duping his readers with religious superstition, as there is no known, established or understandable causal relation between the colour of footwear and the possibility of becoming rich. When Majlesi asserts that whoever puts on his underwear while standing up will not have his wish fulfilled for three days and will become depressed, sick and may even die and therefore recommends that the pious should put on their underwear while sitting down, he gives his readers the impression that he knows of future outcomes of present acts.[14] It could be argued that having appropriated the right of representing Shi'ism, Majlesi is projecting and reading back into religion and Shi'ism his own attachments and mannerisms, thus establishing a religious justification for his private preference for yellow or white slippers and putting one's underwear on while sitting down. In the process of transforming the use of yellow or white footwear to an obligation for the Shi'i, Majlesi imposes his personal taste on the people by forcing them to comply with it as the correct way of being pious. He furthermore defines and shapes Shi'ism according to his selection of the ascribed reports.

Under the last subheading of the topic of dressing, Majlesi enters into the minute details of the proper Shi'i mode of putting on and taking off one's footwear. He informs his readers that when wearing their shoes, they should start with the right foot, whereas when they are taking off their shoes the process should begin with the left foot. In case one sets out to walk with one shoe, Majlesi argues that Satan will overcome the person and he will go mad.[15] Majlesi's detailed account of the correct Shi'i mode of operation in almost every aspect of everyday life provides the necessary pieces of a grand ideological jigsaw puzzle, co-ordinating, regulating and managing the life of the Shi'i based on religious superstition.

BELIEVERS AND HUMAN ACTIVITIES

Majlesi develops a highly elaborate and detailed instructional manual on the manner in which believers should conduct their personal and even intimate affairs. Once again, he seeks public compliance with a very broad range of his opinions on activities, including shaving, combing one's hair and beard, bathing, laughing, weeping, sleeping, dreaming, interpretation of dreams and sexual intercourse, by supporting his prescriptions with religious justifications.

[14] Ibid., p. 10.   [15] Ibid., p. 14.

Majlesi informs his male readers that since the *'olama* are agreed on the
fact that shaving one's beard is prohibited or *haram*, it is best for them not
to shave their beards. He then provides his attributed report-based arguments on the repugnance of plucking one's white hair and beard.[16] Majlesi
enters into his typical irrational argumentations when he tries to impose on
the Shi'i a uniform standard of combing their beard and hair. His treatment of this topic bears his trademark of a high degree of attention to the
most trivial of details. Based on an attributed report, the lines of transmission of which are not cited, Majlesi instructs the Shi'i to comb their
beards seventy times. He does not specify the time limit within which they
should do this, but it seems as if he intended it to be within a day. He then
instructs them to count carefully the times they pass the comb through their
beard. If the counting is done one by one, then Majlesi argues that Satan
would keep away from the person for forty days. The carefully counted
combing of one's beard is here presented as a shield against Satan. Under
the same topic, Majlesi argues that if one combs one's hair, beard and chest
seven times, pains will be chased away.[17] However, combing one's hair
while standing up is considered repugnant. Majlesi argues that combing in
this position will cause poverty, indebtedness and anxiety. Once again, he
relies on religious superstition in order to impose a straitjacket on how
individuals should conduct their private hygiene. In conclusion, on what
he must believe to be religious grounds, Majlesi recommends combing
one's hair while sitting down.[18]

   According to Majlesi's "combing manual", even the direction in which
the beard should be combed is minutely recorded and recommended:
"forty times from the neck up and forty times from the cheekbones
down". Combing the beard in the Majlesi-specified manner is said to
increase daily provisions and improve one's health. Furthermore, the use
of an ivory comb is said to act as an anti-fever medication.[19] Majlesi's
guide for the pious Shi'i on going to public baths on a particular day
(Wednesday), the procedure of bathing, what to do and what not to do
in the bath, what kind of prayers to recite, the medical threats and benefits
involved in bathing and the proper manner of exiting a public bath is
meticulously itemized and highly detailed.[20]

   Based on attributed reports, Majlesi warns believers against "excessive
laughter", which is argued to be an outcome of pride and the work of
Satan. Excessive laughter is argued to cause the wrath of God, dissolve the

---

[16] Ibid., pp. 101–103.   [17] Ibid., p. 106.   [18] Ibid., pp. 106–107.
[19] Ibid., p. 107.   [20] Ibid., pp. 115–118.

faith and impoverish individuals on the Day of Judgement.[21] Without an explanation on what distinguishes laughter from excessive laughter, Majlesi refers to an attributed report and determines the limits of acceptable laughter as "a silent smile". However, he considers witticism and humour as acceptable behaviour, as long as they do not lead to insulting others.[22] While excessive laughter is admonished, weeping and shedding tears is argued to be the worthiest and most blessed act of worshippers in the eyes of God, rewarded by a castle in paradise in the proximity of the prophets and those dear to God.[23]

According to Majlesi, those who sleep alone are damned and may go insane.[24] Sleeping in mosques and on unwalled rooftops is reprobatory (*makruh*). He who sleeps on an unwalled rooftop will be out of the protective reach of God.[25] Majlesi believes that sleeping with one's right hand beneath one's face constitutes the correct mode of sleeping, while sleeping on one's back or on the left hand is again reprobatory (*makruh*). According to Majlesi, sleeping on one's stomach is also unacceptable, and anyone observing another person sleeping in that position should awaken him.[26] Majlesi also writes about how believers should interpret their dreams. Shoes are said to symbolize women, and Majlesi maintains that if a man dreams that his shoes have been stolen, his wife will pass away or will become separated from him.[27]

Majlesi has his own particular recommendations on the correct mode and time of sexual intercourse. Without any reference to a report, he posits that intercourse under a fruit tree will bear a bloodthirsty and murderous child.[28] He strongly recommends against couples talking during sexual intercourse or men laying their eyes on the sexual organ of women. He predicts that a child born out of sexual intercourse during which partners speak to one another will become mute, and if men lay eyes on the sexual organ of the women, the child will be born blind or become blind.[29] Under the title of "times during which copulation is reprehensible (*makruh*)", Majlesi first lists a series of dates and then warns that if couples engage in sexual intercourse during those specified dates, they will be punished. Without citing any reports, he writes, if sexual intercourse occurs on the first day of the month, except Ramadan, or the middle of the month, except the middle of

---

[21] M. B. Majlesi, *'Eyn al-Hayat*, p. 389.
[22] M. B. Majlesi, *Heliyatal-Mottaqin*, pp. 250–251.
[23] M. B. Majlesi, *'Eyn al-Hayat*, p. 366.   [24] Ibid., p. 128.   [25] Ibid.   [26] Ibid., p. 129.
[27] M. B. Majlesi, *Majmu'eh-e Rasel-e E'teqadi*, p. 73.
[28] M. B. Majlesi, *Ekhtiyarat*, p. 125.   [29] Ibid.

Shaʿban, or the last day of any month, the child born from it will have either four or six fingers. Majlesi also rules that a child born as a result of copulation during the eclipse of the sun or the moon will be damaged or impaired.[30] Majlesi employs religious superstition to regulate the most private aspects of people's lives.

BELIEVERS AND INDIVIDUALS OF THE OTHER WORLD

Majlesi's understanding and interpretation of the ascribed *ahadith* leads him to ascertain that the believer can actually solicit and obtain the visitation of the Prophet, Imam ʿAli, or any dead person in his or her dream if the proper prayers are recited before falling asleep.[31] Majlesi cites an attributed report to demonstrate that the Prophet himself had said that seeing him in dreams would be exactly similar to a situation in which he would be seen in a state of consciousness and awakenness.[32] The issue of when and why dreams would come true preoccupied Majlesi. He, therefore, categorized dreams according to their fulfilment and unfulfilment potential.[33] Based on different attributed reports, he provided different theoretical scenarios on dreams and their fulfilment.

According to one attributed *hadith*, as the believer falls asleep, his soul will move towards the sky, and the fulfilment or unfulfilment of his dream will depend on where in this journey the dream actually happens. Whatever is observed by the soul of the believer in the world of angels, up in the sky, will be fulfilled and actualized, and whatever is observed on earth and in the air, between the earth and the skies, will turn out to be false and unfulfilled dreams.[34] Majlesi argues that, according to another ascribed report, the dream of a believer (*moʾmen*) will always be fulfilled, as he is pure and his certitude is unyielding. The believer's dream, according to Majlesi, has the same status as a revelation.[35]

Providing further justification for the claim that the dream of a believer is the same as a revelation, Majlesi argues that, according to a different attributed report, after the Prophet passed away, the flow of revelations discontinued, yet foretelling (*besharat dahandeh*) dreams continued to circulate.[36] The significance and power of a foretelling dream or a revelation is that both have to draw from the same Divine source of information about the future. Majlesi leaves open the possibility of a person's phantasmical claim to have received revelations or foretelling dreams and

[30] Ibid., p. 124.　[31] M. B. Majlesi, *Heliyat al-Mottaqin*, p. 134.
[32] Ibid., p. 137.　[33] Ibid., p. 135.　[34] Ibid., p. 136.　[35] Ibid.　[36] Ibid.

maintains that such a relation between God and humans could happen. By claiming that believers can receive revelations, he places the worldly claims of an individual on a par with that of the Prophet. It seems as if Majlesi wishes to democratize and make available the metaphysical experience of the Prophet with God to any worldly believer who wishes to claim it. By normalizing and banalizing the unique relation between God and his prophets, Majlesi invites greater claims of interaction between the material and hidden world. He opens the floodgates of superstition in the name of religion.

BELIEVERS AND DATES: OMINOUS AND AUSPICIOUS

Majlesi establishes not only what ought to be done or avoided on a particular day of the month, but even foretells detailed events that will occur if a particular day of the week coincides with the changing lunar month. Once again, Majlesi engages in religious superstition, presenting so-called religious justifications for inexplicable causal relations. For Majlesi, Fridays are a most auspicious day. He submits that there is a particular time in every Friday during which if a subject asks God for a favour, God will surely grant him the favour, unless it is religiously prohibited (*haram*).[37] If a person cuts his or her nails on Fridays, Majlesi argues that, according to an attributed report, that person will become immune to insanity, blindness and skin diseases.[38] Majlesi refers to an ascribed report according to which when Abolhamas inquires about what he should do to become more affluent, he is told to cut his nails and trim his moustache each Friday.[39] According to another attributed report, Majlesi rules that whoever of the Shi'i dies on a Friday, that person will not be subjected to the fire of hell and the torture of the first night in the grave.[40]

Through a lengthy and detailed survey of certain events such as the days on which Adam's repentance was accepted by God, Zarathustra claimed prophethood or the day on which the Prophet Mohammad entered Medina, Majlesi develops an elaborate list of auspicious and inauspicious dates and rules on what believers ought to do or not to do on particular days and months of the year. He even makes precise predictions on the outcome of actions undertaken on each particular day or month.

[37] M. B. Majlesi, *Rabi' al-Asabi' (Doaha va A'mal Shab va Ruz-e Jom'eh)* (Qom, 1386), p. 21.
[38] M. B. Majlesi, *Doaha va A'mal Shab va rouz-e Jom'eh*, p. 67.   [39] Ibid., p. 66.
[40] Ibid., p. 22.

Majlesi rules that the first day of the first lunar month, which is an auspicious date, is suitable for getting married, seeking knowledge, visiting kings, going on trips, buying and selling. He rules that on this day of the month, if a slave or a domesticated animal escapes or is lost, it will be recuperated within eight days and whoever falls sick will recover rapidly.[41] However, he foretells that whenever the first day of Mohharam falls on a Saturday a string of ominous consequences will unfold. Winter will be extremely cold, and there will be excessive rainfall. Numerous babies will perish due to a plague. A pox epidemic will break out among children. War will flare up between Arabs and Turks. Fruits will be tasty in Hamadan and Fars. Conflicts will erupt in Yemen and Bahrain and, during one month of that year, a lot of blood will be spilled.[42]

According to Majlesi, if the first day of the Iranian New Year, the first day of spring, which has its origin in pre-Islamic times and is traced back to the time of Jamshid, the mythical first King of Iran, falls on a Tuesday a series of events will ensue. Kings and the nobility will prosper but hardship will befall the ordinary people and their hearts will be filled with sorrow. Commerce will slow down and prices will increase. Civil strife will be on the rise, insects and stinging beasts will multiply, women will quarrel with their husbands and seek divorce, fruits will be damaged, silk will be found in abundance yet its price will increase.[43]

In the opening pages of *Zad al-Ma'ad*, or "Provisions for the Hereafter" Majlesi explains why the supplications, rites and litanies that he reports from the imams and which are to be recited and performed during the three months of *Rajab*, *Sha'ban* and *Ramazan* (*Ramadan*) are so important and special. On the day of resurrection, Majlesi writes, these three months will be addressed and asked about the behaviour and action of God's subjects, during each month. If the three months report that a person has "collected provisions" by petitioning God for "mercy and grace", "endeavoured actively" to obtain His satisfaction and "tried hard" to acquire His favour, then the angels would testify to the righteousness and piety of that person. It is based on this register or balance of religious activities during the special months that people can obtain salvation in the hereafter. According to Majlesi, upon receiving each month's positive record on individuals, God would order the angels to direct the ones who had collected proper provisions towards paradise.

In *Zad al-Ma'ad*, once again, Majlesi is setting out in specific and minute detail the exact rites, rituals and supplications incumbent upon a

---

[41] M. B. Majlesi, *Ekhtiyarat*, p. 4.   [42] Ibid., pp. 48–49.   [43] Ibid., p. 44.

pious Shi'i wishing salvation in the hereafter. He charts out not only the exact words to be pronounced by the Shi'i, but also specifies the precise acts, gestures and behaviour considered as religiously correct during various occasions. Majlesi, for example, writes that if on the day of festivities of *Qadir-e Khom*, commemorating the Prophet's nomination of 'Ali as his successor, a believer smiles on another believer, on the day of resurrection, God will look upon him with blessings, fulfil a thousand of his wants, build him a castle of white pearls and illuminate his face.[44] While one could argue that Majlesi's intention for his writings was only to guide the Shi'i towards felicity in the here and the hereafter, it could also be argued that an element of social, psychological, religious and inevitably political indoctrination, engineering and control of the Shi'i community underlied his detailed accounts. Majlesi's works reflect a clear inclination and trenchant for thinking, deciding and planning for the Shi'i and running their lives in as many aspects as possible. He writes that on the day of 'Ashura, commemorating the day of Imam Hoseyn's martyrdom, "one should not become involved with worldly activities ... should not eat or drink, yet should not intend to fast ... should not store food in one's house or laugh ... should damn the murderers of Imam Hoseyn one thousand times".[45] Majlesi seems to be programming individuals in the Shi'i community according to his own specifications, criteria and details. If daily thought and action is successfully controlled through the internalization of a manual with promised worldly rewards in the here and spiritual rewards in the hereafter and if rational thought is effectively repressed through rendering it religiously reprehensible if not prohibited, the foundations for an unrestricted absolutist political ideology and political system are laid.

Once the illogical relation between a number of particular dates, ominous or auspicious, and a series of random outcomes enters and is registered in the belief system of the common folk as facts and certitudes, superstitious thinking chases out logical thought. The superstitious believer, apprehensive about employing his independent reasoning, since it is presented as an irreligious activity and steeped in internalizing unreasonable argumentations, thus becomes a tool in the hands of the propagators of nonsensical propositions or ideas. Majlesi's manual on the significance of particular dates and their supposed corresponding outcomes can be considered as yet another means of stupefying, dulling and distorting the mind and logical powers of the common folk. One may ask why the coincidence of a day (Tuesday) and the first day of spring should

[44] M. B. Majlesi, *Zad al-Ma'ad*, p. 382.   [45] Ibid., p. 435.

lead to the increase in the production of silk, and if silk is to be found in abundance, everything else held constant, why its price should increase? Or how can and why should the rate of women quarrelling with their husbands and demanding divorce be related to the concurrence of the first day of spring with a Tuesday?

BELIEVERS AND PRAYERS

Having established the proper Shi'i mode of sleeping, Majlesi effectively lists his compilation of various prayers, incantations, supplications, phrases or Qur'anic verses that, if recited prior to falling asleep, would result in a series of rewards, in both this world and the hereafter. The rewards in the hereafter for reciting Majlesi's suggested lines include having all one's sins forgiven, just as if one were a newly born. The rewards guaranteed by Majlesi in this world include becoming immune to and protected from Satan, brigands, pillage, physical paralysis, disasters, poverty, depression and being caught under a collapsing roof. To those who opt for his comprehensive insurance scheme by reciting the suggested incantations or supplications, Majlesi promises a special bonus. He suggests that those who comply by his instructions would live long enough to witness the reappearance of the Hidden Imam.[46] This worldly reward promised for resignation to Majlesism is one that no pious Shi'i, who comes to believe him, would ever want to risk foregoing.

In the meantime, based on his selection of "appropriate" attributed reports, Majlesi presents his followers with an incredible bargain. He suggests that they would be shielded against poverty and destitution in this material world and would also be endowed with ample provisions and eternal happiness in paradise if they would only recite three particular Qur'anic chapters on Friday nights. The fact that the pious would obtain their desirable results only if the recitation is carried out on Friday nights bears the mark of the inexplicable causal relations that typifies Majlesi's superstitious writings. To encourage the Shi'i further to act according to his religious directives, Majlesi argues that the person engaging in such prayers would later – in the hereafter – become wedded to 100 beautiful women (*houri*), the kind that can only be found in paradise.[47]

From among his collection of utilitarian and practical prayers, Majlesi refers to one that functions as a modern alarm clock. He suggests that once

---

[46] M. B. Majlesi, *Heliyat al-Mottaqin*, pp. 129–132.
[47] M. B. Majlesi, *Doaha va A'mal Shab va rouz-e Jom'eh* (Qom, 1386), p. 34.

the believer recites a particular prayer and mentions the time at which he wishes to wake up, God will commission an angel to wake the person up at the specified time.[48] In another case, Majlesi instructs his readers how to shut out nightmares. Once again, he lists the supplications, phrases or verses that once recited would dispel frightful and disturbing dreams.[49]

Throughout his writings, Majlesi employs a carrot and stick or incentive and disincentive method of persuasion, operational in both the material world and the hereafter, to regulate the behavioural pattern of the members of the community. First, he tries to convince the popular masses of the credibility of his position by informing them that the private and social comportment that he promotes is in accordance with the conduct and tradition of the imams. He then threatens the potential dissident and non-compliant elements with some evil consequence if they refuse to follow his prescription, which he claims to be that of the imams.

Through the regimentation of the private and public life of the Shiʿi, in the name of religion, Majlesi engages in a process of cultural homogenization. His writings are intended at persuading the Shiʿi to wear a ring with an agate stone, wear yellow or white shoes, sleep with one's right hand beneath one's face, not engage in a conversation in the middle of sexual intercourse, not laugh excessively and try hard to shed tears in remembrance of the imams. Majlesism imposes conformity and uniformity in the name of correct Shiʿi belief and practice. By constructing an ideal Shiʿi mode of behaviour and presenting its constituent elements, selected by him, as the distinguishing feature or mark of Shiʿism, Majlesi defines the faith and effectively labels the non-compliers as deviant "others". Through the use of compelling religious persuasion if not dictates and a supportive state apparatus, Majlesi creates and imposes a set of behavioural rules on the common folk who were both emotionally attached to Shiʿism and technically unfamiliar with its legal intricacies, functionings and obligations.

Compliance with Majlesi's ideal Shiʿi behaviour, whether it results from sheer coercion or free volition, implies a large degree of internalization and acceptance of superstition and unreasonableness as a mode of reflection, argumentation and life. Majlesism as an ideology aims at immunizing the people to questioning and challenging political and religious authorities by arguing that the justification or legitimacy of what is demanded or imposed by such authorities is beyond the comprehension of common people and only understood by a special category of people, the *ʿolama* and reporters

[48] M. B. Majlesi, *Heliyat al-Mottaqin*, pp. 133–134.   [49] Ibid., p. 132.

of *ahadith*. The common folk drilled and nurtured in Majlesi's culture of irrationality become insensitive and unresponsive to arbitrary and auto-cratic decisions of religious and political authorities. Majlesism numbs independent reasoning and seeks to replace rationality as the criteria of judgement with superstitious explanations inapplicable or irrelevant to our material world. The danger of Majlesism as a tool for social engineer-ing and manipulation is in its use of religion to cast rationality as an anti-religious tool while promoting false cause fallacies and irrationality as the proper yardsticks of the pious. The religio-political grip and hold of religiously supported autocratic rulers over the common folk can be sus-tained as long as the people can be convinced by religious authorities that belief in contrived and illogical quasi-religious causal relations can serve them better than rational and somewhat predictable causal relations. Majlesism as a superstition-based ideology can remain potent as long as the common folk fail to or are prevented from substituting their own common sense and rationality without necessarily abandoning their piety for the opinions and dictates of the producers and propagators of super-stition as Shi'ism. Majlesism fosters political arbitrariness and absolutism by promoting the unquestioning servitude of the people to those who speak in the name of Shi'ism.

9

Reconfigurating the Necessities of Belief

Articulating a State Religion

What does it require to be a Muslim and what else does it require to be a Shiʿi? The proclamation of faith is associated with *shahadat* or the profession of a simple, well-known and cogent line. For the Sunnis it reads, "I give witness that there is no god but God and Mohammad is His Messenger". For the Shiʿi it reads, "I give witness that there is no god but God, Mohammad is His Messenger, and ʿAli is His vicegerent". The original requirement for being considered a Muslim was straightforward; belief in monotheism plus acceptance of Mohammad as His Prophet. Once the person living in the Age of Ignorance (*jaheliyyat*) made this simple attestation, it was implicit that he or she had come to believe that Angel Gabriel informed Mohammad of his mission and that he received revelations from God in which He articulated His designs for His creatures. Addressing the believers (*moʾmenun*), the Qurʾan clearly informs the people what they need to believe in if they wish to be considered Muslims. They need to believe in God (Allah) and His Messenger and the scripture that He has sent to his Messenger and also the scripture that He has sent to those before Mohammad. The Qurʾan subsequently adds that those who deny Allah, His angels, His books, His messengers and the Day of Judgement have gone far, far astray.[1] In terms of correct dogma, all Muslims believe in monotheism (*towhid*), prophethood of Mohammad (*nobovvat*) and the Day of Judgement (*maʿad*).

This constellation of core Islamic beliefs is non-negotiable. Denial of any one of these articles of faith places the denier beyond the pale of Islam. The Shiʿi, however, require members of their creed to believe in two

[1] A. Y. ʿAli (tr.), *The Holy Qurʾan* (4:136), p. 229

additional core articles: *Imamate,* or the leadership role of the twelve
imams after the Prophet, and *'adl,* or Divine justice. The first three principles held in common with Sunnis and the two additional ones specific to
the Shi'i constitute their principles of the faith. Annexed to this five-sided
pentagon, the Shi'i, similar to Sunnis, have a set of practical requirements.
This annex of correct practices identifies the necessary acts, practices, rites
and rituals required of a believer. Once again, both the Shi'i and Sunnis
find themselves sharing the same core of key correct practices or practical
obligations. They both believe in the necessity of prayers, fasting, pilgrimage and the payment of the wealth tax. In fact, the Shi'i believe in the
well-known Sunni "five pillars of Islam" and more. The Shi'i, however,
classify the practices and rituals as branches or derivatives of the religion
(*foru'-e din*) in contrast to the principles or fundamentals of belief in the
faith (*usul-e din*).

Relegating practices to the realm of branches implies that once belief in
principles of Islam is affirmed through choice, the practical aspects of
seeking proximity to and serving God through observing the correct
practices or orthopraxy will automatically grow out of the correct
dogma or orthodoxy. Moving from polytheism to monotheism and then
rising to the position of the believer (*mo'men*) and subsequently transcending to the station of the one who fears God (*mottaqi*) is attainable
by supplementing the belief principles of the faith with the prescribed
practices, rites and rituals of religion. Believers and practitioners of
Shi'ism, however, are expected to adjust and coordinate their lives not
only according to the said principles and branches of the religion, but also
to yet another extension of both, which we shall call auxiliary necessities.

The specific number of Shi'i auxiliary necessities in both the realm of
beliefs and practices and the reason for identifying certain acts, beliefs or
rituals as necessities (*zaruriyat*) of Shi'ism is unclear and somewhat arbitrary. The formulation and presentation of Shi'i auxiliary necessities by
Majlesi has served to establish a set of criteria differentiating the Shi'i from
other Muslims. It would be misleading to suggest that the idea of such
auxiliary necessities originated with Majlesi. Acting as the archaeologist,
the architect and the mason, Majlesi searched, found and prioritized the
information already available in previous Shi'i reports and crafted a standardized model of what Shi'ism was supposed to be in terms of its beliefs
and practices. In the exhaustive list of auxiliary necessities that Majlesi
enumerates, there is hardly an item that is not referred to by Koleyni or
Sheykh Sadduq (Ebn Babawayh). Yet, it may be argued that Majlesi's
construction is of particular significance. He occupied an official state

position giving him the power to implement religiosity. Whereas the compilers of *ahadith* such as Koleyni or Ebn Babawayh before Majlesi were not in a political position to enforce the content of their compilations, Majlesi was. For Majlesi auxiliary necessities could also serve as an extra filter to weed out religio-political "deviations" thereby imposing an ideological purity and uniformity. Once a standardized model of Shi'ism fashioned by Majlesi's auxiliary necessities is established, adherence to it by the public is secured by the autocratic religio-political Safavi state. The official inclusion of auxiliary Shi'i necessities as identifiers of the Shi'i enabled Majlesi to articulate and shape a religion that looked different from the original Shi'i creed defined by its simple principles and practices.

RELIGIOUS RECOMMENDATIONS OR OBLIGATIONS?

In *Heliyat al-Mottaqin*, Majlesi uses a style, which he develops and perfects in his later works. Without explicitly declaring an act as a religious obligation, he introduces and supports it with attributed reports in such a persuasive and forceful manner that it would appear as an obligation to a person incapable of checking and verifying its status. Majlesi effectively creates a wide circle of creedal recommendations based on the practices attributed to the imams. These emphatic creedal recommendations, which take the significance and status of obligations, are net additions – auxillaries – to the original obligations of the faith.

Examples abound in *Heliyat al-Mottaqin* demonstrating Majlesi's method of persuasive recommendation-cum-obligations on issues ranging from the prohibition of shaving one's beard to the obligation of holding hands when two believers meet.[2] As usual, Majlesi's rulings include incentives and disincentives operational in both the here and the hereafter. As long as Majlesi's recommendations, enjoinments and prohibitions were not necessarily binding, they constituted a highly recommended personal code of conduct to be honoured by the virtuous and pious Shi'i. When, however, Majlesi informs his readers that the recommendations and interdictions in his books are directly based on the teachings and the traditions of the imams, in effect, he is reminding his readers that if they do not wish to contradict the practice of the imams, thereby inviting the charge of rejecting the imams and ultimately God, it is in their best interest to comply with his recommendations.[3] Majlesi couches his

---

[2] M. B. Majlesi, *Heliyat al-Mottaqin*, pp. 101, 239.   [3] Ibid., p. 2.

recommendations in such a compelling manner that the common folk find themselves in a moral and religious bind. The fine line between obligatory (*farz* or *vajeb*) and recommended (*mostahab*) acts, on the one hand, and forbidden (*haram*) and reprobated (*makruh*) acts, on the other, become purposefully blurred. Whereas the faith acknowledges five gradations in human behaviour from the obligatory to the forbidden, Majlesi effectively introduces a polarity between obligatory and forbidden by converting those acts deemed as recommended to obligations and those deeds deemed as reprobatory into forbidden.

Infused with a compelling religious sense of duty, the common folk were faced with the strong recommendations of a prominent scholar who was also a politically powerful clergy. Without any possible recourse to verifying and scrutinizing Majlesi's emphatic instructions, his teachings became binding creedal obligations of a state religion in the process of formulation. In this light, Majlesi's books could have served the double purpose of publicizing and popularizing a perception of Shiʻi orthodoxy and orthopraxy with the purpose of indoctrination, as well as gradually forging an official state religion, where the recommendation and chastisements would become legally and politically binding rather than personally privileged. This official state religion would be founded upon Majlesism.

In pursuit of formulating a state religion based on his own perceptions, Majlesi creates a closed and inflexible religious environment in which the pious Shiʻi feel compelled to follow his words as if they were the fundamentals of the faith. For example, Majlesi rules that there is no doubt in ʻOmar's unbelief. He further adds that there is no doubt in the infidelity (*kofr*) of those who consider ʻOmar a Muslim.[4] While historically, ʻOmar is the second Rightfully Guided Caliph of the Muslim *ommat* and an in-law of the Prophet, Majlesi brands him and all those who consider him as a Muslim as infidels. Majlesi seeks to convert the anti-Sunni religious sentiments historically fanned by the Safavis into a systematic component of Safavi Shiʻism or the official state religion.

On issues of orthopraxy, Majlesi engages in a similar process. Whereas the standard obligatory rites and rituals of Islam are commonly known, he insists on certain auxiliary rituals as the distinguishing features of Shiʻism. For example, by elevating the act of participation in mourning sessions to the status of "the supreme act of worship" and the means to "felicity", he articulates a new set of binding creedal obligations.[5] The standard obligatory acts of worship in Islam do not include attending mourning sessions or

[4] M. B. Majlesi, *Jalaʼ al-ʻOyun*, p. 88.   [5] Ibid., pp. 21–22.

wailing the martyrdom of imams. Neither does Majlesi explicitly declare such acts as obligatory, yet he does refer to it as "the supreme act of worship" and the highest means of attaining proximity to God (*a'zam ta'at va ashraf ghorabat*). Again Majlesi's highly persuasive message of enjoining the pious to engage in such practices and participate in such rituals raises the importance of that rite to an equal footing as that of obligatory prayers in the minds of common Shi'i practitioners. Shi'ism is subsequently associated with an auxiliary necessity.

In time, Iranian Shi'ism became increasingly identified with auxiliary religious orthodoxy and orthopraxy, which had taken an obligatory aspect as a result of Majlesi's compelling promotion of them as unassailable Shi'i particularities. To formulate and propagate a popular religious ideology, Majlesi focused on galvanizing an emotionally charged Shi'ism among the common folk, hardly capable of discerning original religious obligations from aggressive recommendations. The accounts in his book *Jala' al-'Oyun* claim to provide the pious Shi'i with key instructions, which if closely followed during the prescribed mourning sessions would substantially augment, if not guarantee, their chances of deliverance and redemption.

THE ORIGIN, SOURCES AND PURPOSE OF NECESSITIES

In a book called *History and Principles of Shi'ism*, written in 1931, Kashef al-Gheta (Kashifu al-Ghita) articulated the Shi'i belief system. Following a standard procedure, Kashef al-Gheta divides religion into two parts: theoretical and practical, or the fundamentals of the faith and its branches. He argues that since belief in monotheism, prophethood and the Day of Judgement constitute the pillars of the faith, anyone who denies one of them is neither a Muslim nor a believer. Belief in the three pillars, however, immediately qualifies the individual as a Muslim.[6] By adding the two additional beliefs of *Imamate* and Justice to the three pillars of the faith, the fundamentals of the faith comes to five for the Shi'i.[7] According to Kashef al-Gheta, in the same way that God chose His Prophet, He commanded His Prophet to appoint an imam as the leader of the community. Just as "the prophet is the messenger of God, the Imam is the messenger of the Prophet".[8] Even though Kashef al-Gheta acknowledges the fact that according to the Shi'i, a person of faith (*mo'men*) is one who

[6] M. H. Kashifu 'l-Ghita, *History and Principles of Shi'ism* (Rome, 1985), p. 36.
[7] Ibid., p. 40.   [8] Ibid., pp. 37–38.

believes in the concept of *Imamate*, he readily concedes that the refusal to acknowledge *Imamate* does not exclude an individual from the Islamic community.[9] According to this definition, the belief in *Imamate* is not a necessity of Islam but certainly is that of Shi'ism.

Shi'i jurists have conceptualized an intricate chain of authority and legitimization demonstrating that what may be required of a Shi'i as a necessity or an obligation is God's command, even though it may not be directly or explicitly identified as a necessity in the Book of God. The line of argument follows as such. God designates the Prophet. The Qur'an is the word of God uttered by the Prophet and the Sonnat is the act and words of the Prophet himself, both binding on Muslims. The Prophet designated Imam 'Ali and subsequently each imam appointed his successor. The infallible imams have their own tradition equally binding on the Shi'i. The culture and tradition that originates from the imams is as binding on the Shi'i as that which originates from the Prophet and God. The words and the acts of the infallible Shi'i imams who are considered as the deputies of God and the Prophet and cannot err is reflected in their attributed *ahadith, akhbar* or reports. The accounts attributed to imams may compliment or extend the practice of the Prophet, establishing what become new necessities or auxiliary necessities. As such, strict adherence to the tradition of imams, as reflected in the reports attributed to them, is as important to the Shi'i as adherence to the word of God and the tradition of the Prophet.

The inclusion of an increasing number of auxiliary Shi'i necessities, legitimized by the claim that they could be deduced from the reports attributed to the imams, left the creed open to the threat of mutation and distortion. Some 580 years before Majlesi, Sharif Morteza, *'alam al-hoda* (d. 436/1044), a prominent Shi'i jurist, had forcefully challenged the uncritical reliance on and veracity of reports attributed to the imams, the cornerstone of Majlesi's formulations. Majlesi had read Morteza's works and commented on them. Morteza, influenced by the rationalist *Mo'tazeleh* (*Mu'tazilite*) believed that the "basic truths of religion are to be determined by reason alone".[10] He is said to have believed that the books belonging to the Shi'i, as well as their opponents, were full of reports containing all kinds of errors and untruths.[11] In reference to a *hadith* in Koleyni's *Usul-e Kafi*, Morteza shed doubt on the *ahadith* and asked, "How many reports whose literal meaning is impossible or false have this man and others of our

[9] Ibid., p. 39.
[10] W. Madelung, 'Imamism and Mu'tazilite Theology' in *Religious Schools and Sects in Medieval Islam* (Hampshire, 1999), p. 25.
[11] Ibid.

companions reported in their books. Most likely this report is forged and foisted".[12] Morteza therefore argued for putting the reports to the critical test of reason and reliable evidence such as the Qur'an.[13] It was therefore not surprising that Morteza rarely quoted reports in his argumentations and, when he did, it was only used as a subordinate proof.[14]

Broadening the sphere of obligatory necessities beyond the five core principles of Shi'i belief (three plus two) and the four standard practices of prayers, fasting, pilgrimage and the wealth tax redefines and reconfigurates Shi'ism. As long as the new auxiliary necessities are presented as binding legal obligations and not voluntary personal recommendations and their status is placed on a par with core principles, non-compliance or disbelief in them provokes retribution or expulsion from the faith. The creation of an "other" within the Shi'i creed begins by redefining what a Shi'i should be and do, couched in new auxillary necessities. The expanded definition of necessities implies that those who fall out of the newly identified circle of the Shi'i become deviants and heretics. The power to add on a set of auxiliary necessities other than the five core principles and four standard practices is effectively equivalent to the artic-ulation of a new definition of Shi'ism, or the presentation of a new creed under an old name. Categorization between insiders and outsiders within the Shi'i community based on auxillary necessities articulated by Shi'i jurists empowers them to determine essentially who is a Shi'i and in what he or she should believe and by what they should abide.

The founders and formulators of auxiliary necessities were the reporters and the compilers of the reports (*mohaddethin*). Yet unlike Majlesi, the majority were not in an official position to impose them. They identified, selected and derived the auxiliary necessities from reports attributed to the imams. Then, as jurists/compilers, they further required the common folk to comply rigorously with the additional necessities they themselves had retrieved or enunciated. The greater the number of binding auxiliary necessities, the more rigidly defined did the conduct of correct Shi'i live-lihood become. Therefore, the decision of compilers of reports on what to select and add on to the core of necessities becomes, crucial, exclusive and conclusive. The redefinition and reconstruction of the creed by reporters and compilers of *ahadith* and jurists on the basis of auxiliary necessities provides the reformulators with tremendous religio-political and cultural power. The religious theoreticians and guardians of the people, especially if they benefited from the political support of kings, occupied the unique

---

[12] Ibid., p. 26.   [13] Ibid., p. 25.   [14] Ibid., p. 26.

position of thinking, leading and managing the people's mode of behaviour, interaction and livelihood in almost all conceivable domains. By adding to the list of doctrinal and practical necessities of Shi'ism, compilers of reports or jurists could effectively alter the private and social codes of conduct of the pious and the definition of being a Shi'i.

THE RELIGIO-POLITICAL SIGNIFICANCE OF NECESSITIES: FROM THE NECESSITY TO BELIEVE IN IMAMS TO THE NECESSITY OF BELIEVING IN TRANSMITTERS AND COMPILERS OF THEIR REPORTS

In the process of defining the Shi'i creed, Majlesi effectively adds new layers of auxiliary necessities while paying formal respect to the core principles. These auxiliary necessities are given an official status as archetypal models and blueprints of Shi'i behaviour and belief. Majlesi's dilution of the importance of core principles by highlighting the significance of auxiliary necessities triggers off a process of replacement. The kernel of core principles is overwritten by the chaff of auxiliary necessities. This development runs parallel with Majlesi's attempt at magnifying the importance of *hadith* or report literature in comparison to the Qur'an as the irreplaceable and unique text that explains and clarifies the Qur'an. In a third parallel line of progression, Majlesi posits that reason and rationality are not the proper tools for discerning the truth, leaving the source of deriving the truth only to the *ahadith* and reports. These three key processes blend together in Majlesi's ideology providing the basis and justification for empowering the clergy, the compilers and the interpreters of the reports with an unassailable position similar to that of the imams.

The importance accorded to reports by Shi'i imams is derived from the belief in *Imamate*, the infallibility of the imams and the notion that the kind of knowledge they possessed and passed on was unique and perfect. Their knowledge was believed to be infinite, rendering them independent of any other source. Based on Koleyni, Majlesi maintains that Imam 'Ali and his children possessed three books containing the "Complete Truth" from the day of creation till eternity, enabling the Shi'i community to have access to all past, present and future knowledge and information. These three books are argued to include all the commandments that would ever be needed by mankind.[15] First, Fatemeh's Holy Book the *Mosahaf* is said to be three times the official Qur'an, without a word of the official Qur'an in it.

---

[15] M. B. Majlesi, *Haq al-Yaqin*, p. 43.

This book is maintained to have been dictated to the Prophet's daughter by the Angel Gabriel who sought to comfort her after Mohammad's death. Second, a two-volume text called the lesser *Jafr* and the greater *Jafr*. This text is said to contain the accumulated knowledge of all prophets, legatees (*owsiya*) and jurists, as well as every single conceivable ruling for all possible wrongdoings. Third, a book called *Jame'* dictated by the Prophet and written by 'Ali, including all that is recommended and forbidden and all religious needs and requirements of every epoch and every single detail of rewards and punishments.[16]

The imams are said to have inherited these books from their fathers and, along with them, they inherited their knowledge. Also in possession of a column of light connecting them to God, Majlesi maintained that the imams were knowledgeable about the condition and state of God's subjects.[17] Until the reappearance of the Twelfth Imam, who is said to possess the three books, the flow of complete knowledge from the imams to the people is believed to be interrupted. The role of the clerical interme-diary in the period when the flow of information from its original source, namely the imams, dries up is to act as a proxy or substitute delivering the established knowledge of the imams reflected in their reports to the people. Majlesi openly refers to this surrogate role of the clergy as the bearer or messenger of the knowledge of the imams. He maintains, "it is incumbent upon Muslims to venerate the reporters of their [imams'] *ahadith* and the messengers or bearers of their knowledge, since venerating them, [report-ers/clergy/jurists] implies, signifies or returns to venerating the imams".[18] This argument would also imply that if people do not venerate the report-ers of the *ahadith*, it would be as if they do not venerate the imams, the Prophet and God.

By justifying the religio-political need for the reporters of the *ahadith* as functional intermediaries between the absent imams and the people, on the one hand, and the politico-military need for the worldly guardian-ship of the kings, on the other, Majlesi endows the clergy and the kings with unlimited authority. Whereas fearful of secularizing the sacred, the Akhbaris refused to recognize anyone, even the *'olama*, as plenipotentiary spokespersons and legatees of the imams, Majlesi succeeded in not only combining but institutionalizing the worldly powers of the King and the spiritual powers of the living jurist as an integral and indivisible unit,

[16] Ibid. See *Koleyni, Usul-e Kafi*, vol. 1, p. 345.   [17] M. B. Majlesi, *Haq al-Yaqin*, p. 43.
[18] M. B. Majlesi, *Hayat al-Qolub*, vol. 5, p. 486.

imbued with the uncontested powers of the absent imam. In their capacity as the guardian, interpreter and propagator of all the Truth handed down from God to Mohammad and from Mohammad to 'Ali and his children, the reporters and compilers of *ahadith* claim that their decisions and rulings in the absence of the Twelfth Imam are binding on the common folk.

Majlesi posits that reverence towards the Prophet and the imams during their lives and after their death, as well as reverence for whatever is attributed to them, such as their holy shrines, relics, reports, those of their progeny who follow their path, the reporters of their *ahadith* (*akhbar*) and those who are the transmitters of their knowledge, is obligatory (*vajeb*).[19] Majlesi creates new obligations and auxiliary necessities. The Shi'i duty of admiring and following the transmitters of the knowledge of imams or the compilers and reporters of *ahadith* is presented as a natural by-product of the necessity of belief in *Imamate*. Shi'i veneration for their imams is extended by Majlesi to new or auxiliary necessities. Once a reverential connection is established between the imams and a souvenir, mementos or relics of them, those associated categories – holy shrines, reports and transmitters of reports – obtain the same status and deserve the same level of adoration as the imams. Majlesi's argument places reverence for the transmitters and compilers of Shi'i reports (*akhbar*) on a par with the admiration for the imams and instantly renders it into a religious duty as new necessities or an auxiliary necessity of Shi'i belief.

According to Majlesi's new formulation, the acceptance of the authority and status of the transmitters of reports and the clergy is no longer optional but a necessity for the Shi'i. Majlesi's call on the Shi'i to venerate and revere the reporters of *ahadith* as strongly as they would venerate and respect the imams and the Prophet is not worded in terms of a recommendation but an obligation.

EXPANDING THE NECESSITIES OF SHI'ISM: A CREED WITH A DIFFERENT EMPHASIS

Once Majlesi formulates the proper Shi'i mode of behaviour in every aspect of human activity and establishes a right for the clergy and an obligation for the people, he proceeds to define new Shi'i necessities on the basis of attributed reports. The sum total of the disparate attributed reports from which he selects and turns into directives on proper Shi'i belief

---

[19] Ibid., pp. 486–487.

and practice in addition to his reinterpretations constitute Majlesi's comprehensive religious ideology. Enumerating a very wide range of new necessities, Majlesi defines what a Shiʿi should believe and do. Since, other than the core principles, there is no exact indication of what precisely constitutes the necessities of Shiʿi belief, the rejection or non-compliance with which would constitute unbelief, the pious Shiʿi seems obliged to act according to Majlesi's maximalist or expanded concept of the necessities. The variety and plurality of new or auxiliary necessities articulated by Majlesi redirects Shiʿism in a different direction from that in which it was poised to move, given its core principles of beliefs and practices.

Majlesi posits that it is obligatory (*vajeb*) to believe in whatever constitutes the necessities (*zaruriyyat*) of the faith, while their denial would constitute unbelief (*kofr*), unless someone has just converted to Islam and is uninformed about its necessities.[20] Referring to Shahid Thani, Majlesi states that belief (*iman*) is acquired through faith in the five basic Shiʿi principles of monotheism, justice of God, prophethood, *Imamate* and resurrection.[21] Yet Majlesi points out that affirming the prophethood of Mohammad as a necessity of belief also implies confirming and acting according to certain obligations that ensues from and is directly connected with the belief in prophethood. These auxiliary obligations or necessities have their origin in reports attributed to the Prophet, such as the questioning of the dead in their tombs, the torment that the dead may be subjected to and Mohammad's physical ascent to heaven.[22] This category of beliefs, as well as rites and rituals attributed to the Prophet and therefore associated with him, automatically generates a new set of auxiliary necessities, the rejection of which would also lead to unbelief.

At first, Majlesi maintains that if a detailed and in-depth knowledge and acceptance of all auxiliary necessities were required to establish belief (*iman*), then the majority of Shiʿi would fall out of the circle of believers, giving the impression that he does not seek to include belief in the auxiliary necessities as a prerequisite of the Shiʿi faith.[23] However, Majlesi adds an important caveat essentially justifying his creation of a whole set of new obligations. He argues that belief in the five established principles and a general, cursory or overall (*ejmalan*) belief in the rites, rituals and practices attributed to the Prophet would categorize a person as a believer, only if he does not deny any of the essential necessities of the Muslim faith *in the process*.[24] A chain process of one core belief engendering a series of equally

[20] M. B. Majlesi, *Haq al-Yaqin*, p. 542. [21] Ibid. [22] Ibid., p. 543. [23] Ibid. [24] Ibid., pp. 543–544.

important connected auxiliary beliefs or practices, as deduced and interpreted by Majlesi from attributed reports, is established as a norm. Majlesi
argues that a person raised among Muslims cannot be ignorant of the
necessity of prayers, fasting and pilgrimage. If such an ignorant person
were to exist, he would not be considered as an unbeliever (*kafar*). Yet if he
were informed of these necessities and rejected them, then he would be
considered an apostate (*mortad*).[25]

In the same manner that Majlesi elaborates a set of Prophet-related
auxiliary necessities based on the principle of prophethood, he launches
into Imam-related auxiliary necessities. According to Majlesi, *Imamate* is a
core principle (*usul*) of the Shi'i faith and not a derivative (*far'*). It is also an
all-encompassing concept that envelops numerous subsets related to the
features and behaviours of the imams, the belief in which are said to be as
important as believing in the imams themselves. Majlesi argues that it is
not enough simply to believe in the imams and, for example, not believe
in their infallibility. In order to qualify as a Shi'i, individuals also need
to believe in "many of their [the imams'] characteristics and qualities
(*sefat*)".[26] Majlesi introduces the auxiliary necessities associated with the
imams by stating that "whatever the imams say is the truth and is being
said on behalf of the Prophet and God".[27] He argues that just as rejecting
the necessities of Islam presupposes the refusal of the Prophet and therefore
places a person outside Islam, the dismissal of the necessities of the
Imamiyyeh (the Twelver Shi'i) is an expression of denying *Imamate* and
the imams, subsequently placing a person beyond the pale of Shi'ism. For
example, Majlesi posits that the belief in temporary marriage or *mut'eh*,
the infallibility of imams, their comprehensive knowledge of all sciences
necessary for believers and the fact that no time or age can exist without the
imams or empty of them obviously constitute the necessities of Shi'ism.[28]
He suggests that belief in certain features or qualities of the imams also
constitute necessities of Shi'ism. Yet he points out that, for example, the
'olama know that after the death of the imams, their bodies are carried up
to the sky by the angels. However, this information, he argues, may not be
known to the common folk, and therefore they will not be considered non-
Shi'i if they do not believe in this concept.[29]

Majlesi maintains that the belief in *Imamate* and reverence for the
imams implies that a Shi'i should believe in all that is connected or related
with the imams. Majlesi's discussion of a particular case in relation to the
imams sheds light on the manner in which he articulates a third circle of

[25] Ibid., p. 544.   [26] Ibid., p. 544–545.   [27] Ibid., p. 545.   [28] Ibid.   [29] Ibid.

necessities, which may be classified as sub-auxiliary necessities. The only factor justifying such a classification is the so-called relation and connection of the subject with the imams. Majlesi seems to argue that a sub-auxiliary necessity of Shi'i belief is the conviction that a fictive and phantasmal city called Jabelqa actually exists. Referring to a report transmitted by Saffar Qomi, Majlesi writes about "a city behind or beyond the West, called Jabelqa". Its inhabitants are said to be 70,000 very pious and sinless individuals. Their only activity is the damnation of Abu Bakr and 'Omar (Umar) and the confirmation of the guardianship position of the Prophet's House (or the imams).[30] Majlesi interweaves the story of Jabelqa with the imams by maintaining that the imams recognize this city and are in contact with its inhabitants. According to Majlesi, it is the so-called recognition of Jabelqa by the imams and their contact with it that imposes on the Shi'i the necessity of belief in this fictive city. Even though Majlesi does not categorically state that the Shi'i ought to believe in Jabelqa as a necessity of their creedal conviction, he typically insinuates that due to the relation established between the imams and Jabelqa, the necessity of belief in the imams ipso facto requires the belief in Jabelqa.

According to Majlesi, the imams are the "saving vessels" of mankind, and if it were not for them and the Prophet, the universe and its inhabitants would not have been created.[31] Therefore, it follows that the Shi'i's love and affection for their imams obliges them to believe in the special features attributed to the imams, as well as all that is reported to be associated with them. In this sense, the belief in Jabelqa, according to Majlesi, becomes a sub-auxiliary necessity of Shi'i belief. Majlesi writes about the mythological city of Jabelqa or the angels visiting the imams with almost the same passion, conviction and intensity as he writes about the necessity of the Shi'i believing in monotheism, the prophethood of Mohammad, the Day of Judgement, *Imamate* and Divine justice.

Some of those particular features attributed to the imams, which Majlesi implicitly requires the Shi'i to believe in as auxiliary necessities, are: (1) the birth of imams with their umbilical cords severed; (2) their ability to proclaim their *Shahadat* upon birth; (3) their supernatural quality of seeing simultaneously what occurs in front of them, as well as what goes on behind them; (4) sleeping while being perfectly conscious and aware of what goes on around them as if they were awake; (5) the concept that they have no shadow; (6) their performance of miracles, such as bringing the dead to life again and returning the eyesight of the blind; (7) their knowledge of all

---

[30] M. B. Majlesi, *'Eyn al-Hayat*, p. 130.   [31] Ibid., p. 133.

languages; (8) their awareness of all future events; and (9) their hosting of
visiting angels.[32] Majlesi does not, however, expressly assert that the Shi'i
are obliged to believe in these features. Yet he clearly states that these
features are only understood by a "perfect believer" whose heart, by
God's grace, has been illuminated by the light of belief (*iman*).[33] Since, on
numerous occasions, Majlesi insists on the belief in particular qualities and
features of the imams as a necessity of Shi'ism, it would be consistent to think
that he would consider the above-mentioned features and more as auxiliary
necessities that have become part of his definition of established Shi'i necessities of belief. For Majlesi, as long as one does not attribute divinity to the
imams, any conceivable praise or ascription of supernatural qualities, exceptional virtues and superlative characteristics to them would be less than
what they would deserve.[34]

Majlesi argues that all those ideas, positions and notions that have
gained such widespread recognition among believers that the faithful are
knowledgeable about them constitute the necessities of Shi'ism.[35] He
warns that certain notions falling short of achieving the status of a necessity, due to their limited acceptance, may in time attain such a position.[36]
The element of public recognition, consent and knowledge of dogmatic, as
well as practical, Shi'i notions is presented as a pillar of this definition.
Majlesi does two things at the same time. He defines and institutionalizes
the prevalent system of beliefs and practices of the Shi'i community, which
he propagates through his works while carving out a free space in case he
needs to add other necessities, reshaping Shi'i behaviour and thought, in
the future. This open-ended concept of the necessities of Shi'i belief leaves
the field open to the ad hoc formulation of an official state religion in tune
with the changing interests of kings and clerics. The absence of clarity on
when an auxiliary necessity is transformed into a necessity of belief for the
Shi'i poses a problem for the pious and introduces a considerable degree of
arbitrariness in terms of judging a person as a Shi'i or a non-Shi'i. The
ability and power to change or redefine the necessities of Shi'i belief
constitutes a highly potent political tool for those religious figures who
can effectuate such alterations. The clergy armed with such a potent tool
can readily manipulate religion for political objectives.

At times, without providing an explanation for why certain auxiliary
notions should become a fixed part of the standard necessities, on a par

---

[32] M. B. Majlesi, *Haq al-Yaqin*, pp. 42–47.   [33] Ibid., pp. 46–47.
[34] Ibid., p. 47.   [35] Ibid., pp. 553, 555.   [36] Ibid., p. 554.

with the five core principles of Shi'ism, Majlesi issues an injunction. For example, he addresses the Shi'i directly and writes categorically that:

you should believe that the Prophet and the imams, as well as all prophets and angels, are infallible and that the family of Mohammad (the family of the infallibles and the pure) are superior to all other prophets and angels, as they are the ones who possess all knowledge of what has happened in the past and will happen until the day of resurrection.[37]

In such cases, Majlesi directly identifies and announces the auxiliary necessities of the Shi'i. In the same vein, Majlesi maintains that one of the necessities of Shi'ism is belief in the fact that Abu Taleb, Imam 'Ali's father, had never been an idol worshipper and was a Muslim.[38] Irrespective of the historical veracity of this affirmation, the manner in which Majlesi commands the Shi'i to believe in or observe certain practices leaves no room to question why these auxiliary necessities have been raised to the status of necessities.

Majlesi rhetorically inquires whether believing in *Imamate* and obedience to the imams are sufficient conditions for belief (*iman*), or whether belief can be ascertained only if one believes in all imam-related and associated issues such as their infallibility and their omniscient.[39] Rejecting the first possibility, Majlesi argues that belief in a number of properties and characteristics associated with the imams has become an integral part of Shi'i necessities. Belief in these characteristics, as an aspect of imam-related issues, constitutes a prerequisite of belief.[40] Based on Majlesi's discourse, it could be argued that belief in the five core Shi'i principles is necessary but not at all sufficient for qualifying as Shi'i believers. Therefore, the belief in the auxiliary and sub-auxiliary imam-related necessities complements and completes the faith, explaining the fact that Majlesi's list of necessities is entirely built on and derived from the reports attributed to the imams.[41] Subsequently, the religious justification of the necessities of the creed rests on attributed reports. The authenticity of the reports in turn rests on the self-declared reliability of their reporters and the authentication, corroboration and transmission inspection process of those who sift the reports and finally the selection preference of the compilers. Majlesi builds his official state religion on the information transmitted by reporters (*rejal/raviys*).

---

[37] M. B. Majlesi, *E'teqadat*, p. 29; M. B. Majlesi, *Haq al-Yaqin*, p. 43.
[38] M. B. Majlesi, *Haq al-Yaqin*, p. 31.
[39] Ibid., p. 544; M. B. Majlesi, *E'teqadat*, p. 28.
[40] M. B. Majlesi, *Haq al-Yaqin*, p. 545.   [41] Ibid., p. 555.

The freedom with which Majlesi uses his discretionary power to add necessities to the core of Shi'i beliefs and practices and therefore reshape it, forms the backbone of Majlesism as a religious ideology. In his book *E'teqadat (On Beliefs)*, Majlesi first points out that there is a plethora of necessities of Islam (*zaruriyyat-e din*) for both the Sunnis and Shi'i. Under the rubric of the necessities of the faith, Majlesi provides a long list of diverse items including rites, rituals, acts and behaviours. This list includes items such as the standard obligations of prayers, fasting during *Ramazan*, payment of *zakat* and performing the *haj* pilgrimage, as well as less well-known necessities such as the belief in accursedness of non-expedient lying and insulting.[42] Majlesi's list of the necessities of the faith can become rather confusing, since, in it, he includes the *mostahabat* or those rites, behaviours and acts that are recommended and not obligatory, such as congregational prayers.[43] In this same list of necessities, Majlesi includes the notion of belief in the "supremacy of science and scientists".[44] Are the pious expected to think that unless they comply by this edict on the status of scientists that they would be branded as infidels? Majlesi warns his readers that anyone denying the necessities of the faith, as he articulates them, is an infidel (*kafar*) and deserves to be put to death.[45]

Having defined the necessities of Islam, Majlesi goes on to present a list of necessities of the *Imamiyyeh* creed (*zaruriyyat-e mazhab Imamiyyeh*). He warns that denying a Shi'i necessity is as grave as denying all necessities, and the denier will join the "opponents of the creed" and will be considered out of the Shi'i creed. Again, Majlesi grafts a series of auxiliary necessities to the five core principles of Shi'i belief and the four necessities of practice, and presents a "package deal" notion of creedal necessities. This single and indivisible corps of Majlesi's Shi'i necessities – doctrinal and practical – is again composed of an array of items. This list includes items such as the belief in *Imamate*, one of the five basic Shi'i necessities of belief, as well as the virtue of visiting the graves of Shi'i imams, temporary marriage, hatred towards the enemies of Imam 'Ali and the other imams and the conviction that the imams possessed the knowledge of all that existed in the past and will occur until the Day of Judgement.[46]

Expectedly so, in his initial description of the necessities of Islam, Majlesi does not mention the issue of *Imamate*. However, he subsequently introduces a clause to the effect that "affection (*mohabat*) and friendship (*mavadat*) for, as well as reverence and obedience (*ta'zim*) towards, all Shi'i

[42] M. B. Majlesi, *E'teqadat*, pp. 27–28.   [43] Ibid., p. 27.
[44] Ibid.   [45] Ibid.   [46] Ibid., pp. 28–29.

imams is a necessity of Islam and those who deny this axiom such as the *Navaseb* and *Khavarej* will become infidels".[47] The term *Navaseb* is the plural for *Nasebi* or one who is usually understood to have enmity towards Imam 'Ali, and is a term usually applied to the Sunni by the Shi'i. By including this important clause, Majlesi effectively rules that even though the belief in *Imamate* is not a necessity for all Muslims, all Muslims need to be kind, reverential and obeisant towards Shi'i imams, otherwise they will be considered as infidels. Incapable of excommunicating Sunnis on the charge of not being Muslims, he introduces an auxiliary necessity that effectively renders them infidels.

From Majlesi's writings, it could be deduced that he expects those Muslims who recognize Imam 'Ali as the fourth Rightfully Guided Caliph as Sunnis do, yet do not recognize him as the first imam, should still be reverential and obeisant not only towards Imam 'Ali but the eleven imams succeeding him. Elevating obeisance to the twelve Shi'i imams to the status of a necessity of a Muslim's belief system, when he knows that Sunnis do not believe in the special status of the imams as Shi'i do, enables Majlesi to categorize Sunnis as infidels. Elsewhere in his writings, Majlesi is much less nuanced about the direct association that he establishes between the non-recognition of Shi'i imams or *Imamate* and infidelity. He maintains that those who deny the *velayat* or rulership of the imams will not enter heaven, even if they fulfil all their other obligations such as prayers, fasting, the payment of zakat and performing the *haj* pilgrimage. According to Majlesi, if a Muslim does not believe in *velayat* or the right of the imams to establish their rule, as is the case with a Sunni, his good and pious acts will not be accepted from him by God.[48] Therefore, without belief in the leadership of imams, the cornerstone of *Imamate* and Shi'ism, Majlesi holds that Muslims would be doomed, since they would not gain access to heaven.

THE SPECIFICS OF NECESSITIES

Majlesi maintains that faith in seven convictions categorizes a person as a Shi'i believer (*mo'men*). He stipulates that the acceptable source of knowledge for determining the necessities of Shi'ism is solely the transmitted reports (*akhbar*) emanating from Shi'i imams. Majlesi argues that on certain issues such as the features or specificities of paradise and hell, there are differences rooted in the *ahadith*. These differences, however,

---

[47] Ibid., p. 28. [48] M. B. Majlesi, *'Eyn al-Hayat*, p. 109.

he argues, do not lead to the rejection of the principles of paradise and hell, which constitute the necessities (*zaruriyyat*) of the Shi'i faith.[49] Even though Majlesi refers to seven items, he ends up citing some eleven necessities. These prerequisites of the Shi'i faith according to Majlesi include items of both orthodoxy and orthopraxy, the denial and rejection of which are not tolerated. Majlesi's list is said to be based on Ebn Babawayh and includes belief in: (1) the unity of God or monotheism; (2) the notion of resurrection and return or *raj'at* of a selected number of friends and foes of Shi'i imams at the time of the return of the Twelfth Imam and before the Day of Judgement; (3) temporary marriage or *mut'eh*; (4) the second part of the complete *haj* composed of *omreh tamatto'* and *haj tamatto'*; (5) the Prophet's ascent to heaven or *me'raj*; (6) questions asked of the dead during their first night in the grave; (7) a stream, pool or fountain in paradise called *Kowsar*; (8) intercession or *shafa'at* by the Prophet and the imams on behalf of believers; (9) the createdness of heaven, hell and the path to heaven (*sarat*); (10) resurrection and the Day of Judgement; and (11) accountability in the hereafter.[50]

In his work entitled *E'teqadat* or "Beliefs", Majlesi discusses some fifteen necessities of belief, expanding his list of eleven necessities cited in *Haq al-Yaqin* by four additional necessary items. First, he argues that it is incumbent upon the Shi'i to simultaneously and concomitantly love the house of the Prophet and the Shi'i imams, as well as hating, despising and damning those who usurped the Caliphate of 'Ali, namely Abu Bakr, 'Omar and 'Osman, in addition to the enemies of the imams.[51] Majlesi identifies the belief in the infidelity of Sunnis and harbouring a deep sense of animosity towards them as a necessary conviction of being a Shi'i. Second, in the list of obligatory beliefs defining the Shi'i, Majlesi introduces a peculiar and surreal addition. This new item is related to the skyscape or architecture of the skies. He maintains that the Shi'i must believe that the skies are not positioned connected to one another but that there are 500 years of distance between each sky, bustling with angels continuously worshipping God.[52] Majlesi does not present this unusual belief as an auxiliary or sub-auxiliary necessity but as if it is a fundamental obligatory Shi'i conviction. He then goes on to transform the belief in the infallibility of angels into another obligatory belief for the Shi'i.[53] Third, another new addition to the list of Shi'i obligatory belief is that on the first night in the grave, the dead will experience pressure weighing upon them. Majlesi

---

[49] M. B. Majlesi, *Haq al-Yaqin*, p. 354.   [50] Ibid.   [51] M. B. Majlesi, *E'teqadat*, p. 28.
[52] Ibid., p. 33.   [53] Ibid.

clearly states that the Shiʻi must believe that this pressure will be borne on their real body and not on their symbolic body.[54] As usual, there is a sub-auxiliary necessity to this seemingly auxiliary necessity. Majlesi maintains that a Shiʻi has to believe that in the grave, non-believers will be subjected to physical pressure, while complete believers will be immune to such pressures. Fourth, the Shiʻi are obliged to believe in the truth of accountability before God and that God has assigned two angels to constantly keep an eye on the acts of every human being. One angel is positioned to the right of individuals, recording all their virtuous acts, and the other, to the left, recording all vices.[55] According to Majlesi, the Shiʻi are also required to believe that at the end of every day, two angels ascend to the skies, taking their reports with them, and another pair of angels descend to replace them and register the nocturnal activities of the people.[56] The obligation in believing that God has designated two angels to record the activities of each person is another auxiliary necessity, which spins off the necessity of belief in accountability on Judgement Day and is turned into yet another necessity.

A good number of these necessities could be categorized as auxiliary and sub-auxiliary necessities of belief. Yet, for Majlesi, the notion of necessities seems to be an umbrella concept, arching over and incorporating fundamental, auxiliary as well as sub-auxiliary necessities. Majlesi's general appellation or label of necessities of belief blurs the differences in importance among these necessities. Calling upon the Shiʻi to believe in a particular architecture of the skies with the same firmness and conviction as that of believing in resurrection on the Day of Judgement, which constitutes one of the major principles of Islam, implies that, for the Shiʻi, these two concepts should be of equal weight and significance.

Majlesi's process of weaving auxiliary and sub-auxiliary necessities out of the fundamentals and then placing them on a par with the principles of the faith can be demonstrated through his analysis of the ascension of the Prophet to heaven and the resurrection of humanity on the Day of Judgement. On the issue of the Prophet's ascent to heaven or *meʻraj*, Majlesi insists that the Shiʻi must believe not only in the conceptual notion of the ascent, but also that the ascent was indeed physical and bodily.[57] Majlesi dismisses the Shiʻi *motakallemin*, or speculative theologians who relied on reason and rational proofs to question the Prophet's physical ascent. He rules that belief in the physical ascension of the Prophet to heaven is a necessity of Islam, and whoever denies this interpretation is a

---

[54] Ibid., pp. 33–34.   [55] Ibid., p. 37.   [56] Ibid.   [57] Ibid., p. 30.

disbeliever. By ruling that a Shi'i is obliged to believe in the physical ascent of the Prophet, Majlesi narrows and shrinks the circle of believers only to those who concur with him on the issue that this is the only possible form of ascension.[58] Majlesi wishes the Shi'i to accept the attributed reports cited in Ebn Babawayh and Saffar's works that, by God's wish, the Prophet ascended to heaven 124 times and, every time, he was informed of the *velayat* or guardianship, rule and *Imamate* of Imam 'Ali and the other imams.[59] By forcing the Shi'i to either abandon their creed or accept the notion of a physical ascent, Majlesi is effectively excommunicating the Shi'i who may wish to interpret the Prophet's ascension in a spiritual manner.

Majlesi's method of imposing what he identifies as religiously correct upon all Shi'i by calling it a necessity of the faith surfaces again in his treatment of resurrection on the Day of Judgement. He warns that the Shi'i are obliged to believe that, on the Day of Resurrection, the soul of the dead will be returned to their physical bodies and that any interpretation of this fact will be considered as infidelity and disbelief.[60] Majlesi lashes out at attempts by philosophers who have provided spiritual or allegorical interpretations of resurrection and argues that such renditions result in apostasy, as it constitutes a rejection of the principle of resurrection.[61] Once again, unless a Shi'i believes in physical resurrection, he will be castigated as an apostate. Majlesi gives birth to an auxiliary necessity, which he then converts into a necessity of Shi'i belief. Majlesi's broad list of necessities becomes an all-inclusive, non-negotiable, inflexible absolute truth, binding upon anyone who considers himself or herself a Shi'i. A Shi'i not conforming to his straitjacket is not a Shi'i.

---

[58] M. B. Majlesi, *Haq al-Yaqin*, p. 30.   [59] Ibid.
[60] M. B. Majlesi, *E'teqadat*, p. 36.   [61] Ibid., pp. 36–37.

Majlesism as an Ideology

The corpus of Majlesi's scholastic-cum-propaganda work presents itself as an ideology aimed at thought manipulation and social engineering with the objective of inculcating the masses with an anti-rational and superstitious world outlook. Majlesi homogenizes society according to the criteria and standards that he chooses and establishes. He spins auxiliary and sub-auxiliary necessities from the fundamental necessities – in the realm of beliefs and rites – and imposes them on believers as religious truths and prerequisites of piety. As with any ideology, Majlesi defines and negotiates the political and religious role of social players with the intention of consolidating the prevailing bipolar power relationship between the masses and the ruling king-cleric duo.

To construct his ideology Majlesi employs and promotes substitute concepts, effectively overshadowing the fundamental necessities of Islam. The ersatz concepts employed by Majlesi are not alien to a Shiʿi hadith-based tradition, but could be categorized as peripheral or marginal issues in relation to the main Islamic discourse. Majlesi's articulation and promotion of a "complementary Shiʿi frame of reference", based on his selection of reports, gradually becomes an "alternative frame of reference" and eventually becomes the hegemonic identifier of Shiʿism. As such, parallels to the fundamental necessities of the faith are developed. According to the Islamic tradition, the four devotional rites of prayer, fasting, pilgrimage and the payment of the wealth tax are the main tools for attaining proximity to God and seeking felicity in the hereafter. Majlesi presents the notion of visiting the tomb of imams as an equally effective tool if not more than the regular *haj* as a "complementary Shiʿi frame of reference". To render his ideology even more appealing to the common folk, Majlesi provides specific "Shi'i shortcuts". He argues that shedding tears while mourning the imams is a tool even more efficient than the standard four practices for securing a place in paradise. To make his alternative construction more palpable and attractive to the common folk, he relies on a superstitious discussion, collapsing the clear differences between the laws of the material and hidden world. In Majlesism, the relation between man and God, as well as the relation between worldly human acts and their positive or negative consequences in the hereafter, are redefined on the basis of what Majlesi argues to be Shi'i proofs. In the same manner that Majlesi redefines the realm of spiritual relations, he presents an ideal type of worldly human relations and interactions in the political and social domain. Through the innovative use of auxiliary necessities, Majlesi promotes intellectual imitation, fatalism and resignation in life, as a precondition for felicity in the hereafter. Sociopolitical acquiescence and accommodation is not only advanced as a prerequisite for individual salvation in the hereafter, but also as an indispensable behavioural pattern for the survival of Shi'ism. The notion of redefining the necessities of belief in Shi'ism enables Majlesi to reconfigure his rendition of Shi'ism according to his objectives and his exegesis of the texts available to him.

In what seems as a dubious attempt to free himself from the constraint of all traditional religious sources, not necessarily articulated by the Shi'i, Majlesi challenges the integrity and entirety of the most important pillar of Islam – namely, the Qur'an. He maintains that Shi'i imams possess the complete Qur'an. In this case, Majlesi champions a highly sensitive complementary/alternative Shi'i frame of reference. He attempts to convince the Shi'i that they should believe in or know that the complete Qur'an is different from the one compiled during the Caliphate of 'Osman.[1] By questioning the completeness of the Qur'an and arguing that the three books of *Mosahaf*, *Jafr* and *Jame'*, said to be in the possession of Shi'i imams, are more complete and integral than the Qur'an, Majlesi undermines the most important source of the faith. In the name of Shi'i imams, Majlesi sheds doubt on what Muslims believe to be the "Book of God" and consequently the Prophet and Islam. The Qur'an as an established and accepted Divine corpus among Muslims is sidetracked by three unavailable texts referred to in Shi'i reports. Majlesi maintains that the complete Qur'an was compiled by Imam 'Ali after he buried the Prophet.[2]

---

[1] M. B. Majlesi, *'Eyn al-Hayat*, pp. 92, 450.   [2] M. B. Majlesi, *Jala' al-'Oyun*, p. 247.

Yet 'Omar refused to accept this compilation, since it included chapters on the hypocrisy (*nefaq*) and unbelief (*kofr*) of some people, as well as the guardianship (*velayat*) of Imam 'Ali and his children. According to Majlesi, Imam 'Ali was angered by 'Omar's refusal and returned the complete Qur'an to his house, promising that "no one would ever see this Qur'an until the reappearance of the Twelfth Imam".[3]

Referring to the so-called complete Qur'an, which is said to be different from the one compiled during 'Osman's caliphate and in use among Muslims, Majlesi argues that after the reappearance of the Twelfth Imam who is in possession of 'Ali's Qur'an, the people will be taught the "new Qur'an".[4] Majlesi's explicit hints at the incompleteness of the Qur'an, as we know it, along with his methodological attempt to subject it to the authority of Shi'i reports indicates that he is not totally satisfied with the content of the existing Qur'an as an ultimate source of Truth. It must be Majlesi's dissatisfaction with the content of the Qur'an that induces him to conjure an alternative fundamental and Divine source instead of or complementary to the accepted Qur'an. Even though Majlesi does not dare reject the Qur'an and regularly refers to it to prove his points, it seems evident that by questioning its authenticity and completion, he wishes to argue for the existence of a "Shi'i Qur'an" in contrast to and perhaps as a substitute for what he probably believes to be a "Sunni Qur'an". According to Majlesi's own chainlike reasoning, once anyone, including an Islamic jurist, dares to question the integrity and content of the Qur'an for any reason, even in defence of Shi'ism, he in effect rejects the completeness of the word of God, which would lead to his own apostasy.

In a similar move, yet in the domain of rites and rituals, Majlesi elevates and promotes a whole set of rituals connected with the memory, vestiges and relics of the imams to the status of necessities of Shi'ism. These rituals are effectively spin-offs from the necessity of believing in the imams or *Imamate*. According to Majlesi, the real ka'beh or that central object of veneration for Muslims, symbolizing the house of God, is "the heart of the imams", which he contends to be superior to the ka'beh of all Muslims. Yet Majlesi cautions his pious Shi'i readers that they may not deny the sanctity of the "apparent ka'beh", which Muslims are required to revere during the *haj*, since such a denial would imply infidelity and apostasy. Paying purely formalistic respect to the official ka'beh, Majlesi suggests that believers should first visit the "seeming or superficial ka'beh and then visit the

---

[3] Ibid., pp. 247–248.   [4] M. B. Majlesi, *Majmu'eh-e Rasael-e E'teqadi*, p. 110.

essential *kaʿbeh* and benefit from both".[5] For Majlesi, the shrines and tombs of the imams are as important a place of worship as the *kaʿbeh*, if not more important. He seeks to inculcate the rite of visiting the grave of Shiʿi imams as a necessity of Shiʿi belief. Majlesi's emphasis on revering the tombs and shrines of Shiʿi imams as a Shiʿi obligation is closely connected with his recurrent theme that God is worshipped through the worship of imams.[6]

Belief in the spiritual and temporal right of the imams to establish their rule as successors of the Prophet encapsulates the Shiʿi creedal principle of *Imamate*. It can be argued that the promotion of imam worshipping is an auxiliary necessity subjectively deduced from *Imamate*, which Majlesism imposes on the Shiʿi, yet it is not explicit in *Imamate*. Subsequently, the obligation to worship, venerate and commemorate all things pertaining to imams, subjectively derived from the auxiliary necessity of imam worshipping becomes a sub-auxiliary necessity binding on Majlesi's Shiʿis.[7] Majlesi refers to reports attributed to the imams and argues that believers should circumambulate the graves and shrines of the imams.[8] Summing up his assessment of certain Qurʾanic verses, Majlesi posits that after the death of imams, believers are obliged to revere, bow down and pay respect to them and their holy shrines.[9] Unable to deny the significance of *haj*, Majlesi submits a "complementary/alternative Shiʿi frame of reference" by effectively shifting the focus of the pious common folk to the imams, their tombs and shrines. In time, certain salient features of this complementary/alternative Shiʿi frame of reference came to overshadow aspects of the original Islamic framework.

Having highlighted a different and specific rite for the Shiʿi, Majlesism posits that felicity in the hereafter is guaranteed by engaging in these specific rites. According to Majlesi, the practice of visiting the shrine of imams, in particular that of Imam Hoseyn, paying homage to the imams and shedding tears for Imam Hoseyn are key tools for securing grace or atonement for all of one's sins and gaining direct admission to paradise.[10] Majlesi argues that, according to successive reports, "reminding and being reminded of, shedding tears and causing others to shed tears and grieving in the memory of the ordeals and trials of the Prophet's household" is "the supreme act of worship". He argues that such rites and rituals would result

[5] M. B. Majlesi, *ʿEyn al-Hayat*, p. 453.   [6] M. B. Majlesi, *Hayat al-Qolub*, vol. 5, p. 497.
[7] Ibid., p. 487.   [8] M. B. Majlesi, *ʿEyn al-Hayat*, p. 453.
[9] M. B. Majlesi, *Hayat al-Qolub*, vol. 5, p. 245.
[10] M. B. Majlesi, *Jalaʾ al-ʿOyun*, pp. 523, 525.

in the strengthening of "belief and certitude".[11] Based on a reference attributed to one of the imams, Majlesi highlights the idea that anyone who reads an elegy for Imam Hoseyn and brings tears to his own eyes or that of one or fifty others will certainly obtain a place in paradise.[12] In case one is incapable of naturally shedding tears while mourning, Majlesi finds and presents a mechanical solution. If the pious force themselves to shed a tear, irrespective of whether they have committed major or minor sins, they too will have access to paradise.[13]

Majlesi is no longer constructing a "complementary Shi'i frame of reference", but effectively a "substitute or alternative Shi'i framework"; the shedding of tears for Shi'i imams becomes the determining pre-condition for access to paradise, the highest conceivable reward in the hereafter. Majlesi claims that rigorous compliance with the key elements of *'ebadat (ibadah)* or worship will not secure a place in heaven for those who refuse to believe in the rulership or guardianship (*velayat*) of the imams.[14] Majlesi goes beyond requiring the Shi'i to believe that the first three caliphs usurped the rulership of the Shi'i imams as a necessity of the creed. According to Majlesi, the real sources of "abomination, evil, dis-belief, sin and transgression" are Abu Bakr, 'Omar and 'Osman, who should also be held responsible for the endurance and persistence of disbelief and sin on earth.[15] Based on reports attributed to the imams, Majlesi argues that "the followers of Abu Bakr, 'Omar and 'Osman will go to hell".[16]

Having demonstrated that the standard Islamic devotional acts may not suffice for entering paradise, Majlesi presents the shortcut. Not only would tears shed in remembrance of imams wash away sins but, according to Majlesi, for each tear shed, the mourner would receive a castle in paradise, decorated with pearls and jewels.[17] To assure the popularization of this rite, Majlesi readily promises a material reward for it, not on earth but in heaven. For Majlesi, the Shi'i are expected to believe that those who are admitted to paradise will be able to enjoy eating, drinking and sexual intercourse as well.[18] Majlesi provides an extravagant and detailed description of the carnal pleasures awaiting pious Shi'i males in heaven.[19] The notion of a physical existence and subsequently sensual pleasure in the hereafter, almost as we know it in our material world, resonates with

---

[11] Ibid., p. 21–22.   [12] Ibid., p. 522.   [13] Ibid., pp. 522, 525.
[14] M. B. Majlesi, *'Eyn al-Hayat*, p. 109.   [15] Ibid., p. 453.
[16] M. B. Majlesi, *Hayat al-Qolub*, vol. 5, p. 60.
[17] M. B. Majlesi, *'Eyn al-Hayat*, p. 248.   [18] M. B. Majlesi, *Haq al-Yaqin*, p. 372.
[19] M. B. Majlesi, *Majmu'eh-e Rasael E'teqadi*, pp. 130–163.

Majlesi's conviction that the laws concerning and governing human beings in the hidden world are basically the same as those in the material world. He believes that the soul of a dead person returns to his corpse once after his funeral and then at the time of his physical resurrection on Judgement Day. Majlesi rejects the notion that humans entering paradise will transform into angels and will therefore be incapable of engaging in carnal pleasures as a relic of Christian thought. Even though Majlesi does not reject the notion of spiritual pleasures in heaven, he argues in favour of the existence of both spiritual and sensual rewards.[20]

Majlesi impresses upon the Shiʿi notions of belief that they may, to different degrees, personally and privately believe in and deduces conclusions from them with a certain political bias. He argues that the Shiʿi need to rely on God's will (*tavakkol*) in their everyday life. Majlesi transforms his interpretation of this concept to a pillar of belief and rules that those who reject it are polytheists (*moshrek*).[21] From his insistence on the details of what constitutes reliance on God's will, an important political agenda can be inferred. One of Majlesi's pre-conditions for the proof of reliance on God's will is for believers to reject categorically any "trust in themselves or others". He encourages believers to have no faith or hope in God's creatures and accept their situation and condition as destined by God.[22] Majlesi insists that the common folk ought to remain resigned to their lot and destiny as a sign of their reliance on God and the acceptance of God's will. Reliance on God would mean believing that "profit or loss" cannot result from God's creatures. Majlesi's interpretation of reliance on God is a dictate for believers to accept the social, political and economic status quo as if it is God's eternal will. Majlesi seeks to dissuade those who do rely on God to reflect, organize, mobilize and forment any social, political or religious movement challenging the existing conditions.

According to Majlesi's reading, change is not part and parcel of God's will and therefore challenging the status quo would constitute a sign of rebellion against submission to Him. The highest level of faith, according to Majlesi is characterized by unquestioned gratification from and acquiescence to whatever is received from God without the slightest complaint.[23] By raising his interpretation of submission to God's will to the status of an auxiliary necessity of Shiʿism, Majlesi transforms the political notions of subservience to existing powers, blind acceptance of one's position and station in life, resignation to one's lot and desisting from

---

[20] M. B. Majlesi, *Haq al-Yaqin*, p. 373.
[21] M. B. Majlesi, *ʿEyn al-Hayat*, pp. 534, 536.   [22] Ibid.   [23] Ibid., p. 535.

challenging and revolting against the status quo to a religious pillar of the creed. He warns the pious against any reflection, questioning or querying about "difficult problems", as such exertions would pave the way for satanic inroads.[24] Here, Majlesism employs the general notion of reliance on God's will over aspects of which Muslims have debated since the day of the Prophet, and converts it into a particular ruling that requires believers to remain unquestioningly loyal and grateful to their political leaders under all circumstances. The individual's spiritual relation of trust with God is codified into a conservative sociopolitical axiom demanding pacifism, resignation and submission in relation to the political, economic and religious powers in place. The particular definition and use of reliance on God's will as an auxiliary necessity of the creed, derived from monotheism, promotes and institutionalizes social and political deresponsibilization and deactivation of believers.

Majlesi articulates another auxiliary necessity of Shi'i belief, the function of which is rather similar to his interpretation of reliance on God's will. According to Majlesi, the Shi'i are obliged to believe in the fact that the Prophet and the imams will intercede in their favour in the hereafter.[25] The interpretation and promise that, through the intercession (*shafa'at*) of the Prophet and imams, the Shi'i will be exculpated of all their sins once again deresponsibilizes the Shi'i. The Shi'i, according to the auxiliary necessity of intercession, are exonerated from their sins, not because of their acts but simply because they are Shi'i. The logical relation between act and consequences of the act is ruptured. Majlesism provides a final guarantee to those who accept and blindly imitate the plethora of rulings and dictates enumerated in the corpus of Majlesi's works. Based on Majlesi's concept of intercession, the Shi'i are assured that God will unfailingly honour His promise of good rewards yet He may not carry out His threat of punishment. For Majlesi, the intercession of the Prophet or the imams could secure the attainment of salvation in the hereafter for a Shi'i sinner.[26] According to Majlesi, in response to the Prophet's intercession on the part of all Shi'i, God expiates "the past and future" sins of all Shi'i.[27] As long as the Shi'i are preoccupied with the private sphere, closely and loyally following the life that Majlesi outlines for them, even if they sin or witness injustice and tyranny and happily comply with it, they are assured of paradise in the hereafter.

---

[24] Ibid., pp. 536–537.   [25] M. B. Majlesi, *E'teqadat*, p. 31.
[26] Ibid., pp. 37–38.   [27] M. B. Majlesi, *Majmu'eh-e Rasael-e E'teqadi*, p. 96.

It may be argued that in order to keep the Shi'i within the private sphere of religious preoccupation and prevent them from actively entering the sociopolitical sphere, Majlesi emphasizes on the importance of dissimulation (*taqiyyeh*) as a key auxiliary necessity of Shi'i belief. Advocating the dissimulation of one's religious beliefs, when faced with a conceived or real threat, as a religious obligation, is a call on the pious to back down from their principles and withdraw intellectually and actively from the public sphere, instead of confronting and redressing the social and political ills. Complying by this auxiliary necessity would imply desisting from reflection, argumentation and taking responsibility for one's beliefs and thoughts. A dissimulating community embraces deresponsibilization and agrees to abandon its right to exert any checks and balances on those who think, decide and govern in its name. Majlesism justifies and promotes dissimulation and passive compliance by the pious in the name of what is necessary for the survival of the faith. The controversial obligation of dissimulating one's belief under duress, when threatened by persecution becomes yet another auxiliary necessity.

The notion of hiding one's faith and beliefs, complying and even falsely pledging allegiance to the dictates of a non-Shi'i and therefore unjust ruler in order to preserve one's true beliefs in a hostile environment, is at the root of religious dissimulation. Concerned with the difficult task of the Shi'i to maintain and safeguard their faith in a Sunni-dominated religious and political environment, religious dissimulation became a tactical necessity to ensure the survival of Shi'ism. Majlesi refers to verses 3:29, 16:106 and 23:28 to provide Qur'anic evidence for this concept.[28] A simple reading of those verses does not demonstrate that dissimulation should be accepted as a necessity of the faith. Having argued that he has grounded the concept in the Qur'an, Majlesi cites thirty-eight reports attributed to the imams in reference to this auxiliary necessity. Almost all the reports attributed to the imams revolve around the pivotal role of religious dissimulation in Shi'ism.

According to reports cited by Majlesi, the concept of religious dissimulation is applicable to all conceivable domains and areas, except that of drinking wine made out of dates and ablution over footwear.[29] Dissimulation is glorified to such an extent that it is claimed that "nine tenths of the creed is comprised of *taqiyyeh* and whoever does not practice dissimulation does not have faith".[30] Even false oaths for the purpose of

---

[28] M. B. Majlesi, *Adaab-e mo'asherat* (Tehran, 1365), p. 250.   [29] Ibid., p. 253.
[30] Ibid., p. 251; M. B. Majlesi, *Hayat al-Qolub*, vol. 5, p. 419.

deflecting harm to oneself are not considered as sin.[31] Among the reports attributed to the imams, Majlesi cites one in which it is emphasized that verily *taqiyyeh* has been established to prevent bloodshed.[32] In this sense, religious dissimulation is presented by Majlesi as "the shield of the believers", behind which they are justified to engage in deception, concealment and hypocrisy. Whereas Majlesi's promotion of dissimulation during the rule of Sunni overlords has utilitarian and pragmatic value, his commitment to raising this concept to an auxiliary necessity during the reign of Shi'i kings is rather confusing. Why should the Shi'i hide their conviction during the Shi'i rule of the Safavis? Was Majelsi trying to prevent the Shi'i from revolting against their impious Safavi kings?

The auxiliary necessity of dissimulation complements Majlesi's interpretation of the concept of reliance on God's will to institutionalize resignation and passive acceptance of the status quo further as an integral part of Shi'ism. By redefining and transforming the twin concept of dissimulation–reliance to auxiliary necessities of Shi'i belief, the pious are encouraged not to apply their critical thought or engage in social, political and religious criticism. They are also effectively prohibited from expressing ideas and performing acts that would challenge the dominant or hegemonic powers to be, since such activities may solicit threatening reactions and retributions.

Majlesism glorifies resignation, cowardice and submissiveness as virtuous behavioural traits, since the ideal Shi'i personality is presented as one who believes in the veracity of Shi'ism yet hides his convictions and, if need be, even condemns them when faced with the possibility of hardship or a threat. Majlesi's exemplary Shi'i would be obliged to live in a duality. On the one hand, believing in a truth – Shi'ism – and wishing to propagate and uphold it yet, on the other hand, being constrained by a particular interpretation of the same truth, namely Majlesism. Promoting good and forbidding evil, an important pillar of a dynamic Shi'ism, is thus trumped by Majlesi's privileging of dissimulation. It is reported that until the return of the Hidden Imam, religious dissimulation would be necessary and its proper practice would become more difficult and intense as the time for the reappearance of the Hidden Imam approaches.[33]

Majlesism breeds confusion among believers who are taught by the fundamentals and the spirit of their faith to take pride in and defend it, yet they are restrained from actively realizing it, if faced with danger. Majlesism encourages them to conceal their faith as if it were a "wrong". His insistence

---

[31] M. B. Majlesi, *Adaab-e mo'asherat*, p. 252. [32] Ibid., p. 255. [33] Ibid.

on dissimulation, within the context of his own times, can best be considered as an invitation to sociopolitical pacifism and quietism. Majlesi's firm belief in the need for the common people to accept their position of submissiveness to rulers, religious or worldly, in all aspects of life, surpasses and outweighs his belief in the Shi'i key concept of *'adl* or justice.

While Majlesi seeks to pacify the Shi'i by inviting them to accept their political and social condition, a crucial part of his state ideology is concerned with constructing a clear target against which the Shi'i would unleash their repressed anger. The passiveness promoted towards domestic authority is balanced by a call to aggressiveness against the external "other". Once sociopolitical consciousness with regard to the shortcomings and corruption of the ruling religio-political Safavi shahs is desensitized through the promotion of dissimulation, Majlesi channels the remaining anger and frustration of the people from the real source of their problems towards the Sunni "other". This is a politically safe mechanism of directing public resentment and discontent to the "foreign enemies" of Safavi shahs, consolidating their rule rather than threatening it. The Shi'i love for their imams or *tavalla* is given a politically and religiously expedient corollary, namely the repudiation of and hatred for Sunnis or *tabarra*. Majlesism presents Sunni bashing as a natural consequence of imam loving and enunciates the two concepts as necessities of Shi'i belief.

THE POLITICS OF THE SHI'I–SUNNI DICHOTOMY

The twin concept of loving the imams by remembering their sufferings and hating the Sunnis as their enemies is popularized, institutionalized and systematized by Majlesi. The regular establishment of mourning ceremonies on a national scale becomes the educational and cultural medium for promoting an inter-religious conflict, to ward off the danger of a political uprising against the Safavis and their religious partners. Mir Mohammad Saleh Khatunabadi, Majlesi's son-in-law, maintains that Majlesi was "extremely adamant" about organizing religious ceremonies. Thousands of people would participate in prayers and worship sessions during special religious occasions and the nights of *ehya* (revitalization in the month of *Ramazan*), listening to and benefiting from Majlesi's useful sermons.[34] Khatunabadi laments that, after Majlesi's death, such mass ceremonies lost their popularity.[35] Even though the practice of holding mourning sessions

---

[34] M. B. Khonsari-Esfahani, *Rowzat al-Jennat*, vol. 2, p. 274.   [35] Ibid.

based on reciting the hardships of the imams had started well before Majlesi, it was he who provided not only a new and revised narrative for the ritual, but also firmly instituted the practice of denunciating and disparaging Sunnis as an integral part of this ritual. In this sense, Majlesi "corrected" what he believed to be Va'ez Kashefi's distorted Sunni-based rendition of events.

One year after Shah Esma'il's reign and the establishment of a Shi'i state (908/1502), a book called *Rowzat al-Shohada*, by Kamaleddin Hoseyn ebn 'Ali Kashefi Sabzevari, known as Va'ez Kashefi, was completed.[36] The book, in Farsi, dealt with the trials and ordeals of the prophets, Mohammad, Fatemeh and the twelve imams. The person reciting the events (*rowzeh khan*) used Va'ez Kashefi's book as a key reference for inciting grief and lamentation among those in attendance causing them to shed tears. These mourning sessions came to be known as *rowzeh khani* or the ritual of reciting the book of *Rowzat al-Shohada*.

The fact that Va'ez Kashefi was a Sunni scholar of the Hanafi sect with Shi'i leanings could not have escaped Majlesi.[37] In the preface to *Jala' al-'Oyun*, Majlesi's emphasis on the point that whatever had been written on the life and tribulations of the imams was partially based on inappropriate texts and unreliable reports is probably a reference to the fact that the authors of such works and their sources were non-Shi'i or of dubious religious leanings. Majlesi's reference was intended to shed serious doubt on the doctrinal credibility of the author of *Rowzat al-Shohada* and therefore the validity of the entire book. Having prepared a "suitable" Shi'i text for mourning the imams, Majlesi was informing his readers why he believed that *Rowzat al-Shohada* had served its purpose and that it was time for it to be replaced by *Jala' al-'Oyun* (Cleansing the Eyes). The structure of *Rowzat al-Shohada*, however, became the blueprint for Majlesi's *Jala' al-'Oyun*. Majlesi assured his readers that his book contained only authoritative *ahadith* obtained from texts written by learned *Imamiyyeh* (Shi'i) *hadith* compilers.[38]

The main purpose of mourning sessions at which certain parts of Majlesi's *Jala' al-'Oyun* would be read was to cause the public to weep and grieve. The act of mourning would seal their faith and help them attain greater proximity to God. In the introduction to his book, *Jala' al-'Oyun* completed in 1089/1678, Majlesi presents his argument in support of the

[36] Z. Safa, *Tarikh Adabiyat Iran*, vol. 5, part 1, p. 87.
[37] H. Kashani, *Rowzat al-Shohada* (Tehran, 1380), p. 5.
[38] M. B. Majlesi, *Jala' al-'Oyun*, p. 22.

significance of mourning the imams. Referring to a report attributed to an Imam, Majlesi quotes him as saying, "whoever remembers us or in whose presence we are remembered and weeps as much as the wing of a fly, then God will forgive his sins even if they were as vast as the seabeds".[39] Painstakingly, Majlesi presents other reports supporting his position that remembering and mourning the imams would be rewarded handsomely by eventually dwelling in paradise.[40]

This ceremony of reminiscing the tribulations of the Prophet and the members of his household through sympathizing and empathizing with their predicament became an important means of propagating the Shi'i culture. Through this exercise, the Shi'i developed a sense of common history, identity and community, distinct from other Muslim sects. The ritual also forged a collective memory and fostered a bonding process, reviving, revisiting and actualizing the tragic circumstances and destiny of the Shi'i imams. Another equally important component of mourning the imams became the practice of identifying, vilifying and cursing their enemies. Majlesi pursued the dual objective of generating a burning and passionate love for the imams while fermenting a deep sense of hatred for their enemies. Both objectives fostered religio-national cohesion and solidarity around the Shi'i–Sunni animosity.

The anti-Sunni sentiment whipped up by Majlesi and played out in mourning ceremonies was further strengthened and heightened by the claim that anti-Sunnism would secure salvation in the hereafter. The presentation of Sunnis and the Ottoman Turks as the embodiments of evil was not divorced from the religio-political legitimization and endorsement of Safavi rule. The portrayal of Sunnis as historical "oppressors" of the Shi'i community and the Safavi kings as Shi'i revivalists and selfless protectors of Shi'ism against Sunni Turks constitutes a key religio-national and political factor in Majlesi's ideological construct.

There is little doubt that the anti-Shi'ism of the Ottomans, as well as their persecution of the Shi'i, played a major role in paving anti-Sunni feelings in Persia. The virulent anti-Shi'ism of Sunni Ottomans added to the historical Shi'i–Sunni schism and facilitated the task of both the Safavi monarchs and their allied clerical establishment to present the Sunni–Shi'i conflict as the most pressing concern of the Shi'i community. It suited the Safavi religious and political establishment to present the Shi'i–Sunni divide as an irreconcilable conflict. Majlesi's *Jala' al-'Oyun* operated as a powerful and emotionally charged potion injecting the masses with a

---

[39] Ibid., p. 25.   [40] Ibid., pp. 26–28.

dichotomous and conflictual religio-political outlook. It promoted loyalty and sympathy for the Safavi Shahs as the upholders, protectors and propagators of Shi'ism and instilled animosity for and fear of the Ottoman state as the advocate and champion of Sunnis. During every mourning session, Majlesi's religious account of the tribulations of Shi'i dignitaries reminded the Shi'i of how extremely privileged they were to be living in the time and under the rule of Safavi kings, who protected them from once again being subjected to hardships and persecutions at the hand of the Sunnis. Majlesi's religious message contained a strong dose of political propaganda.

In *Jala' al-'Oyun*, Majlesi highlights the irreverent character of certain companions of the Prophet to prepare his readers for his assault on them and his final ruling on their infidelity. Having narrated the incident during which 'Omar refuses to oblige the Prophet's wish to write a few lines before his death, Majlesi writes, "Oh dear one! After [having heard] this *hadith* reported by all the *'ameh* [Sunnis] is it possible for reasonable men to doubt the infidelity (*kofr*) of 'Omar and the infidelity of whosoever considers 'Omar as a Muslim?"[41] Here, Majlesi is effectively ruling on the infidelity of Sunnis and even those followers of 'Ali who considered 'Omar not only as a Muslim, but also the second of the Four Rightly Guided Caliphs, despite the fact that they may have believed that Abu Bakr and 'Omar had usurped 'Ali's position. It is important to note that in Va'ez Kashefi's book, *Rowzat al-Shohada*, there is no reference to 'Omar's refusal to allow the Prophet a few lines as his last testament, let alone the ruling on 'Omar's infidelity.[42]

On another occasion, Majlesi refers to an episode when Abu Bakr and 'Omar disobey the Prophet's order to leave Madineh (Medina) with Osameh's army during the last days of the Prophet's life. Majlesi concludes, "Let God's and His Prophet's curse be upon them [Abu Bakr and 'Omar] and also upon whoever considers them as Muslims and also upon whoever stops cursing them".[43] Evoking Abu Bakr and 'Omar's act of disobedience in relation to the Prophet's clear orders is sufficient to convince zealous Shi'i readers of the impiety if not disbelief of the first and second Rightly Guided Caliphs. In *Jala' al-'Oyun*, whenever Majlesi recounts an incident in which members of 'Ali's house are wronged or their rights are usurped by Abu Bakr, 'Omar or 'Ayesheh (Ayesha), the Prophet's wife, he refers to them as the damned or the

---

[41] Ibid., p. 88.   [42] H. Kashani, *Rowzat al-Shohada*, pp. 95–117.
[43] M. B. Majlesi, *Jala' al-'Oyun*, p. 89.

accursed.[44] To leave a long-lasting negative impression on the Iranian Shi'i psyche, Majlesi multiplies his references to such an extent that the term damned or accursed becomes synonymous with the Sunnis. Whereas in *Rowzat al-Shohada*, Fatemeh and Shi'i imams are glorified and honoured without any concomitant disrespect towards Abu Bakr, 'Omar and 'Ayesheh, for Majlesi the glorification of the Prophet and the imams is in tandem with the vilification of Sunni dignitaries.

Majlesi maintains that the Prophet had foreknowledge of the fact that, after his death, Abu Bakr and 'Omar would oppose 'Ali and usurp his rightful position. Right before his death, dejected and disappointed with Abu Bakr and 'Omar, Majlesi claims that the Prophet had announced that he detested Abu Bakr and 'Omar as they detested him.[45] Majlesi quotes the Prophet as saying that the Caliphate of Abu Bakr would usher apostasy, infidelity and hypocrisy and 'Omar's Caliphate would be even worse and more unjust than that of Abu Bakr.[46] In a systematic manner, Majlesi inches towards his ultimate judgment on Abu Bakr, 'Omar and the Sunnis. Based on a report in Ebn Babawayh, Majlesi rules that Abu Bakr and 'Omar never believed in God and the Prophet and that 'Omar was but a bastard who would burn in hellfire.[47] Majlesi accuses 'Ayesheh, Abu Bakr's daughter and Hafseh, 'Omar's daughter, both wives of the Prophet, of having perpetrated the Prophet's death by poisoning him.[48] Majlesi also maintains that Fatemeh's illness, which led to her death, was caused by Abu Bakr and 'Omar's "mistreatment" of her. He, therefore, refers to them as the two "damned ones" and the two "hypocrites" responsible for Fatemeh's death.[49] Majlesi's labelling of Abu Bakr and 'Omar as infidels who never believed in God and Mohammad or hypocrites, who only pretended as though they believed in them, is in effect an excommunication verdict against all Sunnis. Majlesism was too concerned with presenting the Sunnis as hateful scapegoats, thereby channelling the rage of the Shi'i towards them and creating a safety buffer for the Safavis, that it overlooked the inconsistencies of its own arguments. Given the Prophet's foreknowledge of events, as narrated by Majlesi, why would he have befriended Abu Bakr and 'Omar, whom Majlesi considers as infidels, or why would he have accepted to marry their daughters who would according to Majlesi empoison him?

---

[44] Ibid., pp. 102, 145, 146, 151, 245–250, 257, 258, 263, 264.
[45] Ibid., p. 101.   [46] Ibid., p. 102.   [47] Ibid., pp. 238, 251, 276.
[48] Ibid., p. 145.   [49] Ibid., p. 263.

MAJLESI'S LEGACY

Majlesi constructs a rigidly defined discourse and provides believers with only one path to welfare in this world and salvation in the hereafter. Either they accept and act according to his formulations and presentations of Shi'ism or they reject his constructions and are branded as infidels. Once believers accept Majlesi's Shi'ism, they are automatically obliged to accept Majlesi's formulations in all aspects of life, as well as his selection and interpretation of reports as the authentic basis of Shi'ism. According to Turner, "The uncritical acceptance of any Traditions which happened to come his way has led to Majlesi's critics accusing him of opportunism and forgery".[50] Majlesi's rejection of the human agency, reason and rational thought enables him to pass off overstated, exaggerated and even phantasmical propositions as absolute and unquestionable truths. Majlesism does not invite the pious to dialogue and reflect but expects them to accept submissively assertations and edicts that are claimed to be based on reports attributed to the imams and Majlesi's interpretation of them. Aware of the Shi'i's love and respect for their imams, Majlesi wishes to foreclose all questioning and debate by claiming that his formulations are based on the reports attributed to the imams. The stamping out of an inquisitive and reflective society is a prerequisite for the widespread and popular reception and adoption of his ideology. His assertive and unequivocal opinions and ideas blend well with his absolutist ideology. Whereas it is usually accepted among Muslims that Mohammad's miracle was the Qur'an, Majlesi is adamant on proving that a prophet without palpable and material miracles cannot be considered as God's true messenger and therefore seeks to prove miracles for the Prophet.

Majlesi shrouds his subjects of analysis with phantasmical accounts, thereby stifling rational inquiry. According to Majlesi, the Prophet had over 1,000 miracles including: (1) a light that constantly emitted from his forehead; (2) the light that radiated from his fingers like ten candles; (3) the splitting of the moon into two parts; (4) rendering to the blind their eyesight; (5) replenishing a dried-up well with water by spitting into it; and (6) foretelling the future and reviving the dead through prayers.[51] According to Majlesi, whenever the Prophet passed by stones and trees, they would bow down and greet him.[52] Even though the belief in objects such as stones and trees bowing to the Prophet is not raised to the status of

[50] C. Turner, *Islam Without Allah* (Richmond, 2000), p. 172.
[51] M. B. Majlesi, *Haq al-Yaqin*, pp. 20, 25, 26, 29.   [52] Ibid., p. 27.

a necessity of Shi'i belief, Majlesi does mention that the validity of prophet-hood is based on miracles and finally lists the miracles attributed to the Prophet for his Shi'i to believe in.

Majlesi is categorical and unforgiving towards people who disagree with him, even when it comes to Shi'i jurists who have a different interpretation from him, based on the same religious sources. For Majlesi, his opinions and positions are equal to the correct Islamic and Shi'i positions, and all other ideas are just wrong and irreligious, if not idolatrous. For example, Majlesi claims that, from birth to death, prophets are infallible, incapable of committing minor or major sins and inerrant, intentionally or unintentionally. He then goes on to criticize those who have referred to the errors of prophets and attributes such "slander and calumny" to the Sunnis, who have borrowed these ideas from "Jewish books". Majlesi then completes his circle of the undesirable if not despicable "others" who do not hold his interpretations, and adds, "A group of deficient and defective Shi'i have also referred to these ideas in their books".[53] Majlesi's genius is in elevating his choice of reports to the most important source or evidence of the Shari'at and then arguing that as the indisputable expert on reports, he is the sole speaker, formulator and propagator of Shi'ism. By carving out an official and indispensable position for himself, the object of which is mediation between human beings and all that is Divine, Majlesi engraves into Shi'ism his own Majlesism.

The phenomenally deep-rooted and continuing influence of Majlesi on Iranian Shi'ism is undeniable. 'Allameh Tabataba'i, a highly learned and esteemed scholar of the Qur'an and Islam, hailed as one of the brightest contemporary 'olama, disagreed with Majlesi and rebutted one or two of his positions while writing a commentary on *Bahar al-Anvar*. When under pressure from his publisher, Tabataba'i was asked to cut down his commentary and tone down or delete his critical comments, he responded: "In the Shi'i school of thought, Ja'far ebn Mohammad Sadeq (the sixth imam) is more valued and esteemed than 'Allameh Majlesi. When as a consequence of 'Allameh Majlesi's writings and descriptions the infallible imams could become exposed to rational and scientific objections, we are not prepared to sell out those esteemed figures [imams] for the sake of Majlesi. I will not delete a word of what I think is necessary to be written on certain issues". Majlesi's works were subsequently published in Iran without Tabataba'i's commentaries.[54] In his own reserved approach,

---

[53] Ibid., p. 19.

[54] M. Kadivar, 'Aql va Din az Didgah-e Mohaddes va Hakim' in M. Mohrizi and H. Rabbani (eds.), *Shenakhtnameh 'Allameh Majlesi*, vol. 1, p. 127.

Tabataba'i was warning against the fact that, even in the twentieth century, Majlesi's legacy and heritage was so deeply ingrained in the minds
and outlook of the guardians and members of the religious establishment
that one could not even criticize him in defence of the imams. Majlesi is a
towering spokesman of Shi'ism, whose works have influenced generations
after generations. It is not surprising that Shari'ati, one of Majlesi's bold
and outspoken modern critics, himself subjected to 'Allameh Tabataba'i's
criticism, referred to Majlesi as the thirteenth Imam of the Shi'i and
lamented the fact that even in the twentieth century one cannot criticize
Majlesi.[55]

Majlesism promotes the abandonment of independent and rational
thought in favour of superstitious and illogical explanations. It expects
the people to imitate and blindly accept the dictates of those who have been
placed in authority among them, be they the clerical reporters of *ahadith* or
non-clerical men of political and military power. His ideology relies on
vacating the human mind from speculative thought and critical inquiry
and replenishing the intellectual void with the fear of rationality, fatalism
and resignation. Majlesi's Shi'i are invited to accept and appreciate the
virtues of abandoning their own intellectual and rational capacities. They
have to suppress and sublimate their instinct and ability to reflect on and
react to their material and spiritual conditions in favour of the rewards
Majlesi promises them in this world and the hereafter. This same ideology
channels the anger and hatred of the people towards the Sunnis whom, at
the time of Majlesi's writings, did not present a domestic danger to the
Safavi rule.

Majlesism as an ideology identifies a set of goals and objectives by
which the pious should adjust their private and social lives. With the aid
of the Safavi state, Majlesism seeks to impose its subjective interpretations
and formulations. Majlesism envisions a bipolar society. The masses or the
ruled should renounce any claim to individual reflection and initiative;
distrust their own human capacities, as well as the efforts of their fellow
beings; desist from participating in social organizations, the object and
purpose of which flows from their autonomous and individual thoughts.
Forsaking the power to think and act independently, they should embrace
the guidance of Shi'i scholars in every aspect of their life. At the apex of the
ruling class sits the Safavi Shah, graced by God and ruling by the power of
the sword. The Shi'i Shah is closely aided in ruling and managing the

---

[55] A. Shari'ati, Collected Works 1, p. 9 and C.W.18 (Tehran, 1361), p. 172.

masses by the Shiʻi scholars. Majlesism seeks to defuse and neutralize any opposition to the status quo.

Majlesism reinterprets the faith and reads into Shiʻism a conservative, complacent, irrational, timid and obesient ideology. A key objective of this ideology is to demonstrate or prove that Shiʻism is incompatible with a belief in the powers, promises and capacities of individuals. Majlesism wishes to hide its own ideological incompatibility with and disdain for the common folks' sense of self-reliance and self-respect by claiming that such tendencies are sacrilegious and heretical. An underpinning feature of Majlesism is its fear of the Shiʻi liberated from its dominion, believing in both God and His creatures and their power to reason.

Conclusion

Societies go through critical phases where crises in their prevailing collective thought, perception or world outlook, having reached the culmination of their gestation period, lead to shifts in thought, belief and paradigms. There are no scientific rules determining the duration of this gestation period of crises. Before and after the shift becomes operational and institutionalized, different discourses continue to compete with one another. Until the ascending discourse transforms its ideas and perceptions into laws and policies and even after it succeeds to do so, it will be nudged and challenged by the ideas that preceded it and held its political realization in check. The reshaping of the prevailing collective thought in Iran, triggered by the historical encounter between modernity and religion dating back to the Iranian Constitutional Revolution of 1906, is still underway. The intellectual production of those segments of society involved in this encounter has gone through a clear process of crystallization. Ambiguous understandings of terms and concepts have distilled and sharpened. An idealistic, voluntaristic and cavalier acceptance of ready-made formulas not necessarily corresponding to the socio-economic and religious realities of Iran have given way to more nuanced, and therefore realistic, synthesis and analysis.

In the process of this historical encounter, two loosely labelled outlooks – anti-religious modernists and religious anti-modernists – have pretended to be interested in participating in the dialogue within the main body of society, sometimes latent and sometimes overt, on modernity and Islam. The proponents of both of these positions, hardened and bloodied over the years, have *pretended* to be interested in dialogue because neither are committed to the process of debate and argumentation but are seduced by the final outcome of converting the other. Both are out to conquer not to understand and seek cognition. Both anti-religious and anti-modernists believe in repudiation and rejection and, if pushed to the logical end of their positions, could concede to containment, confinement and repression of the other, through legal means or otherwise.

The anti-religious modernists do not possess solid domestic historical roots. Their outlook is not the result of a long-term internal encounter reflecting the development of native intellectual forces, but it is an imported outlook. There is nothing wrong with importing social, political and philosophical ideas rooted in different socio-economic experiences and geographical environments. Imported ideas, if in tune with human nature and ideals of the times, may take hold among one segment of society but take much longer to become accepted and integrated with the domestic culture of a larger segment of society. In the interim, imported ideas may face serious resistance and undergo undesirable mutations. Ideas enriching in the native society may not prove to be equally enriching in the imported one. Historically, anti-religionism was an imported idea that was not associated with the prevalent religious sentiments of the majority of the people and therefore remained confined to small intellectual circles. It could be argued that Islam was also imported or imposed, but it dates back to centuries ago and it has since become almost indistinguishable from a native or Iranian culture.

The religious anti-modernists have deeper roots, but dream of society as an airtight vacuum, static and frozen in time or one that should be kept that way. To them, society is not a living organism capable of development, endogenous and exogenous. They firmly believe that, armed with their singular interpretation of religion, which they believe suffices all times and ages, they will be able to steer society clear of any deviationist temptations and impulses on the path that it has "always" been. At the heart of this position rests the notion that the common folk will always remain an indistinguishable and undifferentiated mass incapable of independent and critical thought, and if they were to possess it, society would be endangered by divisiveness, strife and ultimately heresy.

Broad historical sweeps risk gross generalizations. But to make a point in a short space, its use becomes indispensable. Sweeping statements are unrefined, carrying half-truths and in need of being evaluated cautiously. Anti-religious modernists and religious anti-modernists are two stereo-typical dogmatic positions, each seeing the other as anathema. In the past 100 years of Iranian history, they have viewed one another as funda-mental threats to society, its development and well-being. Segments of the religious anti-modernists have even gone as far as liquidating those whom they have deemed as enemies of the faith. Yet neither perception has really observed what the people may think and want. For both, their respective ideal constructs are so perfect that the people cannot but welcome and aspire to them for their own good. One of the key characteristics of the religious anti-modernists is their disregard for the will and preference of people.

During the past 100 years, Iranians have experienced modernization with mixed enthusiasm. On some occasions, they sought it and gallantly fought for it, and on others, it was imposed upon them and they resisted it. Naturally, they have been exposed to the fruits of modernity, material and intellectual, political and economic, institutional and organizational, from which society at large has benefited. At times, when the tangible outcomes of modernity demanded a mindset that would come to clash with their traditional way of thought, life or their religious mindedness, then it was for the people to negotiate their dilemma. Usually what the religious anti-modernists or the anti-religious modernists said, promulgated or even made into law did not prevent the people to seek out and live with their own acceptable and alternative synthesis. Even after the Iranian Revolution of 1979, the interaction of Iranians with or exposure to modernity did not imply a fundamental trade-off between religiosity and modernity. For the common folk, the pre-revolution modernization drive from above in its multifarious aspects was not associated with a frontal assault on their religiosity and religion. In sum, it seems as if Iranians of different social classes have in general tried to harmonize their religiosity with the modernization process, creating a space for a budding civil society.

Moments of social and political unrest and revolution can be traced to historical instances when either the religious or the modernization zeal of those in power have pressed ahead with their own convictions overlooking the fine balance of the two – modernity and religiosity – in the mind and practice of Iranians. Placing the historical relation between religion and modernity as the core explanatory factor of events in Iran is a useful and necessary exercise. Yet if this relationship is not nuanced and explained by a serious study of the historical, social and economic context and its evolution, its explanatory power will prove incomplete, if not faulty. A thorough and meaningful analysis would need to look at the material historical development of the Iranian society to understand how different classes and social strata came to adopt, reinterpret, attenuate, extend, reject or combine religiosity and modernity.

The trade-off presented by the two extreme positions of the religious anti-modernists and anti-religious modernists is usually not an acceptable scenario to the majority. Combining modernity – including democracy/good government and some form of capitalism – with Shiʿism, the exact content of which other than belief in monotheism, prophethood, the Day of Resurrection, *Imamate* and Justice, need not be specified, probably provides the majority of Iranians with the ideal spiritual and material combination. In their minds, this combination probably assures them of greater economic welfare, increased political and social participation, enjoyment of their mental and material capacities and the continued possession of their traditional spiritual serenity, beliefs and peace of mind. Let us assume that modernity is characterized by: (1) the development and use of science and technology; (2) free application of reason; (3) the development of capitalism; (4) the institutionalization of democratic procedures; (5) respect for individual and collective rights and freedoms; (6) respect for the rule of law; (7) separation of powers, the judiciary, legislative and executive. If it is agreed that modernity includes the above characteristics, then it seems obvious that in a modernizing society with strong religious affiliations, even in the absence of the anti-religious modernists and the religious anti-modernists, traditional religious beliefs and modernism would need to enter into a debate or an argument for a renegotiated outcome. Today, the key debate revolves around the most suitable political system that would best reconcile modernity and spiritual Shi'ism without subjecting one to the dictates of the other. A democratic political system based on the division of state and religion holds up the greatest hope.

The European experience, which could be learned from but is not assumed to be an ideal model, demonstrates that a space for critical dialogue or debate within Catholicism did present itself in the sixteenth and seventeenth century. Setting the stage for the idea of modernity including democracy, a historically crucial in-house criticism occurred in Christian Europe. Catholic priests, firmly grounded in their Christian teachings of the times, challenged the dogmatic, hierarchical, authoritarian and worldly practices of their own religious institution. The Church, as the most significant and powerful institution of medieval Europe, faced a challenge from within. The debates and criticisms of the challenging priests and protestors were couched in the same Scripture as those whom they criticized. Protesting Catholic monks and priests questioned the teachings, dogmas and relevance of the institution that gave them a preferential status as compared to the laity. It was not the laymen who laid claim to the powers of the priests, even though they too were involved in the debate, but it was the priests, wishing to empower the lay that most threatened the Church. The individual and natural rights of the underprivileged were reclaimed by the privileged. The intermediaries between God and men were renouncing their own position as unchristian and extending to all

Christians the right of interpreting the Scripture. The reformists acknowledged that the individual believer had the capacity to reflect upon God, establish and regulate his relation with God, lead a pious life and have faith in his own reasoning and individual conscience without blindly following the edicts and practices of the Church. "Priesthood of all believers" became the popular slogan of the Protestants. Some of the challenging priests sought to reform both their own religion and the absolutist states and rulers. The reformers of religion such as Calvin and Zwingli became associated with anti-monarchism and pro-republicanism.

This in-house debate led to the Protestant movement and reformation in Europe, changing the path of European and subsequently world development. A similar systematic in-house criticism spreading through the land, impacting the people and leading to a broad movement did not occur in Shiʿi Iran. Even though in the name of reforming the faith, individual and interspersed criticisms of actually existing Shiʿism did clearly occur, it failed to gain any real momentum, let alone attain the status of a movement. Shiʿism has always positioned and identified itself as a religion of protest against the deviations, injustices and excesses of the worldly caliphs, especially after the death of Imam ʿAli. As such, it could claim to be the Protestant movement of Islam. Even though the *mavali* – Iranians living among the Arabs – had always been close to the Shiʿi, Shiʿism only became truly Iranian after it was made the state religion by the Safavis. Several factors, in contrast to the Catholic Church, may partially explain why the in-house debates in Shiʿism after the death of the imams did not result in a major reformation movement. At its apex, Shiʿism has been a decentralized institution lacking a hierarchical, central command claiming infallibility. The openness of the gate of *ijtihad* in Shiʿism allowed for the general acceptance of different yet equally legitimate religious opinions by jurists. The possibility of coexisting diverse religious opinions of Shiʿi *mujtahid*s provided a political as well as a religious safety net for criticism and venting of popular discontent. Perhaps the diffused Shiʿi system allowed for some degree of dissent without ex-communicating dissident Shiʿi. Shiʿism proved capable of incorporating and co-opting challenges such as the *akhbari* and *usuli* school. Twelver Shiʿism has demonstrated its ability to accommodate diversity within its confines just as much as it has demonstrated intolerance towards those whom it considers to have transgressed its confines, abrogated it and created a new faith rooted in Shiʿism, such as the Bahaʾis. The lifestyle of non-court Shiʿi guardians of the faith was far from opulent and ostentatious. The non-court clerics were viewed as the protectors and sanctuary of the common people against the injustices, repression and corruption of the state. In the absence of an official fusion of judicial and executive power in the hands of the Shi'i clergy, the excesses of the state, except until after the Iranian revolution, was not associated with the clergy.

The sense of elation and enthusiasm that followed the institution of Shi'ism as the official state religion during the Safavi period united the Shi'i jurists behind the state and the monarchs. The recognition, as well as the religious and political power granted to Karaki by Shah Tahmasb, the second Safavi King, endowed Shi'i jurists with an unprecedented position and prestige in running the political, legal and administrative affairs of the state. Yet as much as the clergy obtained power under most Safavi kings, from the people's perspective, they were in general not at the origin of social, political and religious ills. They were considered as forces who wished to attenuate the excesses of the shahs. The sudden ascendancy of Shi'i jurists to spiritual and political power and their increasing involvement in the administration of the state was not concomitant with any social movement focused on critical soul-searching or reflection on Shi'ism and the clerical institution. In the minds of Iranian Shi'i jurists, Shi'ism under the Safavis had finally been given the recognition that it had historically deserved and longed for. The newly gained status was not to be disturbed or threatened by internal strife or dissent. The few critical voices received no attention, as the coffers of the state seemed to finance the livelihood of Shi'i jurists and the seminary students.

During the Constitutional Revolution, the clergy took different sides on a political issue. Even though the struggle between constitutionalist clerics and the anti-constitutionalist Sheykh Fazlollah Nuri was based on the question of Islam's compatibility with a constitution or a social contract based on the right of people to legislate and could have led to more profound speculative and theological debates on Shi'i Islam, it did not. Once religio-political positions on concrete issues hardened during the debates and written works, the key participants backed down. The compromise solution of five jurists acting as the guardians of the Islamicness of legislations moderated the rift between the clerical modernists and the traditionists. A number of young, promising and bright clerics with a taste for speculative reasoning who had participated in the Constitutional Revolution and later became notable figures in Iranian history shed their religious garb and became laymen. This self-exclusion process by what could have become a core of reformist clerics, starting at the end of the Qajar dynasty, gained momentum during the rule of Reza Shah.

From the Safavi period to the rule of Reza Shah, the relation between the clergy and the state was one of either fascination and acquiescence or anger and revolt. In either case, they closed ranks, shielding their collective religious identity under the banner of Shiʿi Islam thus leaving no room for internal dissent. When the clergy found the state and the monarchs generous, receptive to their ideas and not directly and blatantly contradicting their interpretation of the Shariʿat, they walked in tandem with political power, legitimizing and supporting it. When they fell out with the shahs, as did Mirza Hasan Shirazi, even though he was not residing in Iran, they acted almost in unison in censuring the monarchs. Reza Shah's attempt at breaking the influence of the clergy and isolating them enhanced their popularity, unified them and in effect worked against those clerical voices such as Shariat Sangelaji who were gradually articulating a reformist discourse. Under attack from Reza Shah, the clergy closed ranks, pulled together and consolidated their energy, dismissing all attempts at questioning their religious discourse as anti-religious agitation by elements in collusion with Reza Shah. The official religious institution (*rowhaniyyat*) brushed aside attempts by the clergy and lay at cleansing Majlesi-inspired Shiʿism from superstitious and phantasmical ideas as ruses and plots by agents in the pay of Reza Shah.

ʿAli Shariʿati, who in the 1970s conducted a passionate campaign both against the political despotism of Mohammad-Reza Shah Pahlavi and the religious obscurantism of Safavi Shiʿism, Majlesi and his clerical supporters in order to revive, actualize and make Shiʿism attractive to the Iranian youth, was not spared from the religious institution's invectives, denunciations and even excommunication. Even after Shariʿati's death, Ayatollah Mesbah Yazdi remained one his main detractors and antagonists. The magnitude and intensity of the attacks against Shariʿati demonstrated the official clergy's deep anxiety faced with the success of an anti-Majlesi dissident Shiʿi discourse. Just as in the Constitutional debate, some sixty years later, Shariʿati was engaging the official clergy on political grounds. He chastised them for their submission to and collaboration with despotism in order to secure their own political and economic interests. In the process of explaining why the official clergy acted in the way they did, Shariʿati developed his concept of Safavi Shiʿism as a creed opposed to ʿAli's Shiʿism.

In his quest to induce and spur an "Islamic Protestant Movement", Shariʿati sought a Shiʿism free from the monolithic interpretations of its official clergy, in which the discriminatory barriers between the clergy and the lay would be broken down and Shiʿism would become liberated from what he called "the confines of medieval churches" and cleansed from superstitious and deviationist ideas. As much as Shari'ati's intellectual assault against the official religious establishment was serious, popular and influential, it failed to become a religious reformist movement. His audience was much more interested in the political implications of his religious discourse than the religious discourse itself.

Shari'ati had two major handicaps. First, his audience was not the traditional pious common folk imbued with Majlesi's Shi'ism, but the intellectuals, university students and those who were already interested in a discourse that would reject the dichotomy between reason and faith. Shari'ati's audience believed that independent thought and reflection was their right, as well as their God-given gift. They were, therefore, naturally inclined towards Shari'ati's conclusion that Majlesi's religious superstition was a distortion of the faith for political purposes. Second, and probably most important of all, Shari'ati was himself a layman and not a cleric. He was not a *mojtahed*, with the authority and respect that such a status commanded among common believers in his time, but a Western-clad, Western-educated outsider. As an outsider, his words and his teachings did not have the weight of the men of the cloth among the traditionalist folk.

After the institution of the Islamic Republic, Mohammad Mojtahed Shabestari, 'Abdolkarim Sorush, Mostafa Malekian, Mohsen Kadivar and Hasan Yusefi Eshkevari made important theoretical contributions with an attempt to reform Shi'i Islam. From the above, three – Shabestari, Kadivar and Eshkevari – were clerics, although only one – Kadivar – still dons the religious garb. Many other influential clerics and laymen have sought to reform the Islamic Republic, primarily from a political perspective. From within the traditional religious establishment, Ayatollahs Montazeri and Yusef Sane'i emerged as the leaders of a new Shi'i reformist movement. As they distanced themselves from the tradition-alist Safavi or Majlesi discourse of Shi'ism through their *fatwas*, they effectively became the leaders of a Shi'i reformation movement that found its social base in the Green Movement of post-June 2009.

After the death of Montazeri, it is primarily Sane'i who stands at the head of this Shi'i reformation movement, which traces its lineage to the Constitutional Revolution. As long as Ayatollah Khomeyni was alive, aspects of the Majlesi discourse, which emphasized the inability of laymen to think and reason, belittled the public will, propagated superstitious ideas and found the idea of people's rule disdainful, were somewhat kept in check. Yet Khomeyni's emphasis on the absolutist rule of the Shi'i jurist in running the affairs of the state provided the proponents of the Majlesi discourse with an ideal opportunity to revive these aspects once Khomeyni had passed away, in order to constrain if not abolish the Republic. The post-Khomeyni era opened up a new breathing space for the Majlesi discourse to bounce back into full swing, reinvent itself and come to the aid of Khomeyni's successor who was not in any way as secure in his popularity as Khomeyni.

The tenacity of Majlesi's religio-political ideology and methodology, reflected through its survival through the centuries, albeit with mutations, alterations and adaptations, is a definite sign of its strength and appeal. Some 400 years after Majlesi, the core of his ideology is being resurrected and once again promoted by a man of the cloth. Majlesi was very close to the Safavi centre of political and economic power and considered the Safavi shahs graced and driven by God. He had tied Shiʿism, as well as his own fortune and future as its spokesperson, to the rule of the Safavi shahs. Ayatollah Mesbah Yazdi, and the clerics close to him are committed to the Leader of the Islamic Republic, consider him as the successor and representative of the Hidden Imam and believe that whoever "opposes him and disregards or rejects his words and edicts" is a polytheist.[1] Majlesi did not believe in human reasoning as a beacon for human felicity and salvation and therefore strongly advocated its abandonment in favour of blindly imitating the Shiʿi jurists. Mesbah Yazdi is of the opinion that the masses are unenlightened, incapable of understanding or identifying the problems and issues at hand and often unable to distinguish right from wrong. He therefore shares Majlesi's belief on this issue and considers the thoughts and behaviours of the masses as untrustworthy.[2]

Majlesi called on the people to disengage from intellectual, social and political inquiries, leaving all aspects of their affairs to the connoisseurs of the *ahadith*, who in his esteem were the sole authorities, entitled to think for the people. Mesbah Yazdi argues that people should listen to what God and the Prophet enunciate, and, at present, he opines that they should blindly follow the words of the Guardian Jurist.[3] Majlesi believed that his perception of Shiʿi Islam was the only correct one endorsed by the Shiʿi imams, therefore reclaiming the total adherence of the Shiʿi community to his views. Today, Mesbah Yazdi denounces pluralism and multiple readings and understandings of religious texts, arguing for the validity of a

---

[1] M. T. Mesbah Yazdi, *Pasokh Ostad be Javanan Porseshgar*, p. 53.
[2] H. A. ʿArabi, *Haqiqat Sharq*, pp. 185–186; M. T. Mesbah Yazdi, *Dar Partoy-e Azarakhsh* (Qom, 1382), p. 42; M. T. Mesbah Yazdi, *Naqsh Taqlid dar Zendegiye Ensan*, p. 59.
[3] H. A. ʿArabi, *Haqiqat Sharq*, p. 196.

single reading of Shiʻism – naturally his – and labels other readings and interpretations as a "satanic ruse", "polytheism" and a *"fetneh"* (*fitna*) or sedition.[4] Mesbah Yazdi's use of the term *fetneh* in this context well precedes the use of the term by the political status quo after the June 2009 uprisings.

While Majlesi nourished and replenished the assumed "deficient minds" of the common folk with superstitious and irrational causal relations to stupefy and prevent the emergence of critical consciousness, in the twenty-first century, Mesbah Yazdi's task is much more complicated. Even though, faced with a less culturally, educationally, intellectually, economically and professionally homogeneous society, Mesbah Yazdi develops a multiple discourse with different emphases when addressing his different audiences. Yet his mainstream arguments are similar to those made by Majlesi in the seventeenth century. Mesbah Yazdi encourages the common folk to vote for the presidential candidate that he actively supports by arguing that the Twelfth Imam supports him. He whips up support for the Leader, Ayatollah Khamenehʼi, by attributing to him the ability to hear Divine messages. Mesbah Yazdi spurs pious believers to visit the Jamkaran mosque where they may meet the Twelfth Imam and see the realization of their dreams through miracles.[5]

The religious identity and binding official state religion that Majlesi formulated is preciously guarded by Mesbah Yazdi, whose crusade against the "cultural onslaught" of the West is reminiscent of Majlesi's attempts to formulate a standard norm of private and public behaviour based on his vision of the religiously approved social code of conduct. Just as Majlesi sought to tighten the circle of the Shiʻi by rejecting, branding and excluding those who refused to comply with his vision of Shiʻism and its necessities as irreligious and infidel "others", Mesbah Yazdi considers those who disagree with his vision of Shiʻism as hypocrites, polytheists, enemies of the faith, agents of Satan and lackeys of foreigners. To Mesbah Yazdi, even if hundreds and thousands are to be killed, the Islamic system that he guides, supports and benefits from needs to be upheld.[6] Finally, in the tradition of Majlesi, who prayed for the long-lasting rule of the Safavi kings until the appearance of the Hidden Imam, Mesbah Yazdi prays that God keep Iran safe under the grace of the Twelfth Imam and the leadership of the guardian of the affairs of Muslims until the return of the Hidden Imam.[7]

[4] *Bayan* (22 Farvardin 1379); M. T. Mesbah Yazdi, *Dar Partoy-e Azarakhsh*, pp. 145, 147, 159.

[5] M. T. Mesbah Yazdi, *Tahajome Farhangi* (Qom, 1387), p. 119.

[6] H. A. ʻArabi, *Haqiqat Sharq*, p. 189.

[7] M. T. Mesbah Yazdi, *Dar Partoy-e Azarakhsh*, p. 114.

Ayatollah Mesbah Yazdi has repackaged Majlesism as the official discourse of the Shi'i religious establishment. The leader of the Islamic Revolution has given Mesbah Yazdi the responsibility to impose his Majlesi-based ideology on society, when necessary, through the repressive force of an emerging politicized security and military apparatus. Since June 2009, the overconfident status quo has been both confronted with a religious reformation movement led by Ayatollahs Montazeri and Sane'i and supported by a growing number of clerics, as well as a political and social reform movement led by a layman and two clerics. After thirty years of experience with an Islamic Republic, which, by definition, fused religion with politics, the Iranian reformist movement is intensely engaged in two different but merged debates. Shi'i Iran is experiencing another phase in its historically long process of articulating and negotiating its political and religious identity. The intense struggle is, on the one hand, over the ideal polity, its system of governance and institutions and, on the other hand, on the appropriate Shi'i mode of life or what it means to be Shi'i and modern.

The ruling religio-political and military bloc views the successful continuation of its rule in enforcing homogeneity, stamping out dissent and differences at whatever price. It believes in an exclusivist, absolutist, mono-vision and definition of politics, society and religion, barring any alternatives as a threat to the nation and God's religion. The notion of checks and balances and consequently accountability to the people does not sit well with the ruling bloc, as it presupposes that the ordinary people should only act as followers. The absolutist exclusivists, who share the cultural and political aspects of the religious anti-modernist discourse, do not believe in the rational capacities and sound judgement of those outside the closed circuit of their like-minded fraternity. The ruling classes' ideal of a homogeneous society or community, with a single mind, opinion and voice is invariably rooted in an almost necrophiliac social outlook, as standardization requires stunting fertility, life and diversity. They see no virtue or merit in human beings with ideas other than themselves. Consequently, wherever they look, they see conspiracies, chicanery and foul play or apostasy. They agonize over the incessant proliferation of divergence and plurality in society, despite their incessant imposition of straitjackets on religion, society, culture and polity to achieve their desired homogeneity. They wishfully think that the imposition of a single manual of livelihood and a unitary code of religious behaviour similar to the one articulated by Majlesi and equally superstition-based is possible on twenty-first century Iran. They do not wish to accept that the Iranian community's average common sense can no longer be moved and influenced by religious

superstition and political unaccountability, both of which rely on the public's resignation to and acceptance of irrational, supernatural and inexplicable causal relations.

Their reformist challengers, the "rainbow of greens", have learned to
become both politically and religiously tolerant, inclusivist and pluralist.
They repudiate any single preconceived and forcefully imposed reading,
position or voice, unapproved by a popular mandate as outdated, unrepresentative and therefore harmful to both the general welfare and Shi'ism.
Based on their perception of human nature and their understanding of
Shi'ism, the reformists find the methods of ruling through violence, intim-
idation and fear as irreligious and inhuman from an ethical point of view
and inefficient and futile from a tactical and technical perspective. They see
differences and dissent as natural, healthy and religiously condoned. The
reformist inclusivists believe in a Shi'i culture accommodating the plurality
of modes of life, interpretations and preferences. The reformist movement
is now grounded in a community common sense, which has surpassed a
historically and socially outdated narrow vision and interpretation of
religion, politics and society. Today, this prevalent public common sense
finds itself and its aspirations restrained and repressed by the political and
religious ghosts of the superstitious past.

The Iranian reformist movement, both political and religious, moves
from the premises that to allow for maximum participation of all in
society, polity and faith, differences should be respected and understood,
ideas should be debated and old fears of "others" overcome. They have
come to believe that foes could be befriended and individuals need to
become accepted and respected as part of a nationwide circle of equal
citizens, without anyone abandoning their right to disagree and object. The
project of reviving Majlesi's ideology of superstition and irrational fear and
hatred through numbing individual and public judgement to secure the
political leadership of an unrepresentative and unaccountable ruling bloc
seems no longer viable and attainable, given the rational transformation of
the average common sense of Iranians.

Material and spiritual development has undone the appeal and magic of
superstition and unexplained phenomena. Yet the ruling bloc perceives the
longevity of its tenure in tenaciously holding on to the belief that the triad
of irrationality, arbitrariness and superstition can bring people back into
the fold of obedient followers. When this belief has proven false, the ruling
bloc has resorted to the ultimate irrationality of using force against those
whose collective interests it is supposed to defend and further. The forceful
imposition of a minoritarian common sense upon a majoritarian one

invariably leads to bloodshed, even when the majoritarian side is deeply committed to change through non-violence.

What needs to be seen is whether the political success of the Iranian reform movement will also automatically achieve the ends of a Shi'i reformation movement. Will the fate of the religious reformation movement be tied to the political reform movement? Will one happen without the other? Will historians look back on the 1990s and the first decade of the twenty-first century and earmark it as the beginning of Iran's Shi'i reformation movement?

Bibliography

Works in Persian

'Abedi, A., 'Naqd Bahar al-Anvar dar Dayeratolma'aref Tashayo' in M. Mohrizi, and H. Rabbani (eds.), *Shenakhtnameh 'Allameh Majlesi*, vol. 2 (Tehran: Vezarat Farhang va Ershad Eslami, 1378).

Anonymous, *'Alam Aray-e Safavi* (Tehran: Entesharat Keyhan, 1363).

'Akef, S., *Khakhaye Narm Kushk* (Mashhad: Molk Aazam, 1387).

'Alavi, E., 'Majlesi az Didgah-e Mostashreghan va Iranshenasan' in M. Mohrizi and H. Rabbani (eds.), *Shenakhtnameh 'Allameh Majlesi*, vol. 2 (Tehran: Vezarat Farhang va Ershad Eslami, 1378).

'Alikhani, A., *The Diaries of Asadollah 'Alam*, vol. 1 (1347–1348) (USA: New World Ltd., 1992).

'Alikhani, A., *The Diaries of Asadollah 'Alam*, vol. 2 (1349–1351) (Bethesda: Iranbooks, 1993).

'Alikhani, A., *The Diaries of Asadollah 'Alam*, vol. 3 (1352) (Bethesda: Iranbooks, 1995).

'Alikhani, A., *The Diaries of Asadollah 'Alam*, vol. 4 (1353) (Bethesda: Ibex Publishers, n.d.).

'Alikhani, A., *The Diaries of Asadollah 'Alam*, vol. 5 (1354) (Bethesda: Ibex Publishers, n.d.).

'Alikhani, A., *The Diaries of Asadollah 'Alam*, vol. 6 (1355–1356) (Bethesda: Ibex, 2008).

Anousheh, H., 'Astarabadi' in *Encyclopaedia of Shi'a*, vol. 2 (Tehran: Bonyad-e Shat, 1372).

Ansari Qomi, N., 'Sharh Zendegiye 'Allameh Kabir Mohammad Baqir Majlesi' in M. Mohrizi and H. Rabbani (eds.), *Shenakhtnameh 'Allameh Majlesi*, vol. 1 (Tehran: Vezarat Farhang va Ershad Eslami, 1378).

Aqatehrani, M., *Soday-e Ruy-e Dust* (Qom: Markaz Entesharat Moa'seseh Amuzeshi va Pajuheshi Emam Khomeyni, 1386).

'Arabi, H. A., *Haqiqat Sharq* (Qom: Zolale Kowsar, 1381).

'Aref Arzerumi, *Enqelab al-Eslami Beyn al-Khass va al-'Am*, vol. 1 (Tehran: The National Library of Iran – F/1634, 1308).

Asef, M. H., *Rostam al-Tavarikh* (Tehran: Amir Kabir, 1352).

Asgharizadeh, M., *Arefan Vesal* (Qom: Sabet al-Nabi, 1386).

Baqi, A., *Dar Shenakht Hezb-e Qaedin-e Zaman* (Qom: Nashre Danesh Eslami, 1362).

Baqeri, A., *Khaterat-e 15 Khordad* (Tehran: Entesharat Soureh Mehr, 1388).

Davani, A., *Mafakher-e Eslam* (Tehran: Entesharat Markaz Asnad-e Enqelab-e Eslami, 1375).

Davani, A., 'Sharh Hale 'Allameh Majlesi' in M. Mohrezi and H. Rabbani (eds.), *Shenakhtnameh 'Allameh Majlesi*, vol. 1 (Tehran: Vezarat Farhang va Ershad Eslami, 1378).

Faqih Imani, M. B., *Foze Akbar* (Qom: Atr-e Etrat, 1382).

Ghanipour, H., *Jebhe'y Jonoub* (Tehran: Sureh Mehr, 1386).

Ja'fariyan, R., *Din va Siyasat dar Dowreh Safavi* (Qom: Ansarian, 1370).

Kadivar, M., ''Aql va Din az Didgah-e Mohaddeth va Hakim' in M. Mohrizi and H. Rabbani (eds.), *Shenakhtnameh 'Allameh Majlesi*, vol. 1 (Tehran: Vezarat Farhang va Ershad Eslami, 1378).

Kadivar, M., ''Ayar Naqd dar Manzelat 'Aql' in M. Mohrizi and H. Rabbani (eds.), *Shenakhtnameh 'Allameh Majlesi*, vol. 1 (Tehran: Vezarat Farhang va Ershad Eslami, 1378).

Kaempfer, E., *Safarnameh Kaempfer*, K. Jahandari (tr.) (Tehran: Kharazmi, 1360).

Kashani, H., *Rowzat al-Shohada* (Tehran: Eslamiyeh, 1380).

Khatunabadi, A.-H., *Vaqaye' Alsanayen val Avam* (Tehran: Eslamiyeh, 1352).

Khomeyni, R., *Hokumate Eslami* (n.p., n.d.).

Khomeyni, R., *Sahifeh Nur*, vol. 12 (Tehran: Vezarat Ershad Eslami, 1361).

Khonsari-Esfahani, M. B., *Rowzat al-Jennat*, vols. 1 and 2 (Tehran: Eslamiyeh, 2535).

Khonsari-Esfahani, M. B., *Rowzat al-Jennat*, vol. 5 (Tehran: Eslamiyeh, 1360).

Khoramshahi, B., 'Bahar al-Anvar dar Dayeratolma'aref' in M. Mohrizi and H. Rabbani (eds.), *Shenakhtnameh 'Allameh Majlesi*, vol. 2 (Tehran: Vezarat Farhang va Ershad Eslami, 1378).

Khoramshahi, B., 'Tahrifnapaziri-e Qur'an' in *Encyclopaedia of Shi'a*, vol. 4 (Tehran: Entesharat 'Elmi va Farhangi, 1373).

Koleyni, *Usul-e Kafi*, vol. 1 (Tehran: Entesharat Golgasht, 1375).

Lowhi, M. Hoseyni Musavi Sabzevari, *Ketab Arba'eyn. Ketab Kefayat al-Mohtadi* (Handwritten Manuscript, Ketbkhaneh Majlis Shoray-e Melli Iran, Shomareh Daftar: 833).

Mahdavi, M., *Zendeghinameh 'Allameh Majlesi*, vols. 1 and 2 (Tehran: Vezarat Farhang va Ershad Eslami, 1378).

Majlesi, M. B., *Adab-e Mo'asherat* (tarjomeh jeld shanzdahom-e Bahar al-Anvar) (Tehran: Eslamiyeh, 1365).

Majlesi, M. B., *'Eyn al-Hayat* (Tehran: Ketabfrushi Eslamiyeh, n.d).

Majlesi, M. B., *Bahar al-Anvar*, vol. 7, Book 3, On Emamat, M. Khosravi (tr.) (Tehran: Ketabfrushi Eslamiyeh, 1363).

Majlesi, M. B., *Bahar al-Anvar*, vol. 7, Book 4, On Emamat, M. Khosravi (tr.) (Tehran: Ketabfrushi Eslamiyeh, 1364).

Majlesi, M. B., *Ekhtiyarat* (Tehran: Ketabfrushi Eslami, n.d.).

Majlesi, M. B., *E'teqadat* (Qom: Resalat, 1378).

Majlesi, M. B., *Haq al-Yaqin* (Tehran: Entesharat-e Rashidi, n.d.).

Majlesi, M. B., *Hayat al-Qolub*, vol. 1, 'Tarikh-e Payambaran' (Qom: Entesharat Sorour, 1375).

Majlesi, M. B., *Hayat al-Qolub*, vol. 2, 'Tarikh-e Payambaran' (Qom: Entesharat Sorour, 1375).

Majlesi, M. B., *Hayat al-Qolub*, vol. 5, 'Emamshenasi' (Qom: Entesharat Sorour, 1376).

Majlesi, M. B., *Heliyat al-Mottaqin* (Tehran: Ketabfrushiye Eslamiyeh, 1373).

Majlesi, M. B., *Jala' al-'Oyoun* (Qom: Entesharat Sorur, 1373).

Majlesi, M. B., *Majmu'eh-e Rasael-e E'teqadi* (Mashhad: Astan-e Qods Razavi, 1368).

Majlesi, M. B., *Raj'at* (Mashhad: Ketabkhaneh Abdolhamid Mowlavi, book number 69, n.d.).

Majlesi, M. B., *Rabi' al-Asabi' (Doaha va A'mal Shab va Ruz-e Jom'eh)* (Qom: Entesharat Masjed-e Moqadas-e Jamkaran, 1386).

Majlesi, M. B., 'Resaleh-e Majlesi dar bareh Hokama, Ousuliyoun va Sufiyeh' in R. Ja'fariyan, *Din va Siyasat dar Dowreh Safavi* (Qom: Ansarian, 1370).

Mashayekh, M. H., 'Akhbariyeh' in *Encyclopaedia of Shi'a*, vol. 2 (Tehran: Bonyad-e Shat, 1372).

Mesbah Yazdi, M. T., *Aftab Velayat* (Qom: Markaz Entesharat Moaseseh Amuzeshi va Pajuheshi Emam Khomeyni, 1384).

Mesbah Yazdi, M. T., *Amuzesh 'Aqayed* (Tehran: Sherkat Chap va Nashr-e Beynolmelal, 1385).

Mesbah Yazdi, M. T., *Azarakhsh Karbala* (Qom: Markaz Entesharat Moaseseh Amuzeshi va Pajuheshi Emam Khomeyni, 1384).

Mesbah Yazdi, M. T., *Dar Partoy-e Azarakhsh* (Qom: Markaz Entesharat Moaseseh Amuzeshi va Pajuheshi Emam Khomeyni, 1382).

Mesbah Yazdi, M. T., *Hokumate Eslami va Velayat Faqih* (Tehran: Sazeman Tabliqat Eslami, 1369).

Mesbah Yazdi, M. T., *Kavoshha va Chaleshha*, vol. 1 (Qom: Markaz Entesharat Moaseseh Amuzeshi va Pajuheshi Emam Khomeyni, 1379).

Mesbah Yazdi, M. T., *Kavoshha va Chaleshha*, vol. 2 (Qom: Markaz Entesharat Moaseseh Amuzeshi va Pajuheshi Emam Khomeyni, 1382).

Mesbah Yazdi, M. T., *Naqsh Taqlid dar Zendegh'i-ye Ensan* (Qom: Markaz Entesharat Moaseseh Amuzeshi va Pajuheshi Emam Khomeyni, 1384).

Mesbah Yazdi, M. T., *Negahi Gozara be Basij va Basiji* (Qom: Markaz Entesharat Moaseseh Amuzeshi va Pajuheshi Emam Khomeyni, 1386).

Mesbah Yazdi, M. T., *Pasokh Ostad be Javanan Porseshgar* (Qom: Markaz Entesharat Moaseseh Amuzeshi va Pajuheshi Emam Khomeyni, 1385).

Mesbah Yazdi, M. T., *Rahiyan Kuy-e Dust* (Qom: Markaz Entesharat Moaseseh Amuzeshi va Pajuheshi Emam Khomeyni, 1384).

Mesbah Yazdi, M. T., *Tahajom-e Farhangi* (Qom: Markaz Entesharat Moaseseh Amuzeshi va Pajuheshi Emam Khomeyni, 1387).

Mesbah Yazdi, M. T., *Velayat Faqih, Porseshha va Pasokhha*, vols. 1 and 2 (Qom: Markaz Entesharat Moaseseh Amuzeshi va Pajuheshi Emam Khomeyni, 1379).

Mirahmadi, M., *Din Va Mazhab dar 'Asr Safavi* (Tehran: Amir Kabir, 1363).

Mir'azimi, J., *Masjed-e Moqadas-e Jamkaran Tajaligah Saheb Zaman* (Qom: Entesharat Masjed-e Jamkaran, 1385).

Mirkhandan, S. H., *Mohammad-Taqi Majlesi bar Sahel Hadith* (Tehran: Sazeman Tabliqat Eslami, 1374)

Mirza Saleh, Q., *Reza Shah: Khaterat Soleyman Behbudi, Shams Pahlavi, 'Ali Izadi* (Tehran: Tarh-e No, 1372).

Mohrizi, M., and Rabbani, H., *Shenakhtnameh 'Allameh Majlesi*, vols. 1 and 2. (Tehran: Vezarat Farhang va Ershad Eslami, 1378).

Montazeri, H. A., *Mabani-ye Feqhi-ye Hokumat-e Eslami*, vol. 1 (Tehran: Ettela'at, 1367).

Musavi Gilani, R., *Doctrine Mahdaviyat* (Qom: Bonyad Farhangi Hazrat Mehdi-ye Mo'ud, 1387).

Nasiri, M. I., *Dastur-e Shahriyaran* (Tehran: Bonyad-e Moqufat-e Mahmud-e Afshar, 1373).

Niazmand, R., *Reza Shah* (London: Foundation for Iranian Studies, 1996).

Pahlavi, M. R., *Pasokh be Tarikh*, (n.p.: Mard-e Emrouz, 1371).

Pahlavi, M. R., *Ma'muriyat Baray-e Vatanam* (Paris: Parang, 1366).

Parsadust, M., *Shah Esma'il-e Aval* (Tehran: Sherkat Enteshar, 1375).

Podaat, B., *Safar be Sarzamin Nur* (Tehran: Farhang Menhaj, 1385).

Qomi, A., *Safinat al-Bahar*, M. B. Saidi (tr.) (Mashhad: Ketabfrushiye Ja'fari, n.d.).

Rajabi, F., *Ahmadinejad, Mo'jezeh Hezareh Sevom* (Tehran: Nashr-e Daneshamouz, 1385).

Safa, Z., *Tarikh Adabiyat Iran*, vol. 5, part 1 (Tehran: Entesharat Ferdowsi, 1363).

Safa'i, E., *Reza Shah Kabir dar Ai'eneh Khaterat* (Tehran: Edareh Kol Negaresh Vezart Farhang va Honar, 1365).

Safari-e Forushani, N., *Ghallian* (Mashhad: Islamic Research Foundation, 1999).

Saleh, M., *Jame'eh-e Modaresine Howzeh 'Elmiyeh Qom az Aghaz ta Aknoun*, vol. 2 (Tehran: Markaz Asnad-e Enqelab-e Eslami, 1385).

Salehi-e Najafabadi, N., *Asay-e Musa ya Darman-e Bimariy-e Gholov* (Tehran: Omid Farda, 1380).

San'ati, R., *Goftoman Mesbah* (Tehran: Markaz Asnad-e Enqelab-e Eslami, 1387).

Sanson, *Safarnameh Sanson*, T. Tafazoli (tr.) (Tehran: Ibn-Sina, 1346).

Sefatgol, M., *Sakhtar, Nehad va Andisheh Dini dar Iran-e asr Safavi* (Tehran: Rasa, 1381).

Sha'banzadeh, B., *Tarikh Shafah'ie Madreseh Haqani* (Tehran: Markaz Asnad-e Enqelab-e Eslami, 1384).

Shariati, A., *Collected Works*, vol. 1 (Tehran: n.p., n.d.).

Shariati, A., *Collected Works*, vol. 9 (Tehran: Entesharat-e Tashayo', 1359).

Shariati, A., *Collected Works*, vol. 18 (Tehran: Elham, 1361).

Tabataba'ifar, M., *Nezam-e Soltani* (Tehran: Nashr-e Ney, 1384).

Taheri, H., *Velayat Faqih* (Qom: Daftar Entesharat Eslami, n.d.).

Talafiy-e Daryani, A. A., 'Bahar al-Anvar, Dayeratolma'aref Shi'i' in M. Mohrizi and H. Rabbani (eds.), *Shenakht nameh 'Allameh Majlesi*, vol. 2 (Tehran: Vezarat Farhang va Ershad Eslami, 1378).

Taremi, H., *'Allameh Majlesi* (Tehran: Tarh No, 1375).

Tonokaboni, M., *Qesas al-'Olama* (Tehran: Entesharat 'Elmiyeh Eslamiyeh, n.d.).

Yazdi, M., *Khaterat Ayatollah Mohammad Yazdi* (Tehran: Markaz Asnad-e Enqelab-e Eslami, 1380).

Works in European Languages

ʿAli, Abdullah Yusuf (tr.), *The Holy Qurʾan* (Hertfordshire: Wordsworth, 2000).

Amir-Moezzi, M. A., *The Divine Guide in Early Shiʿism* (New York: State University of New York, 1994).

Boussuet, J.-B., *Sermons Choisis de Boussuet* (Paris: Librairie de Firmin Didot Freres, 1845).

Chardin, J., *Voyages de Monsieur le chevalier Chardin en Perse et autres liux d'Orient*, Tomes 2, 4, 6 (Amsterdam: J. L. de Lorme, 1711).

Cohn, N., *The Pursuit of the Millennium* (London: Pimlico, 2004).

Hume, D., *Essays, Moral, Political and Literary* (Indianapolis: Liberty Fund, 1987).

Kashifu ʿL-Ghita, M. H., *History and Principles of Shiʿism* (Rome: Islamic European Cultural Centre, 1985).

Kohlberg, E., *Belief and Law in Emami Shiʿism* (Hampshire: Variorum, 1991).

Madelung, W., 'Imamism and Muʿtazilite Theology' in *Religious Schools and Sects in Medieval Islam* (Hampshire: Ashgate, 1999).

Modarressi, H., *Crisis and Consolidation in the Formative Period of Shiʾite Islam* (Princeton: Darwin Press, 1993).

Omidsalar, M., 'Jamshid in Persian Literature' in *Encyclopedia Iranica*, vol. XIV, Fascicle 5 (New York: Encyclopaedia Iranica Foundation, Inc.).

Spinoza, B. A., *Theologico-Political Treatise and Political Treatise*, R. H. M. Elwis (tr.) (New York: Dover Publications, 2004).

Rahnema, A., and Nomani, F., *The Secular Miracle, Religion, Politics and Economic Policy in Iran* (London: Zed Books, 1990).

Rodinson, M., *Europe and the Mystique of Islam* (London: I. B. Tauris, 2006).

Thomas, K., *Religion and the Decline of Magic* (London: Penguin, 1991).

Turner, C., *Islam Without Allah?* (Richmond: Curzon, 2000).

Wiesehofer, J., *Ancient Persia* (London: I. B. Tauris, 1996).

Index

List of Books in the Series

For EU product safety concerns, contact us at Calle de José Abascal, 56–1°,
28003 Madrid, Spain or eugpsr@cambridge.org.

www.ingramcontent.com/pod-product-compliance
Ingram Content Group UK Ltd.
Pitfield, Milton Keynes, MK11 3LW, UK
UKHW020400140625
459647UK00020B/2567